THE OFFICIAL GUIDE

Corel**PHOTO-PAINT 10**

THE OFFICIAL GUIDE

Corel**PHOTO-PAINT 10**

Dave Huss

Osborne/**McGraw-Hill**

New York   Chicago   San Francisco
Lisbon   London   Madrid   Mexico City
Milan   New Delhi   San Juan
Seoul   Singapore   Sydney   Toronto

Osborne/**McGraw-Hill**
2600 Tenth Street
Berkeley, California 94710
U.S.A.

To arrange bulk purchase discounts for sales promotions, premiums, or fund-raisers, please contact Osborne/**McGraw-Hill** at the above address. For information on translations or book distributors outside the U.S.A., please see the International Contact Information page immediately following the index of this book.

Corel PHOTO-PAINT 10: The Official Guide

1234567890 CUS CUS 01987654321

ISBN 0-07-212752-X

Publisher: Brandon A. Nordin
Vice President and Associate Publisher: Scott Rogers
Acquisitions Editor: Megg Bonar
Project Editor: Jennifer Malnick
Acquisitions Coordinators: Alissa Larson and Cindy Wathen
Technical Editor: Jennifer Campbell
Copy Editor: Robert Campbell
Proofreaders: Carroll Proffitt and Linda Medoff
Indexer: Jack Lewis
Computer Designers: Roberta Steele, Kelly Stanton-Scott, Tara A. Davis
Illustrators: Lyssa Sieben-Wald, Beth E. Young, Michael Mueller
Series Design: Mickey Galicia & Peter F. Hancik
Cover Illustration: Cristina Deh-Lee

This book was composed with Corel VENTURA™ Publisher.

Dedication

This book is dedicated to my son Jonathan, who is more than a son—
he's a close friend.

About the Author...

In the last seven years, Dave Huss has authored or co-authored ten books on Corel PHOTO-PAINT, which have been translated into six languages. He was seen on CNN, and his photo montage with PHOTO-PAINT, titled *Beautiful Lady,* won Grand Prize in the 1997 Corel World Design Contest. During the day, Dave's job title is Senior Technical Writer and graphic illustrator for Motorola in Austin, Texas, where he lives with his wife of 26 years, Elizabeth. (Note: she isn't 26, their marriage is.) He also writes articles in several computer magazines and teaches at conferences in both the US and Europe. In his spare time—who is he kidding?—what spare time?

Contents At A Glance

Part I   **The Basics of PHOTO-PAINT 10**

   1 An Introduction to PHOTO-PAINT 3
   2 Learning About Digital Images 21
   3 Opening, Creating, and Saving Images 53
   4 Image Fundamentals—Viewing and Modifying Images 75
   5 Tools for Layout, Undoing, Redoing, and Replacing 109

Part II   **Masks and Objects**

   6 The School of Masks 131
   7 Exploring Objects and Text 161

Part III   **Photo-Correction Tools and Techniques**

   8 Repairing and Restoring Photographs 199

Part IV   **Painting with PHOTO-PAINT 10**

   9 Filling with Color or Patterns 227
  10 Corel TEXTURE and Corel KnockOut 269
  11 Finding the Right Color 289
  12 Exploring Corel PHOTO-PAINT's Brush Tools 313

Part V   **Those Incredible Filters**

  13 Exploring PHOTO-PAINT Enhancement Filters 375
  14 Exploring the PHOTO-PAINT Effect Filters 421

Part VI   **Advanced PHOTO-PAINT Topics**

  15 Scanners, Digital Cameras, and the Web 489

16   Using PHOTO-PAINT to Create Web Graphics   517
17   Using Advanced Masks and Channels   533
18   Automating PHOTO-PAINT Tools and Features   563
19   Customizing Corel PHOTO-PAINT 10 Preferences   577
20   Getting the Best Printing Using PHOTO-PAINT   597

Index   609

Contents

Acknowledgments xxiii
Introduction xxv

PART I | **The Basics of PHOTO-PAINT 10**

CHAPTER 1 | **An Introduction to PHOTO-PAINT** **3**

An Introduction to Corel PHOTO-PAINT 10 4
    A Brief History of PHOTO-PAINT 4
    Before We Get Started 5
    PHOTO-PAINT 10: A Premier Photo-Editing Program 6
    Changing Reality (Virtually) 7
A Quick Tour of PHOTO-PAINT 10 11
    Elements of the PHOTO-PAINT Screen 11
    The Menu Bar 12
    The Title Bar 12
    Dockers 12
    Rulers and Guidelines 12
    Toolbars 13
    The Image Window 13
    Toolbox/Flyouts 13
    The Status Bar 14
    Mask and Mode Icons 14
    The Property Bar 14
    The Standard Toolbar 14
    Where to Find Help 16
Setting Up Your System—Do You Have What It Takes? 18
    Hardware Considerations 18
    RAM 18
    CPU 18
    The Hard Disk 19

CHAPTER 2 | **Learning About Digital Images** **21**

Basic Terms in Digital Imaging 22
    Bitmap and Vector Images 22

Pixels   26
Color Depth   27
An Introduction to Screening   31
Gamma   39
"Resolution"—A Term with Too Many Definitions   40
Resolution and the Size of the Image   40
Resolution and Printers   46
Basic Color Theory   47
Color Models   48
Describing Colors   49
Color Matching   49
RGB Versus CMYK   50
Hue, Saturation, and Brightness   50
Color Gamut   51
In Summary   51

CHAPTER 3   Opening, Creating, and Saving Images   53
Overview of Image File Management   54
Welcome to PHOTO-PAINT   54
Opening an Existing Image   55
More File Opening Features   56
Reopening Images   58
Opening Photo CDs   59
Tips and Tricks for Opening Photo CDs   60
Opening Vector Images   61
Setting Up the Import Into Bitmap Dialog Box   62
Opening 3D Images   64
Creating New Images   67
Defining Your New Image   67
Creating Images from the Clipboard   69
Saving Your Work   69
Saving Versus Exporting—
They're the Same but Different   69
Understanding File Formats   71
File Compression   74
In Summary   74

CHAPTER 4   Image Fundamentals—Viewing and Modifying Images   75
Zoom and Navigation Tools   76
Hazards of Bitmap Zooming   77
Working with Zoom Levels   77
The Zoom Tool (Z)   80
The Hand Tool (H)   80

Navigator Pop-up   81
Fitting Images to Your Display   82
Changing Shape and Placement of Images   83
The Flip Command   83
The Rotate Command   84
The Price of Custom Rotation—Distortion   85
Using Custom Rotate   87
Rotation Demonstration   88
The Duplicate Command   89
Changing the Size of an Image   91
Why You Shouldn't Resize or Crop an Image in
Other Applications   91
The Resample Command   92
Cropping an Image with the Crop Tool   98
Crop to Selection   98
Crop to Mask   99
Crop Border Color   100
The Paper Size Command   101
Paper Size Demonstration   102
Changing the Color Mode of an Image   105
The Mode Command—
It's More than Color and Grayscale   105
An Alternative to Grayscale Conversion   106
In Summary   108

CHAPTER 5   **Tools for Layout, Undoing, Redoing, and Replacing** **109**
Rulers, Guidelines, and Grids   110
Rulers   110
Grids   115
Guidelines   117
Rules about Rulers, Grids, and Guidelines   118
Zoom and Navigation Tools   119
The Hand Tool (H)   119
Navigator Pop-up   119
Tools for Correcting Mistakes   120
The Eraser Tool   121
The Local Undo Tool   121
The Checkpoint Command   124
The Undo/Redo Docker—Try It, You'll Like It!   124
Clone from Saved—the Ultimate Undo Tool   125
Color Replacer Tool   126
In Summary   126

PART II	**Masks and Objects**	
CHAPTER 6	**The School of Masks**	**131**
	What Is a Mask?	132
	Black, White, and Gray	134
	Displaying Masks	135
	Marquees Are Okay, but Overlay Is Where It's At	137
	The Mask-Creation Tools	138
	Mask Transform Tool	138
	Regular Mask Tools	139
	Mask Modes	143
	Color-Sensitive Masks	147
	The Grow and Similar Commands	156
	Properties of Mask and Selection	158
	The Mask Transform Tool (M)	158
	The Mask Brush Tool (B)	159
	In Summary	160
CHAPTER 7	**Exploring Objects and Text**	**161**
	Pixels and Crazy Glue	162
	Objects Defined	162
	Expanding the Definition	163
	The Objects Docker and Property Bar	164
	Object Modes	165
	A Guided Tour of Objects	166
	Clip to Parent	171
	Looking Deeper into the Objects Docker	171
	Clip Masks	174
	More Stuff About Clip Masks	179
	Object Transparency Tools	180
	The Interactive Dropshadow Tool (S)	180
	Managing Drop Shadows	185
	Transform Modes	187
	Additional Tips for Working with Objects	188
	How to Group Objects	189
	The Text Tool	190
	Paragraph Text and Corel PHOTO-PAINT	190
	Text on a Path (Finally)	190
	Text and the Path	194
	Basics of the Text Tool	194
	In Summary	195

PART III   **Photo-Correction Tools and Techniques**

CHAPTER 8   **Repairing and Restoring Photographs** **199**
               Discovering Hidden Treasure in Dark Backgrounds   200
           Fixing Digital Camera Photographs   207
               Some Digital Camera Basics   208
               Color Fundamentals   208
               What Color Should We Make the Orange?   210
               An Exercise in Color Correction   211
           Repairing Noncolor Photographic Problems   217
               Cropping—It's Quick and Easy   217
               Cropping in PHOTO-PAINT Reduces File Sizes   217
           In Summary   223

PART IV   **Painting with PHOTO-PAINT 10**

CHAPTER 9   **Filling with Color or Patterns** **227**
           The Fill Tools…So Many Choices   228
               Selecting the Right Fill   230
           More Fills Than You Could Have
               Thought Possible   232
               Meet the Fill Buttons   233
           Fill Status Line   234
           The Uniform Color Fill Mode   234
           The Fountain Fill Mode   235
               Fiddling with the Fountain Fill Dialog Box   235
               Putting Fountain Fills to Work   242
           Bitmap Fill   244
               Loading a Bitmap Image   245
               How the Bitmap Fill Operates   245
               Controlling the Size and Position of the
                   Bitmap Tiles   246
               Loading Bitmap Images   247
               Putting Bitmap Fills to Work   248
           The Texture Fills   249
               What's in a Name?   249
               Exploring the Texture Fill Dialog Box   250
               Doing Something with Texture Fills   253
           Interactive Fill Tool   255
               Type   256
               Paint Mode   256

Interactive Fill Style 257
   Great, So How Does It Work? 258
Transparency Controls 258
   Flat 259
   Linear 259
   Elliptical 260
   Radial 261
   Square, Rectangle, and Conical 261
The Disable Fill Button 261
The Shape Tools 261
   Width and Roundness of Borders 262
   The Rectangle Tool 264
   The Ellipse Tool 265
   The Polygon Tool 266
   The Line Tool 266
In Summary 267

CHAPTER 10   **Corel TEXTURE and Corel KnockOut** **269**
What Is Corel TEXTURE? 270
   How Does It Work? 271
   Before You Can Launch It, You Must Find It 271
   How to Make a Texture 274
   Making a Seamless Tile 276
   Changing the Texture Size 278
   Making a 3D Button 279
Corel KnockOut 282
   RAM Requirements for KnockOut 283
   How KnockOut Works 283
   Your Next Stop—The Transition Zone 284
   Once the Mask Is finished 285
In Summary 287

CHAPTER 11   **Finding the Right Color** **289**
The Trio of Colors—Paint, Paper, and Fill 290
Changing Colors—It's Easier Than You Think 291
   Picking Colors from the Palette 292
Picking Palettes 292
What's in a Name? A Rose by Any Other Name 294
Getting the Right Color with the Eyedropper Tool 297
   Eyedropper Tool Hot Key 297
   Eyedropper Sample Size 297
   Notes on Using the Eyedropper Tool 298
Selecting a Paint Color 299

The Paint Color Dialog Box 299
  Pick Your Own Color Models Selection 299
Color Models 301
  Color Model Options 301
  How to Select or Create a Color Using
   Color Models Mode 302
  Colors by the Numbers 303
  Name That Color 303
  Checking Out the Options Button 304
  Saving a New Color to a Palette 305
The Mixers Mode 306
  Color Harmonies 307
  Color Blend 309
Palettes Mode 310
  Viewing Palette Selections by Name 311
In Summary 312

CHAPTER 12 **Exploring Corel PHOTO-PAINT's Brush Tools** **313**
More Tools, Same Controls 314
  Selecting and Configuring Brush Tools 315
  Quick Start Brushes—the Artistic Media Docker 315
  Constraining and Automating the Brush Tools 316
  Brush Nibs—Everything Else Is Details 317
  The Brush Settings Docker 318
  A Quick Tour of the Brush Settings Docker 319
  The Stroke Style Section 320
  Nib Properties Control and Selection 323
  Stroke Attributes 326
  Dab Attributes 327
  Brush Texture 330
  Orbits/Color Variation 331
  What Can You Do with Orbits? 333
  The Pen Settings Roll-Up 335
  Configuring Your Pen 336
  Pen Settings Roll-Up Buttons 337
The Symmetry Toolbar 338
The Paint Tools 339
  Creating Custom Nibs from Masks 340
The Effect Tools 343
  The Smear Tool 345
  The Smudge Tool 346
  The Brightness Tool 347
  Thoughts About Retouching Photographs 347

The Contrast Tool   348
The Hue Tool   348
The Hue Replacer Tool   349
The Sponge (Saturation) Tool   350
The Tint Tool   350
The Blend Tool   351
The Sharpen Tool   352
The Undither Tool   352
Dodge and Burn Tool   352
The Power of the Clone Tool (C)   353
How the Clone Tool Works   353
The Clone Tool Settings   357
Aligned and Nonaligned Clone Modes   358
Clone   359
Impressionism Clone   359
Pointillism Clone   359
Clone from Saved   360
Clone from Fill   361
Advanced Cloning Stuff   361
The Image Sprayer Tool   363
How the Image Sprayer Works   364
How to Create Your Own Image List   364
Image Sprayer Presets   370
Painting with the Image Sprayer   371
Real Art with the Image Sprayer   371
In Summary   372

PART V   **Those Incredible Filters**

CHAPTER 13   **Exploring PHOTO-PAINT Enhancement Filters** **375**
Understanding Plug-In Filters   376
Installation of Filters   376
Managing Your Plug-Ins   378
Introducing the Filter Dialog Box   380
Preview Options   380
Panning and Zooming   381
Other Effects   384
Repeat and Fade Last Commands   384
The Last Effect and Repeat Effect Commands   384
Fade Last Command   385
The Sharpen Filters   385
What Is Sharpening?   386
When to Apply Sharpening   388
How Sharpening Affects Noise   388

Unsharp Masking Filters (USM) 389
The Unsharp Mask Filter 389
The Adaptive Unsharp Filter 389
The Directional Sharpen Filter 390
The Sharpen Filter 390
The High Pass Filter 390
The Tune Sharpen Filter 391
The Blur Filters 391
The Gaussian Blur Filter 392
    Subtle Emphasis by Creating a Depth of Field 393
    Depth of Field 393
    Removal of Banding Using the Gaussian Blur Filter 394
The Motion Blur Filter 396
The Jaggy Despeckle Filter 398
    Using the Jaggy Despeckle Filter 399
The Radial Blur Filter 399
Zoom Filter 400
The Directional Smooth Filter 400
The Smooth Filter 400
The Soften Filter 400
Getting It All Together—The Tune Blur 401
Smart Blur Filter 401
The Low Pass Filter 403
Noise Filters 403
The Add Noise Filter 404
    The Add Noise Filter Dialog Box 404
    Noise Filter Effects 406
    Noise and Focus 407
Removing Noise Without Buying Earplugs 407
The Diffuse Filter 408
The Dust & Scratch Filter 408
    Using the Dust & Scratch Filter 409
Messing with Masks 409
    Maximum Filter 410
    The Minimum Filter 411
The Median Filter 412
    Unleashing the Real Power of Median 412
The Remove Moiré Filter 415
    Moiré Patterns 416
The Remove Noise Filter 417
    Tuning Up the Noise 418
In Summary 419

CHAPTER 14   **Exploring the PHOTO-PAINT Effect Filters** **421**
3D Effect Filters   422
The 3D Rotate Filter   422
  The 3D Rotate Dialog Box   423
  Using the 3D Rotate Filter   423
The Cylinder Filter   424
The Emboss Filter   424
  The Emboss Dialog Box   425
The Glass Filter   426
  The Glass Dialog Box   426
  Glass Raised Text Using the Glass Filter   430
Page Curl   433
  The Page Curl Dialog Box   433
The Perspective Filter   434
The Pinch/Punch Filter   435
  The Pinch/Punch Dialog Box   435
The Sphere Filter   437
  The Sphere Dialog Box   437
The Boss (Emboss) Filter   438
  The Boss Dialog Box   439
The Creative and Art Stroke Filters   442
Creative Filters   442
  The Crafts Filter   442
  The Crystalize Filter   443
  The Fabric Filter   443
  The Frame Filter   444
  The Glass Block Filter   445
  The Mosaic Filter   446
  The Particles Filter   448
  The Scatter Filter   448
  The Smoked Glass Filter   449
  The Stained Glass Filter   449
  The Vignette Filter   449
  The Vortex Filter   449
  The Weather Channel, er, Filter   450
The Art Stroke Filters   452
  Charcoal   452
  Conté Crayon   453
  Crayon   453
  Cubist   453
  Dabble   454
  The Impressionist Filter   454
  The Palette Knife   454

The Sketchpad 454
Watercolor 455
The Contour Filters 455
The Edge Detect Filter 456
Find Edges 457
The Trace Contour Filter 457
Alchemy Effects 457
Starting Alchemy Effects 458
The Alchemy Effects Dialog Box 458
The Band Pass Filter 458
The User Defined Filter 459
Bump Map 459
The Distort Filters 460
The Blocks Filter (Formerly Known as the Puzzle Filter) 461
The Displace Filter 462
More Technical Information About Displacement Maps . . 463
The Mesh Warp Filter 463
So . . . What Can You Do with It? 464
The SQUIZZ! Filter 465
Grid Warping 466
Brush Warping 466
What Can You Do with SQUIZZ!? 467
The Offset Filter 467
The Pixelate Filter 468
Using the Pixelate Filter 468
The Ripple Filter 469
Controlling the Ripple Filter 469
The Shear Filter 469
The Swirl Filter 470
The Tile Filter 471
The Wet Paint Filter 472
The Whirlpool Filter 473
The Wind Filter 473
Before We Leave Distort 474
The Render and Fancy Filters 474
The Render Filters 474
3D Stereo Noise 475
Lens Flare 475
Lighting Effects Filter 476
Setting Up the Lighting Effects Filter 476
The Fancy Filters 478
Julia Set Explorer 2.0 478
The Terrazzo Filter 479

An Overview of Terrazzo 479
Tiles, Motifs, and Patterns 479
The Terrazzo Motifs 481
Selecting a Symmetry 482
Creating Seamless Patterns 483
The Mode Settings 485
The Opacity Slider 485
Previewing Tiles 485
Saving a Tile 485
In Summary 486

PART VI   **Advanced PHOTO-PAINT Topics**

CHAPTER 15   **Scanners, Digital Cameras, and the Web** **489**
Scanners and Scanning 490
What Your Mother Never Told You About Scanners 490
All Scanners Are Not Created Equal 491
What Resolution and Bit Depth Actually Mean to You . . . 492
Final Musings on Choosing a Scanner 493
Scanners, PHOTO-PAINT, and TWAIN 494
Previewing the Scan 496
The Story of TWAIN (Not Mark) 497
Some Facts About Scanning 500
Scanning and Resolution . . . Making It Work for You . . . 501
A Trick Question About Resolution 502
Why You Shouldn't Scan at Excessively
   High Resolutions 503
Scanning Printed Material, or the Dangers of Moiré 503
Working with Digital Cameras 506
Getting from the Digicam into Your Computer 507
Loading Images Directly into PHOTO-PAINT 508
Video Capture—It's Easier Than You Might Imagine 508
Corel Scrapbook Docker Window 510
Getting Great Screen Shots Using Corel CAPTURE 511
In Summary 515

CHAPTER 16   **Using PHOTO-PAINT to Create Web Graphics** **517**
The World of Internet Colors 518
Two Paths to Smaller File Sizes 518
To GIF or Not to GIF, That Is the Question 519
Button, Button, Who Made the Button 519
Beyond What the Designer Had in Mind 522
Making a 3D Web Page Button 523

Making Green French Fries for Your Web Page 528
Using the Glass Block Filter to Make
a Multimedia Background 531
In Summary 532

CHAPTER 17   Using Advanced Masks and Channels **533**
Saving a Mask 534
Saving a Mask with the Image 535
Loading a Mask 536
Saving a Mask As an Alpha Channel 538
Managing Masks and Channels 538
The Channels Docker 539
Removing a Mask 539
Inverting a Mask 540
Select All 540
Manipulating Masks 540
Feather Mask 542
The Shape Category Mask Commands 544
Using Masks to Create Deteriorated Metal 547
What Is POM? 549
Holy Corrosion, Batman! 550
Variations on a Theme 551
The Color Mask 552
The Color Mask 552
Replacing a Background Using the Color Mask 553
Additional Information About the Color Mask 556
Using the Color Mask More Productively 558
Paths 559
Stroke Mask/Path Command 559
In Summary 562

CHAPTER 18   Automating PHOTO-PAINT Tools and Features **563**
Batch Process (Formerly Known as Batch Playback) 564
The Recorder Docker (It's Just Like Your VCR, Sort Of) 566
Creating a Script 570
Scripts Docker 575
In Summary 576

CHAPTER 19   Customizing Corel PHOTO-PAINT 10 Preferences **577**
Toolbars 578
Fitting the Toolbar to Your Monitor 578
Changing the Toolbar Size and Shape 579
Building Your Own Custom Toolbar 583

Menus and Keyboard Commands 585
Making Your Preferences Known 586
The Workplace Settings 587
The Customization Page 593
The Document Guidelines Group 593
The Global Bitmap Effects Group 593
Onscreen Palette 595
In Summary 596

CHAPTER 20 **Getting the Best Printing Using PHOTO-PAINT** **597**
Color Correction vs. Ink Jet Printers 598
Color Printers vs. Color Photo Printers 600
General Dos and Don'ts of Printing with PHOTO-PAINT 600
Making Your Own Wallet-Size Pictures 603
Making Photos That Fit Without Alterations 606
Fitting Several Different Photos on a Page 607
In Summary 608

Index **609**

Acknowledgments

If you are reading this part of the book, you are either one of the many excellent editors who work so hard to give you the impression that I passed high school English, or your cable is out. Let's face it, the acknowledgement portion of a book is like a secret compartment—generally only those mentioned in it ever read it.

It is the evening of the 2000 presidential election, and this book is ready to be put to bed (with milk and cookies, of course). It's nearly midnight (I do my best writing when everyone else is asleep), and the nation is listening to dozens of political prognosticators predicting the outcome, which, by the time you read this, will be very old news. After a book is finished it's pleasant to look back and think about all that was involved to get this book into your hands.

Of course, my family once again must be thanked for giving up father and husband in exchange for the grumpy old man that I become when writing a book under a deadline. As always, my family got to see more of the back of my head than the front.

The creation of a technical book is always a challenge to everyone involved. To have a book ready to ship shortly after that product shipped meant it was necessary to write about things in PAINT during the beta cycle. Now, *that's* entertainment. A typical telephone conversation began with, "When I move the cursor, it changes shape. Is it supposed to do that or is it a bug?" I think we were successful because of the efforts of several people up Ottawa way. (Ottawa, Canada, is where Corel is—you knew that, right?) I first and foremost must thank Sean McClenan, who heads up the PHOTO-PAINT development team and who once again endured a ceaseless barrage of questions during the creation of this book. My other PHOTO-PAINT technical wizard is David Garrett, who never ceases to amaze me with what he knows about the product—must be why they do PHOTO-PAINT quality assurance. Here is a safety tip I received from David Garrett: "Never clean your PHOTO-PAINT brushes with kerosene." My thanks also go to Kristin Divinksi at Corel, who has worked behind the scenes to help spread the word about this book—through Corel's Web site and other fine marketing efforts.

My thanks to Jennifer Campbell, who worked during weekends and part of her family vacation to complete the copy edit so we could get this book completed in time. I felt bad that it took away from her vacation, but how exciting can Idaho be? Just kidding—please, no e-mail from Idaho.

Finally (it keeps going and going and…), thank you to my acquisitions editor and friend Megg Bonar, who makes the task of getting a book out on time almost fun. Also essential to getting the book completed are Cindy Wathen and Alissa Larson, who make sure all parts of the puzzle that make up a complex book project like this one are turned in on time. Once again, I would be remiss if I didn't mention the head honcho at the Osborne ranch, Scott Rogers. You've been mentioned.

Last, but surely not least, my daughter Grace (now 20) wanted to remind all of you reading this book that she is still looking for a boyfriend. (I guess the boyfriend-in-a-box I bought her last week didn't work out.) So if you are either Prince William or some other dashing member of the opposite gender, send her an e-mail at my address (davehuss@austin.rr.com). And if you are really interested, remember: I own a gun and a shovel.

Introduction

So, there you stand next to a multicolored wall of computer titles, most of which are nearly as thick as phone books for major metropolitan cities. You ask yourself, "Will this book help me learn PHOTO-PAINT 10, or will it become another dust collector?" Your puzzlement is understandable. After all, the word "idiot" or "dummy" doesn't appear anywhere in the title. By now you have already looked at the dazzling color inserts and noticed it wasn't the typical collection of award-winning art produced by people with years of experience and way too much time on their hands. Instead you've seen a large collection of images that *you* will create using the step-by-step exercises in this book. If you own one of the previous editions of this book, you have also noticed that the exercises are different from the previous editions. Yet, you may hear that still-small voice in the background (not to be confused with the store announcement of the half-off sale on all organic chemistry textbooks) saying you won't be able to do stuff like that. Let me assure you that you will.

 This book contains exercises and information about digital photo-editing that could be harmful to your non–computer literate status.

My "day job" (as in "don't give up your day job") for several years involved talking to thousands (OK, dozens) of people every day who began their conversations by telling me how stupid they were regarding their computer knowledge. That was generally just before they handed the phone over to their eight year old. These people are not stupid. However, they have come to believe that they are—convinced by a legion of techno-babble-talking computer types, many of whom simply need to date more often. In creating this book, I have worked with the following assumptions:

- You have not received the Nobel Prize recently.

- Your IQ is higher than that of mayonnaise.

- You would like to learn to use the computer for something other than solitaire or Quake.

- You are not a graphics arts expert; in fact, you may even be wondering if graphic art is the stuff they hang in motel rooms and sell by the truckload at "Starving Artist" sales.

In short, if you want to learn PHOTO-PAINT, this book is for you. There is one tiny secret I must share with you if you really want to learn how to use PHOTO-PAINT: READ THE BOOK and DO THE EXERCISES! Contrary to rumors in the computer industry, you cannot learn anything in this book by any of the following methods:

- **Osmosis**   Keeping the book near you at all times so the knowledge of the product migrates into your mind.

- **Sleep Teaching**   Sleeping with a copy of the book as a pillow, hoping that it will somehow jumpstart one or more of your brain cells.

- **Super Speeder Reader method**   Thumbing through the pages, wondering what all of the pictures mean.

- **Proximity method**   Placing the book close enough to the computer so the PHOTO-PAINT program can make your computer smarter and do what you want it to do.

- **The *Annie* method**   Bet your bottom dollar that tomorrow it'll make sense.

- **The Impress Your Friends method**   Keeping a copy of this book on your shelf so your friends (or your boss) will think you are really getting into the program. Actually, this technique does work, except you never really learn anything—you just impress your friends.

Enough already. Here is the short version. Using PHOTO-PAINT isn't brain surgery; it's electronic finger-painting without the mess to clean up afterward. As I always tell people at the PHOTO-PAINT seminars, if you're not having fun with PHOTO-PAINT, you're probably doing something wrong. Buy the book and then check out that sale of organic chemistry books.

PART I

The Basics of PHOTO-PAINT 10

CHAPTER 1

An Introduction to PHOTO-PAINT

An Introduction to Corel PHOTO-PAINT 10

Y ou are about to begin an incredible journey into the world of photo-editing and digital wizardry. (Does that last sentence sound like the preview for a new movie?) This was once the exclusive domain of multimillion-dollar computer systems and dedicated graphic artists.

With Corel PHOTO-PAINT 10, you will quickly correct and produce images that can make your desktop projects dazzle. Photo-editing programs have traditionally been labor intensive. They required many hours of tedious effort to manipulate images (removing trees, adding people, changing sky color, and so on). PHOTO-PAINT 10 greatly simplifies this time-consuming process. Just as CorelDRAW enables you to achieve professional computer graphic effects with little effort, Corel PHOTO-PAINT 10 will allow you to reach that same professional level in the manipulation of photographs, paintings, and other bitmap images. The bottom line is that PHOTO-PAINT 10 is fun to work with, period. The fact that you can quickly produce professional results is a bonus. Next, Dave's genuine history of PHOTO-PAINT.

A Brief History of PHOTO-PAINT

Corel PHOTO-PAINT began its life as a software product called Photofinish, created by Z-Soft. It was introduced as Corel PHOTO-PAINT 3 in May 1992. It was, at best, an interesting bitmap-editing package that was very similar to Microsoft Paint, which Z-Soft also wrote.

When Corel PHOTO-PAINT 4 was released in May 1993, there were many improvements, and only a small amount of the original Z-Soft program remained. PHOTO-PAINT 4 had limitations in the size of the image files it could handle, and the absence of several other key features prevented it from being a first-class product. In fact, it resembled Microsoft Paint on steroids.

PHOTO-PAINT 5, which Corel originally released in May 1994, showed marked improvement. There were many changes still in progress when the product had to ship. Those changes appeared when the maintenance release (E2) was shipped in September. PHOTO-PAINT 5 began to draw serious attention from the graphics community with its support of objects and layers and its other features.

PHOTO-PAINT 6 entered the world of 32-bit applications, offering a robust set of photo-editing tools coupled with the power of a 32-bit architecture. If all this talk about 32-bit power is confusing, then—to borrow some terms from *Star Trek*—think of 32-bit power as warp drive and 16-bit as impulse power.

PHOTO-PAINT 7, which was released in November 1996, remains a 32-bit-only application that ranks among the best in the area of photo-editing applications. While retaining the general form and structure of PHOTO-PAINT 6, it provided greatly improved speed and functionality over the previous release. During its brief reign as Corel's premier photo-editing application, it won the coveted Editor's Choice award from *PC Magazine.*

PHOTO-PAINT 8, released in November 1997, had as its most notable change the addition of advanced mask functions like Clip Mask and Clip to Parent. Exciting new paint brush controls like Orbits and Symmetry were added. In addition, PHOTO-PAINT 8 marked the beginning of the migration from roll-ups to dockers.

PHOTO-PAINT 8 for the Power Macintosh was released a few months later. Building on the success of PHOTO-PAINT 8, the product won rave reviews from the Mac community press.

With PHOTO-PAINT 9, the program continued to build on its previous successes. New filters added a whole new range of effects to an already robust package. Many of the improvements in PHOTO-PAINT 9 were "under the hood," meaning they weren't new features but performance-enhanced existing ones.

The latest version of this program, Corel PHOTO-PAINT 10, features a variety of image-enhancing filters to improve the quality of scanned images, and special effects filters that dramatically alter the appearance of images, such as the new Red Eye Removal and Smart Blur filters. Corel PHOTO-PAINT 10 provides a redesigned and fully customizable UI, enhanced mask effects, and the ability to disable common warning messages to reduce interruptions to the creative process. Corel PHOTO-PAINT 10 also gives users text tools that have been significantly enhanced for easier text creation, more control over drop shadows by using new color and update features and Shadow Feathering and Shadow Opacity controls, and enough new material to add many pages to this book.

Before We Get Started

One thing that makes PHOTO-PAINT such a powerful package is that there are so many combinations of tools and functions available. Of course, these qualities also make PHOTO-PAINT confusing for the novice. If you are new to photo-editing programs, I have included a section in this book to help you understand the sometimes-complex world of bitmap images.

PHOTO-PAINT 10: A Premier Photo-Editing Program

Corel PHOTO-PAINT 10 is first and foremost a photo- or image-editing program.
It is in the same league as Adobe Photoshop, but it costs hundreds of dollars less.
As a photo-editing program, it offers all the features you should expect from a
professional photo-editing package, and in several areas you can do more with
PHOTO-PAINT 10 than with its main competitor. In case you are wondering why
I mention Adobe Photoshop, it's because before PHOTO-PAINT came along,
Adobe Photoshop was the unchallenged leader in digital photo-editing. Corel
PHOTO-PAINT is not so quietly changing that.

One of the more useful tasks you can perform with PHOTO-PAINT 10 is to
take a poorly composed, underexposed photograph and make it look as if the
photographer did a great job. Figure 1-1 is a before-and-after photograph of a
woman who can carry more beers than I can. In the original (a), the foreground is
brightly lit but the background is underexposed. This problem is not uncommon
when using flash photography. Using a combination of several PHOTO-PAINT
tools, we are able to restore the background and also remove the customer's
cigarettes (the beer hall is now smoke-free) and his empty beer stein (b).

FIGURE 1-1 a) The background is black due to flash; b) Using PHOTO-PAINT, it is possible to restore the background and clear the customer's table

People tend to get excited about all the breathtaking, surrealistic effects they can achieve with photo-editing packages such as PHOTO-PAINT 10. In truth, I get excited, too. But it is the everyday work of making the images in documents look as professional as possible, with the least amount of effort, that makes PHOTO-PAINT 10 such an important addition to your desktop publishing library.

Changing Reality (Virtually)

With PHOTO-PAINT 10 and this book, you will learn how simple it is to add people or objects to existing images. You can easily make static images come to life as shown in Figure 1-2. Better yet, you may want to create things that don't exist, as shown in Figure 1-3, or, more commonly, remove unwanted objects like scratches, stains, or old boyfriends, as shown in Figure 1-4. You will even be able to change the way people look. I recently did a brochure for our church. The photo of one of the pastors had been taken several months and over 20 pounds ago. No problem. With PHOTO-PAINT 10 I took off those excess pounds in less than an hour—which is more than the pastor or the diet industry can say.

FIGURE 1-2   With PHOTO-PAINT 10 we can modify exiting photographs into something more dynamic

FIGURE 1-3   Feeling a little surrealistic? With PHOTO-PAINT, it's easy to do

FIGURE 1-4   Breaking up may be hard to do, but removing a boyfriend (a) from a photograph is simple using PHOTO-PAINT 10 (b)

Altering people's appearance (removing blemishes, changing hair color, and so on) has been done by professionals for a long time. I knew a guy who was one of the kings of the airbrush (back in the predigital days) and was greatly appreciated by more than one model whose photo appears on a foldout page. Now, like my friend, you will be able to change the way people look. The only difference is that PHOTO-PAINT 10 doesn't require an airbrush, long hours, or years of experience.

In Figure 1-5 we have an easy shot. My CorelDRAW counterpart, Gary Priester, wrote a book titled *Corel Studio Techniques.* It's a fantastic book about how to use PHOTO-PAINT and DRAW together and…oops. Anyway, we needed a picture of the two of us for the chapters entitled "Back to Back." No sweat. Gary lives near San Francisco and I live in Austin, Texas. So I had a picture taken of me leaning against a tree and Gary had his taken of him just standing there with a smug expression on his face. With PHOTO-PAINT it was easy to put us both in the same picture as well as to make us the same height (Gary is 4 inches taller) and shave about 40 pounds off of me. I am real good at that last part.

FIGURE 1-5   Why is Gary (left) smiling? Because he knows he is several inches taller, and I used to be several inches wider

What else can you do with PHOTO-PAINT 10? We have been talking up until now about changing existing images, but you can also create original images. If you're not an artist, don't feel excluded from this discussion. Like CorelDRAW, PHOTO-PAINT 10 lets you take clip art and assemble it to make exciting images. Corel has provided an assortment of objects that can be placed together to make a composite image. Using the PHOTO-PAINT filters and its powerful editing tools, you will quickly learn to create all kinds of original images, logos, and what-have-you (and still maintain your I'm-not-an-artist standing). You can take the background from one photograph and place it seamlessly with another. Figure 1-6 shows how you can make an object stand out by replacing the background. Can you find the can of Coke? It's hidden under his paw—and I wouldn't want to fight him for it.

FIGURE 1-6   Background replacement enhances the subject

A Quick Tour of PHOTO-PAINT 10

There's a lot of useful information in this chapter, so I urge you to look through it. If you are a first-time user of PHOTO-PAINT, I recommend that you familiarize yourself with (don't memorize) the terms and concepts described in this chapter before you begin to use the program. Time invested here will pay off in later chapters.

Elements of the PHOTO-PAINT Screen

Figure 1-7 shows the Corel PHOTO-PAINT 10 main screen. Your screen may look quite different depending on how it is configured (you'll learn about this in Chapter 3). The following are the key elements that make up the PHOTO-PAINT screen:

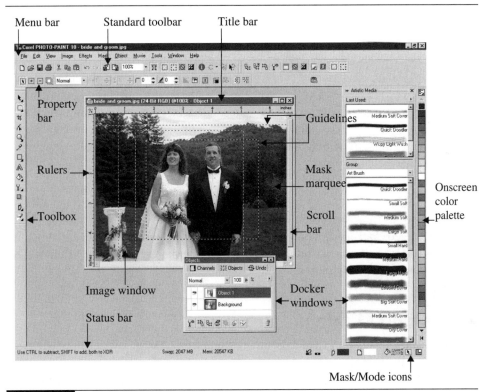

FIGURE 1-7   The main screen in Corel PHOTO-PAINT 10

The Onscreen Color Palette

The *onscreen color palette* is used to select the *Paint* (foreground color used by the brushes), *Paper* (background), and *Fill* colors. These three terms are used throughout PHOTO-PAINT, so you should try to remember them. To choose a Paint color—that is, to change the color of a brush—click a color on the palette with the left mouse button. To choose a Fill color, click with the right mouse button. To select a Paper color, hold down CTRL and click the left mouse button.

The Menu Bar

Select any menu heading in the *menu bar* to access dialog boxes, submenus, and commands. Access is also available by pressing ALT followed by the highlighted or underlined letter in the command.

The Title Bar

The *title bar* displays the application title or the image title (image filename). New in PHOTO-PAINT 10 is that the title bar now displays information about the image in the windows. While it's nice to know the title, the important thing about the title bar is the background. The background color of the title bar indicates whether an image window is selected, which is important when you have several image files open and want to know which one you are about to apply an effect to.

Dockers

The successor to roll-ups, which were last seen in PHOTO-PAINT 8, docker windows, called *dockers,* are parked on the side and provide the same functionality as the equivalent roll-up. In PHOTO-PAINT 10, there are 13 dockers listed in the Window | Dockers pop-up menu.

Rulers and Guidelines

Selecting View | Rulers or the keyboard combination CTRL-R toggles the display of the rulers on the image.

Rulers are important in PHOTO-PAINT because they provide the only visual indicator of how large an image actually is. We will explore why this happens in Chapter 2. For now, be aware that it is possible for a photograph to completely fill the screen and yet be smaller than a postage stamp when you print it.

Toolbars

Toolbars were first introduced in PHOTO-PAINT 6 and are similar to the Ribbon bars found in many other Windows applications. Choose Window | Toolbars to see the list of available toolbars. You can also make your own toolbars, which you will learn to do in Chapter 3. I recommend displaying six of them at all times: *menu bar, standard bar, Mask/Object, property bar, Toolbox,* and *status bar.* Buttons on the toolbars provide quick access to commonly used commands. All the functions available on the toolbars can also be accessed through the menu bar. The appearance of the toolbar and the number of buttons visible depend on which tool is selected.

The Image Window

This is the image-display window. The zoom factor of each image window is controlled independently by the Zoom control in the Standard toolbar. The default setting of Opening Zoom—100%—is set in the General page of the Options dialog box (CTRL-J). If you have a medium- to high-performance graphics board in your system, you can choose Best Fit. But for an accurate representation of the image on the screen, you should always use 100%.

TIP	*When you choose a zoom factor that is less than or greater than 100 percent, the image may have a poor appearance. This is a result of the way it's displayed by the graphics adapter under Windows 98 and does not reflect the actual image quality.*

Toolbox/Flyouts

The *Toolbox* contains all the tools used for image editing. Many of the buttons in the Toolbox have flyouts to allow access to additional related tools. Most flyouts are identical to their toolbar. A flyout is actually a toolbar containing all of the tools in that category.

NOTE	*Availability of a flyout is indicated by a tiny black arrow in the lower-right corner of the button.*

To open a flyout, you can click and hold the cursor on the button for more than a second, or click directly on the black arrow. If you click one black arrow and you pass the cursor over the other tools with a black arrow, each flyout will open without being clicked. Clicking any tool in the flyout places the selected tool button in the Toolbox.

The Status Bar

The *status bar* contains a wealth of information. By default, it is located at the bottom of the screen. Refer to Chapter 3 for information on how to customize the status bar for your desktop needs.

Mask and Mode Icons

The mask icons are displayed in the status bar. The two icons are the Mask Mode and Mask Present icons. The two mask icons are more important than you might imagine. Suppose you try to apply an effect or use a brush stroke, and either nothing will happen, or what happens is not what you expected. More often than not, this is because you have a mask somewhere in the image that is hindering you, or you have the mask in something other than Normal mode. Make a habit of looking for the Mask icon when things don't work as planned.

The Property Bar

The *property bar* is a great productivity enhancement. Most of the common tool settings items now appear on property bars, relieving the screen from overcrowding by too many toolbars. Put simply, the property bar displays the most-often-used commands for whatever mode is selected by the user.

The Standard Toolbar

The *standard toolbar* is enabled by default. The nine buttons of the standard toolbar are common Windows functions. The remaining buttons of the standard toolbar will be discussed in greater detail as we learn to use them.

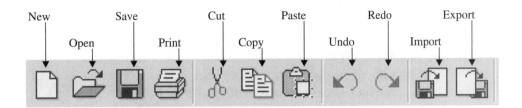

- **New**   Activates the Create a New Image dialog box for creating new image files.

- **Open**   Activates the Open an Image dialog box to open existing files.

- **Save**   Saves the currently selected image. This button is grayed out (unavailable) until the selected image has been modified.

- **Print**   Allows printing of the selected image.

- **Cut**   Cuts (removes) the defined (masked) area and copies it to the Clipboard.

- **Copy**   Copies a defined (masked) area to the Clipboard.

- **Paste as Object**   Pastes (copies) the image in the Clipboard into the selected image as an object. Note: Unlike the Paste *command,* which gives you a choice of pasting as an object or as a new document, the Paste As Object *button* does not give you a choice.

- **Undo**   Undoes the last PHOTO-PAINT command or action.

- **Redo**   Reapplies the last action that was undone with the Undo command.

- **Import**   Used to import graphic files into PHOTO-PAINT that cannot be opened with the File | Open command.

- **Export**   Used to make a copy of the currently selected image in another graphics format.

Where to Find Help

Most users don't take advantage of the extensive help features built into products. I can't say for sure why they don't use them, but I can say that Corel has built a lot of help features into PHOTO-PAINT 10. These help features will answer many questions for you without the need to reference either this book or the manual that shipped with the product. Here is a brief summary of what and where they are.

CorelTUTOR

It's hard to miss this one—it's one of six possible choices on the opening screen. Selecting CorelTUTOR opens the CorelTUTOR main menu. This is a step-by-step tutorial that teaches you how to use PHOTO-PAINT 10 to accomplish many tasks in photo-editing.

> **TIP**   *If you cannot find some of the buttons mentioned in this section, there is a good chance their current setting is too large to fit on your display. To change the size of the buttons, select Window | Toolbars and change the button size from the dropdown list so that all the buttons in the standard toolbar fit the display.*

Context Help

The button with the question mark and the arrow, shown next, is the Context Help button, located on the standard bar. Clicking this button changes the cursor to an arrow with a question mark. It remains in this mode until clicked on an item, which brings up the context-sensitive help screen that explains the purpose of the item clicked.

What's This?

Place the cursor on a feature anywhere on a tool or feature inside a dialog box, hold down the right mouse button for two seconds, and release it to produce a small rectangle with the message "What's This?" as shown next. This provides a brief description of the function selected. The trick to making it work is to click the "What's This?" message box with the left mouse button *after* you right-click the feature. If other options are available with the feature you clicked, the "What's This?" option is at the bottom of the list.

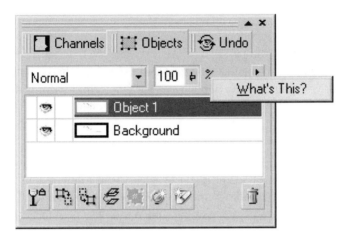

TIP

Don't forget to click the message box that contains the message "What's This?" to access the information.

The Help Manual

Throughout the book I have included tips to direct you toward the more useful help files. These files provide all the information that you would expect to find in the PHOTO-PAINT 10 reference manual. Speaking of which…

The manual shipping with the CorelDRAW 10 suite is an excellent, albeit abbreviated, reference manual that is a vast improvement over the 48-page insert that was included with the original CorelDRAW 5 release.

Help on the Web

There are several Internet sites that provide answers to questions, including the Corel Web site (www.corel.com). Another useful site is a site owned by Corel called www.designer.com. As Corel PHOTO-PAINT continues to increase in popularity, expect to see an even greater number of resources appearing.

Before finishing this chapter, we need to discuss some hardware requirements that are recommended for those about to venture into the land of PHOTO-PAINT 10.

Setting Up Your System—Do You Have What It Takes?

This is more than just a cute title. Corel PHOTO-PAINT 10 requires some substantial systems resources to work properly. To make sure that you have sufficient system resources, it is necessary to spend a little time understanding what's "under the hood" with the system you already have. (Good news for you techno-wizards: If you already know everything about hardware, go directly to the next chapter.)

Hardware Considerations

The minimum requirement to run PHOTO-PAINT 10 is that you must have Windows 98 or Win2K (includes Windows ME) already installed and running. While the minimum hardware necessary to run Windows is not insignificant, it is not sufficient for photo-editing. Let's consider some realistic system requirements for using PHOTO-PAINT 10.

RAM

If you can afford it, I recommend your running with a minimum of 128MB RAM installed. I am running with 348MB RAM while working on this book. The reason for this large amount of RAM is that the price of RAM is low right now, and it was too good a deal to pass up. The performance increase you will realize with additional RAM installed greatly outweighs the dollar/benefit increase you will see with almost any other hardware purchase.

CPU

I used to recommend a Pentium system—now it is mandatory. While working on this book, I am using an Intel Pentium III (500 MHz) processor and it is no longer really fast. I also have tested a 1 GHz CPU unit from AMD. How fast is that, you ask? I can actually finish a photo-editing project before I start. Now that's fast!

The Hard Disk

Your hard disk drive should have at least several gigabytes of capacity. If that figure gave you a start, take a look at your local computer superstore. In late 2000, 40GB drives were selling for $189 or less. So how big a drive do you need? After CorelDRAW10 is loaded, you should have at least 50 to 100MB of free disk space remaining. Bitmap images take up a lot of space. So does Windows, for that matter. If you are going to be working on a lot of images and not constantly archiving them on tape or floppies, get yourself a drive large enough to handle the load. I am currently using a system with two 20GB drives, and I have already filled up most of it. Scary, isn't it?

That's all for this chapter and the first part. Next we will learn about digital images, resolution, and color. If you think that pixels are mythical winged creatures that fly in the forest, you really need to read Chapter 2.

CHAPTER 2

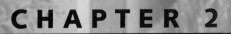

Learning About Digital Images

As the field of digital imagery expands, many people with little or no background on the subject are getting deeply involved with computer graphics. While there are many books about graphics, most of them assume that the reader knows the terminology and the technical material that serve as the foundation of computer graphics. The end result is a frustrated user. This chapter will try to help you fill in some of the gaps you might have in your graphics background.

Basic Terms in Digital Imaging

Before we dive into computer terms and acronyms, there is something you must understand first: There are many terms in the computer industry that are nonstandard, colloquial, or just plain dumb. This has led to one of my theorems regarding computer terminology: *The only thing that is universally accepted in the computer industry is that nothing is universally accepted in the computer industry.*

I don't expect the Pulitzer prize for that one, but it helps explain why there are so many different terms to describe the same thing. I am also a strong believer in using the terminology in common use rather than the technically correct term. When it comes to communicating ideas, the popular or commonly used term is more important. In this book, I will always try to use the commonly used term (even if it isn't accurate) as well as the technically correct term. Here are a few terms you need to know something about.

Bitmap and Vector Images

Computers can only understand 1's and 0's. When it comes to displaying art on computers, it is necessary to convert the images into something the computer can understand—1's and 0's. There are two ways to display images: *bitmap* (sometimes called "paint" or "raster") and *vector* (also called "freehand").

The photograph of a hamburger shown in Figure 2-1 is a typical example of a bitmap image. The image file is composed of millions of individual parts called *pixels* (picture elements). The color or shade of each part is determined by a numerical value assigned to each pixel. This photograph is small, yet it contains 289,224 pixels. Since each of these pixels requires some number of bits to define its shade or color (some require up to 32 bits), you can see why bitmap files tend to be large. The original image is color and it weighs in at 1.3 megabytes (MB). These bitmap images are displayed by using the pixels in the bitmap image to control the intensity of individual pixels on the monitor.

FIGURE 2-1   A bitmap image is composed of millions of tasty pixels

NOTE   *Adobe® refers to black-and-white images as "bitmaps." For the rest of us on the planet, a bitmap is any image composed of pixels.*

The other way to display images involves creating a series of instructions for the output device (a computer display, a printer, and so on) to follow. The hamburger shown in Figure 2-2 from a CorelDRAW clip-art collection is a relatively simple *vector* image. The image contains no pixels. The file it was created from contains hundreds of lines of instructions that define where each line segment and curve is to be placed in the image, as well as the type, size, and color of fill for each object. If the instructions were in English, and they're not, they might look like the following:

```
001 Go to row 00, column 00
002 Draw a line (direction 090) to row 00, column 80
003 Draw a circle at row 23, column 22, radius 34
004 Fill circle with a radial fill
```

This means each time the image is opened, the software application (such as CorelDRAW) must read the instructions and create the image on either the display or the printer. The advantage of this approach is that the image can be changed to almost any size. After it is resized, the application recreates it according to the modified instructions. When a bitmap image is resized, the image is distorted.

Vector images tend to be complex—meaning they may be composed of thousands of individual objects—and yet they have a much smaller file size than their bitmap equivalent. The file containing the hamburger vector image is only 17 kilobytes (K).

FIGURE 2-2 A vector image is made of less tasty vectors and curves

Figure 2-3 shows a comparison of the resulting file sizes of the two hamburgers shown in Figures 2-1 and 2-2.

What have we learned so far? Vector images can easily be resized, and their resulting file size is smaller. If we limited our comparison to the two hamburgers previously shown, it would appear that vector images are limited in their ability to look realistic. Actually, if you are willing to put in the time and effort, vector images can look like photographs—as the entry from the 1996 Corel Design Contest by James L. Higgins III shows in Figure 2-4.

FIGURE 2-3 Which burger is the light burger? The one made with vectors

FIGURE 2-4   Is it real or a drawing? Complex vector drawings approach vivid realism

The complexity of the vector-based image necessary to create the illusion is shown next in a zoomed-in view of a portion of the image as it appears (wireframe view) in CorelDRAW. Corel PHOTO-PAINT only works with bitmap images, so when a vector-based image file (like the "light" hamburger) is loaded into PHOTO-PAINT, it must first be converted, or *rasterized,* to a bitmap as it is loaded.

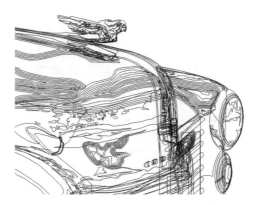

To work effectively with bitmap images in PHOTO-PAINT, it is necessary to understand how these bitmap wonders work. Let us begin by defining our terms.

Pixels

Pixels are not little elf-like creatures that fly through the forest at twilight. As we said before, bitmap images are composed of pixels. A *pixel* is the smallest variable element on a computer display or in a computer image. The term "pixel" is short for "picture element" and is used to describe several different items in graphics. At this point in the chapter, we are concerned with pixels as a way to describe the number of discrete horizontal and vertical elements in an image. The term "pixel" has replaced an earlier contraction of picture element, called the pel. As shown next, a pixel is one of several units of measure in PHOTO-PAINT.

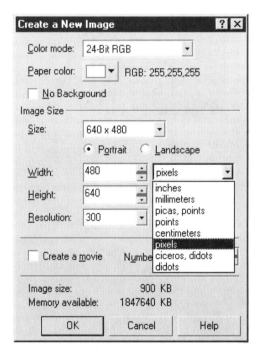

Unlike the other choices—centimeters, inches, and so on—a pixel is not a fixed size. A combination of resolution and the physical size of the image determines the size of the individual pixels that make up an image on a computer screen or on hard copy. For example, your computer monitor displays 96 pixels per inch if it is a Windows-based computer, making each pixel 1/96 of an inch square.

One way to understand pixels is to think of a mural created with mosaic tiles. When you get close to a mural made of mosaic tiles, it looks like someone had a bad LEGO day. This is because you are so close that you are looking at individual tiles. But step away a few feet from the mosaic, and the individual tiles begin to

2

lose their definition and to visually merge. The tiles have not changed their size or number, yet the farther back you move, the better the image looks. Pixels in bitmaps work much the same way.

I have created a sample image, shown in Figure 2-5, to illustrate how pixels make up an image. The part of the hamburger surrounded by the white circle on the left has been zoomed in to 1,000 percent and displayed on the right. It shows that as you zoom in on an image, the individual pixels begin to stand out more; the image they produce becomes less and less evident. Returning to our mosaic tile analogy, there are, of course, major differences between pixels and mosaic tiles. Pixels come in a greater selection of decorator colors (more than 16.7 million), and pixels don't weigh as much as tiles. However, mosaic tiles and pixels operate in the same way to produce an image.

Color Depth

What is *color depth?* It is the number of bits necessary to describe an individual pixel color. If a color image has a depth of 4 bits, that means there are 16 possible combinations of bits ($4^2 = 16$) to describe the color in each pixel. In other words, there are 16 possible colors available, or the image has a 16-color palette.

There are several different color depths available with PHOTO-PAINT. They are 1-bit (2 colors), 4-bit (16 colors), 8-bit (256 colors), 16-bit (65K grayscale),

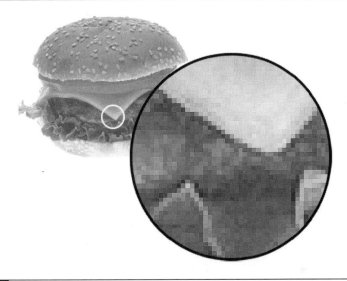

FIGURE 2-5   The pixels that make up the image become apparent at high zoom levels

24-bit (16.7 million colors), and 48-bit (281 billion colors!). There is also 32-bit color, but it is used for prepress and essentially only represents 16.7 million colors using a different type of color model.

The greater an image's color depth, the more shades of color it contains, as shown in Table 2-1. In turn, as the color depth of an image changes, the file size changes. An image whose color depth is 8-bit (which is also called *paletted*) and has a size of 400K becomes almost 800K when converted to 32-bit CMYK. Color depth is explored in depth (pardon the pun) near the end of this chapter.

> **NOTE**   *PHOTO-PAINT does not support conversion of an image to 16-bit color depth, although it will allow 16-bit color images to be opened and saved as 24-bit color images.*

All image file formats have some restrictions regarding the color depth that they can accommodate, so it becomes necessary to know what color depth you are working with in order to recognize what kinds of colors and other tools you can use with it. Don't worry about memorizing this information; PHOTO-PAINT already knows these limitations and will only let you use file formats that can accommodate the attributes of the image you want to save.

If color depth is new to you, you may be wondering, "Why do we have all these different color depths? Why not make all the images 24-bit and be done with it?" There are many reasons for the different image types. One of the major factors of color depth is the physical size of the file that each type produces. The greater the number of bits associated with each pixel (color depth), the larger the file size. If an image has a size of 20K as a black-and-white (1-bit) image, it will become

Color Depth	Type of Image	Color(s) Available
1-bit	Black-and-white	2 colors
8-bit	Grayscale	256 shades of gray
4-bit	Color	16 colors
8-bit	Color	256 colors
16-bit	Color	65,000 colors
16-bit	Grayscale	65,000 shades of gray
24-bit	Color—also called RGB color	16.7 million colors
32-bit	Color—also called CMYK	16.7 million colors
48-bit	Color	281 billion colors

TABLE 2-1   Color Depth for the Different Image Types

more than 480K as a true-color (24-bit) image. If an 8 × 10-inch color photograph is scanned in at 600 dpi (don't ever do it!) at a 24-bit color depth, the resulting 64MB+ file will probably not even fit in your system. Not to mention that every operation performed with this image will be measured in minutes instead of seconds. There are other factors associated with the different color depths.

While not all monitors are set to display 24-bit color, the ones that can are capable of displaying the full-color detail of 24-bit RGB images, which can contain almost 17 million different colors (16,777,216 to be exact). The result can be vibrant, continuous-tone, photographic-quality display. Nevertheless, 24-bit images pose certain size problems for the World Wide Web—no one wants to spend 10 minutes downloading those really cool images you create. Let's take a closer look at the various types of color depth used in the industry today.

NOTE *If you're not sure how many colors your monitor displays, try this: right-click your Desktop and select Properties. A dialog box similar to the one shown next opens, displaying your current monitor settings. This Display Properties dialog box is found in Windows 98, so yours may look slightly different.*

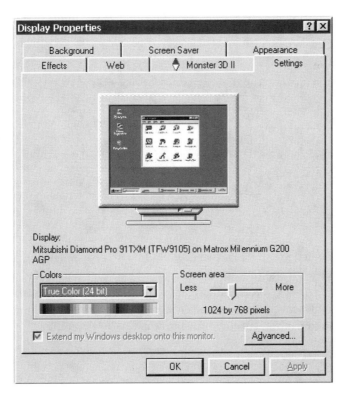

Black-and-White Images

The term "black and white" has caused some confusion in the past because old movies and television shows are referred to as being in black and white. They are actually grayscale, not black and white. Don't try to educate anyone on this subject. Just remember that the old *Andy Griffith* and *Dick Van Dyke* shows are really in grayscale, not black and white.

In real black-and-white images, one bit of information is used per pixel to define its color. Because it has only one bit, it can only show one of two states, either black or white. The pixel is turned either on or off. It doesn't get any simpler than this.

Black-and-white images are more common than you would imagine. The following illustration shows a royalty-free, black-and-white image of a Windows user who has discovered a different way to adjust her display settings. This image was downloaded from www.arttoday.com, which contains a wealth of clip art for a small yearly subscription fee. It is common to associate black-and-white images with old Victorian woodcuts, but as you can see next, black and white is still in use today. Probably one of the most common forms of black and white now are logos on business cards. They are usually very small, and the business card that you have been asked to scan is wrinkled, stained, and…never mind. Where were we?

A lot can be done with a black-and-white image, also called *line art*. Adobe refers to black-and-white images as bitmaps; no one else does. Also, this can be confusing, since most photographic images are referred to as bitmaps. To best understand how Corel converts images to black and white, I recommend taking a little side trip to the box entitled "An Introduction to Screening."

2

An Introduction to Screening

Printing is simple. A given spot on a printed page either has ink (or toner) or it doesn't. Printing does not understand shades of gray. Therefore, photographs and other material containing shades of gray must be converted to spots of pure black on a field of white.

The traditional method of doing this is called *screening*. Screening essentially simulates shades of gray by converting light grays (they are like regular grays, but have only half the calories) to tiny black dots on a white background (paper color). Conversely, dark grays are represented by large black dots. Because of the way our eyes work, these dots or, in the case of more sophisticated screening techniques, configurations of dots, appear as various shades of gray to the viewer.

A continuous-tone image, like a photograph, after being screened is known as a *halftone*. If you look at a halftone in a newspaper or magazine under a magnifying glass, it consists of a regular grid of dots. The grid is made fine enough so those individual dots are inconspicuous to the viewer. The exception to this definition is the late Roy Lichtenstein, who made a fortune creating large comic-strip panels with the dots very visible.

If an area in the photograph is 90 percent black, the halftone would be a white area occupying 10 percent of the area and black dots filling the remaining 90 percent. If another area is 30 percent gray, there would only be 30 percent of the image filled with black dots while the rest is white. Magnified, this area would look like a checkerboard, but to the viewer it appears as a gray area.

The quality of the halftone image depends on both the fineness of the grid of dots and on the number of possible dot shapes for each dot. Yes Virginia, the dots come in different shapes.

The printing industry measures the grid of dots using the term *screen ruling*. Screen ruling is equivalent to dots per inch (dpi), but it is measured in lines per inch (lpi). Screened photographs in your local paper are typically 85 lpi, while the halftones you see in magazines are typically 150 lpi. It's not that the newspapers don't like quality pictures; the screen ruling is determined by the paper type and the printing presses used.

Now that you know something about screening, you can understand how PHOTO-PAINT converts images to black and white a little better.

It is possible to use black-and-white (1-bit) images to produce photographs that appear to be grayscale by a process called *dithering*. Dithering can be thought of as pseudo-grayscale when it comes to black-and-white images. While dithering can simulate grayscale, quality suffers greatly if a dithered image is resized later.

In addition to line art, there used to be three different types of dithering available for black-and-white images: Ordered, Error Diffusion, and Halftone. Not anymore. PHOTO-PAINT 10 has seven ways to convert an image into a 1-bit black-and-white image.

> **NOTE**   *With color printers becoming so common, why would I want to convert an image to black and white? Because many times your work is reproduced on photocopy machines, and converting photographs to black and white using error diffusion offers the best results.*

The image conversion options are shown in Figure 2-6. Selecting Black and White (1-bit) opens the Convert to 1-Bit dialog box. When you click the Conversion down arrow, a list of seven options appears, as shown here.

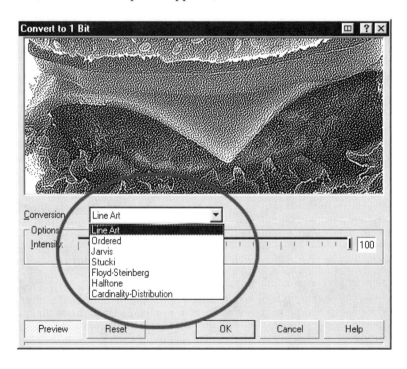

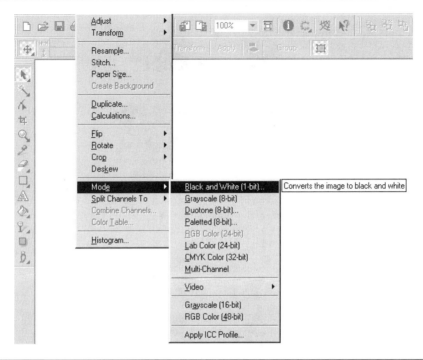

FIGURE 2-6   Selecting Mode opens a wide selection of choices for image conversion

A picture is still worth a thousand words (when adjusted for inflation). To illustrate the differences between them—and save 7,000 words—I have converted our hamburger, which is beginning to get cold, using each of the seven conversion techniques. The examples appear in Figures 2-7 through 2-13.

For more information about halftones than you might ever want, look in the Help files (Index) under Halftones.

Grayscale Images

What we call black-and-white photos are, in fact, grayscale images. Photographs (color and grayscale) are *continuous-tone* images, so called because the photo is composed of continuous areas of different colors or shades. This is unlike a digital

FIGURE 2-7 Converting the hamburger using Line Art conversion loses a lot of image detail, not to mention the bottom part of the bun

FIGURE 2-8 Using Ordered conversion is an improvement over Line Art, but the bottom of the bun is still missing

FIGURE 2-9 The Jarvis conversion offers photographic quality and the bottom of the bun

FIGURE 2-10 Stucki conversion, like Jarvis, offers photorealism and the entire hamburger; it is still a 1-bit image

FIGURE 2-11 Floyd-Steinberg conversion—the name sounds like a law firm—gives arguably the best error diffusion

FIGURE 2-12 Halftone, a classic conversion, is shown with one of its six Screen Types (Fixed 4 × 4)

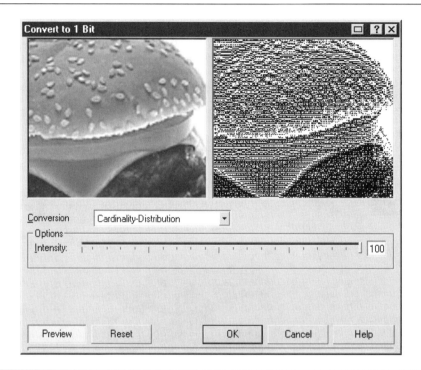

FIGURE 2-13 Cardinality-Distribution—Creates a textured look by applying a calculation and distributing the result to each pixel

image, which is composed of square pixels. To represent a black-and-white photograph in a digital format requires dividing the image into pixels using eight bits of information for each pixel, producing 256 possible shades of gray. The shade of each pixel ranges from a value of white (0) to black (255). Grayscale is used for many other things besides "black-and-white" photos. When you learn about masks (beginning in Chapter 6), you will find out that most of the masks used in photo editing are actually grayscale images.

Four-Bit and Eight-Bit Color

With the explosive growth of the use of Web pages on the Internet, 256-color (8-bit) images have become very popular. If you are using PHOTO-PAINT to create images for the Web, you will be using the 8-bit color depth a lot. (Four-bit color is rarely used.) Referred to as *paletted* or *256-color,* an 8-bit color image can only have one out of 256 combinations of color assigned to each pixel. This isn't as limited as you might imagine.

Why 256 Colors Is Really 216 on the Web   For images that will appear on Web pages, you will usually want to choose from a palette that is limited to the 256 colors that most computer users can display. Users with very high-quality display monitors and adapters that provide a 24-bit variation for each pixel can view more than 16 million different colors. However, many Web surfers have displays that can only handle 8-bit colors. If your images use a range of colors or a palette that is larger than the viewer's display or browser can handle, the browser will dither the colors. In other words, the browser will find colors within its palette that it can substitute for any color that is outside its palette. The result can get downright ugly.

Now for the big surprise: Mac and Windows browsers do not have identical color palettes. In the standard 256-color palette, only 216 are common to both platforms, but 40 are different and require dithering by one of the browsers. The good news is that Corel PHOTO-PAINT provides a Web Safe Colors palette, so your images will always look their best.

When an image is converted to 8-bit, PHOTO-PAINT creates a *reference palette* (also called a "table") to which all the colors used in the image are assigned—hence the term "paletted."

Getting a Little Technical   Here is some technical stuff that is not necessary to know but that I thought you might find interesting. The Web Safe Colors palette is based on a simplified version of the *color cube* (the color cube is another term for the color model used by browsers). The traditional 24-bit RGB color cube is based on mixing the colors red, green, and blue in varying values from 0 to 255. So, black would be represented by 0, 0, 0—no red, no green, and no blue—while white would be represented by 255, 255, 255—100 percent red, 100 percent green, and 100 percent blue. This method results in 16,777,216 colors, which are represented by 24 bits of data: three 8-bit bytes.

The 8-bit color palettes for Netscape Navigator and Microsoft Internet Explorer are based on the same idea, but using a much smaller scale. Instead of 256 values, only six values are used. These correspond to the normal color cube values of 0, 51, 102, 153, 204, and 255. Instead of resulting in the enormous 16.7 million colors, this method results in a mere 216 colors, which conveniently (and intentionally) fits within the 256 colors of an 8-bit color system.

Many people think that 8-bit color is markedly inferior to 24-bit color. That used to be true, but the process of converting the image from 16- or 24-bit to 8-bit color has been so dramatically improved that in many cases it is difficult, if not impossible, to tell the original image from the paletted one.

16-Bit Color (Thousands of Colors)

Using 16 bits to define the color depth provides approximately 65,000 colors. This is enough for almost any color image. I have seen 16- and 24-bit images side by side, and it is almost impossible to tell them apart. All things being equal, most of the photo-editing public could work with 65K color from now until the Second Coming and never notice any difference. What are the advantages of 16-bit color? Faster performance on video cards with less video RAM, because you are moving one-third fewer bits. When will you use 16-bit color? Even though PHOTO-PAINT doesn't export images in 16K color, it can open them and save them in a different color depth. You may discover that your video card is set to display in 16-bit color. This is usually the case with video cards with a limited amount of video RAM when you increase the resolution setting of your monitor. When that happens, the display adapter will change the display color depth from 24-bit to 16-bit to conserve the limited amount of video RAM.

TIP *If your display adapter is set to display 16-bit color, it does not affect the image color depth—only the display of the image.*

24-Bit (True Color)

True-color images may use up to 16.7 million colors. They are so closely associated with the RGB color model that they are sometimes referred to as RGB 24-bit. (We will talk about color models later in this chapter.) "RGB" stands for red-green-blue. Your monitor makes all its colors by using combinations of these three colors. Your eye perceives color the same way: red, green, and blue. The three colors that make up the RGB models each have eight bits assigned to them, allowing for 256 possible shades of each color. Your monitor creates colors by painting the images with three electronic beams (called *guns*). The mixing together of three sets of 256 combinations produces a possible 16.7 million color combinations. While True Color doesn't display every possible color, it gets pretty close. It is the model of choice for the desktop computer artist.

32-Bit Color

Back in Table 2-1, did you notice anything unusual about 32-bit color? Although the color depth is increased by 25 percent over a 24-bit image, the number of colors remained the same. Why is that?

There are two answers, because there are two types of color depth that involve 32 bits: a 32-bit image and an image using 32-bit color. The first is more commonly seen on the Mac side of the world. A 32-bit image uses a 24-bit RGB model with an additional 8-bit *alpha channel*. Apple reserved the alpha channel, but it has never specified a purpose for this data. The alpha channel has come to be used by most applications to pass grayscale mask information. The second use of 32-bit color is to represent the four colors that are used in printing—cyan, magenta, yellow, and black—or as they are more commonly known, *CMYK*. (*K* is used as the designator for the color black, since the letter *B* already designates the color blue.)

NOTE	*Most of the graphic processors are advertising that they offer 32-bit, 64-bit, and now 128-bit graphic processor boards. This has nothing to do with color depth. It is a reference to the width of the data path. The wider the data path, the greater the amount of color data that can be moved, and therefore the faster the screens are redrawn.*

48-Bit Color

The availability of 48-bit color can be blamed on the people who market scanners. Many of the scanners today scan color depths greater than 24 bits, then extract the best information out of the scan and send it to the computer in 24-bit format. In their headlong rush to make scanners bigger and better, someone came up with the idea of making all the unprocessed digital information available to the computer. The result is huge files of questionable worth, and you still must convert to 24- or 32-bit color to print the image.

Gamma

Gamma is an important component of an image. *Gamma* can be intimidating, but really you can think of it as a brightness control with attitude. How bright or dark an image appears on a computer display depends on several factors including the software gamma setting on the computer, the physical brightness setting of the monitor, and ambient light (the light in the room).

Before we all started displaying our pictures on the Internet, life was simpler. I never thought of displaying my photographs on a Mac, just as my Mac user counterpart never thought his creations would ever grace a PC screen. The Internet has changed all that. Because of different gamma settings inherent in the hardware, images prepared on a Mac will look too dark on a PC, and images prepared on a PC will look too bright on a Mac. One option is to adjust the gamma so the resulting image is somewhere in the middle. This way, images will appear just a little too bright on the Mac, and a little too dark on the PC. The common gamma setting on the Macintosh is 1.8, so a good compromise would be to set it to 2.0 when images will be displayed on the Web.

"Resolution"—A Term with Too Many Definitions

Without an understanding of resolution and its effects, you may find yourself creating beautiful images that fill the entire display screen in PHOTO-PAINT, yet appear to be smaller than postage stamps when you print them. Resolution is a very misunderstood concept in desktop publishing. The confusion is compounded because this term may have entirely different meanings depending on the device you are talking about. In this chapter, we will learn what resolution is and what it does for us in PHOTO-PAINT. The information about resolution that is discussed in this chapter applies to all image-editing applications, not just PHOTO-PAINT.

Resolution and the Size of the Image

As I said, the term "resolution" represents one of the more elusive concepts of digital imaging. In a vector-based program, we describe an image's size in the popular unit of measure for the country we live in. In the United States, we refer to the standard letter-size page as being 8½ × 11 inches. Image size in photo-editing programs is traditionally measured in pixels. The reason for using pixels is that the size of an image in pixels is fixed. So when I speak of an image being 1,200 by 600 pixels, I know, from experience, approximately how big the image is. If we use a unit of measure other than pixels—say, inches—the dimensions of the printed image are dependent on the resolution of the image.

So, What Is Resolution?

Resolution takes the density of pixels per inch (ppi) that make up an image and describes it in dots per inch (dpi). In other words, it is a measure of how closely each pixel in an image is positioned to the one next to it.

Let's assume we have an image that is 300 pixels wide by 300 pixels high. So how big will the image be when I import it into another application? This is a trick question. There is not enough information. Without knowing the resolution of the image, it is impossible to determine the size when it is imported into another application. If the resolution of this image is set to 300 pixels per inch, then the image dimensions are 1 × 1 inch when imported. If the resolution is *doubled* (set to 600 dpi), the image would be *half* the size, or ½ × ½ inch. If the resolution is *reduced by half* (150 dpi), the image size *doubles* to 2 × 2 inches. We can see that resolution exhibits an inverse relationship. The physical size of an image in PHOTO-PAINT is most accurately expressed as the length (in pixels) of each side. Resolution tells you how many pixels are contained in each unit of measure.

To show the effect of changing resolution, I duplicated our hamburger with PHOTO-PAINT, making three copies. Next, I changed *(resampled)* the resolution of each of the copies so that I had three photographs at three different resolutions. Even though each of the images in Figure 2-14 is a different resolution, they appear the same size in PHOTO-PAINT because PHOTO-PAINT only cares about how many pixels are in the image. When all three files were imported into CorelDRAW, the results were as shown in Figure 2-15. Why do the photos appear to be the same size in Figure 2-14, you ask? Because the physical size of the images (in pixels) remained unchanged—only the resolution changed.

Screen Resolution

No matter what resolution you are using, Corel PHOTO-PAINT displays each pixel onscreen according to the zoom ratio. That is why all the photos in Figure 2-14 appear to be the same size even though they are at different resolutions. At a zoom ratio of 100 percent, each image pixel is mapped to a single screen pixel. This is why the size of the image remains unchanged regardless of the image resolution. The display's zoom setting has no effect on the actual image file. If you are a little fuzzy on monitors and pixels, read on. If you know them cold, skip ahead to "Resolution and Printers."

FIGURE 2-14 Although each photograph is a different resolution (size), they appear the same size displayed in PHOTO-PAINT

When you bought your monitor and/or display card, you may have been bewildered by such tcrms as "640 × 480," "800 × 600," and so on. These figures refer to the number of screen pixels that the monitor can display horizontally and vertically. For example, let's say you have a plain-vanilla VGA monitor. The standard resolution for this monitor is 640 pixels wide by 480 pixels high (640 × 480). If you open a file that is over 1,000 pixels wide, the image at 100% zoom is too large to fit into the screen, as shown in Figure 2-16. With the screen resolution changed to 800 × 600 (Super VGA) the same display area now contains a width of 800 pixels by a height of 600 pixels. Since the size of the display didn't change, the pixels must be getting smaller. The image, shown in Figure 2-17, appears smaller than the photograph in the previous figure, but it is still too large to fit

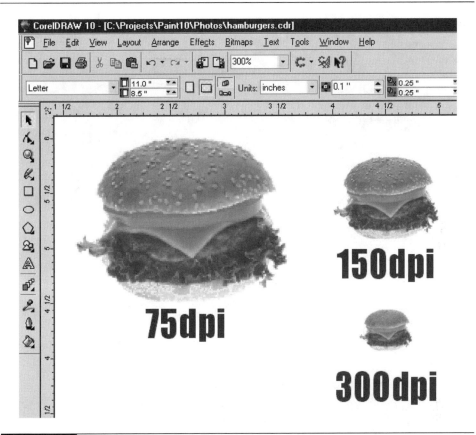

FIGURE 2-15 When the same photos are displayed in CorelDRAW, the image resolution causes them to be displayed at the size they would appear if printed

into the screen area. The size of the photograph hasn't changed, but the screen (or display) resolution has. To make more pixels fit into the same physical screen dimensions, the actual pixels must be smaller. With the resolution changed to 1,024 × 768 (Figure 2-18), most of the original photo can be seen on the screen. Again, the photograph remains unchanged; only the screen resolution has increased. Screen or display resolution operates under the same principle we discussed in the previous paragraph. As the screen resolution increases, the image size decreases proportionally.

NOTE *Because the original photograph used in Figures 2-16 through 2-18 was so large, Figures 2-17 and 2-18 had to be scaled down to fit them onto the page.*

FIGURE 2-16   Displaying a photograph that is 1,400 pixels wide using a VGA
(640 × 480) screen resolution

FIGURE 2-17   Increasing the resolution to Super VGA (800 × 600) makes the pixels
smaller, and more of the photograph can be seen

2

FIGURE 2-18   Only by increasing the resolution to 1,024 × 768 can all of the image be seen

Many people have been surprised to discover that after spending a lot of money to get a high-resolution monitor and display card, their screen images appeared smaller rather than sharper. Now that you know the secret of the screen resolution game, have your friends buy you lunch and you can explain it to them, too.

Screen Setting Recommendations

With all the exciting ads for high-resolution displays and graphics adapters, it is difficult not to get caught up in the fever to upgrade. If you have a 14- or 15-inch monitor, you should be using the VGA or Super VGA screen resolution setting on your graphics card. If you go for a higher resolution on a 14- or 15-inch display, even if your monitor supports it, your friends may start calling you Blinky, because you will be squinting all the time to read the screen. Also, be cautious about recommendations from the retail clerk/computer expert at your computer superstore. Remember that last week your "expert" might have been bagging groceries and may know less about computers than you do.

With the price of 17-inch displays dropping, more people are investing in a few extra inches on their display. Just because you have a 17- or a 21-inch monitor does not mean you have a moral obligation to run it at the highest resolution that your display adapter will support. Using the wrong resolution for your monitor can sometimes damage the monitor or cause something worse, as shown next. I use a setting of 1,024 × 780 most of the time with my 21-inch monitor, and it works very well. Some display adapters only support 24-bit color up to 800 × 600 without adding extra memory to the video card.

Resolution and Printers

If this were a perfect world, image resolution would be the same as printer resolution (which is also measured in dpi). Then, if we were printing to a 600-dpi printer in our perfect world, we would be using a 600-dpi-resolution image, because each image pixel would occupy one printer dot. However, it is not a perfect world. First of all, pixels are square and printer dots are round. When we talk about printer resolution, we are talking about the size of the smallest dot the printer can make. If you are using a 600-dpi laser printer, the size of the dot it produces is 1/600th of an inch in diameter. The dot it creates is either on or off—there is either a black dot on the paper or there isn't. If we are displaying a grayscale photograph, we know that each pixel can be 1 of 256 possible shades. So how does the laser printer create shades of gray from black-and-white dots? Using halftone cells. What? Read on.

Creating Halftones

If I take an area on the paper and create a box that has a width of 10 dots and a height of 10 dots, it would have a capacity to fit 100 dots in it. If I were to place printer dots at every other possible point, it would only hold 50 printer dots. The

2

result when printed on paper would appear to the eye as gray or 50 percent black. This is the principle behind the *halftone cell.* The halftone cell created by the laser printer is equivalent to the pixel—not exactly, but close enough for the purposes of discussion. The number of halftone cells a laser printer can produce is a function of its *line frequency,* which some of us old-timers still refer to as "screen frequency." Companies that produce advertisements to sell their printers to the consumer marketplace never discuss line frequency, expressed as lpi (lines per inch). And why not? Because, in this hyper-advertised computer marketplace, bigger is better (except for price). And which sounds better—a 600-dpi printer or a 153-lpi printer? The 153-lpi printer would have a resolution of around 1,200 dpi. Names and numbers are everything in selling a product. This resolution-specification hype also confuses the scanner market as well.

So what resolution should you use? I have included the values in Table 2-2 for use as general guidelines when setting up the resolution of an image in PHOTO-PAINT.

In the next chapter we will take a look at color to understand some basics of how it works and, more importantly, how to get what comes back from the printer to look like what we see on the display.

Basic Color Theory

Color is everywhere. Even black and white are colors. Really. Color has the greatest and most immediate effect on the viewer of any factor in graphic design. Psychologists confirm that color has an enormous capacity for getting our attention. To use color effectively, we must have a basic understanding of it.

Image Type	Final Output	Recommended Resolution
Black-and-white	Laser printer (600 dpi)	600 dpi
Black-and-white	Display screen	Convert black-and-white image to grayscale and use 72–96 dpi
Grayscale	Laser printer	150–200 dpi
Grayscale	Imagesetter	200–300 dpi
Grayscale	Display screen	72–96 dpi
Color	Color ink-jet printer	100–150 dpi
Color	Imagesetter	150–200 dpi
Color	Display screen	72–96 dpi

TABLE 2-2   Recommended Resolution Settings

If you were looking for a detailed discussion on the complex mathematics of color models, you won't find it here. What you will find here is a nontechnical discussion of the basic concepts and terminology of color.

Knowing how color works in the natural world and how this "real-world" color operates in a computer will help you when dealing with the complexities of the color models. It will be simple, and I think you will find it interesting.

Color Models

Color is made up of light components that, when combined in varying percentages, create separate and distinct colors. You also learned this in elementary school when the teacher had you take the blue poster paint and mix it with the yellow paint to make green. Mixing pigments on a palette is simple. Mixing colors on a computer is not. The rules that govern the mixing of computer colors change, depending on the color model being used.

There are many color models available in PHOTO-PAINT. They provide different ways to view and manipulate an image. To view different color models, you need to load the Paint Color dialog box, which is done by double-clicking a Paint swatch in the status bar and then selecting the Models tab. These color models fall into one of two basic categories: *additive color* and *subtractive color.* Additive color (also known as RGB) is the system used by color monitors, scanners, photography, and the human eye. Subtractive color (also known as CMYK) is used in four-color publishing and printing. Let's take a closer look at both.

Additive Color (RGB)

This model is said to use the additive process because colors are produced by adding one or more colors. RGB (red-green-blue) involves transmitted light as the source of color. In the additive model, color is created by adding different amounts of red, green, and blue light.

Pure white light is composed of equal amounts of red, green, and blue. For the record, red, green, and blue are referred to as the *additive primary colors,* so called because when they are added (combined) in varying amounts, they can produce all the other colors in the visible spectrum.

Subtractive Color (CMYK)

The subtractive model is so named because colors are subtracted from white light to produce other colors. This model uses the secondary colors: cyan, magenta, and yellow. As you have already learned, this is called the CMYK model, because combining equal amounts of cyan, magenta, and yellow only produces black, in theory. When printed, they produce something closer to swamp mud than black; so, to create a vivid picture, black is added to compensate for the inability of the colors CMY to make a good black. As noted earlier, K is used as the designator for the color black, since the letter *B* already designates the color blue.

CMYK is a printer's model, based on inks and dyes. It is the basis for almost all conventional color photography and commercial color printing. Cyan, magenta, and yellow dyes and inks simply transmit light better and are more chemically stable than red, green, and blue inks.

Describing Colors

If someone were to ask me to describe the color of my son's Ford pickup, it would be easy. It is black. The color of my wife's car is more difficult. Is it dark metallic green or deep forest green? The terms generally used to describe color are subjective. Even for simple classifications involving primary colors like red and blue, it becomes difficult to describe the exact color. Is it deep-sea blue or navy blue? In the world of color, we need a way to accurately describe the *value* of color.

When creating or picking out a color in PHOTO-PAINT, you can specify the color either by defining values for its component parts or by using a color-matching system. When using the RGB model in PHOTO-PAINT (it is the default color model), color values are expressed in shades of RGB. The maximum number of shades a color can contain is 256. For example, the value of red in an RGB model is defined as 255, 0, 0. In other words, the color contains the maximum amount (255) of the red component and a value of zero for the green and blue components. *Let me interject here that in PHOTO-PAINT, you still pick colors from color palettes that contain recognizable colors like red, green, and blue. You won't have to sit with a calculator and figure out the value of puce.*

In CMYK, the component values are traditionally expressed as a percentage, so the maximum value of any color is 100. It should be noted, however, that PHOTO-PAINT allows you to express CMYK values in both percentages and shades (0–255). The color red in the CMYK model is 0, 100, 100, 0. In other words, mixing the maximum values of magenta and yellow with no cyan and no black creates the color red.

Color Matching

While defining colors as either number of shades in the RGB model or percentage of tint in CMYK is accurate, it is not practical. Given that we cannot assign names to the millions of shades of color that are possible, we need a workable solution. The use of color-matching systems like the Pantone™ Spot colors provides a solution. The designer and the printer have identical books of print samples. The designer wants to use red in a two-color publication and specifies PANTONE Red 032 CV. The printer looks up the formula in the Pantone™ book for the percentages of magenta and yellow to mix together and prints the first sample. The output is then compared with the book of print samples, called a *swatch book*. Most corporate accounts will use one of the popular color-matching systems to specify the colors they want in their logos and ads. Color matching in the digital age is less than 10 years old. It has come a long way in its short life and is now finding its way into the design of Internet Web sites. No longer restricted to four- and six-color printing, the color-matching systems are dealing with the important issues of colors looking correct on the Internet, too. Color correction on the Web is critical for companies selling products. For example, if the color of the sweater you saw on the Web isn't even close to what arrives in the box, the product will probably be returned. To accurately display colors in images has become invaluable.

RGB Versus CMYK

Each color model represents a different viewpoint. Each offers advantages and disadvantages. If you are using Corel PHOTO-PAINT to create multimedia and Web pages, or just printing to ink-jet or color laser printers, knowing how to get what you need out of RGB will more than satisfy your requirements. If you must accurately translate color from the screen to the printed page, you must get more deeply involved in CMYK.

Hue, Saturation, and Brightness

The terms hue, saturation, and brightness (also called "luminosity") are used throughout PHOTO-PAINT. *Hue* describes the individual colors—for example, a blue object can be said to have a blue hue. *Saturation* is technically the purity of the color. In practical terms, it is the balance between neutral gray and the color. If an image has no saturation, it looks like a grayscale image. If the saturation is 100 percent, it may look unnatural, since the image's midtones, which the gray component emphasizes, are lost. *Brightness* is the amount of light reflecting from an object determining how dark or light the image appears.

Color Gamut

It may come as a surprise to you, but there are a lot more colors in the real world than photographic films or printing presses can recreate. The technical term for this range of colors is *gamut*. There are many gamuts—for monitors, scanners, photographic film, and printing processes. Each gamut represents the range of colors that can actually be displayed, captured, or reproduced by the appropriate device or process. The widest gamut is the human eye, which can see billions of colors. Further down on this visual hierarchy is the color computer monitor, which can display 16 million colors. Photographic film can only capture 10,000 to 15,000 colors, and a high-quality four-color printing process can reproduce from 5,000 to 6,000. We won't even discuss the limitations of color ink on newsprint.

In Summary

If you have read through this chapter, you should have enough background to understand how the tools and commands in PHOTO-PAINT work. The good news is, there won't be a test. Now let's begin to work with PHOTO-PAINT 10. Were you thinking we weren't ever going to get to the actual program?

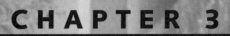

CHAPTER 3

Opening, Creating, and Saving Images

Before you can apply all of the fantastic effects described in this book to your favorite photo, you first need to get that image into PHOTO-PAINT. After you have finished your masterpiece, it then needs to be saved in the appropriate format so that it can be displayed or printed. Whether you are scanning photos, importing them from a digital camera, or downloading images from the Internet, there are so many ways to get images in and out of PHOTO-PAINT it is necessary to set aside a chapter just to explore this subject.

Overview of Image File Management

Corel PHOTO-PAINT contains very powerful file import features, which means that you can open up just about anything except possibly a Swiss bank account. Not only can you open existing bitmap graphic files but you can also open and convert vector files into bitmaps. PHOTO-PAINT also offers the ability to import and render 3D models to add objects to your images that are photo-realistic. Once an image is in PHOTO-PAINT, it can be saved or exported into just about any industry standard graphic format, including some proprietary formats like Adobe Photoshop®.

Most of the operations involved with opening, closing, and saving files in PHOTO-PAINT are common to all Windows applications. To save both time and precious pages, I will assume that you already know how to do basic Windows file operations, and so I will concentrate on features that are unique to PHOTO-PAINT.

This chapter explores procedures and options for opening existing graphic files and how to save or export these files into one of many other graphic formats.

Welcome to PHOTO-PAINT

The first time you launch PHOTO-PAINT, the welcome screen, shown next, is displayed offering you six choices, including two options that open files. Even though this seems really friendly, don't feel obligated to choose any of them; you can just close the welcome screen window. If you uncheck Show This Welcome Screen at Startup, it won't appear the next time you launch PHOTO-PAINT. You can restore the welcome screen by opening Options (CTRL-J) and changing the On Startup setting in the General page of the Workspace settings.

Opening an Existing Image

Assuming that the image you wish to work with has already been saved as a graphic file, here is what you need to know to open it. Choosing File | Open, clicking the file open icon in the Standard toolbar, or using the keyboard shortcut CTRL-O displays the dialog box shown in Figure 3-1. If the dialog box doesn't have its Options button enabled, most of the buttons and icons displayed represent

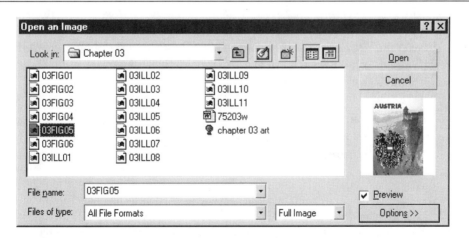

FIGURE 3-1   The Open an Image dialog box offers many options for opening graphic files

standard Windows features for opening files. To open an image, select the file, and click the Open button. That's all there is to it.

> **TIP** *When you are looking for files in a folder containing lots and lots of files, you can speed up the search by using Files of Type to limit the types of files displayed in the dialog box to a specific graphic format. Be aware that this setting remains where you put it last, so if later on you are looking for a different format file, you might get a little frustrated wondering where the file went before realizing that the dialog box is not set for All File Formats.*

More File Opening Features

When you check the Preview box, PHOTO-PAINT displays a thumbnail of the selected image file. This is a great feature when you want to preview some images or you can't remember what filename you used to save a particular image you are now trying to find. The Preview feature has a downside, though—it can slow things down. This is especially true when the images are on a slow reading medium such as a floppy disk or a CD-ROM. If you know the name of the file you want to open, I recommend leaving the Preview box unchecked.

> **TIP** *You can select and open several files at once. If the files are all together on the file list, click the first one and then SHIFT-click the last one. This selects all of the files in between. If the files are scattered throughout the folder, CTRL-click each file before using the Open button. The preview feature is automatically turned off when multiple files are selected.*

We still are not finished. If you click the Options button on the Open an Image dialog box, you get a bigger dialog box (at no extra charge), as shown in Figure 3-2. The larger dialog box displays more information about the selected image file plus a few neat, if rarely used, options.

Modifying the Image As It Opens

PHOTO-PAINT can remove part of an image (cropping) or make the image smaller (resampling) as the file is opened. Unless you change this option from the Full Image setting, PHOTO-PAINT opens the entire image without applying any changes.

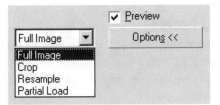

If the image is going to be either cropped or resized after it is opened, you should consider using either the Crop or Resample option. Cropping or resampling an image as an image is opened saves system resources (especially if it is a large image or you have limited system memory) and time. The topics of cropping and resampling are covered in greater detail in Chapter 4.

FIGURE 3-2   Clicking the Options button provides more file information and options

Size, Format, and Notes

With the Options button enabled, you can see additional information about files you have selected: image size, color mode (depth), and file format. If notes were attached to the file when it was saved, they are displayed as well.

Checking for Watermarks

Corel PHOTO-PAINT includes the PictureMarc plug-in from Digimarc, which allows you to embed and read digital watermarks in an image. These watermarks contain information about copyrights and authorship and provide a persistent identity, which travels with the image wherever it goes. The watermarks are not visible to the viewer. Digimarc watermarks do not prevent someone from using your images, but they do prove who created the image.

If you're opening a file format other than Corel PHOTO-PAINT (CPT) with this check box checked, if a watermark is present a copyright symbol appears after the filename on the title bar as shown next. You can obtain information about the watermark by reading the embedded message and by linking to the contact profile of the creator of the image in Digimarc's database. For more information about Digimarc, see www.digimarc.com.

imagination © (24-Bit RGB) @100% - Background

Reopening Images

There are two ways to quickly reopen files that you've already worked on. When you open the File menu, the last four files that were opened will appear at the bottom of the list. Just click the filename and it will open. Another way is to click the down arrow of the File Name field in the Open an Image dialog box to display a drop-down list containing the names and paths of the last five files that were opened.

TIP   *If PHOTO-PAINT isn't running, you can click the Windows Start button and choose Documents. If the PHOTO-PAINT file appears on the list, click it and Windows will launch PHOTO-PAINT and load the image. How's that for service?*

3

Opening Photo CDs

Once upon a time Kodak attempted to set the standards for consumer digital photography, and part of that attempt was a new file format known as Photo CD (PCD). Although Kodak was unsuccessful in that venture, it appeared for a short while that the PCD format was going to become the preferred format for stock photographs. The increased popularity of the Internet made the JPEG format a more popular choice. These days the PCD format is most often seen on older CDs with stock photography collections and from photos put onto a CD by your friendly neighborhood Kodak developer.

While opening a PCD image in PHOTO-PAINT 10 is much simpler than in previous versions of PHOTO-PAINT, you still have a few terms and concepts to be aware of when opening a PCD file. When a PCD file is opened, a secondary PCD Import dialog box appears, as shown next. From this dialog box you can specify the size of the image (Kodak insists on referring to the size as resolution), select the color depth (called image type), and apply color correction.

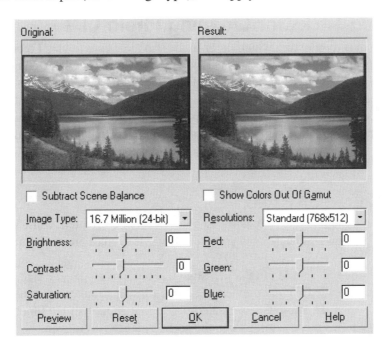

Using the Photo CD Dialog Box Preview

The dialog box has two options for previewing the effects of the changes you are applying. In the upper-right corner of the dialog box is a button that switches the preview from the Original-Result format (which the rest of the planet calls before-after) to a single result screen. The Preview button in the lower left must be enabled for the Result window to show the changes.

To zoom the image in the preview in and out, place the cursor in the preview window (the original window with the Original-Result display) so that it becomes a hand. Click the left mouse button to zoom in and the right button to zoom out. Simple, right? The quality of the preview will become poor as you zoom in, because you are looking at a thumbnail and not the actual image.

 PHOTO-PAINT can only open Photo CD (PCD) files; it cannot save existing images as PCD files.

Tips and Tricks for Opening Photo CDs

When it comes to selecting which color mode (Image Type) to use, I recommend always choosing 16.7 million (24-bit) color, or 256 Color Grayscale if the image will be used where color is not required. If you need to use the image on the Web, you can very easily convert it to 256-color in PHOTO-PAINT. Many editing features and effects in PHOTO-PAINT are only available when the image is either 24-bit color or grayscale. Later it is a simple matter to convert the image to 256-color before saving it in a suitable format for the Web.

Color Correction Issues

Before you are tempted to play with the color or tonal correction, consider that your only preview of the changes you are making is a small preview thumbnail. It is best to apply correction in PHOTO-PAINT.

One setting you should always investigate is the Subtract Scene Balance check box under the Original preview. The photofinisher makes the scene balance adjustment when the Photo CD is created. I find that about half the time the color in the image looks more natural when the scene balance is removed.

Finding the Right Image Size

You have a lot of choices when it comes to selecting image size, as shown by the drop-down list shown next. The size selection, called "Resolutions," actually selects the dimensions of the completed image in pixels. Don't worry about the names of the sizes; like everything else in this dialog box, these were terms chosen by Kodak. Always choose a size large enough for the work you have to do. You can always resample the image and make it smaller. I recommend using a size no smaller than Standard.

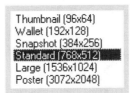

When opening an image on a CD, you will see a message box as shown next. While its message is obvious, it can become irritating after opening the twentieth image on a CD. To turn this feature off, open the Options dialog box (CTRL-J), select the Warnings page, and uncheck the Read-only status warning.

That wraps up Photo CDs, so let's look at another unique type of file you can open with PHOTO-PAINT.

Opening Vector Images

While opening bitmap images in PHOTO-PAINT involves few choices, opening a vector file like a CorelDRAW (CDR) or Windows Metafile (WMF) file requires some additional information from you to complete the process. PHOTO-PAINT must convert the vector image to a bitmap through a process called rasterization; therefore when a vector file is opened, a secondary dialog Import to Bitmap box opens, as shown in Figure 3-3.

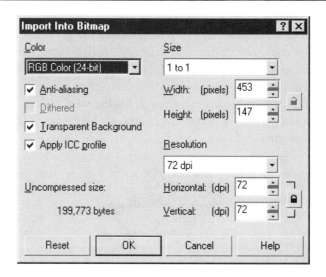

FIGURE 3-3 The Import Into Bitmap dialog box allows you to control the conversion of vector files into bitmaps

Setting Up the Import Into Bitmap Dialog Box

This dialog box appears a little complicated the first time you see it. Especially if you weren't expecting it to appear. Let's take a look at it, and we will discover what the controls do and consider some suggested settings.

Choosing the Optimum Color Mode

The first choice is the Color setting, which offers a choice of six different color depths. If the file you are importing is color, I recommend the setting "RGB Color (24-bit)" because it is the native color depth of PHOTO-PAINT. Unless it is absolutely necessary, avoid using the 16 colors or Paletted (8-bit) options. You will see consistently superior results by making the conversion to the desired color mode using PHOTO-PAINT.

Picking Size and Resolution

Next is the Size setting, which should be left at 1 to 1. At this setting, the ratio of height to width (aspect ratio) of the image will remain unchanged. If you use one of the other fixed aspect ratio choices on the drop-down list, the resulting bitmap may be distorted if the aspect ratio is different than the ratio of the vector file being rasterized. Below the Size setting, the dimensions of the resulting bitmap are displayed if 1 to 1 is selected. You can also enter your own dimensions into the value boxes—if you are really sure of what you're doing.

The Resolution settings can be selected from a long drop-down list containing many preset resolutions, or the desired resolution for the bitmap can be entered directly into the value boxes. I suggest one of the preset Resolution values using 72 or 96 dpi for images that will appear on the Web or a higher resolution (200 and up) for graphics that will be printed. The projected file size appears in the lower-left corner of the dialog box.

Options to Consider—Briefly

The remaining choices are check boxes beginning with the Anti-Aliasing check box, which should be checked. The Dithered check box is only available when Black and White, 16 Colors, or Paletted (8-bit) color is selected. While Dithering reduces banding, it also makes the image difficult to resize without developing moiré patterns. The Apply ICC Profile check box embeds the appropriate ICC profile information into the bitmap so that color accuracy can be obtained on systems that support this form of color management.

Using Transparent Backgrounds

My favorite check box is Transparent Background. When enabled, the vector image is converted to a bitmap object without a background. This means that the resulting image can be placed in another image without the need to create a complex selection mask as done in previous releases of PHOTO-PAINT. To show how this can be used, the CorelDRAW clip art seen in Figure 3-4 was opened in PHOTO-PAINT. The checkered pattern represents the transparent background.

FIGURE 3-4 Vector clip art can easily be converted to bitmaps in PHOTO-PAINT

Once the converted vector image is in this format, it is a simple matter to drag the image onto a photograph, as shown in Figure 3-5. On the photograph, the former clip art becomes a floating bitmap image that is called an *object*. It can be resized or rotated and have a whole array of effects applied to it. See Chapter 7 to learn more about PHOTO-PAINT objects.

Opening 3D Images

One of the unique types of files that can be opened and used by PHOTO-PAINT is three-dimensional model files. You can open any 3D model file saved as a QuickDRAW Meta File (3DMF), QuickDRAW Binary 3D (B3D), or QuickDRAW McGraw (sorry). While these are older 3D graphic formats (meaning you won't find

FIGURE 3-5   Combining vector images and photographs is easy with PHOTO-PAINT

a lot of free examples on the Internet), Corel ships and has shipped a lot of 3D models to play with. What makes a 3D model different from any other image you can open is that when the dialog box is open, you can actually change the viewing angle and lighting of the image.

Once you open a 3D image a secondary dialog box (shown next) opens. At this point, you are looking at a 3D viewing engine, and you can rotate the model as well as add and remove lighting. When the model is finished, the image is imported into PHOTO-PAINT as a bitmap (2D) image with a transparent background and has lost all of its 3D information. In Figure 3-6, I used the Laptop.3DMF file from a Corel 8 CD. In the Import 3D Model dialog box, I repositioned the model to the angle I wanted for the ad I was creating and clicked OK to render it. Next, I dragged the laptop bitmap onto a stock Corel photo and added some text. Just for fun, I used CorelCAPTURE to capture the screen with the ad I was working on, and pasting it as an object, I changed its shape and placed it in the laptop's screen.

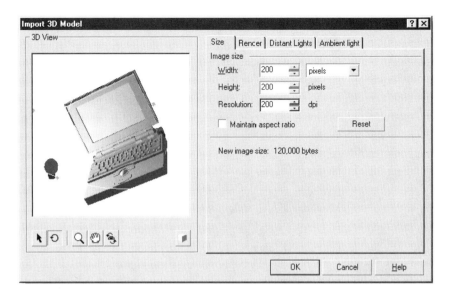

While I think the operation of the Import 3D Model dialog box is intuitive, you can get detailed information on how to control the lighting and other settings in the Corel PHOTO-PAINT User's Manual.

FIGURE 3-6   3D model images can also be imported into existing photographs

Creating New Images

Up until now, we have been looking at how to open existing images. While most of the work you do in PHOTO-PAINT will involve existing images, there are times you will need to create an image from scratch. While it isn't complicated to create a new image, let's take a look at the procedure and the dialog box used to create the image.

Defining Your New Image

One of the most common remarks I hear from CorelDRAW users when they open PHOTO-PAINT for the first time is "Where's the blank page?" I can't find fault with these users, since I made the same remark the first time I opened PHOTO-PAINT 4. To make a new image, select File | New, CTRL-N, or the paper icon on the menu bar. Either way, the Create a New Image dialog box opens as shown in Figure 3-7. Don't let the number of settings alarm you; it will be a rare day that you change more than two or three of the settings.

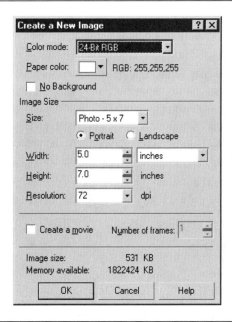

FIGURE 3-7   Changing settings in the Create a New Image dialog box

Understanding the Create a New Image Dialog Box

This is usually the first dialog box that new PHOTO-PAINT users see, and the effect on someone new to bitmap editing can be intimidating. When you get past all of the drop-down lists and value boxes, this dialog box controls color modes, paper color, image size, and a few options. Let's see how this beauty works.

Picking the Right Color and Background

The Color Mode list box gives you a choice of eight different settings. The general rule I use for this setting is: if it is color, use 24-bit RGB; if it is not, choose 8-bit grayscale. Here is my reasoning for this simplistic rule: even if I will eventually convert the image to CMYK for printing or to 8-bit Paletted for the Web, I will do all of my work on a 24-bit RGB image and convert it to the appropriate color mode as a final step.

The Paper Color setting is a "no brainer." Pick a color for the background (which is called Paper in PHOTO-PAINT). You will find that most of the time you will use white.

The No Background check box creates an image that only contains one transparent object. This feature is very handy for making images for the Web or to create objects for other images.

Picking the Right Size

The settings in the Image Size section of the dialog box are closely interrelated. The preset settings available in the Size drop-down list change to match the units of measure. For example, if the unit of measure is set to Pixels, the size presets include: 640 × 480, 800 × 600, and so on. If it is changed to inches, the presets change to include Photo 3 × 5, Photo 5 × 7, Letter, Legal. If millimeters are chosen, the presets reflect European sizes such as A3, A4, B5. Of course, you can directly enter the height and width of your image in the appropriate value box. Although Resolution has preset values, you can enter any value you want into the value box. When selecting a resolution, remember that if you are not exactly sure about the size of the new image, make it too large rather than too small. Images suffer much less quality loss when made smaller than when they must be made larger.

Options and Features

Want to make a movie? Selecting the Create a Movie check box allows you to specify how many frames your animation/movie will contain. Don't be too concerned about how many frames are required to make your movie. You can always add more frames later.

Before we leave this subject, I should point out that at the bottom of the dialog box are two values that you should be aware of. The Image Size refers to the projected size of the image you are creating, while Memory Available is there to give you some idea how much room your image is going to take up in memory. Back when memory chips (before SIMMS) cost more that gold, it was necessary to keep a close eye on these values. Now, with even low-cost (sounds better than cheap) systems sporting 128MB of RAM, you rarely need to be concerned about these numbers.

Creating Images from the Clipboard

If you capture an image into the Windows Clipboard, you can use it to create a new image. This is really handy when you are using a screen capture program like Corel CAPTURE. Select File | New From Clipboard and the contents of the Clipboard are pasted into an image that is the dimensions of the Clipboard contents. A word of caution here: more times than I would like to admit I have forgotten that I had just copied a large amount of text to the Clipboard and when I created a new image with it, PHOTO-PAINT almost threw a hairball trying to rasterize all of that text.

Saving Your Work

Once you have created or opened an image and then completed all of your work, you are going to want to save it. Fortunately, that is very easy. Your choices are pretty much standard Windows fare, but there some features Corel included to make your image management easier.

Saving Versus Exporting—They're the Same but Different

There are three basic commands for saving image files: Save, Save As, and Export. Using File | Save or CTRL-S opens the Save an Image to Disk dialog box as shown in Figure 3-8. This will save the file to the directory that Windows is currently pointing to. There is one caveat to the Save command: You can only save the image in a format that will keep all of the current contents of the image without modification. In other words, if I want to save a PHOTO-PAINT image

FIGURE 3-8   Saving images to disk

that contains objects and masks, the only choices available in the Files of Type drop-down list will be formats for PHOTO-PAINT and Photoshop (which is compatible with PHOTO-PAINT).

If the image is on a CD-ROM (or some other write-protected source), it can only be saved by using File | Save As or the Export command (CTRL-E). Just as with the Save command, your choice of graphics formats is limited to formats that can contain all of the image's content without modification.

Export saves a copy of the selected file in just about any format your heart desires. If changes need to be made (for example, objects are merged), a message box will appear advising you of the modification made to the exported file that you must OK. (An example is shown next.) Even though the copy is modified, the original remains unchanged. Unlike with the Save and Save As commands, the name of an exported file doesn't appear on the file history list.

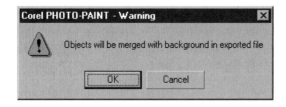

Options for Saving Files

There are only a few unique options on this dialog box, and some of them interact with one another. The Files of Type setting offers a large number of different graphic formats into which you can save your masterpiece. When you open the list to find a graphic format, you will discover that there is a large selection of graphic formats available, as discussed in the following sections. The format you select will control whether or not the Compression Type feature is enabled. For example, if you're saving a file in Corel PHOTO-PAINT native format (CPT), compression is not available because automatic compression is part of the format.

The "Selected Only" check box   The Web_safe_filenames option, when enabled, will ensure that the filename you use to save your file doesn't violate Web file naming conventions. Several file formats call up secondary dialog boxes when you save the file so that you can make adjustments to their settings. Checking the Do Not Show Filter Dialog feature tells PHOTO-PAINT to use the last setting for this format and not to open the secondary dialog box. It is always a safe practice to uncheck this feature the first time you save an image, just to make sure what its current settings are.

The ability to add notes to an image is a neat feature for attaching all kinds of textual information about the image you are saving. Just type what you want into the dialog and when you save, the text will be attached to the image file. Now that you know how to use this dialog box, let's review some of the more popular graphic file formats.

Understanding File Formats

The file format we choose defines the way an image's data is stored in a file and any related information in a way that other programs can recognize and use. Each format has its own unique form, called a *file structure*, for saving the image pixels and other related file information such as resolution and color depth.

Each format is unique and is generally identified by its three-letter file extension. For example, in the filename BUGS.CPT, the three-letter extension "CPT" identifies the file format as a Corel PHOTO-PAINT file. Images that will be used on a PC Windows platform need to have the right three-character extension so that the application can select the appropriate Import filter. If the wrong extension or a unique extension is used, it may be difficult, perhaps impossible, to import the image. If you know the file will be opened on a PC, be sure to add the correct extension to the filename.

When saving a file, Corel PHOTO-PAINT is aware of the color depth of the image and changes the selection of available file-format choices automatically.

For example, if you have a 32-bit color image, the drop-down list will be reduced from the normal selection to the few file format choices that support 32-bit color.

Because there are dozens of file formats, it would be confusing to try to cover them all. Instead, we will look at the major ones supported by Corel PHOTO-PAINT and discuss a few of their strengths and limitations.

CPT (Going Native)

CPT is a native format of Corel PHOTO-PAINT. The term *native* means it is unique to the application. Corel PHOTO-PAINT format is the best one for your originals because it retains all of the unique PHOTO-PAINT information about the image being saved. Saving in other image formats may result in the loss of this information. Another feature of the CPT format is that it automatically compresses the image when saved (using lossless compression) and loads faster than any other format.

PHOTO-PAINT has two different CPT formats, each one for different releases of PHOTO-PAINT. The two versions are PHOTO-PAINT 7/8 (which I hope is self-explanatory) and PHOTO-PAINT, which works with versions 9 and 10. It is best to save your work in the native format of the version you are currently using. Then if you need to send the work to someone or somewhere else that does not have that version, you can use the Export command to convert it to the desired file format.

Windows Bitmap (BMP, DIB)

BMP (Windows Bitmap) is the native image format for Microsoft Paint, which is included with every copy of Microsoft Windows and supported by nearly every Windows program. Corel PHOTO-PAINT supports BMP images up to 24-bit color (16.7 million colors). This is a popular format that decorates everyone's computer screen these days, but it may not offer compression and is generally used only for small image files (less than a few hundred kilobytes in size).

Graphics Interchange Format (GIF)

CompuServe created GIF (Graphics Interchange Format) a long time ago as a means of compressing images for use over their extensive online network. GIF has become a very popular format, especially now that everyone is jumping on the Internet. As a way to send pictures over phone lines, it can't be beat. Its single limitation is it only supports 8-bit (256-color) images. Corel PHOTO-PAINT does not offer an option to compress images saved as GIF files because it is already a compression format. The principal advantage of GIF is the support of transparent backgrounds.

NOTE *There is a detailed discussion of both the JPEG and GIF formats in reference to using them on the Web in Chapter 16.*

PICT

Apple developed PICT as the primary format for Macintosh graphics. Like PostScript, it is a page-description language. While it is a default format for the Mac platform, it is a troublesome format. If you are going to save a PHOTO-PAINT image for use in a Macintosh application, use TIFF instead.

TIFF (Tagged Image File Format, TIF)

TIFF is probably the most popular full-color bitmap format around, supported by every PC and Mac paint program I have ever seen. TIFF is clearly the image format of choice for graphics that are going to be printed or used in other applications. It is used as a default format setting for every scanning program on the marketplace today.

There are many different versions of TIFF, a fact that can conceivably cause some compatibility problems when moving images between programs. To date, the only problems we have experienced with TIFF files have involved saving images as 24-bit color TIFF files and trying to read them on an application that doesn't offer 24-bit color support.

Corel PHOTO-PAINT supports all color-depth settings in TIFF format, including 32-bit color (CMYK). However, don't save your images in 32-bit color unless it is specifically requested. Because 32-bit color (CMYK) is not supported by all programs that can import TIFF files, you may end up with a TIFF file that some older applications cannot read. Remember that 32-bit (CMYK) TIFF contains the same color information as 24-bit color TIFF.

Photoshop (PSD)

Yes, for all of these references I make to Photoshop, it is good to know PHOTO-PAINT can both read and save in PSD format. You might be surprised to know that with the exception of CPT, the native format for PHOTO-PAINT, the PSD format allows preservation of more PHOTO-PAINT internal data (channels, masks, and so on) than any other file format. This is also a very handy format to use when giving your artwork to a Mac service bureau.

Now that you understand a few of the file formats, let's move on and learn about the subject of file compression.

File Compression

As the file size of images increases, so does our need for a method of compressing the image information so as to get the most information in the smallest possible space. The file compression we use in graphics is not related to any compression that you may already be using on your disk drive. Although several compression schemes are either built into the file formats or offered as options when saving the file, we need to know a few things about compression and its benefits and drawbacks. Compression is generally divided into two categories: lossless and lossy.

Lossy Compression

Lossy compression offers the greatest amount of compression, but at a price. As the name implies, some of the image quality is lost in the process. Lossy compression schemes can reduce very large files from several megabytes in size to only a few kilobytes. Most of the time the loss in quality is not apparent. The most popular example of lossy compression is the JPEG format. Another compression method that is becoming popular is Wavelet compression, which also supports 24-bit color. This file format stores bitmap information at very high compression levels.

Lossless Compression

Lossless or non-lossy compression has been around longer than lossy compression. It generally offers a significant amount of compression without any loss of image information (quality). Most of these compression schemes offer compression ratios between 2:1 to 4:1. The more popular versions of lossless compression found in Corel PHOTO-PAINT are LZW and Packbits. There is little noticeable difference between LZW and Packbits.

In Summary

If you read the entire chapter, you probably know more about opening, creating, and saving files than most PHOTO-PAINT users. Now let's learn how to change the size and placement of the images.

CHAPTER 4

Image Fundamentals–Viewing and Modifying Images

In the previous chapter, you learned how to manage image files. In this chapter, you will discover the tools in Corel PHOTO-PAINT for viewing and navigating around those images, after which you will learn how to manipulate them.

Zoom and Navigation Tools

One of most necessary tools for photo editing and photo-retouching is the Zoom tool. When you are attempting to do fine detail work on a photograph, you will discover that zooming in on the spot you are working on makes the job easier—especially if you are using a mouse rather than a stylus.

The Zoom levels and the Zoom tool in Corel PHOTO-PAINT, shown in Figure 4-1, provide several ways for viewing and working on your image from as close up or as far away as necessary. Zoom features magnify or decrease the size of your onscreen image without affecting the actual image size. When an image either is too large or has a zoom level too high for the entire image to fit on the screen, two navigational

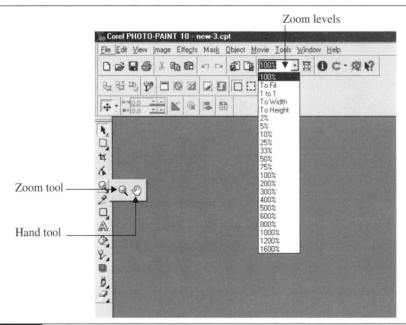

FIGURE 4-1   The Zoom and Navigational tools of Corel PHOTO-PAINT make image editing more accurate and easier

tools—the Hand tool and the Navigator Pop-up (not shown in Figure 4-1)—allow us to quickly get around the image. Before we learn how the Zoom tools work, we need to learn a few things about how the zoom feature affects the display of bitmap images.

Hazards of Bitmap Zooming

4

If your experience using the zoom feature is limited to vector programs like CorelDRAW, you will discover that using the Zoom tool on a bitmap image has some limitations that affect how images appear. When using a vector program, selecting a different zoom level causes the program to redraw the image at the requested level resulting in a accurate zoomed image. When the zoom level is changed, Corel PHOTO-PAINT resizes the image pixels to create an image display at the requested zoom level. Remember that the image size is unaffected by the change to the displayed image. At a zoom level of 100 percent, each pixel in the image is mapped to a screen pixel producing the most accurate display of the image. When the zoom level is changed from 100 percent, the 1:1 ratio of the image to screen pixels is no longer possible. To illustrate what happens when the zoom level is changed, a photograph of a pocket watch face displayed at 100 percent is shown (see Figure 4-2a). When Zoom to Fit was applied, the Zoom level changed to 87 percent, as shown in Figure 4-2b. Both pictures have been increased in size by 300 percent to make the distortion caused by this minor change in zooming more apparent. This is not a design flaw of PHOTO-PAINT or your computer. Quite simply, when the image is resized, the screen pixels of your display (whose size is fixed) no longer align with the image pixels. The result is varying degrees of distortion of the image being displayed. Even after using PHOTO-PAINT for years, I got tripped up by this phenomenon. I was teaching a PHOTO-PAINT class in London and was trying to correct some jaggies that were present in an image I had just scanned. Try as I might, I could not correct the problem. Fortunately, someone in the class pointed out that my zoom level was at 83 percent. I changed it back to 100 percent and the problem went away. Learn from my mistakes.

Working with Zoom Levels

You can change the zoom level in PHOTO-PAINT several different ways. The most direct is choosing a preset zoom level from the pop-up menu in the standard toolbar as shown in Figure 4-1. You are not limited to the preset values on that list, except to choose something between 2 percent and 1600 percent. You can enter a value into the Zoom Level box and press ENTER. In addition to the percentile preset zoom level settings, there are seven other zoom settings: To Fit, 1 to 1, To Width, To Height, To Active, To Selected, and To All. When the Zoom tool is selected, the property bar displays the available choices as icons, as shown in Figure 4-3.

FIGURE 4-2   The effect of the Zoom on a photograph shown at (a) 100 percent (b) 87 percent

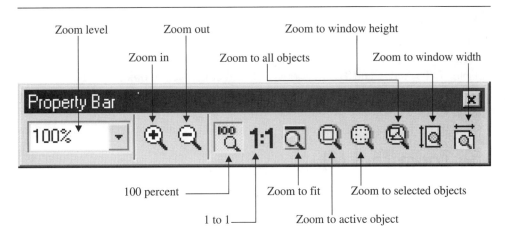

FIGURE 4-3   The Zoom Property Bar displays all of the Zoom options

Zoom 100 percent Versus Zoom 1 to 1

The first time I saw these two zoom presets, I thought they did the same thing. I was wrong. Zoom 100 percent (CTRL-1) matches pixels in the image with screen pixels in the display. Zoom 1 to 1 should be called "display in actual size," since it changes the zoom level to display the image at its physical size.

Zoom to Fit

The Zoom to Fit setting is very handy when you want to quickly see the entire image. Choosing Zoom to Fit changes the zoom level so that the image fits into the current window. The keyboard shortcut is F4.

> **TIP** *When you use Zoom to Fit, your zoom setting may change from 100 percent, so you may no longer be viewing an accurate representation of the image.*

To Width/To Height

Selecting the To Width or To Height option changes the zoom level so that either the entire width or height fits in the image window.

To Active/To Selected/To All

These three Zoom options are only available when the image contains PHOTO-PAINT objects. If you haven't learned about objects yet, don't worry: that's covered in Chapter 7. To Active and To All zooms fit to either the Active object or all of the objects. These objects are always in the list when an image has objects. To Selected appears in the list when an object is selected.

The Zoom Tool (Z)

You may zoom in on a specific area of an image by using the Zoom tool, shown here, which is found in the Toolbox. To use it, click the image to zoom in to the next preset level, right-click to zoom out to the next preset level, or click and drag a rectangle around the area you wish to zoom in on.

 The quick way to activate the Zoom tool is to depress the Z key (you don't need to continue holding it down) while any other tool is selected. After you have finished using the Zoom tool, press the SPACEBAR to return to the previously selected tool.

The Hand Tool (H)

If you zoom in enough so that the entire image no longer fits on your display, Windows provides a way to move around the image by clicking the scroll bars that appear at the side and bottom of the image window. A better method is to use the Hand tool and drag the image. As you click and drag the image, it moves inside the window much faster than the scroll bars. You can select the Hand tool from the Zoom tool flyout. If the image is smaller or the same size as the image window, the Hand tool doesn't do anything.

> **TIP** *A quick way to select the Hand tool is to press the H key. The Hand tool is selected as indicated by the cursor becoming a hand. Press the SPACEBAR to return to the previously selected tool.*

Navigator Pop-up

The Navigator pop-up is an easy-to-use image navigation tool, which is also available whenever the entire image no longer fits in the image window. Placing the cursor on the icon in the lower-right corner of the image where the scroll bars meet and holding down the mouse button displays the Navigator pop-up, as shown in the following illustration. The Navigator remains open as long as the mouse button is held. The cursor moves the rectangular box in the Navigator and, as the box moves, the image moves. Releasing the mouse button closes the Navigator. This is a quick way to navigate around an image. The only reason I don't use it as often as I could, is I forget it's there.

You can also activate the Navigator pop-up with the N key. You navigate in this window by moving the mouse and close the window by clicking the mouse button in the desired area.

> TIP
>
> *The aspect ration of the Navigator pop-up is determined by the aspect ratio of the image.*

Fitting Images to Your Display

One of most important things you must do to work on images in Corel PHOTO-PAINT is to figure out the best way to fit the image to the size of display you are using. You may have noticed that PHOTO-PAINT has lots of menu bars, dockers, and so on that compete for the limited space on your display. Corel has put some features in PHOTO-PAINT that help in getting the optimum amount of image displayed on you monitor.

The Maximize Work Area Command

This command on the Window menu provides you with a little more room by making the status bar and PHOTO-PAINT title bars disappear. You can open up the Window menu as just shown, but an easier way is to press the BACKSPACE key. Pressing it a second time toggles it back to normal.

Automatic View Resize

This feature is found in the Options settings. When enabled, it automatically resizes the image window to fit the currently selected zoom setting. You can enable it in the General page of Options (CTRL-J). This feature, at times, can be a mixed blessing. While it is a great feature, the automatic resizing can make photo retouching difficult as you zoom to different levels to work on a photo. My suggestion is to leave it off when doing touchup work.

Full Screen Preview

This feature offers a quick way to see the whole picture. I use this feature all of the time because it is very easy to toggle the F9 key and see the image you are working on. As great as this feature is, remember that it zooms the image to fit the display. If the image is too large to fit, it is automatically zoomed down. I am telling you this so that you are aware that the image you see in the full-screen preview may not accurately represent the image.

Now that you know how to find your way around these bitmap images, let's learn how to flip them around and turn them upside down.

Changing Shape and Placement of Images

Just as images don't always come in the desired size, they also don't always come in the desired orientation. When you are laying out a newsletter, for instance, it seems that when you get the images you want, they are inevitably facing the wrong direction. You usually want them facing inward if they are on the outside edge, and facing outward if they are on the inside edge. (I knew you knew that; I just thought I would throw it in.) Corel PHOTO-PAINT offers a collection of commands to allow the image to be reoriented, resized, and duplicated and even to have multiple images stitched together; most of this chapter is committed to these commands, which are found in the Image menu.

The Flip Command

The Flip command (vertically) seems to be the perfect solution for images that are scanned upside down, but it is not limited to that. Many times, an image just looks better when it has been flipped horizontally, as shown in Figure 4-4. The Flip command makes either a vertical or a horizontal mirrored copy of the original image; using it is a no-brainer, select Image | Flip and choose Flip Horizontally or Flip Vertically.

FIGURE 4-4   The original photograph (a) was facing the wrong way; flipping it horizontally (b) allows it to be used for a hard hitting exposé

TIP

Before you decide to use the Flip command, I recommend you examine the image carefully to make sure that the image doesn't contain any text. More than once I have seen ads of nationally recognized sports figures holding footballs or basketballs on which the text was backward.

The Rotate Command

Rotate offers the ability to rotate the entire image. Again, this may not seem like much, but there are many things you can do with this little command. The most common use is to reorient a photograph that was too wide for a scanner. For example, a while back I needed to scan the panorama photo shown in Figure 4-5. The photo was 12 inches wide and 6 inches high, but my scanner could only accommodate a width of 8.5 inches. I flipped the photo 90 degrees on the scanner so that its width ran the length of the scanner. After scanning it, I used PHOTO-PAINT's Rotate command to rotate it 90 degrees to return it to its original orientation.

FIGURE 4-5 To scan subjects too wide for your scanner, scan them lengthwise and rotate them in PHOTO-PAINT

  There are also Flip and Rotate commands in the Object menu. Their effect is limited to a single object, while the ones we have been looking at in this chapter affect the entire image.

To rotate an image, choose Image | Rotate and another menu appears with the available choices in 90-degree increments. The last choice is Rotate Custom, which opens the Custom Rotate dialog box, shown next.

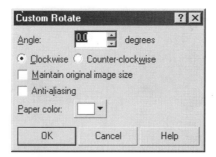

The Price of Custom Rotation—Distortion

Before going further, we should discuss the subject of custom rotation versus image integrity (sounds like a sermon title, doesn't it?). As we discussed in Chapter 2, an image is made of square pixels and each pixel is assigned a single color. When an image is flipped or rotated in 90-degree increments, all the pixels that make up the image are rotated along their axes. The pixels still line up with the horizontal and vertical of the image area, and the integrity of the image remains unchanged. Figure 4-6a shows a representation of nine pixels with a single pixel with a grayscale value of 70 percent surrounded by pixels that are 30 percent gray.

When an image is rotated at some angle that is not at a 90-degree increment, the sides of the pixels no longer line up with the horizontal and vertical axes of the image, as shown in Figure 4-6b. To correct this, PHOTO-PAINT must read the color value of each pixel and its adjoining pixels to create a new pixel (resample) containing a color value that represents the original value plus the color value from the adjacent pixels.

The result is that the image suffers a small amount of distortion. The most common distortion effect is a general softening of the image, which is produced by PHOTO-PAINT's antialiasing feature. The distortion is most apparent in areas of high contrast with limited shades of colors. How bad is this distortion? The image of the rotated pixels in Figure 4-6b was rotated using PHOTO-PAINT. They look pretty good on the page, but when viewed on the screen, you can see that the text and lines in the rotated part of the figure are softer than the original. So, what have we learned? You can rotate an image, but always keep in mind you are introducing mild distortion.

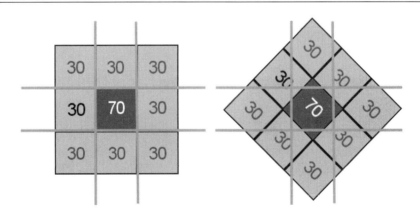

FIGURE 4-6 After being rotated 45 degrees, the middle pixel now contains color values from adjacent pixels

Using Custom Rotate

There are some handy options when using Custom Rotate that enable you to quickly make some pretty slick graphics. The operation of the Degrees and direction settings in the Custom Rotate dialog box is pretty obvious. Antialiasing, when enabled, reduces aliasing (also known as the "jaggies") on rotated images, but it also may soften the image being rotated. If you have any doubt about the use of this feature, apply the desired rotation without antialiasing once and you will see why it was included.

Controlling Image Size and Paper Color

When Maintain Original Image Size is selected, the image height and width dimensions are fixed. Figure 4-7 shows an example of how the Maintain Original Image Size affects the image when it is rotated. If Maintain Original Image Size is left unselected, the dimensions of the image are automatically adjusted to fit the edges of the rotated image as shown in Figure 4-7b. The rotated image is cropped at the image boundaries as shown in Figure 4-7c. The part of the image vacated by the rotated image is replaced with the Paper color. The Paper Color part of the dialog box lets you select a different Paper color.

FIGURE 4-7   The Maintain Original Image Size determines if the photo (a) is enlarged (b) or cropped (c) when rotated

NOTE | *If the original image has objects, they will all become visible in the rotated copy. They will not be merged. This includes the hidden objects. (If you are bewildered by those last few sentences, they will become clearer when you get to Chapter 7.)*

Rotation Demonstration

Here is a simple demonstration of how to quickly create a graphic element for a Web page or newsletter. When you want to get a reader's attention, place the subject matter at an angle.

1. First, I rotate the photo 15 degrees with Maintain Original Image Size checked and a Paper color selected that is darker than the existing background, as shown in Figure 4-8.

2. Ensuring the Fill tool tolerance is set to a low value, such as 5, I selected a bitmap texture called "Lightning" in the Samples 9 library and filled in the four areas that were the Paper color.

3. Add the text with a drop shadows and you have the Web graphic in Figure 4-9.

FIGURE 4-8 The Rotate command gives a new "twist" to a stock photograph

FIGURE 4-9   This graphic took less than a minute to create thanks to the Rotate command

The Duplicate Command

When doing photo editing, at times you will need to make a duplicate of the image you are working on. This is especially handy when you want to show different effects applied to the same photograph. In Figure 4-10 I have made two duplicates from the original photo and applied the Slant filter to the one on the right and the Swirl filter to the one on the left.

TIP   *I used Window | Tile Vertically to align all of the image windows for a screen shot. It sure beats trying to line them up even manually.*

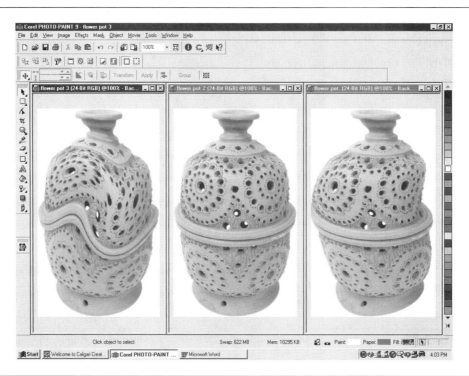

FIGURE 4-10 Using the Duplicate command, it is easy to show different effects on the same photograph

The Duplicate command produces a new file that is a copy of the original image. When you select Duplicate in the Image menu, a dialog box opens. You have two decisions to make. First, you either enter a name for the duplicate file or accept the name generated by Corel PHOTO-PAINT, which is usually something original like "New-01." Second, you must decide whether to use Merge Objects with Background. If you don't know what objects are, don't be concerned; they are explored in Chapter 7. For now, objects can be thought of as bitmap images that float on top of the picture. The Merge Objects with Background option gives you the choice of making the duplicate image either with all of the objects as they are in the original or with all of the objects merged into the background. Once they are merged, they are no longer objects.

Changing the Size of an Image

Images never seem to come in the right size. Whether it is a Web page, a book, or a newsletter, the photograph or the scanned clip art is either too small or too large. There are two ways to change the size of an image: resizing (sometimes called scaling) and resampling. Changing the size of an image in PHOTO-PAINT is easy, but there is more to it than you might imagine. In the following sections, we will learn the difference between resizing and resampling, although they are both accomplished with the Resample command. Before we begin, many readers have questioned the need to resize a photo in PHOTO-PAINT, since they can do it in their word processor or page layout program.

Why You Shouldn't Resize or Crop an Image in Other Applications

Many page layout programs like Corel VENTURA, PageMaker, and Quark offer graphic cropping and resizing as part of the program. These features are usually fine for very minor image adjustments, but for any significant changes you should open the files in Corel PHOTO-PAINT and make the changes there. There are several reasons for doing so, as follows:

- If you crop a large image file in a word processing or page layout program, most of the time the file size remains unchanged. Even if you use only five percent of a 16MB image file, the entire file remains as part of the document file. Large document files create problems with lengthy print times and difficulty in transport to a service bureau. If you crop that same 16MB file in Corel PHOTO-PAINT, it becomes an 800K file.

- Resizing bitmap files in these applications can cause image distortion, which often shows up as unwanted moiré patterns over the entire image.

There are many different ways to change the size of an image once it has been loaded into Corel PHOTO-PAINT. Most of the commands are found in the Image menu. Commands in the Image menu affect the entire image and cannot be applied to a portion of the image.

In the old days, when we needed to change the size of an image, we made a PMT (photo-mechanical transfer) of the image, which involved a camera the size of a Buick. We would take a photograph of the original that would be reduced or enlarged. Cropping was done with an Xacto knife. Fortunately, Corel PHOTO-PAINT provides several much simpler ways to change both the size and the surrounding working area of an image. There are several ways to change the size of an image. They include *resampling* and *cropping* and their variations.

Resizing Methods	Description
Resizing	Changing the resolution of the image, thereby affecting the printed size without adding or subtracting pixels.
Resampling	This command makes the image larger or smaller by adding or subtracting pixels.
Crop tool	This tool acts like a traditional cropping tool. It allows you to define a specific area of an image and to remove all of the area outside the defined area.
Paper Size	This handy command uses a combination of resampling and cropping. The Paper Size command increases the overall image size by increasing the size of the base image. It is as if you put a larger sheet of paper under the original. It can also be used to crop the image.

The Resample Command

Both resizing and resampling of an image is done by the same Resample command. Resampling actually recreates the image, adding or subtracting pixels as required. Resampling changes the image size in pixels, and therefore the file size will vary; it must, in order to store the different number of pixels. Selecting

Maintain Original Size changes the future printed image size in inches, but nothing happens until the image is displayed in a program like CorelDRAW or printed.

Increasing the size of the image is also called *upsampling,* and this usually introduces distortion in the form of softening. Decreasing the image size is called *downsampling,* and while it also causes distortion, the effect is less apparent because of the optical effect of a reduced size. Each method changes the size of the printed size, and each has its own advantages and disadvantages.

| TIP | *Be aware that adding or subtracting pixels from an image decreases the quality of an image. Having said that, resampling remains the best way to change the size of an existing image. If you must resample, downsample (making the image smaller) and avoid upsampling (making the image larger) if possible.* |

Resizing

Resizing the image by changing the resolution is accomplished by choosing Image | Resample and, after the Resample dialog box opens, clicking the button labeled Maintain Original Size. Next, change the values in the value boxes to the desired size or percentage of reduction or increase that you want. Enabling Maintain Original Size forces PHOTO-PAINT to resize the image by keeping the file size (total number of pixels in the image) unchanged. This results in the resolution changing to fit the newly requested image size.

When resizing, you cannot see any physical change in the displayed image because PHOTO-PAINT maps each pixel of the image to a pixel on the display, regardless of the resolution setting. To see the effect, you must display the resized file using a program like CorelDRAW or you must save the image and print it.

To illustrate this concept, look at the two watches displayed in PHOTO-PAINT in Figure 4-11. They are both displayed at a zoom level of 100 percent and appear to be the same size, but look carefully at the rulers. Actually, the image on the left was resized, reducing its resolution from 300 dpi to 45 dpi (which is too low, but I am trying to make a point); the watch on the right remains at 300 dpi. Now, let's import these two watch photos into CorelDRAW as shown in Figure 4-12. Quite a difference and yes, that rectangle behind the watches represents an 8.5 × 11-inch sheet of paper.

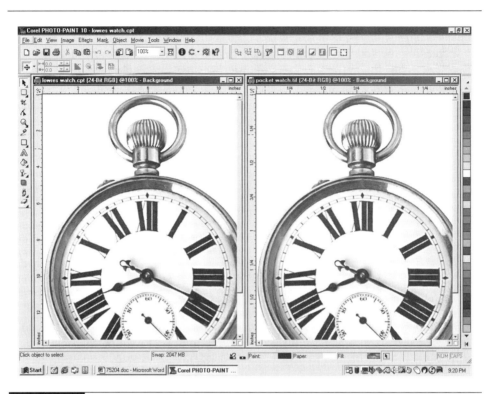

FIGURE 4-11   Two watches appear to be the same size…or are they?

The advantages of this method are that the file size remains unchanged and the operation is instantaneous. The reason it happens so quickly is that the image is not physically altered. Only information in the file header is changed because that is where the resolution information is maintained.

The disadvantage to this method is the loss of image detail that could result from the lower resolution. In most cases, if you keep the resolution at the recommended levels for the type of image you are working with, you should be able to resize the image without any noticeable loss of image detail. You can safely allow the resolution to be reduced to 150 dpi for grayscale and 100–120 dpi for color images.

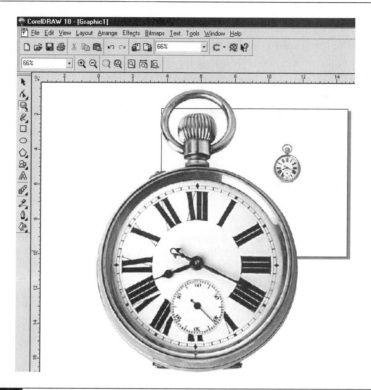

FIGURE 4-12   When they are imported into CorelDRAW, we can see the watches are not the same size

Resampling

There are times when you don't have a choice and you must resample the image to get the needed size or resolution. With this method, none of the parameters of the image are restricted. The dimensions of the image are either increased or decreased, and the resolution can be changed as well. Once you have entered the values you want into the Resample dialog box, Corel PHOTO-PAINT either adds or subtracts pixels from the image to make it fit the new dimensions entered.

When the number of pixels in the image increases, Corel PHOTO-PAINT creates more pixels through a process called *interpolation.* This is the same process your scanner uses when scanning at resolutions much higher than its optics can resolve. PHOTO-PAINT resamples by examining every pixel throughout the entire image, comparing pairs of adjacent pixels and creating pixels that represent the average tonal value. I told you that so that you would know why your computer might seem to take so long to resample a large image.

Conversely, when the dimensions of the image decrease, PHOTO-PAINT subtracts pixels from the image. This sounds ideal, doesn't it? Actually, you always lose some detail when you resample an image, regardless of whether you add or subtract pixels. There is no magic here. The greater the amount of resampling, the greater the amount of image degradation introduced.

If you disable the Maintain Aspect Ratio feature shown in the Resample dialog box shown next, it is possible to change one dimension without causing the other to change. Whenever you change the aspect ratio of an image, you introduce perspective distortion. The distortion will be noticeable if the values entered vary too greatly from the original aspect ratio. In Figure 4-13, our watch was resampled with the Maintain Aspect Ratio disabled and the Width reduced by 50 percent.

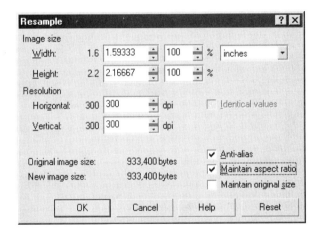

So what would be the advantage to changing the aspect ratio? Sometimes you can make small changes to the aspect ratio to make an image fit properly in a page layout or Web page and the distortion is not apparent to the viewer. Natural subjects such as clouds or trees hardly show perspective distortion. Figure 4-14 shows two photographs that were resampled. One had the aspect ratio maintained, and the other had the ratio changed by 40 percent on one side. Take a look and see if you can figure out which is the original. The answer is at the end of the chapter.

FIGURE 4-13   When the aspect ratio is not maintained, distortion is the result

FIGURE 4-14   Which photo is the original? Perspective distortion isn't as apparent with natural subjects as it is with watches

Cropping an Image with the Crop Tool

Cropping involves the removal of part of an image either to change its size, enhance the composition, or remove a former boyfriend. The Crop tool is in the Toolbox, and there is also a Crop command in the Image menu. If that weren't enough, there's a Crop option on the Open an Image dialog box. There are several different ways to crop an open image:

- Crop to Selection
- Crop to Mask
- Crop Border Color

Crop to Selection

This is the method of choice for 9 out of 10 PHOTO-PAINT users. After you select the Crop tool, draw a rectangular bounding box that surrounds the subject and excludes the area you wish to crop. PHOTO-PAINT will darken the area that will be removed to give you some idea of what the resulting cropped image will look like, as shown in the next example. Once you have the bounding box in place, you can move it around or resize it using the handles that surround the box. Double-clicking within the rectangle crops the image to the shape of the rectangle. Double-clicking outside of the rectangle cancels the Crop command.

4

Crop to Mask

This option operates like Crop to Selection except that it crops to a mask rather than to a rectangle created by the Crop tool. The Crop to Mask option is grayed out (not available) if there are no masks in the image. To crop an area, begin by surrounding it with a mask. Select the Crop tool and right-click inside of the mask to see a choice of crop selection options as shown next. Choose Crop to Mask.

↶ Undo Mask Rectangle|Ctrl+Z		Ctrl+Z
↷ Redo		Ctrl+Shift+Z
Crop To Selection		
Crop To Mask		
Crop Border Color...		

Regardless of the type of mask you place on the image—circle, trapezoid, and so on—the Crop to Mask feature will calculate a rectangular area that will fit all of the points on the mask

Crop Border Color

The Crop Border Color command removes borders of a particular color from an image. An example would be the ugly black border that seems to surround so many of the early photo-CDs. The idea is to select the color of the border and click the button, and the black border disappears. In theory, that is the way it is supposed to work. The problem is that nearly all borders are irregular and, since all crops must be rectangular, pieces of the original border do not get cropped.

The operation of the Crop Border Color option is a two-step process. After you select the Crop tool, you right-click the image to be cropped and select Crop Border Color from the pop-up menu. This opens the Crop Border Color dialog box, as shown next.

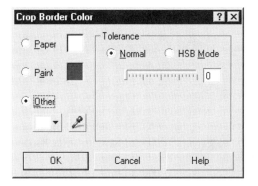

Crop Border Dialog Box

It is from the Crop Border Color dialog box that you select the color that will be used as the border color to be removed. The Crop Border Color dialog box lets you crop out the paper color, paint color, or a custom color you select from an image. The sensitivity of the cropping is controlled using the Tolerance sliders associated with the two modes, Normal and HSB. These sliders control just how many shades of colors will be included in the cropping action.

A Little Bit of Tolerance Is Necessary

A word of warning here. If the Tolerance slider is set to zero, only an exact match of the Paint color will be cropped. While the black on the border looks like the black Paint color, it may only be a close approximation. As you go through the book, you will learn about shading and numerical color values. To crop to the border color, you can increase the Tolerance (a setting between 5 and 10 will suffice); don't go crazy and set the Tolerance to a large value such as 95. When the Tolerance value gets large enough, it reaches a threshold that I call the "avalanche point." When it is set at such a point, almost all colors in the image are included in the border color.

Best Color Selection

For border colors that are not black or white, I recommend that you use the Eyedropper tool to select the color from the image to be cropped. Your chances of finding the right color in a standard palette are very slim. When using the Eyedropper tool to get a color match, remember that most border colors are not uniform and you will still need to increase the Tolerance if you are going to include the entire border. Of the two Tolerance modes to choose from, Normal and HSB, stay with Normal and don't worry about the HSB for the Crop Border Color command.

The Paper Size Command

Another command in the Image menu to change the size of the image area is called Paper Size. This command is used to extend the edges of an image, leaving the original image unchanged on larger or smaller paper (background). It is called Paper Size because Corel refers to the background as "Paper." The new background (Paper) color is determined by the Paper Color setting. If the Paper Size is smaller than the original image, the image is cropped; if the paper size is larger, the image is placed according to the Placement selection made in the dialog box, shown next.

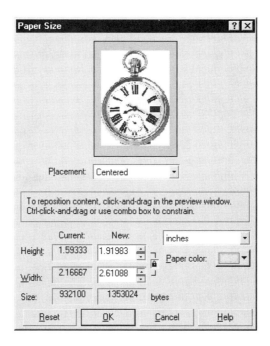

The Paper Size Dialog Box

The Width/Height values determine the new width and height of the paper according to the units of measurement. If the lock icon is enabled, the aspect ratio is maintained. The placement of the original is determined by selecting presets or placing the cursor in the preview window (cursor becomes a hand) and moving the image to the desired location.

TIP *Try using Paper Size several times on the same image with complementary colors to make a quick border.*

Paper Size Demonstration

The Paper Size command offers a quick way to change the size of an image without changing its resolution or resampling. It also is the best way to do either precision crops or add a border to an image. My favorite use of Paper Size is to create composite images. The image shown in Figure 4-15 began as the unusual photo, shown next, that I discovered on a Corel PHOTO-PAINT 8 CD. Although there are several ways to do this, here is Paper Size way.

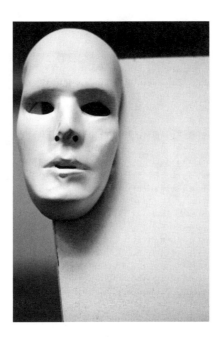

4

1. Mask the entire image (CTRL-SHIFT-A) and then double the width of the image using Paper Size, selecting Center Left for placement, shown next.

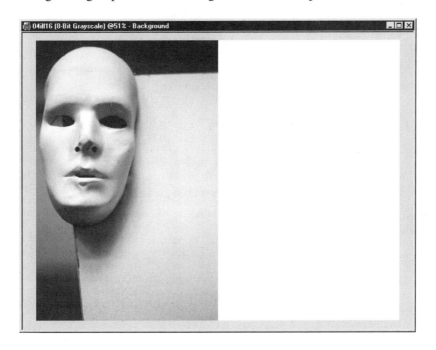

2. Copy the contents of the mask to the Windows Clipboard (CTRL-C) and remove the mask (CTRL-SHIFT-R). Now, Paste (CTRL-V) the image onto the image. At this point it is an object on top of the original. Use the arrow keys to nudge the object so that it aligns with the original image on the left. But now the object is facing the wrong direction.

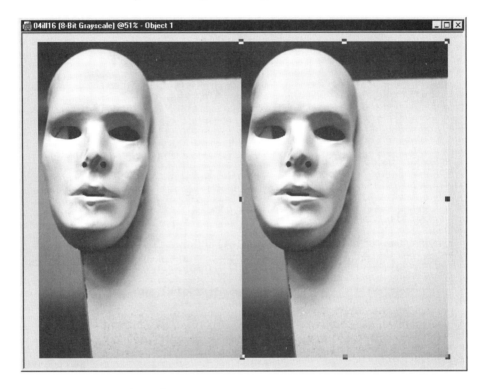

3. Select Object | Flip | Horizontally. Combine the object with the background (CTRL-DOWN ARROW).

4. As a final touch, I isolated parts of the masks and applied several Distort filters to make the faces look different before adding the text.

FIGURE 4-15   Paper Size is the command of choice when it comes to making weird images like this

Changing the Color Mode of an Image

One of the many features of PHOTO-PAINT is its ability to convert images from one color mode to another. Located in the Image menu, selecting Mode offers a ton of choices (okay, maybe it's a little less than a ton) for changing the color mode of an image. All of that said, you shouldn't need to change color modes very often. If you are switching color modes a lot, you need to ask yourself why you are doing it.

The Mode Command—It's More than Color and Grayscale

Before you begin switching modes, you should save a copy of the file you are going to change; because this process, unlike Export, does not create a copy of the image; the original will be converted. Color information in the file is permanently lost in the converting from one mode to another because different modes have different color spaces. If you do not want to change the original, use the Export command to change the format or use the Save As command in the File menu to save the file under a new name before you convert it.

The actual conversion is quite simple. With an image selected, open Image | Mode and choose the desired color mode from the drop-down list. The modes that are unavailable are grayed out. With a 24-bit RGB image, for example, the 24-bit RGB option is grayed out.

So, Why Change?

There are situations that require changing the format of an image. For example, I am a graphics illustrator at Motorola and use PHOTO-PAINT to create marketing material that must go to a color printer. No one has ever said, "Dave, just send it in any mode your 'ol pea-picking heart desires." No, the printers I work with, like those everywhere, have very specific size, file format, and color mode requirements. Most of our conversations sound like someone reading a launch preflight sequence for the space shuttle.

Most of the time the need to change modes is restricted to the following:

- Converting an RGB file to CMYK for printing. If you are working on a file that is destined for a commercial printer, do all of your work in RGB and then convert the file to CMYK.

- Converting an image to 8-bit Paletted color. If you need to save an image in the GIF format, then you must first convert the file to 8-bit Paletted color.

- Converting an image to grayscale. Converting color images to grayscale can save enormous amounts of disk space when producing graphics that will be printed in grayscale. Converting a 24-bit color image to grayscale reduces the image file to one-third of its original size. For example, if the original 24-bit color image is 1.1MB, converting it to grayscale will result in a file size of approximately 250–300K.

An Alternative to Grayscale Conversion

When you are printing a color image on a laser printer, you may find that converting the image from color to grayscale causes some colors to blend together. In Figure 4-16, the figure on the left was converted to grayscale and the colors in the figure (red and green) almost appear to be the same color. The figure on the right in 4-16 was converted to grayscale using the technique I am about to show you.

1. Select Image | Mode | Lab Color (24-bit). Wait until the image title bar shows the change from RGB to Lab Color before doing the next step.

2. Choose Image | Split Channels to | LAB. Now you have three images in addition to the original, as shown next.

4

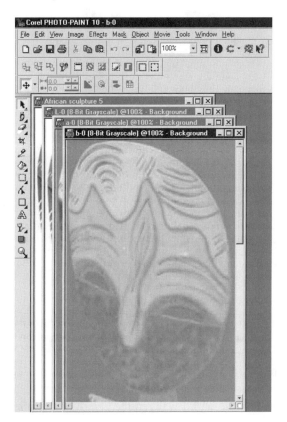

3. Delete the a-0 and b-0 images. Select the L-0 channel image and using either Save As or Export, save the image. That's all there is to it.

FIGURE 4-16   Traditional grayscale conversion (left); Lab Color L Channel (right)

In Summary

We have covered a lot of information in this chapter, and it is now time to move on to the next chapter and learn about tools for layout, correction, and replacement. See you in the next chapter.

Answer to Figure 4-14's question: The photograph on the left is the original… or was it the right? Just kidding. The photo on the right was resampled with the aspect ratio disabled and the width was reduced by 40 percent less than the height.

CHAPTER 5

Tools for Layout, Undoing, Redoing, and Replacing

Corel PHOTO-PAINT 10 provides an assortment of tools to make working on images easier. In this chapter you will discover rulers, grids, and guidelines that are provided for aligning and positioning objects and masks in an image. While alignment tools such as these are generally associated with vector-based (CorelDRAW) or page layout (Corel Ventura) programs, you will learn how they work great in PHOTO-PAINT for something other than positioning of graphic elements. In addition, you will learn about all the navigation tools that help you quickly get around large images and about Zoom tools that magnify areas for accurate retouching and other image manipulation. As capable as these tools are, the most important are those that help us undo our mistakes. Fortunately, PHOTO-PAINT 10 offers a lot of ways to help us recover from our mistakes. In the early versions of PHOTO-PAINT, Undo could only undo the last action. Now, it is almost limitless. So, let's begin by getting acquainted with our layout tools.

Rulers, Guidelines, and Grids

Apart from providing one of the few visual indicators that show the physical dimensions of a PHOTO-PAINT image, rulers also serve as the only source of guidelines that are very useful when cropping an image or aligning elements in an image to a fixed point. The grids, which are nonprintable, serve as both an alignment tool for placing graphic elements in an image and a way to proportionally arrange them.

Rulers

In Chapter 2, you learned it is possible for a photograph to completely fill the screen, yet print smaller than a postage stamp. By displaying rulers on an image, you can actually see the dimensions of the image if it were printed at its current resolution. Here is a quick exercise to familiarize you with the rulers and to visibly demonstrate the effects of changing the resolution of an image.

1. Select Open from the File menu (CTRL-O). From www.osborne.com, download the file named Balloon4.CPT, shown next.

2. Select Duplicate from the Image menu and, when the dialog box opens, name the duplicate image Duplicate. The check box for Merge Objects with Background should be unchecked. Reposition the two identical copies so that they fill the screen, as shown next.

3. With Duplicate active, choose Image | Resample. We will explain resampling in more detail throughout the book. For now, you only need to know that it changes the size of the image. When the Resample dialog box opens, as shown next, check the Maintain Original Size check box. In the Resolution section, double-click the value for Horizontal, change it from 300 to 75, and click the OK button. Wow! Nothing appears to have happened.

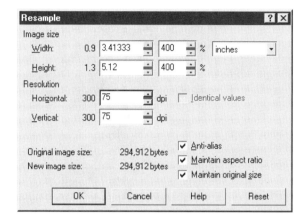

4. With Duplicate still active, display the rulers (CTRL-R, or select Rulers from the View menu). Click the title bar of Balloons4 and display its rulers.

NOTE

If the rulers are displayed in pixels or some other unit of measure like didots (what are those anyway?), double-click the ruler to open the Options dialog box, or select Grid and Ruler Setup in the View menu. Enable the Same Units for Horizontal and Vertical Rulers check box and select inches from the Horizontal pop-up menu in the Units section. Click the OK button. Even though both images appear to be the same size, an examination of the rulers shows that they are not.

TIP

The quickest way to open the Grid & Ruler Setup dialog box is to right-click a ruler and select from the options in the pop-up menu.

5

5. To see the images in their actual size, make sure that the Balloons4 image is still active. In the standard toolbar, change the Zoom level from 100 percent to 1 to 1, which tells PHOTO-PAINT to change the zoom level so that the image is displayed at its physical size. Select the Duplicate image and change the Zoom level to 1 to 1. The following illustration shows the result of changing the resolution of both images when they are displayed using 1 to 1 Zoom level.

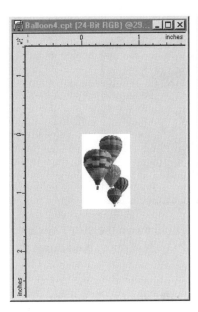

Ruler Properties

The operation of the ruler isn't very exciting, but here are some points to be aware of. The ruler normally uses the upper-left corner of the image window as its point of origin. To change this, click and drag the origin point to the new desired position. The origin point is where the two rulers intersect.

You can place a ruler anywhere on an image. There are times when moving the ruler to a different location on the image allows you to see dimensions of a graphic element in the image more clearly.

To reposition either ruler, hold down the SHIFT key, click the ruler you want to move, and drag it to a new position. The ruler outline will appear as double-dashed lines as you move it. In the illustration that follows the rulers have been repositioned and the origin point is indicated.

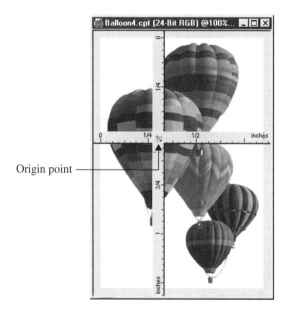

Origin point

If you need to move both rulers at once, hold down the SHIFT key and drag the intersection point of the two rulers. To return both at once, hold down the SHIFT key and double-click a ruler.

NOTE *When you reposition and release a ruler, the image may jump a short distance (the width of the ruler—five pixels) the first time it is moved. When you click and drag the ruler and reposition it a second time, the image will not jump.*

When you change the Zoom settings of the image, the scale of the ruler will change. To illustrate this, I next show a composite image using the Duplicate command and setting each image to a different Zoom level. The numbers in the titles indicate the zoom setting of the underlying image. Notice what the rulers in each image read. The size of the image has not changed, but when the zoom level was changed the ruler's scale changed. Another important thing to notice is how happy my daughter's good friend Eric is to finally be finished with high school.

Grids

Grids in PHOTO-PAINT 10 are nonprintable, a feature that I have been asking the PHOTO-PAINT team to change since PHOTO-PAINT 5 Plus. Still, even though they are seen but not printed, they can still be used for a variety of design functions. In Figure 5-1, I have shown a simple tile pattern that was created using a grid, a mask, and The Boss filter. The actual design of the pattern would have been impossible without the grids and the Snap to Grid feature. When you work with objects and layers, you can align objects and masks to grids or use them for reference when applying perspective transformation to an object. The tile in Figure 5-2a was made much like the one in Figure 5-1 except that a different wood bitmap fill was used and I added the metal ornament in the center. In Figure 5-2b, the image was tiled and rotated to give the appearance of a paneled wall or door.

The Real Nitty-Gritty of Grids

Grids are simple, so we don't need to spend a lot of time learning about them. Select Grid in the View menu to make the grid visible or invisible. Right-click

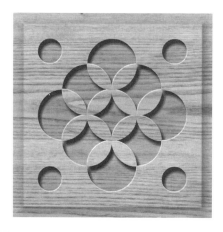

FIGURE 5-1 The pattern for this wood tile would have been impossible to create without grids

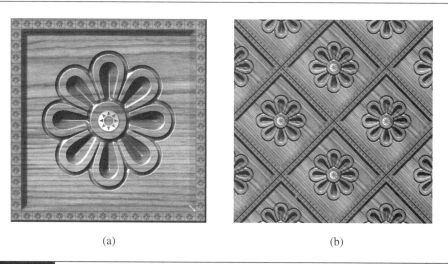

(a)   (b)

FIGURE 5-2 Using grids, masks, and The Boss filter, the single tile (a) was created and then used to create the tiled background (b)

a ruler and select Grid Setup to open the Options dialog box, where you can change the frequency of the grid (number of grids per unit of measure) and other grid properties. Even though grids are not printable, there may be occasions when you want to include the grid in the image. This can be done (as shown in the following illustration), but only by using a screen capture program, such as Corel Capture 10, and bringing the image into PHOTO-PAINT. The appearance of a grid or graph overlaying an image gives a technological appearance to most any photo. When using the grid overlay as part of a graphic, be aware that the grid is always on top.

| NOTE | *Did you know that selecting a Zoom of 1600% will turn the grid on automatically?* |

5

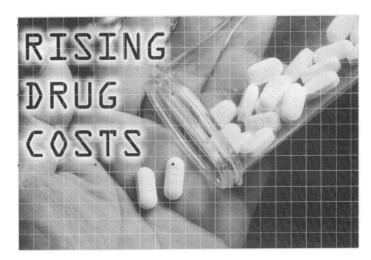

Guidelines

Guidelines are created by clicking the ruler with the mouse button and dragging a guideline into the image. The guidelines come in two flavors: horizontal and vertical. For all practical purposes, you can make as many guidelines as you want. Double-clicking a guideline with the Object Picker tool opens the Guidelines Options dialog box, as shown next. While there are several different guideline settings that can be controlled in this dialog box, the one to remember is the Clear button. This removes all of the guidelines you created with a single action. For more details on the settings for the guidelines, refer to either the online help or the *PHOTO-PAINT 10 User's Manual.* With the Snap to Guidelines feature enabled from the View menu, guidelines can be used like the grids, but with the added advantage of being placed where needed rather than at fixed intervals like grids.

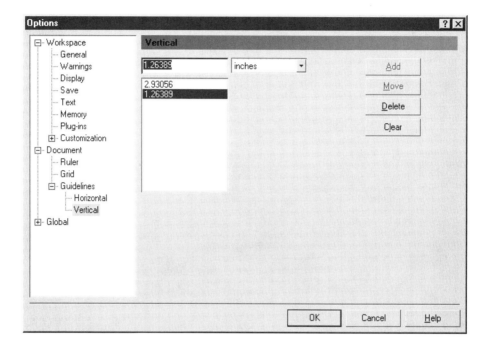

Guidelines are very handy for situations where you need to line up several objects in an image. You can use PHOTO-PAINT's built-in alignment commands to align both multiple objects and masks, but what PHOTO-PAINT considers the center of an object isn't necessarily the center. It is at times like this when you need a guideline to align the visual center of multiple objects in an image. In such cases, you will discover that they are very useful tools indeed.

Rules about Rulers, Grids, and Guidelines

Here are some little-known facts about rulers, grids, and guidelines:

- When a file is saved and later reopened, it uses its last ruler and grid settings. Guidelines remain as well.

■ The grid and ruler are not always visible when a file is opened, even if they were visible when the image was saved.

■ The Show Grid and Snap-to-Grid modes are turned off when an image is first opened.

■ Guidelines are now saved with files so that when you open the file the guidelines appear.

Zoom and Navigation Tools

The Zoom tools of PHOTO-PAINT 10 provide many ways of viewing and working on your image from as close up or as far away as necessary. To learn more about using the Zoom tools, see Chapter 4. When an image is either too large or has a zoom level too high for the image to fit on the screen, two navigational tools—the Hand tool, shown next, and the Navigator Pop-up—will come in handy.

The Hand Tool (H)

If you zoom in enough that the entire image can no longer fit on the display, you can move around the image using the Microsoft Windows method—in other words, clicking the scroll bars that appear at the side and bottom of the image window. A better way is to use the Hand tool and drag the image. As you click and drag the image, it moves inside the window. You can select the Hand tool from the Zoom tool flyout or from the property bar when the Zoom tool is selected.

A quick way to select the Hand tool is to press the H *key. The Hand tool is selected as indicated by the cursor becoming a hand. Press the* SPACEBAR *to return to the previously selected tool.*

Navigator Pop-up

The Navigator pop-up is an easy-to-use image navigation tool available whenever the entire image no longer fits in its window. Placing the cursor on the icon in the lower-right corner of the image where the scroll bars meet and holding down the mouse button displays the Navigator pop-up, as shown in the following illustration. The Navigator remains open as long as the mouse button is held. The cursor moves the rectangular box in the Navigator, and as the box moves, the image moves. Releasing the mouse button closes the Navigator.

You can also activate the Navigator pop-up using the N key. You navigate in this window by moving the mouse and close the window by clicking the mouse button in the desired area.

Tools for Correcting Mistakes

Corel PHOTO-PAINT 10 has several tools for fixing mistakes, which fall into two overlapping categories: those that remove previous actions and those that remove portions of the image. There are three tools in the Undo flyout in the Toolbox (shown next): The Eraser tool, the Local Undo tool, and the Color Replacer tool. The Edit menu has an Undo command and the Checkpoint/Restore to Checkpoint commands. There is also the Undo/Redo docker window, which can be opened by choosing from the Dockers list in the Window menu. This docker lists the actions you have performed in sequence. Besides having as many Undo levels as your system memory resources allow, the Undo list actually works very fast. And then there is the Clone from Saved tool. Let's explore them all.

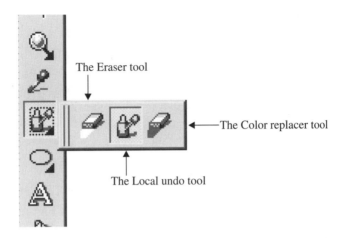

The Eraser tool

The Color replacer tool

The Local undo tool

The Eraser Tool

Found on the Undo Tool flyout in the Toolbox and on the Undo toolbar, the Eraser tool, shown here, is as simple as it gets. The Eraser tool replaces the color value of pixels in the image with the Paper (background) color as it is dragged over them. This makes it look like that portion of the image is erased, though nothing actually is. The Eraser tool has a soft edge that makes the erased area less jagged. Don't confuse this tool with the Eraser icon with the gray shadow; that is the Color Replacer tool.

> **TIP** *Double-clicking the Eraser tool button erases the selected object. Only one object can be selected and erased with this method. Notice that the object remains on the Objects docker but is cleared. If the background is selected, it completely clears the image. Think about this the next time you want to open its property bar by double-clicking the button. If I had a nickel for every time I had accidentally done this...well, be careful.*

The Local Undo Tool

Also located on the Undo Tools flyout (Toolbox) and the Undo toolbar, the Local Undo tool allows the selective removal of the last action that was applied to the image.

Here's a Slick Trick Using the Local Undo Tool

While the Local Undo tool works fine at removing portions of the last applied actions, it can also be used to create some interesting effects. Long before Pleasantville was a movie, advertisers were drawing attention to products by making everything in the ad black-and-white except for the product. The first time I saw this was an ad for 7-Up®. Everything in the commercial was grayscale except for the red dot on the can. Here is a way to use the Local Undo tool to create that same effect with a photo.

1. Download the image named Bride and Groom Color.CPT from www.osborne.com. The photo, shown in Figure 5-3, was taken with a early model of a digital camera, so the color quality is less than sterling—no problem.

2. Choose Image | Adjust | Desaturate and it appears to be a grayscale image, but the title bar tells us it is still a color RGB image.

FIGURE 5-3   A grainy digital photo of bride and groom can be made more interesting using the Local Undo tool (see color insert for comparison)

3. Select the Local Undo tool and change its settings in the property bar so that its Transparency is 80 (percent) and the Shape Soft Edge is 50 (percent), as shown next. The Transparency setting will restore the color at 80 percent of its original value, so it won't overpower the image (but give it a slightly hand-tinted look). The Shape Soft Edge gives you better control when restoring the color. Too much soft edge and the applied area would have a slight color glow where the edge of the brush bleeds over an edge.

4. Apply the brush to the bride and the groom and their color is restored (mostly). Since showing it in grayscale would be rather pointless, you can see the before and after photo in the color insert of this book.

TIP

The Local Undo tool has a limited capacity to undo what you are undoing. Wasn't that really clear? Because the tool is undoing the last action, you will find limited success using the Undo command to correct a mistake. If you make a goof, try Undo (CTRL-Z) if all else fails, use File | Revert and start all over again.

The Checkpoint Command

Before unlimited Undo and Redo capability was added to PHOTO-PAINT, the Checkpoint command, located in the Edit menu, was one of the most frequently used commands when photo-editing. It lets you save a temporary copy of the current image that you can return to anytime.

 When doing any kind of work on an image, you should get in the habit of automatically selecting the Checkpoint command each time you begin to experiment with different effects and techniques.

The temporary file created by the Checkpoint command is closed when the image file is closed or when exiting PHOTO-PAINT (whether you planned to exit the program or it crashes). To return to the image saved by Checkpoint, select the Restore to Checkpoint command located below the Checkpoint command. This command is only available after the Checkpoint has been activated.

 The Checkpoint command is linked to the image; you cannot save a Checkpoint file in one image and open it in another.

The Undo/Redo Docker—Try It, You'll Like It!

The Undo docker window shown in Figure 5-4 is essentially a command recorder that frees you to experiment by providing a way to remove or restore one or more actions. If you make a change to an image that doesn't come out the way you thought it would, you can undo the change or a series of changes, or even redo the changes you have just undone.

As you make changes, a list is created in sequence. By selecting an action in the list with a click of the mouse, the removed actions become grayed out. You can restore actions by clicking them again. You cannot, however, restore or remove selected actions out of sequence.

This list continues to grow until the file is saved or the Checkpoint command is enabled. At that time, the list is cleared. The more actions on the list, the longer it will take your system to replay the entire list without the commands you removed, and the greater the possibility that it may not replay perfectly. Don't let that last sentence scare you. If you haven't used the Undo docker, I strongly recommend you try it. You will be impressed—I guarantee it.

Corel has placed several handy buttons at the bottom of the list as shown in Figure 5-4.

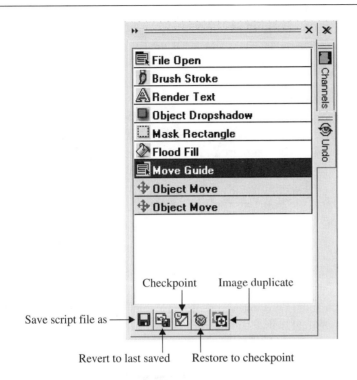

FIGURE 5-4   The Undo Docker lets you backtrack and undo and redo multiple
PHOTO-PAINT actions

The Save Script File As button allows you to save the Undo list as a script.
The Revert to Last Saved button reverts the selected image back to what it was the
last time it was saved. Checkpoint and Restore to Checkpoint we discussed a few
paragraphs ago. You do remember, don't you? Image Duplicate makes a duplicate
of the image.

Clone from Saved—the Ultimate Undo Tool

The Clone from Saved tool is found by selecting the Clone tool in the Paint flyout
on the Toolbox and selecting the icon with the floppy disk in the pop-up list at the
far left corner of the property bar. The Clone from Saved tool is actually a brush
tool that uses the contents of the last saved version of an image as the source and
paints it onto the same portion of the current image.

NOTE *If you have changed the size of an image since opening it, the Clone from Saved tool will not be available because the original and current images are no longer the same size.*

Color Replacer Tool

 The last tool in the Undo flyout is the Color Replacer tool. On the surface, it appears not only simple but useless. It is a brush that replaces any pixels containing the Paint (foreground) color with the Paper (background) color. If only one color is replaced with another, its use would be restricted to the areas of uniform color, of which there are darned few in a color photograph.

Well, the truth is, this little gem can replace a range of colors with a single color. Among other things, users can change day scenes to night or remove the matting that sometimes appears on the edge of an object. In Figure 5-5, on the left is a photograph of a TV remote controller (which someone at Corel categorized under computer equipment in a previous version). Around the edge of the controller is the remainder of the original white background that got included when it was made into an object. (Later in this book you will learn several different techniques to reduce or remove this fringe, formally referred to as *matting*.) If you select the color of the fringe for the Paint color and a color similar to the background for the Paper color, the Color Replacer can instantly replace the ring around the controller as shown on the right in Figure 5-5. To use the Color Replacer tool, use the Eyedropper tool to select the desired Paint and Paper colors and apply it selectively with the Color Replacer brush.

In Summary

We have covered a broad range of PHOTO-PAINT tools. While I realize that some of them may seem about as interesting as 40 pounds of wet fertilizer, they make the day-to-day job of working with PHOTO-PAINT easier and more productive. Now that we know how to use the tools to handle an image, in the next chapter we are going to learn how to manipulate the image itself.

FIGURE 5-5   The original photograph (left) has a white fringe around it; the Color
Replacer tool is used to blend it into the background (right)

PART II

Masks and Objects

CHAPTER 6

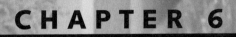

The School of Masks

131

Without masks, editing photographs on a computer would be torture. Masks make it possible to produce many special effects in photo-editing that we take for granted. Apart from lasting peace in the Middle East, masks may represent the most important development in the twentieth century. Okay, maybe that last statement was a little over the top; but when you work on photos every day, it 0seems true. Using masks is essential for you to succeed in photo-editing. In this chapter, we will learn a lot about creating and controlling masks. In Chapter 16, we'll learn about some of the advanced features of these masks. With that said, let's begin this chapter by introducing masks.

What Is a Mask?

Put simply, a *mask* protects part of an image or the entire image, allowing us to control exactly where on the image an effect will be applied. For example, in Figure 6-1 we have a photograph of the famous Taj Mahal in India. Fantastic

FIGURE 6-1   A perfect photograph of the Taj Mahal, except you can't see the mountains

structure, but the neighborhood looks a little bleak. To change the background without affecting the foreground, we must make a mask that protects the foreground. Next, we place a photograph of the city of Innsbruck, Austria, and use the mask to remove the parts we don't want to see. Now, we can have the beauty of this magnificent structure and a great view, as shown in Figure 6-2, looking much like an Ansel Adams photograph. When I first created this little optical illusion, my son immediately noticed that the trees were missing (it would have taken much longer to mask) and that the mountains weren't seen in the reflecting pool. Using the clone tool, we are able to remove the reflected trees and include the reflection of the Alps in the pool.

The concept of a mask is simple. You used masks long before you bought PHOTO-PAINT. If you have ever painted a room in a house, you know that the objective is to get the paint on the wall but not on the windows and baseboards. You can either paint very carefully (and slowly) or put masking tape over the area you don't want painted. Masking tape protects the windows and baseboards; it acts

FIGURE 6-2   Soon we can start making travel posters for Ski India

as a mask. That's why it's called "masking tape." A mask can also be likened to a stencil. When a stencil is placed over an object, only the portion of the stencil that is cut out allows paint to be applied to the surface; the remainder of the area is masked by the stencil.

PHOTO-PAINT masks act just like the previous two examples. They protect the part of the image they cover and select the part that is uncovered. The best part is that they are much more versatile than a stencil or masking tape (and not as difficult to remove when you have finished).

> **NOTE** *While Photoshop and PHOTO-PAINT share similar methods to select/protect image areas, they use different naming conventions for the parts. PHOTO-PAINT uses the term "mask" to describe both the selected area and the resulting mask created by the selection. In Photoshop, the part selected is called a "selection," and the image (mask) produced is called a "mask."*

Black, White, and Gray

Masks in PHOTO-PAINT are not composed of tape or stencil material. A mask is actually a separate image that covers the image you are working on. A photograph and its mask are shown in Figure 6-3. The original photograph (top) shows a leaf against a complex background. The leaf is masked, as indicated by the marquee surrounding it. The image shown at the bottom of the figure is what the mask looks like. The parts of the image covered by 100 percent black (opaque) are protected, while any part of the image under the 100 percent white (transparent) is not. Simple, right? Now let's get a little more complicated.

The bottom image in Figure 6-3 looks like a black-and-white (line art) image, but it's not. In Figure 6-4, the area indicated by the circle has been zoomed at 800 percent to show that the mask is actually a grayscale image. If the pixels in the mask can have transparency, it means that these transparent pixels will only partially protect areas of an image. The zoomed-in area (shown in the circle) shows the mask we saw in Figure 6-3 after it has been feathered. Having the opacity of a mask gradually increase as it approaches the edge produces blurred edges of semitransparent pixels. A blurred edge allows effects to blend into the protected areas of the image. In other words, smooth transitions in an image fool the eye of the viewer.

> **NOTE** *For those used to Photoshop, the mask tools referenced in this chapter are called "marquee tools" in Photoshop.*

Mask marquee
indicates the
mask boundary.

The white areas
of the mask
are selected but
not protected.

6

FIGURE 6-3   The leaf in the photograph (top) has been selected as indicated by the
marquee surrounding it; the actual mask created by the selection is the
black portion (bottom)

Displaying Masks

Corel PHOTO-PAINT provides a large selection of both mask-creation and
mask-selection tools. All these tools do basically the same thing—create masks.
Although a mask lies on top of an image, it is normally not visible to the user.
Let's face it, invisible things are difficult to work with. Therefore, the thoughtful
programmers at Corel put several features in the program to display them.

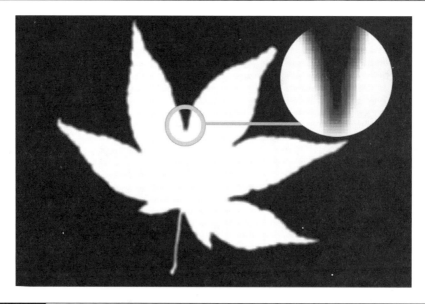

FIGURE 6-4   Feathering the mask produces a blurred image that allows PHOTO-PAINT actions to blend into the image

The Marquee de Mask

The primary way to display a mask is the marquee. When this feature is enabled, selecting an area with a mask produces a visual display of the mask boundary called a *marquee*. The marquee appears as a moving pattern of dash marks that is commonly referred to as "marching ants." Latest scientific research has determined that they are not ants at all, but rather pixels marching around the marquee carrying tiny picket signs protesting the senseless erasing of pixels in an image (sigh). Because all those moving dashes can, at times, be more of a distraction than a help, PHOTO-PAINT allows the display to be toggled on or off by use of CTRL-H or the Mask Marquee icon in the standard toolbar, or you can go the long way through the menus: Mask | Marquee Visible. I recommend the Show Mask Marquee button, which is part of the Mask/Object toolbar in Figure 6-5. Two sets of tools are used when working on masks—mask creation tools and mask manipulation tools. The mask tools in the Mask/Object toolbar are used to manipulate the mask, whereas the first four buttons on the left and the last one on the right of the toolbar involve operations with objects, which are explored in the next chapter.

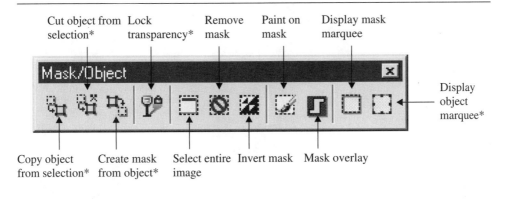

Cut object from   Lock   Remove   Paint on   Display mask
selection*   transparency*   mask   mask   marquee

                                                                    Display
                                                                    object
                                                                    marquee*

Copy object   Create mask   Select entire   Invert mask   Mask overlay
from selection*   from object*   image

*Object tools

| **FIGURE 6-5** | The Mask/Object toolbar |

When you're working with a black-and-white mask, the decision of where to place the marquee is simple—on the mask boundary. But suppose the pixels that make up the mask boundary are gray—where does PHOTO-PAINT display the marquee? Its position, in reference to the mask, as well as the color of the marquee, is controlled by Display settings in Options (CTRL-J). See Chapter 20 for information about adjusting this jewel.

Marquees Are Okay, but Overlay Is Where It's At

Now that I have given you the hot scoop on mask marquees, I need to confess that in over three zillion hours of using PHOTO-PAINT, I have never had an urge or a need to change the threshold setting. Why? Because mask overlay is better. The marquee shows where edges of the mask are. Mask Overlay, which is toggled on and off from the Mask menu, places a tint over the image that shows the actual mask. The next illustration is a composite image showing the mask overlay and the marquee. In real life, enabling the Mask Overlay feature temporarily turns off the marquee. In the zoomed area, notice where the marquee says the edge of the mask is and where the actual edge is (it is the white glow surrounding the glass). Are marquees useless? Of course not. They provide a quick visual indication of the status of a mask when you're working on an effect involving extensive mask manipulation.

Mask overlay does not in any way affect the image, only the display of the image. If you don't like the default color (which looks like Barbie™ pink), you can change the overlay color in the same way we changed the marquee color (CTRL-J and Display).

The Mask-Creation Tools

Mask Transform Tool

These eight tools can be selected from the Mask Tools flyout in the Toolbox or by pressing the shortcut key. Don't be concerned about the names of mask tools for the moment. We will be examining each one of these so that you can understand their functions and the best times to use them. I have also included the Path tool, since, indirectly, it can be used to create a mask. The mask creation tools follow:

Mask Tool	Shortcut Key
Rectangle mask tool	R
Circle mask tool	J
Freehand mask tool	K
Lasso mask tool	A
Scissors mask tool	4
Magic Wand mask tool	W
Mask Brush tool	B
Mask Transform tool	M
Path (Node Edit) tool	. (period)

There are two types of mask creation tools: those used to create regular masks and those that are referred to as the color-sensitive mask tools. The regular mask tools—Rectangle, Circle, and Freehand—create masks defined by the user. Their size, shape, and location within the image are controlled by use of the mouse or other pointing device. This is unlike the color-sensitive masks whose boundaries are determined by PHOTO-PAINT from information you enter about the color values of the image. Color-sensitive masks are like an old Texas bloodhound. You tell the program what color or shade you are interested in, and they will look through the entire image to find every pixel that matches the color or range of colors you asked for. PHOTO-PAINT then creates a mask based on that information. Color-sensitive mask tools are the Lasso, Scissors, and Magic Wand. After a mask is made, we can use any mask creation tool, including the Mask Transform tool, to edit the mask.

NOTE *The default shortcut key for each tool is shown in parentheses after the tool name.*

Regular Mask Tools

These three tools create masks when you click and drag a cursor on the image. The Rectangle and Circle mask tools make masks in the shape that their name implies. The Freehand mask tool is used to create more complex shapes.

The Rectangle Mask Tool (R)

In case the name of the tool didn't give it away, the Rectangle mask tool is used for making square- and rectangle-shaped masks. To create a mask, you only need to select the tool, click and hold down the mouse button, and drag until it has the size and shape you want.

Mask Tool Modifiers   Based on the e-mail I have received over the years, this next feature of the mask tools has confused many users. Pay close attention—there may be a quiz.

Two keys are used as mask tool modifiers: CTRL and SHIFT. That was the easy part. The action produced by pressing a modifier key depends on whether the modifier key is enabled before or after clicking the mouse button.

> **NOTE**   *If a modifier key is held down* before *the mouse button is clicked, it will temporarily enable the mask mode as long as it is held. Mask modes are discussed later in this chapter. The keys only work as mask tool modifiers when held down* after *the mouse button is clicked.*

If you hold down CTRL after clicking the mouse button, the shape of the mask is constrained to a square, as shown here:

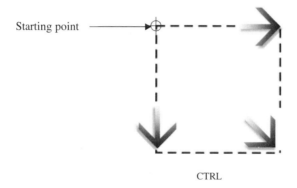

Starting point

CTRL

Key	Action
CTRL—before mouse click	Subtractive mask mode while held
CTRL—after mouse click	Constrains the shape of the mask to a square
SHIFT—before mouse click	Additive mask mode while held
SHIFT—after mouse click	Produces a mask that expands outward from the starting point
CTRL-SHIFT—before mouse click	XOR mask mode while held
CTRL-SHIFT—after mouse click	Produces a square mask that expands outward from the starting point
CTRL-ALT-SHIFT-3-J-Q-[	Produces cramps in fingers

TABLE 6-1   Mask Tool Modifier Keys

The modifier key can be used both as a mask mode control and as a constrain key. Hold down CTRL, click the mouse button, release CTRL, and then hold it down again. Aren't you glad you know that?

Holding down SHIFT produces a mask that expands outward from the starting point, while holding down both CTRL and SHIFT creates a square mask that expands outward from the center, as shown next.

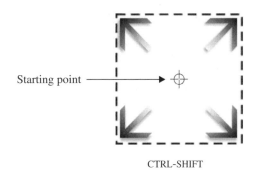

Starting point

CTRL-SHIFT

 ## The Circle Mask Tool (J)

The Circle mask tool, shown here, is used to create elliptical or circular masks. This mask tool works just like the Rectangle mask tool, except that holding down CTRL after the mouse button is clicked constrains the mask to a circle.

 This is one of the most useful masking tools for defining an irregular shape. Almost any curved edge can be selected by changing the mask mode to Additive mode and creating the edge of the curved edge with multiple overlapping elliptical shapes.

 ## The Freehand Mask Tool (K)

The Freehand mask tool, shown here, is really two tools in one.

As long as the mouse or stylus button is held down, the mask tool is in Drawing mode and acts much as a pencil or pen would. The mask boundary is created as you draw an outline surrounding the area you want to edit. When the pointing device button is released, the Freehand mask tool reverts to Polygon mode (what Photoshop users call a "Polygonal lasso"). In this mode, you need only click at different points in your image to define the boundaries; between each click, PHOTO-PAINT creates a straight line. When you have finished with your mask, either double-click the last point or hold down ALT and click the mouse/stylus button to complete the mask.

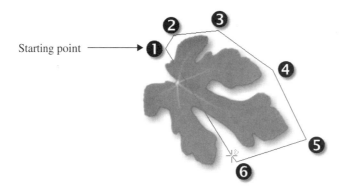

Starting point

To illustrate how the Polygon mode of the Freehand tool works, look at the example just shown. The mask begins by clicking at point 1. As the cursor is moved to point 2 on the example, a continually updated display of the mask shape is shown. Each time the cursor is clicked, a new point of the mask boundary is created. Clicking DEL removes the last point. Clicking at points 3–6 produces the shape shown in the preceding illustration. The cursor still appears, because the mask has not yet been completed. A straight line is continuously displayed between the current cursor position and the starting point.

Freehand Mask Tool Modifier Keys   Just like the other mask tools, the Freehand mask tool has modifier keys. Holding down CTRL and the mouse button in Drawing mode constrains the mask cursor movement to horizontal or vertical strokes. To change the direction of the constraint, use CTRL-SHIFT. In Polygon mode, CTRL constrains creation of strokes to 45-degree angles. DEL is used in either mode to remove the last point on the mask. Each time DEL is pressed, another point is removed; this "undoing" of the mask can continue all the way back to the starting point.

TIP   *When clicking at multiple mask boundary points in Polygon mode, ensure you don't click the button too fast, or else PHOTO-PAINT will misinterpret it as a double-click and complete the mask. If I had a nickel for every time I did that, I'd be a rich man today.*

When Two Tools Are Better Than One   Corel's dualistic approach to the Freehand mask tool offers two advantages over the traditional freehand tool. Traditionally, a freehand-type tool is difficult to use because the mouse, being a relative motion device, does not have the control necessary to accurately trace a complex line. If you doubt this, try writing your name using a mouse. If you can write your name with a mouse, you need to date more. The other limitation of the Freehand mask tool becomes apparent the first time you release the mouse button: Traditionally, a freehand mask is completed with a straight line back to the starting point as soon as the button is released, regardless of whether you have finished. In other words, when you begin to make a mask with a traditional freehand tool, you cannot release the button until the mask is finished.

In PHOTO-PAINT, the Freehand mask tool simply changes mode when the mouse button is released, allowing you to rest when creating a lengthy and detailed mask. Combining the Drawing mode and the Polygon mode makes it possible to use a mouse to mask irregularly shaped objects with some degree of accuracy.

6

> **TIP**   *For irregular mask creation with a mouse, I recommend using the Polygon mode of the Freehand mask tool. If you use a stylus, the Drawing mode will allow you to quickly create a mask.*

> **TIP**   *I strongly recommend changing the shape of the tool cursor to a Crosshair when using the Freehand tool to trace complex shapes. It is much easier to see and, thereby, follow an edge with this cursor. To change the cursor shape, open Preferences (CTRL-J); and from the General setting, set the Cursor Type to Crosshair.*

Mask Modes

If it were a perfect world, every mask you make would be perfect, never needing modification. Alas, the world is not perfect; and if you've worked in photo-editing for any time at all, you've spent a lot of time adding to and subtracting from masks.

Whenever a mask tool is selected, one of four tiny icons appears in the lower-right corner of the status bar and is also visible in the property bar. These icons tell us what mask mode the mask tool is in. These tiny icons are your friends. They will save you a great deal of frustration once you train yourself to look for them.

> **NOTE** *The mask tools do not retain individual mask mode settings. For example, if you are using the Rectangle mask tool and the XOR mode is selected, any other mask tool you select will also be in XOR mode.*

Normal Mask Mode

In Normal mask mode, masks are mutually exclusive. In other words, making a mask deletes any existing mask in an image. This is handy housekeeping when creating simple masks. If a mask doesn't look right, just make another one. With more complex masks, the Normal mask mode prevents modification of masks. As you may have guessed, the purpose of the other mask modes is to allow us to add to, subtract from, and otherwise modify to our heart's content any existing mask. Three of the four mask modes are pretty much self-explanatory. They are

- **Normal**   Every time you make a mask, any existing mask is removed.
- **Additive**   Each mask tool action adds to the existing mask.
- **Subtractive**   Each mask tool action subtracts from the existing mask.
- **Exclusive OR (XOR)**   If the portion of the new mask being added overlaps an existing mask, the mask properties of the overlapped area are inverted. That's clear as mud, isn't it? You'll learn more about this shortly.

Selecting the Mask Modes

Mask modes can be selected from the Mask menu, through keyboard shortcuts, or through toolbar buttons. The mode of the currently selected mask tool is indicated by an icon displayed in the status bar and by the shape of the cursor. Figure 6-6 shows the mask mode icons that appear in the property bar and status bar when the Rectangle mask tool is selected.

You can also select a mask mode using the following keyboard shortcuts; I never can remember them, but maybe you can.

- **Normal**   ALT-NUMPAD . (period)
- **Additive**   ALT-NUMPAD +
- **Subtractive**   ALT-NUMPAD -
- **XOR**   ALT-NUMPAD *

Additive

Subtractive

XOR

This is the Mask Style setting and has nothing to do with mask modes.

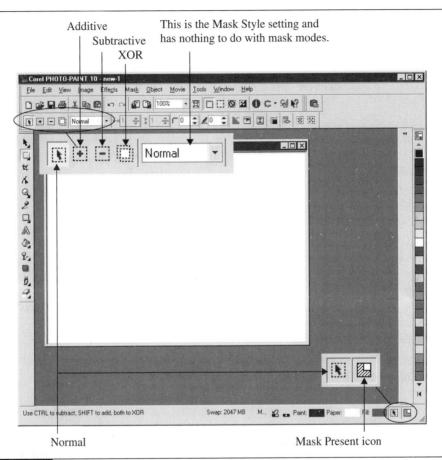

Normal

Mask Present icon

FIGURE 6-6 Corel has placed icons relating to mask modes just about everywhere

If you recall, all the mask tool modifier keys previously described in this chapter required holding down the key after clicking the mouse button. To *temporarily* change the mask mode, click the keys just referenced *before* clicking the mode. Releasing the modifier key reverts the mask to its previous mode. Here are the simple rules for using modifier keys to create masks:

- CTRL enables Subtractive mode.

- SHIFT enables Additive mode.

- CTRL-SHIFT enables XOR mode.

■ Clicking the mouse key before holding down SHIFT creates a new mask that expands or contracts (depending on the direction you are dragging the mouse) from the center.

The preceding rules apply only to mask creation.

If you are unable to apply an effect to an image, check first to see if the Mask Present icon is displayed. Even if you can't see the mask, the computer will prevent you from applying any effect.

Additive and Subtractive Mask Modes

These modes do what their names imply. When in Additive mode, each time you use a mask tool, you add to the previous mask. Of course, if you select an area of the image that is already selected, nothing will change. Conversely, any mask tool actions taken in Subtractive mode remove the portions from the selected area.

XOR Mask Mode

"XOR" stands for a term used in computer logic called "Exclusive Or." With XOR mask mode enabled, if you

■ Create a mask on an image that doesn't have a mask, the mask will act normally.

■ Add a second portion to the mask that doesn't overlap the first mask, it will act like Additive mode.

■ Add a second portion that falls entirely within the existing mask, it acts like Subtractive mode.

■ Add a mask that overlaps a portion of an existing mask, the portion of the image already selected by a mask covered by the XOR mask will be inverted.

■ Know the identity of the Lone Ranger, don't tell anyone. It's a secret.

Is the Glass Half Full or Half Empty?

This is a good time to ensure that you understand an important concept in masks. Here is a little test, much like the famous glass test. Look at Figure 6-7. I have enabled the grid and used the Circle mask tool to create the circles indicated by the mask marquee. How many masks do you see? The correct answer is one mask composed of eight selected areas. The actual mask is shown at the right of the image. Now for extra credit, is the mask half full or half empty?

Color-Sensitive Masks

This category of tools allows you to create incredibly complex masks quickly—if you know how to use them. The color-sensitive mask tools are Lasso, Magic Wand, Scissors, and Color. The Color mask tool is the only mask tool not located on the mask flyout. It is accessed through the Mask menu.

6

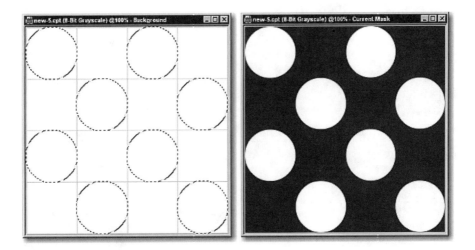

FIGURE 6-7   How many masks can you find in the image on the left? The answer may surprise you

The photograph in Figure 6-8a is an example of a photograph that needs to have the shadow areas lightened without making the lighter areas any lighter. This is where color-sensitive masks really earn their pay. By using the Color mask, we have been able to isolate the shadow portion of the photograph from the light areas, and using Gamma we have recovered the detail in the shadow area and have a much more balanced photograph, as shown in Figure 6-8b.

The success of the three color-sensitive mask tools discussed here depends on the Color Similarity setting the user applies in the property bar. The higher the value, the greater the number of colors that will be included in the resulting mask. The key to finding the optimum tolerance level is experimentation. There are two modes: Normal and HSB. The Normal method bases its selection strictly on the color similarity of adjacent pixels, while the HSB method lets you fine-tune the selection according to the similarity of a combination of hue, saturation, and

a   b

FIGURE 6-8   Using a color sensitive mask, we are able to isolate the shadows in the original (a) and apply correction to recover detail in the shadows (b)

brightness levels between adjacent pixels. Now let's take a look at these tools and how they operate.

The Lasso Mask Tool (A)

The Lasso mask tool is used to create an irregular mask based on an image's color values and the Tolerance level. The lasso metaphor is perfect for this tool. I know a lot about lassoes; I've seen *City Slickers* more than ten times. On a dude ranch, a lasso surrounds an object; and when you pull on the rope, the lasso closes until it fits tightly around the object. The Lasso tool works in much the same way, but without the rope.

When you click the starting point of the mask, PHOTO-PAINT samples the color value of the pixels under the starting point. A mask is created in the same manner as with the Freehand mask tool. Once you have surrounded the subject you want selected with the Lasso mask tool, double-click the mouse button and the marquee shrinks until it surrounds an area with color values that fall within the limits set by the Color Similarity slider in the property bar.

Replacing a Background (Project)   Here is a simple exercise that gives you an opportunity to try the Lasso mask tool and get a preview of an advanced mask feature. In this session, we are going to replace the background of a photograph of a tomato.

1. Choose File | Open and, from the Open an Image dialog box, select TOMATO.CPT, available for download from the Osborne Web site. The image may be too large to fit on most displays (including mine), so use Zoom to Fit (F4).

2. Select the Lasso mask tool from the Mask flyout. In the property bar, ensure Normal is chosen, and change the Color Similarity level to 10. This tells PHOTO-PAINT to include pixels that are greater or less than 10 shades from the starting pixel value.

3. Click the cursor at the point outside the tomato to establish the starting (anchor) point. Now click at points around the tomato as shown next. The exact placement doesn't matter, because the Lasso tool is using the value of the anchor for its calculations.

4. Double-click at the last point indicated to close the mask. If the marquee isn't displayed, press CTRL-H to select Mask Marquee Visible. The mask should outline the tomato, as shown next.

5. You have just isolated the tomato from the background. To replace the background, we need to invert the mask (CTRL-SHIFT-I). Now, choose Edit | Fill. When the Edit Fill & Transparency dialog box opens, click the Texture Fill button and then click the Edit button. Select Styles in the Texture library and Sky 2 Colors in the Texture list. Click OK and then OK again to apply the fill to the masked area. Voilà! We have a lovely sky background for our tomato, as shown next. Close the file and don't save the changes.

The Scissors Mask Tool (4)

The Lasso mask tool is great when you have a background with very similar colors, like the one in the previous exercise. When the background contains many different colors, you can use the Scissors mask tool, which automatically detects edges in your image and places the mask marquee along those edges as you are outlining the mask. This tool has a new added feature in the PHOTO-PAINT 10 release—it works! Yep, Corel has been very honest about the fact that this tool hasn't worked correctly since its initial release in PHOTO-PAINT 8. The good news is it works great now.

Like all color-sensitive masks, the Lasso mask uses the Tolerance setting to control its operation. The Scissors mask tool also uses Color Similarity values in the property bar within the area of the tool's *bounding box*. When you select this mask tool, an invisible bounding box surrounds the Mask Tool cursor and remains centered at each successive point on the mask. If you recall, the Lasso mask tool makes all of its decisions comparing the color value of the starting point and the colors in the image. The Scissors mask tool doesn't look at the color content of the entire image; it only looks at the area inside the bounding box.

How the Scissors Mask Works This is a cool tool, but its operation is a little tricky to explain. The first click is placed near the edge of the subject you want to select. This first point establishes the color sample used for Color Similarity comparisons. The Scissors mask tool evaluates all of the pixels within the 200 × 200–pixel bounding box to determine where to place the edge. As you move the cursor along the edge you want to select, a line appears indicating where the mask will be placed. Every time you click the cursor along the edge, it creates a new center for the bounding box. When using this tool, here are some rules to make it work better. If the area you want to select contains a lot of similar colors, you need only click the tool at a few points and the tool won't have any trouble detecting the edge. If the background contains many different colors, you need to reset the center of the bounding box more often. This is because as you approach or go beyond the edge of the current bounding box, the tool has greater difficulty detecting the edge.

One problem you may experience is when the color/shades that define the edge between the foreground and the background are too close. When this happens, either click many points close together, or click and drag the mouse like a Freehand mask tool. This technique works best when used with a stylus instead of a mouse.

The Magic Wand Mask Tool (W)

The Magic Wand mask tool is the converse of the Lasso mask tool. It creates masks by *expanding* from a starting point until all the adjacent colors meeting the selection criteria are included. As with the other color-sensitive mask tools, the ability of the Magic Wand to make an accurate mask depends on the Color Similarity settings in the property bar and the actual color-value composition of the image.

How the Magic Wand Mask Tool Performs Its Magic   Two simple facts about the Magic Wand tool are (1) there is nothing magic about it, and (2) it is very simple to use once you understand the concept behind its operation. In theory, you simply click the area that needs to be masked and PHOTO-PAINT does the rest. There are actually times when this will work as intended.

PHOTO-PAINT reads the color value of the starting pixel and, using the Color Sensitivity level, *expands* the mask selection pixel by pixel until it can no longer find pixels that are within the limits. For example, if the starting pixel has a value of 60 and the Color Sensitivity value has been set to 50, the mask will expand from its starting point until every adjacent pixel with a value between 10 (60 minus 50) and 110 (60 plus 50) has been included in the mask.

> **TIP** *When you're using the Magic Wand mask tool, the most important decision to make is the choice of whether to mask the object or the area around the object. If the area to be protected is filled with a wide variety of colors or colors with a wide tonal range, then look at the area surrounding it. Remember that it only takes one click of the button to invert a mask.*

Taking the Magic Wand Mask Tool for a Test Drive   Remember the photograph of the tomato earlier in the chapter? In this hands-on exercise, we will use the Magic Wand tool to do a simple background replacement like we did with the Lasso mask tool and the background. We will also learn a few ways to improve the resulting mask.

1. Choose File | Open and select TOMATO.CPT, available for download from the Osborne Web site. Click the Open button.

2. Select Image | Paper Size; and in the dialog box, click the padlock icon to maintain this aspect ratio, and then change the Width to 2.5 as shown. Click OK.

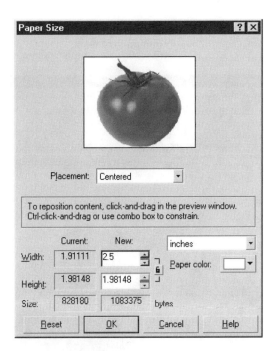

Paper Size

Placement: Centered

To reposition content, click-and-drag in the preview window.
Ctrl-click-and-drag or use combo box to constrain.

	Current:	New:	inches
Width:	1.91111	2.5	
			Paper color:
Height:	1.98148	1.98148	
Size:	828180	1083375	bytes

Reset   OK   Cancel   Help

3. Select the Magic Wand tool from the Mask flyout in the Toolbox, or use the quick way by clicking the W key. Refer to Figure 6-9 and ensure the mode is Normal and the Color Similarity value is set to 10. Turn on Antialiasing to allow the mask to smoothly follow the edges of the tomato.

4. Click anywhere on the white background of the image, and voilà—the entire background is selected—or is it? Choose Mask | Mask Overlay and you will see a tiny part of the original white background lurking under one of the leaves of the tomato. To include this part in the mask of the background, change the Color Similarity to 10 (the change is necessary to prevent the highlights on the tomato from being selected) and choose Mask | Shape | Similar. This causes PHOTO-PAINT to add additional areas to the mask that contain the same colors as the original mask, which takes care of the area below the leaf.

5. Choose Edit | Fill. Select the Paint Color button and click OK to apply the fill. You will notice that the tomato has a white fringe, as shown next (at a zoom of 800 percent), which was part of the original background. Undo the fill (CTRL-Z). Now let's learn how to correct this fringe.

Normal color   Color similarity   Antialiasing
tolerance mode

FIGURE 6-9   Property bar settings control the operation of the Magic Wand mask tool

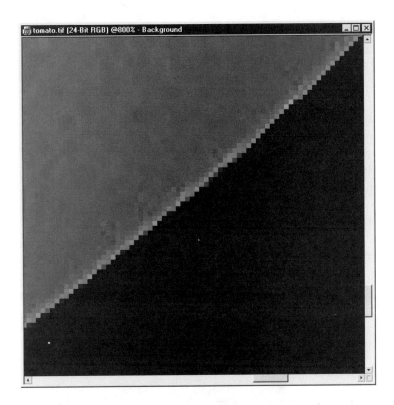

6. Choose Mask | Shape | Expand, which opens another dialog box, as shown next. Change the value to one pixel. Usually, it only takes a small value of a few pixels to remove the fringe.

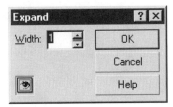

7. To see the results, reapply the bitmap fill. In Figure 6-10, one of the wood bitmap fills was used. Please notice that the white area under the tomato leaf has been replaced with the new bitmap fill.

 In Figure 6-10, an airbrush tool was used to paint the shadow below the tomato. It was simple to add this realistic touch, since the tomato was already protected by its mask.

 Believe it or not, the Grow and Similar commands in Photoshop not only operate like those in PHOTO-PAINT, but also have the same names. Go figure.

The Grow and Similar Commands

In the previous exercise, we used the Similar command; so it seems an appropriate time to understand what Similar and its counterpart, Grow, actually do. These two

FIGURE 6-10 The addition of a new background and a shadow created by an airbrush makes the tomato look much more appealing

commands increase the size of an area selected by a mask. Both commands determine which pixels are included in the mask according to the current tolerance setting of the Magic Wand mask tool.

Grow

With an existing mask on the image, choose Mask | Shape | Grow to include all pixels that neighbor the existing mask and those that fall within the range of colors included in the mask. All the pixels eligible for selection by Grow must be contiguous (adjacent to one another). The color range of pixels selected is determined by the Color Similarity setting. If you need to change the setting, it is first necessary to select the Magic Wand mask tool.

Similar

With an existing mask on the image, choose Mask | Shape | Similar. The Similar command acts like the Grow command, except that the eligible pixels do not need to be adjacent to one another. As long as the pixel's color value falls within the color range specified by the Color Similarity setting, it will be included regardless of where it is in the image.

Color Similarity and Magic Wands

The Color Similarity is critical to getting satisfactory results with the Grow and Similar commands when used in conjunction with the Magic Wand. When you apply the Magic Wand using a relatively high setting (>30), applying the Grow command without changing the Color Similarity value will result in a blown mask—that is, a mask that overruns most color boundaries. This happens because of the cumulative effect of applying the Magic Wand with a setting of 30 percent on top of a 30 percent Grow setting. The best way to use it is either to use low values for both selections, or to use as high a setting as necessary for the Magic Wand to do its job and then decrease the setting of the Grow command.

NOTE *The figure of 30 percent is not some PHOTO-PAINT magic threshold figure for the color-sensitive tools. It is a relatively high-threshold figure I used for an example in the previous paragraph.*

Properties of Mask and Selection

Let's review some of the properties we observed when using the mask tool in the previous tutorial. First, if you move an existing mask using a mask tool in Normal mode (except the Mask Brush or Mask Transform tool), it becomes a selection. If ALT is held down when the selection is created, the original image in the masked area remains; if not, it is replaced with the current Paper color if it is a flat image with no objects. A selection can be moved around an image, even beyond the edge of the image borders, and it will still maintain both its shape and its contents. If a selection is dragged completely off the image, it becomes a new image.

The Mask Transform Tool (M)

The Mask Transform tool is found on the flyout with the Object Picker tool. The Mask Transform tool is actually a mask modifier. All masks created with the mask tools can be moved, scaled, rotated, skewed, or have perspective applied; in other words, you can do just about anything you want to a mask with this tool.

When the Mask Transform tool is selected, eight handles appear on the existing mask. Clicking inside the mask changes the shape of the handles, indicating the transform mode. The transform mode also appears in the property bar. Figure 6-11 shows the control handles associated with the different modes and functions. There are many ways to manipulate a mask using this tool, but you will find its most commonly used function is to move a mask on an image or to change the size (scale) of a mask. The other transform functions are mostly used when working with objects.

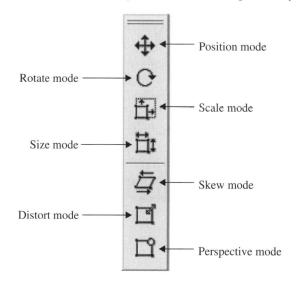

Position, Scale, and Size modes   Distort mode   Perspective mode   Rotate and Skew modes

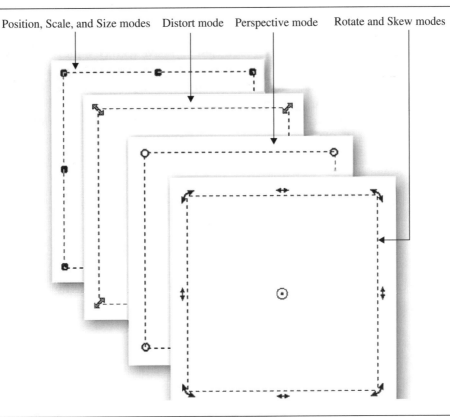

FIGURE 6-11   The handles indicate the selected mask transform mode

TIP
Whenever you apply a transformation to a mask, be sure to double-click the mask to complete the transform action. Until you complete the action, most of the PHOTO-PAINT commands will be unavailable.

The Mask Brush Tool (B)

The remaining button on the Mask Tools flyout is the Mask Brush tool, which is used to modify both the regular and the color-sensitive masks. This is the ultimate mask clean-up and touch-up tool. The Mask Brush tool enables you to brush or paint an area to be masked. Unlike a regular brush tool that applies color to an image, the Mask Brush tool can be used to apply or remove a portion of a mask using the Additive and Subtractive modes. The size and shape of the Mask Brush tool are set from the property bar.

In Summary

If you have gone through each of the exercises, you have learned a lot about masks and how they work. While using masks may at first seem to be more trouble than they are worth, don't get discouraged if they don't act the way you want them to the first few times use them. If you make a habit of using them, their operation will become second-nature to you and soon you'll wonder how you could ever work without them. In the next chapter, we will continue to learn more about these powerful tools.

CHAPTER 7

Exploring Objects and Text

One of the more powerful features of PHOTO-PAINT is the ability to create and control objects. The use of objects falls into a category I call fun stuff. There is a tabloid sold in the United States called *The Sun,* which may be one of the leading forums for unique photo-editing. If you live in the United States, you have probably seen *The Sun* while standing in grocery lines. One headline read "Baby Born with Three Heads." The photograph showed a woman holding an infant who fits the headline's description. Someone on *The Sun* staff had masked the face of a small child, made it into an object, duplicated several copies, and placed them on the body of the baby. Like I said, this is fun stuff. If you are an avid reader of *The Sun,* do not take what I say as criticism of the tabloid. I love *The Sun!* I stand in a lot of grocery lines, and it provides entertainment while waiting for the person with 35 items in the 10-item express line to check out. In this chapter, we will explore objects, the Text tool, and all that can be done with them.

Pixels and Crazy Glue

Traditionally, with bitmap programs like Corel PHOTO-PAINT, there used to be only the background. If we take a brush from the Toolbox and draw a wide brush stroke across an image, every pixel the brush touches changes to the color assigned to the brush. The brush color does not go on *top* of the original color; it replaces it. It is as if every pixel that is applied has super glue on it. When an action is applied to an image, it "sticks" to the image and cannot be moved. Anyone who has spent hours and hours trying to achieve an effect with these older bitmap programs will testify that the process by which bitmaps merge into the background was the major drawback of photo-editing programs. And then, along came objects.

Objects Defined

So what is an object? Here is one definition:

> *An object is an independent bitmap selection created with object tools and layered above the base image.*

Let's expand that definition. In Corel PHOTO-PAINT, an object is a bitmap that "floats" above the background, which is also called the *base image.* Because the object is not a part of the base image, it can be moved as many times as needed without limit. Objects can also be scaled, resized, rotated, and distorted. We also have the ability to apply Perspective transformations, which greatly increase the flexibility of many of the tools. You are about to learn how to do some amazing things with objects. Most of the rules you learned in previous chapters regarding masks also apply to objects.

Expanding the Definition

Figure 7-1 appears to be a single image, and yet it is composed of a background and six separate objects. Figure 7-2 shows the background and six objects that make up the image, and the Objects docker that lists them. The misconception that the object only exists to its visible edge is reinforced by the Object marquee, which displays the "edge" of an object. In reality, an object may be composed of both opaque and transparent pixels. If Figure 7-1 were observed from the side, we

Fig07-01 (24-Bit RGB) @100% - Background

FIGURE 7-1   How many objects do you see in this picture? The answer might surprise you

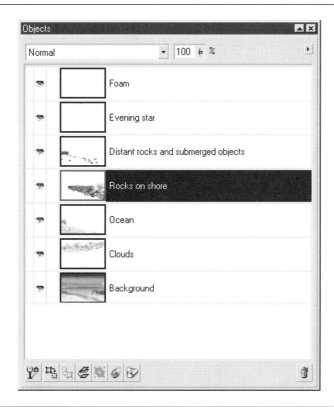

FIGURE 7-2   The Objects docker shows not only what objects are in the image but where they are located

would see that each object is actually the same size and dimensions as the background. It may help to think of the object as on a large sheet of clear acetate, rather than as a cutout placed on the background.

The Objects Docker and Property Bar

The Objects docker, Figure 7-3, can be opened by selecting Window | Dockers | Objects or with the keyboard combination CTRL-F7.

The Objects docker is the control center for all object manipulations. The following is only a partial list of the functions that can be accomplished through the property bar and the Objects docker:

■ Render to object.

creates an object from the background

- Select object.

√ - Lock or unlock object transparency.

- Make objects visible or invisible.

√ - Create objects from masks.

√ - Create masks from objects.

- Move objects between layers.

- Change rate of the transparency/opacity of objects.

- Apply transformations to individual objects.

- Select merge modes for individual objects.

- Label different objects.

- Combine objects with the background. */creates an object from the background*

√ - Combine individual objects. */combine object together*

- Delete objects.

- Get a babysitter on a Saturday night (okay, that might be pushing it).

⊃ new lens   ⊃ new objects

Object Modes

How an object acts or reacts to a PHOTO-PAINT operation is determined by the mode the object is in. Here are some definitions to describe modes in the Objects docker.

- **Selected**   If an object is selected, the name is highlighted. It can be moved, grouped with other objects, or merged with the background or with other objects. An object is selected by clicking its thumbnail or label. To select multiple contiguous objects, select the first one and SHIFT-click the last one. To select multiple noncontiguous objects, CTRL-click each object you want selected. Selected objects are not subject to PHOTO-PAINT actions (sharpening, blurring, and so on) unless they are active.

- **Active**   An object is active when its thumbnail has a red border. Only one object can be active at a time. An object that is active is also selected.

- **Lock Object Transparency**   When enabled, it protects transparent areas of the object from PHOTO-PAINT actions.

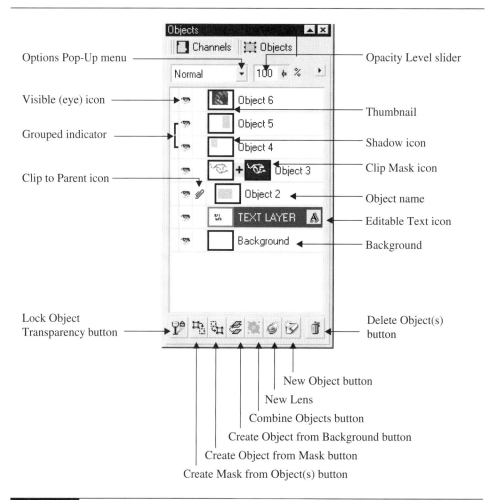

The Objects docker is the control center for nearly all operations involving objects

A Guided Tour of Objects

This is a tutorial to help you get a better feel for what objects and all their features do and do not do. It looks complicated because there is a lot of text explaining what we are doing, so jump right in.

1. Open the downloaded image OBJECTS from the Corel Web site. Shown next is a background that I created for this exercise using a fountain fill background, the Image Sprayer tool for the clouds, and noise for the sand.

2. Select the Text tool in the Toolbox and, on the property bar, change the font to Futura XBlt BT at 150. Type **COREL**. The placement of your text is not important as long as it fits within the image completely. Select the Object Picker tool. Look in the Objects docker and you will see that the text is now an object. Also note the letter "A" on the right side of the Object name. This icon tells us that the text is an editable object.

7

3. There is a lot of information available to us at this point. Place your cursor on the object, and after a moment the box shown next will appear giving details about the object underneath. It shows the object is both active and selected. It also tells us that its Opacity is at 100 percent, the merge mode is Normal, and the size of the object is 499 × 113 pixels. The Objects docker includes some of the same information. The object is labeled COREL. (Text objects use their text string as their object name.) It is highlighted (selected), and the thumbnail has a red border (indicating it is active).

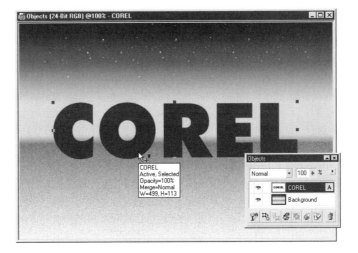

4. Click the middle-top handle of the text. Hold down the CTRL (constrain) key and drag the text up. Nothing will appear to happen until you hit a point where the text's height is 200 percent. Let go of the mouse button first and then the CTRL key. Either press the ENTER key on your keyboard or click the Apply Transformation (tiny green) button on the property bar to apply the transformation. At this point, we have scaled the text object vertically to 200 percent.

5. Select the Text tool again. Click the text. A warning box appears, as shown next, warning you that if you click OK, some of the changes made to the text will be lost. This represents a change in PHOTO-PAINT 10. In previous versions, all changes would be lost; while in PHOTO-PAINT 10, only changes made to fill, distortion, and perspective revert to the original state. Got it? Click OK on the warning box, since the change we made to the text will not revert.

6. Choose File Import (CTRL-I) and, when the dialog box opens, select the downloaded exercise file CHECKERED FLAG.JPG and click Open. A thumbnail of the image we are importing appears attached to the cursor. Click anywhere in the image window and the checkered flag we just imported covers the entire image shown next. Notice that in the Objects docker it is an object floating above the text and the background.

7. In the Objects docker, click in the column to the right of the eye icon and a paperclip icon appears indicating the Clip to Parent mode. We will discuss this mode in the following sections; but for now, try this. Click the text in the Objects docker to select it. Now drag the text and notice that only the portion of checkered flag directly over the text can be seen. Now select the flag and move it. Again, only the portion over the object (text) is visible.

TIP   *You can select objects in an image by clicking them with the Object Picker tool. The background can only be selected in the Objects docker.*

8. That's all for now. We are going to use this file again, so either keep it open or save the file as Guided Tour. Don't forget where you park it.

| NOTE | *For purposes of clarification, the terms "object" and "layer" are used interchangeably. This is because each layer can contain only one object, and without an object there cannot be a layer. Photoshop calls them layers; PHOTO-PAINT calls them objects. A rose by any other name. . . . In this chapter, we will use the term "object" to avoid confusion.* |

Clip to Parent

So what is this Clip to Parent? Clip to Parent sounds like what happens to me when I get the phone bills my children have run up. In PHOTO-PAINT, this option causes the object's shape to be clipped to the shape of the object below it in the object list. This feature is activated by clicking in the column to the right of the eye in the Objects docker. A paperclip icon appears to show that Clip to Parent is active. Before returning to our guided tour, let's look at the controls of the Objects docker a little closer.

Looking Deeper into the Objects Docker

The Objects docker is composed of the Thumbnail display area, the Dialog Display options, the Multifunction buttons, and the Merge/Opacity controls. Let's find out a little more about these wonders.

Thumbnail Display Area

The Thumbnail display is divided into four columns. The column on the far right shows the thumbnail and the name of the object. The bottom object is automatically named Background. It cannot be renamed or moved; but if you click the Create an Object from the Background button on the bottom of the Object Docker, the background title disappears and the background becomes an object. Unless it is text, each time an object is created, Corel PHOTO-PAINT assigns a default name to it. The object name can be edited by double-clicking its name, or by right-clicking the name or thumbnail and selecting Properties; this opens the Object Properties dialog box, shown next. You can give the object any name your heart desires, as long as it is less than 39 characters.

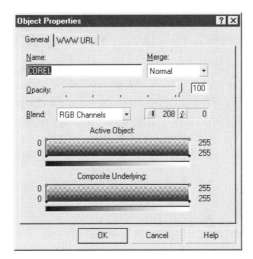

The entire bottom portion of the Object Properties dialog box contains a wide assortment of controls for controlling the blending of the object with an underlying object. These controls may appear a little intimidating because they are. The following section describes how this feature of the Object Properties dialog box works. It is advanced material, and you may want to skip over it now and refer back to it later.

Controlling the Blend of Objects

You can blend objects to define how their pixels mix with the objects that lie under them in the stacking order. You can use the x-axes (sliders) of the Active Object and Composite Underlying graphs to specify the grayscale values of the object pixels on a scale from 0 (black) to 255 (white). The y-axis controls let you specify the opacity of the pixels on a scale from 0 (transparent) to 100 (opaque). Pixels in the active object that fall outside the specified range are hidden so that the pixels of the underlying object are visible. The Help files contain information on the use of this feature.

Returning to the Objects docker, you will notice that next to the Thumbnail is a column that can contain the Clip to Parent icon. This looks like a paper clip and can only be enabled when there are two or more objects. The eye icon in the center column indicates the object is either visible (black) or invisible (grayed out). When an object is invisible, it is automatically protected from any PHOTO-PAINT actions. The narrow column to the far left is used to display any groupings of objects.

Objects Docker Display Options

To the right of the Opacity slider on the top of the Objects docker is a small
right-arrow button that is called the Flyout Option button. Pushing it opens a
pop-up menu, as shown next, that determines the size of the thumbnails displayed.
The choices are Object Properties (same one we met in the previous section
"Thumbnail Display Area"), No Thumbnails, Small, Medium, Large, and
Update Thumbnails. Why is there a No Thumbnails option, you ask? Turning
off the thumbnails speeds up PHOTO-PAINT, especially on slower systems.

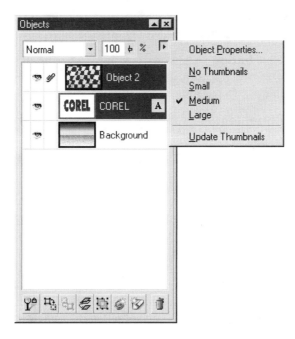

Multifunction Buttons

There are several buttons on the bottom of the Objects docker. The assortment
and availability of the buttons are dependent upon the mode you are in.

- **Lock Object Transparency button**   With this button enabled, the
  shape of an object doesn't change when you edit it. When Lock Object
  Transparency is disabled, the shape of an object can change when you
  apply an effect or when you edit the object using a tool.

- **The Create Mask from Object(s) and Create Object from Mask buttons**   These provide a quick method to convert masks into objects, and vice versa.

- **Create an Object from the Background button**   Allows you to create an object by using the entire image background, or by using an editable area that you define on the image background or another object. When you create an object from an editable area, you can include only the visible elements in that area.

- **The Combine Objects button**   Merges all selected object(s) with each other. Objects that are not selected are unaffected.

- **The New Lens button**   Creates a new lens covering the entire image. Clicking the button opens the New Lens dialog box, from which you can choose one of the 23 possible lens settings.

- **The New Object button**   Creates an empty transparent object that covers the entire image. This button is not available when the Lock Transparency option is enabled. It is the same as selecting Create | New Object in the Object menu.

- **The Delete Object(s) button**   If you select the objects and click this little button, the objects go screaming into the night, where they are never heard from again (unless you evoke the powers of the Undo).

Merge Mode and Opacity

The Merge box determines the way in which the colors of the object and the colors of the background image are combined when the two are merged. You can preview the result of using each merge mode directly in the Image window. The Opacity slider determines the opacity or transparency of the selected object. Some people are confused by opacity and transparency. Remember that 100 percent opacity is zero transparency or 100 percent transparency is zero opacity. You can call it either opacity or transparency. It's an "Is the glass half empty or half-full?" kind of question.

Clip Masks

The Clip mask is a mask that is attached to an individual object. There can only be one mask on an image, but you can apply a Clip mask to any object. One of the primary uses of the Clip mask is to provide a nonpermanent transparency. Later in this chapter, you will learn about the transparency tools that achieve the same effect as the Clip mask. The advantage of the Clip mask, however, is that the transparency action can modify the object at any time and becomes permanent only when you combine the Clip mask with the object. Let's return to our guided tour and it will make more sense:

1. Open the file we made previously, called Guided Tour.

2. With the Object Picker tool, select the text object in the Objects docker. Create a mask of the text (CTRL-M). Save the mask to a channel (Mask | Save | Save as Channel) and, when prompted, name the mask channel **Text**.

3. Before doing our Clip mask thing, we are taking a very brief side trip. You will like the effect, and it will make the image smaller, therefore allowing your system to work a little faster. Select the brush tools and, on the property bar, choose the Airbrush and the Soft Wide Cover brush type. Make the following changes: Nib size: 40 and Transparency: 60. The Brush Type now reads Custom Airbrush.

4. Ensure the Paint color is Black. In the Objects docker, select the checkered flag object. This is because we want to apply the airbrush strokes to the flag texture. Choose the Stroke Mask button on the property bar, shown at left; and when a dialog box opens, choose Middle of Mask Border and OK. Repeat this again. The result is shown in Figure 7-4.

5. At this point there is no advantage in keeping the text and the checkered flag object in the Clip to Parent relationship, since it takes resources of PHOTO-PAINT to maintain this relationship. Hold down the SHIFT key and select the text. Both objects should be selected at this point. Click the Combine Objects button at the bottom of the Objects docker. The text and the object have become a single object. Also note that the name has changed to Object and that the "A" icon is no longer there. Since we combined the objects, the text can no longer be edited as text.

6. If there is a mask on your image, remove it (CTRL-SHIFT-R). At the bottom of the Objects docker, click the New Object button. From the Brush tools flyout, select the Image Sprayer tool. On the property bar, choose Brown Rope. Click and drag a rope roughly the shape of the one shown next. Note that the Objects docker, like all dockers, can be grouped or change shape.

7

FIGURE 7-4   Stroke to Mask gives our text a three-dimensional quality

During the course of this guided tour, you will see several different combinations in the illustrations.

7. Now we are going to use Clip mask and have some fun while we are at it. With the Object Picker tool, ensure the top object (the rope) is selected. Create a mask of this object (CTRL-M). Now we are going to make this mask into a Clip mask. Choose Object | Clip Mask | Create | From Mask (whew). Notice the change in the Objects docker window shown next. Another thumbnail representing the Clip mask has appeared and is active, as indicated by the red rectangle around it. This means that any action we take on the image now is applied only to the Clip mask.

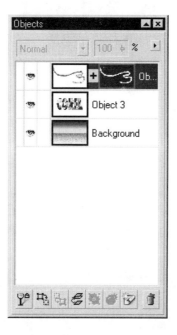

8. We are about to thread the rope through the letters. Before we can do this, we need some protection so that we remove only the part of the rope that coincides with the text. Load the mask we saved in the channel. Choose Mask | Load | Text. The Clip mask and a regular mask can exist on the same image at the same time. If your mask marquee is on, you can see the regular mask, but there is no visual indication on the image of the Clip mask.

9. We are almost ready. Select the Brush tools and change the brush from the Airbrush to the Art Brush; the style should be Quick Doodler. With the Paint color still Black, paint on the rope that crosses the letter "C." Note that you are actually painting black on the mask. Everywhere on the mask you paint black, the rope becomes transparent. The text mask we loaded keeps the transparency from going beyond the boundaries of the text. The result is shown next.

10. Continue to paint on the rope where you want it to be transparent. If you decide to change your mind, you can change the rope's transparency by setting the Paint to White and brushing on the Clip mask. My completed Clip mask rope is shown next; yours probably will look different.

11. Okay, we've done a lot. Close the file and don't save the changes.

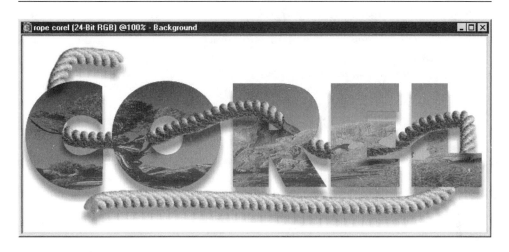

rope corel [24-Bit RGB] @100% - Background

FIGURE 7-5   This image was easy to construct using PHOTO-PAINT's advanced features

Figure 7-5 is an example of both Clip to Parent (photo in the text) and Clip mask (rope through the letters).

More Stuff About Clip Masks

Everything we did to the rope in the previous exercise we could have done with the object transparency tools. The big difference is that the changes made with Object Transparency tools are permanent, while the changes made with the Clip mask are only there until you remove or change the mask. To make the changes permanent, select Combine (which is now available as a choice from the Clip mask part of the Object menu) or right-click the Clip mask in the Objects docker; a pop-up menu will appear, as shown next. Choosing Disable Clip Mask will turn off the effects of the Clip mask, but it will still be there. Selecting Combine Clip Mask will permanently apply the mask effects to the object. If Remove Clip Mask is selected, then the mask is discarded and the object returns to its pre-Clip mask appearance.

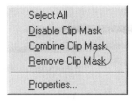

Object Transparency Tools

You can change the transparency of an entire object, or you can change the transparency of part of an object. When you change the transparency of an object, you change the grayscale value of its individual pixels. Grayscale values range from black, which has a value of 0 (transparent), to white, which has a value of 255 (opaque).

Up until now, we have learned about changing the transparency of an object evenly, revealing the image elements that lie beneath the object. You can change the transparency of parts of an object by using the three object transparency tools in the Toolbox. The Object Transparency brush tool lets you change the transparency of an object by applying brush strokes. You can use the Object Transparency tool to apply a transparent gradient to an object, or you can use the Color Transparency tool to make specific colors (or ranges of colors) transparent. To change the transparency of an object in relation to underlying image elements, you can use the Blend controls in the Object Properties dialog box to specify which pixels are visible.

Three object transparency tools—the Object Transparency tool, the Color Transparency tool, and the Object Transparency brush tool—are located on a flyout in the Toolbox.

The image in Figure 7-6 was made using the original photograph of the steps on the bottom and another photograph of a different set of stairs on top of it. The Object Transparency tool was used to gradually blend the two together.

Using all the transparency tools was necessary to create the image shown in Figure 7-7, which won Grand Prize in the 1997 Corel World Design Contest. The major tool employed was the Brush Transparency tool, which was used to remove parts of other photographs. Unlike when using Clip masks, when I removed a portion of the photograph with the transparency tools, it stayed gone.

The Transparency tool is identical in operation to the Gradient Fill tool. You click to place a starting point, and then drag the point out to an ending. I have created a little work session to demonstrate the tool.

The Interactive Dropshadow Tool (S)

The Interactive Dropshadow tool in the Toolbox creates objects that look like shadows. There are two types of drop shadows you can add to an object: flat and perspective. *Flat* drop shadows silhouette objects and can be used to create a glow effect. *Perspective* drop shadows (Pers.) create three-dimensional depth. So, how does PHOTO-PAINT know which type of shadow you want? By the part of the object you click with the Dropshadow tool. Click the edge, and PHOTO-PAINT

FIGURE 7-6   Using the Object Transparency tool, you can seamlessly blend photos together

FIGURE 7-7   All the transparency tools were instrumental in the creation of this Grand Prize winner

assumes you want a perspective shadow. Click anywhere in the middle of an object, and PHOTO-PAINT makes a flat shadow.

You can add a drop shadow to any object by applying a preset drop shadow. When you apply a preset, you can modify it to create a custom drop shadow. For example, you can change its direction and its distance from an object; its color and opacity; and the feathering of its edges. You can also copy a custom drop shadow or save it as a preset.

The best part about the shadows created with this tool is that when you change the shape or transparency of an object to which you've applied a drop shadow, the drop shadow automatically changes to mirror these changes.

Here an exercise that will demonstrate some of the features of the tool:

1. Create a new image using the Size preset Photo—5 × 7 at a resolution of 72 dpi. Ensure that the Landscape button is enabled.

2. Change the Paint color to red or your favorite color. With the Text tool, change the Font to Impact and the size to 150. Click the cursor inside the image and type a word, as shown next.

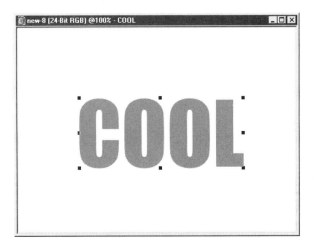

3. Select the Interactive Dropshadow tool (S), click the text, and drag a shadow to the upper left, as shown next.

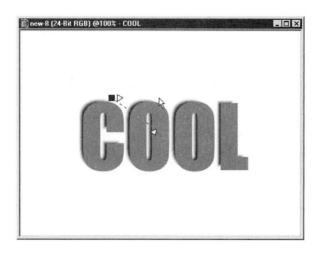

4. The shadow presets appear in the left side of the property bar when the
Dropshadow tool is selected. Because we created the shadow interactively,
the current setting shows Custom. Select the Presets and a drop-down list
appears. As you move the cursor down the list, visual representations of
the shadow pop up, as shown next.

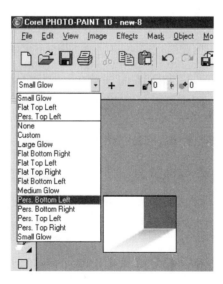

5. The line at the top of the drop-down list displays the last three presets used. Select Pers. Top Left. The result is shown next.

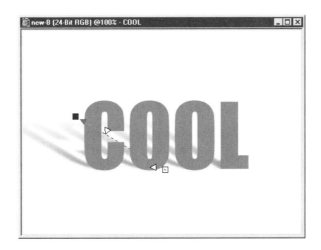

6. Now, change the preset to Medium Glow; and from the far right end of the property bar, select a different shadow color. While we are here, several other settings on the property bar deserve mention. On the property bar shown next, you can control the Shadow Feather Direction and Shadow Feather Edge. If you select A Feather Direction of Average (and I recommend you always use Average), then the Shadow Feather Edge is grayed out. You can make any changes to the resulting shadow either through settings on the property bar, or interactively by moving the sliders that control feather and opacity, or the end point, which controls distance of the shadow from the object.

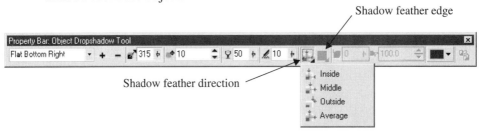

7. Close the file but don't save it. Now let's learn about something else you can do with the Interactive Dropshadow tool.

Managing Drop Shadows

Once you have created a drop shadow, you can see it on the image; it also appears as an icon to the right of the object's name in the Objects docker (if the object is text, the icon does not appear). To control the drop shadow, it is necessary to open the Drop Shadow menu by right-clicking the object in the Objects docker, as shown next. You can delete the shadow, combine it with the object (which will cause it to cease to act like a shadow), or select Split Shadow to make the shadow into a separate object. Did you notice the reference to the shadow having a relationship to the object?

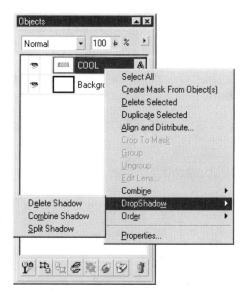

Once you apply a drop shadow to an object, PHOTO-PAINT treats it as a shadow; when the object is changed, the shadow is changed. For example, if the object is made smaller, the shadow becomes smaller. Here is a slick little feature: if an image with a perspective shadow is rotated, the shadow remains in the same relative position. To demonstrate this feature, I rotated the text from the previous exercise; PHOTO-PAINT repositioned the shadow, as shown next.

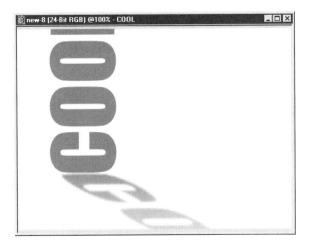

When working with shadows, you can use yet another feature that Corel has added in PHOTO-PAINT 10. You can copy the shadow properties from one object to another. In the illustration that follows, I have created another text object, selected the Interactive Dropshadow tool, clicked Copy Shadow Properties on the property bar, and clicked the object with the original shadow. The new object takes on a shadow that looks as if it was produced by the light that created the shadow on the original text.

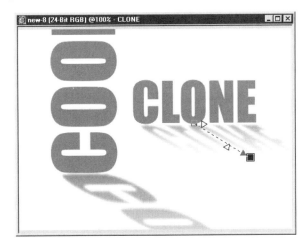

Dave's Shadowy Rules

When working with shadows, observe some basic rules:

- If the object is to appear far away from the background, the shadow should be larger, very transparent, and blurred.

- If the object is to appear close to the background, the shadow should be much darker (less transparent), be very close to the size of the object, and have only a small amount of blurring.

- To add some glow to an object, apply a drop shadow and set the Distance to zero, and increase the Feather width. The Opacity setting will determine how much go you put into your glow.

- Never ever forget that the shadow is to fool the eye. It is not and never should be the center of attraction. If you apply a shadow, and someone viewing the picture makes a comment on how lovely the shadows are, you did something wrong.

Now let's move on to the object transform modes. It's boring reading, but great reference stuff when you get stuck and are wondering why something doesn't work.

Transform Modes

There are seven different transform modes that provide all of the control that you could ever dream of when it comes to manipulating and transforming objects. With the Object Picker tool selected, all of these modes are available either through the property bar or by clicking the object to cycle through the modes.

7

The property bar for objects provides a very powerful and easy way to make precise manipulations of objects. There are seven selections from the pop-up menu that control the following:

- Position mode
- Rotate mode
- Scale mode
- Size mode
- Skew mode
- Distort mode
- Perspective mode

The transform modes are explained in painful detail in the Corel PHOTO-PAINT User's Manual and the Online Help file.

Additional Tips for Working with Objects

Using objects in PHOTO-PAINT makes the creation of unusual and complex images not only possible, but it is sometimes a lot of fun. Like all tools, there are rules regarding their operation, and I have included some handy tips so you won't waste a lot of time trying to figure out why the objects are not doing what you want them to do.

■ Transform options will be unavailable when anything other than the Object Picker tool is selected from the Toolbox.

■ Objects do not have to be the same size as the image. You can paste or drag and drop an object into an image that is larger than the page size, and not have the area outside the image boundaries clipped.

It is the ability to create, modify, and position objects that makes Corel PHOTO-PAINT 10 such a powerful photo-editing program. We have only covered the basics to this point.

How to Group Objects

To group objects, you must have two or more objects selected. There are several ways to select objects for grouping in an image:

■ Using the Object Picker tool, you can drag a rectangle over (marquee-select) the objects you want grouped together.

■ From the Objects docker, you can select the objects you want selected by clicking them.

■ If you want to select all of the objects in the image, you can choose Select All . . . from the Object menu.

■ You can select the first object, and then, holding down the SHIFT key, select more objects. Each time you select an object, it is added to the number of objects selected. The action is a toggle; so if you select an object you do not want, click it again to deselect it. (Did you know "deselect" is not a real word? Isn't it amazing what we learn from our spell checkers?)

After you have selected the objects, press CTRL-G. All of the selected objects will become grouped together. How will you know the objects are grouped together? Looking at the Objects docker gives a visual clue of what objects are grouped. When objects are grouped, they are joined together with a black bar in the left column of the Objects docker. To ungroup the objects, select the group, and press CTRL-U or choose Arrange | Ungroup from the Object menu. You may also toggle the Group/Ungroup Objects button on the property bar, shown at left.

The Text Tool

The text capabilities of Corel PHOTO-PAINT 10 have changed somewhat since PHOTO-PAINT 9. The text no longer looks crummy while transformations are being applied. As mentioned earlier, transformations are no longer lost when text is reedited. Only when the text is combined with the background does it cease to be editable. When the Text tool is used in combination with the fill capabilities and layers/objects, stunning effects can be produced quickly. The major change in the way fonts work is that you can now have multiple fonts in different colors and sizes on the same line. You know what I mean, the stuff they tell you never to do in most page layout books, we can now do in PHOTO-PAINT.

Paragraph Text and Corel PHOTO-PAINT

As great as Corel PHOTO-PAINT's text capabilities are, if you are planning to add paragraph-style text to a Corel PHOTO-PAINT image, it is best to use another program, such as CorelDRAW. It is a simple procedure. Just finish whatever enhancements to the image are needed and save it as a PHOTO-PAINT file. Next, import the file into CorelDRAW or a similar graphics program, and add the text at that time. While I have mentioned this before, it bears repeating. When text is created in Corel PHOTO-PAINT, it is a bitmap image that is resolution dependent. Text in a program like CorelDRAW is resolution independent. This means that text placed in Corel PHOTO-PAINT will be the resolution of the image. If it is 300 dpi (dots per inch), then the text will be a bitmap image that is 300 dpi, regardless of whether it is printed to a 300-dpi laser printer or a 2,450-dpi imagesetter. If the same text is placed in CorelDRAW, it remains text. If it is output to a 2,450-dpi imagesetter, then the resolution of the text will be 2,450 dpi. The result is sharper text.

Text on a Path (Finally)

It took a long time for PHOTO-PAINT to finally get text on a path, but we now have it. You'd think that with the incredibly powerful text engine in CorelDRAW, they would let the PHOTO-PAINT team borrow it. Nevertheless, I am glad we now have the ability to apply text to a path, and here is how it is done.

1. Select the Path tool (.). Click in the image at the point you want the path to begin. Move the cursor to the point at which you want the path to end, and click again. Wait, there's more. At this point, you have a straight line, so if

we align the text to it, we haven't accomplished much. Let's put a curve in
our path.

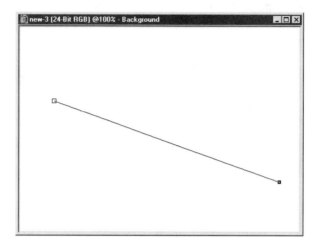

2. With the Path tool still selected, click the Shape tool on the property bar
   and then enable the Make Curve Node button—also on the property bar.
   Now click the nodes and drag the handles to make curves, as shown next.

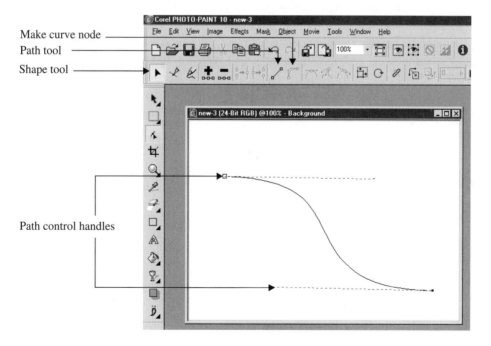

3. Add or select text and choose Object | Text | Fit Text to Path (CTRL-ALT-F). The cursor changes shape, and you must now select the path to which the text is to be contoured ("fixed" doesn't sound right; my dog is watching me as I type this). When the cursor is near a path, the letter "a" appears as part of the cursor, as shown next.

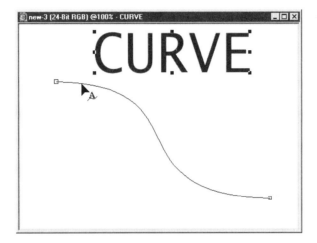

4. Click the path where you want the left end of the text to begin. Be aware that if you click the right end of the path, all of the characters will fit into the limited space remaining on the path and will become a big jumbled mess. In the following example, I clicked a spot very near the beginning of the path.

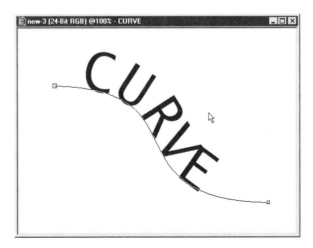

Adjusting Your Text on a Path

Now you have the text on a path (looks kind of ugly, doesn't it?). Here's how to
adjust the text.

1. Select the text using the Text tool. You will receive a warning about losing
   all of the changes; ignore it and click OK.

2. Double-click the text and it will become highlighted, as shown next.

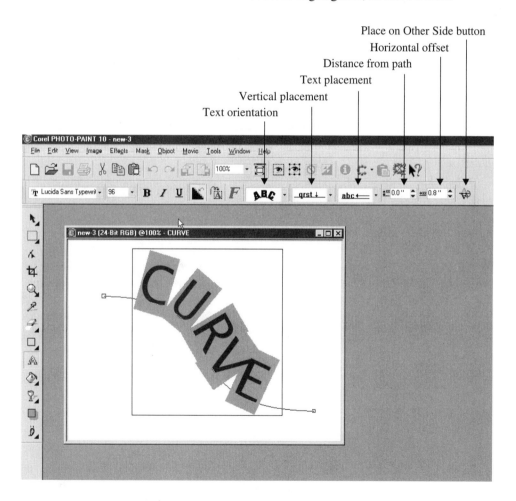

Place on Other Side button

Horizontal offset

Distance from path

Text placement

Vertical placement

Text orientation

3. On the property bar, choose a setting from any of the following list boxes:

- **Text orientation** Lets you specify the orientation of text
- **Vertical placement** Lets you specify the vertical position of text
- **Text placement** Lets you specify the placement of text
- **Distance from path** Lets you specify the distance between the text and the path
- **Horizontal offset** Lets you specify the horizontal position of text
- **Place on Other Side button** Places text on the other side of the path—obviously

> **TIP** *You can adjust the orientation of the text by holding down CTRL, selecting the text using the Object Picker tool, and dragging the selection handles.*

> **TIP** *You can change the horizontal position of text along a path by dragging character nodes using the Path tool.*

Text and the Path

Once the text is linked to the path, it is interactively linked. This means that any changes to the path are reflected in the text. In other words, change the shape of the path and the text follows the new path. At some point, you are going to want to get rid of the path. If you delete the path without first rendering the text, the text will be deleted as well. Choose Object | Text | Render As Object. At this point, the text is no longer linked to the path, so you can select the path with the Path tool and eliminate it. The text is now an object and can no longer be edited like text.

Basics of the Text Tool

Text is, by default, an object that floats above the image background. Text properties—the font, style, size, kerning, leading, and other effects—are determined through the property bar. You can manipulate, edit, format, and transform the text object while it is still an object. Once you've combined the text object with the background, you can no longer edit it as text. The Render Text to Mask button on the Text tool's property bar, when selected, converts the text automatically to a mask. It is a real time-saver.

If you have worked with recent versions of word processors in Windows, everything on the property bar should be familiar to you. The first box shows all of the available fonts that are installed. The second box displays the selected font sizes in points (72 points = 1 inch). The Font Size pop-up list shows a long list of available sizes, but you can select any size you need by typing the desired font size (in points) in the Font Size box. Any change you make on the Text toolbar is instantly reflected in the text displayed in the image area. You can also move the rectangle containing the text by clicking its edge and dragging it with the mouse.

There are no system default settings for the Text tool's font selection. The typeface is always the first element of the list of installed fonts. Since lists are maintained alphabetically, the typeface whose name is first alphabetically (say, AARDVARK) will always appear as the default. The last settings of the Text toolbar remain until changed again or Corel PHOTO-PAINT is shut down.

Here are the facts about the Corel PHOTO-PAINT Text tool:

- The color of the text is determined by the setting of the Paint (foreground) color. It is very easy to change the color of the text in Corel PHOTO-PAINT. To color each letter individually, change the Paint color before typing the letter. To change the text all at once, quickly click it until it is all selected, and then click the desired color swatch in the onscreen color palette.

- When you select existing text with the Text tool, distortion and perspective transformations that have been applied to that text will be lost.

- To correct a text entry, use the BACKSPACE key.

- To check the spelling of text, use a dictionary. Sorry, no spell checker.

- There is no automatic line wrap (soft carriage returns) of text. This is because Corel PHOTO-PAINT has no idea where to wrap the line.

In Summary

Now that you have been introduced to the world of text and objects, it is up to you to spend hours exploring the depths of these tools to see what wonderful and fantastic things can be done. While it isn't necessary to give up your social life to become proficient with these tools, any time spent playing with them will reap enormous benefits when you are under a deadline and need to use them. Now, let's move on to a really interesting subject: correcting, retouching, and restoring photos.

PART III

Photo-Correction Tools and Techniques

CHAPTER 8

Repairing and Restoring Photographs

Photographs seem to be coming at us from every direction these days. It wasn't that long ago that the key to good graphics in a publication was either the effective use of drop caps or some black-and-white clip art. With the cost of color reproduction getting cheaper by the minute, the placement of color photographs in a brochure or a newsletter is no longer extraordinary. It is expected.

The major sources of these photographs can be divided into two general groups—professional photos from stock photography houses such as you find on Corel Professional CD-ROMs, and pictures (either digital or film) taken by ourselves or other equally gifted amateurs—or not gifted, as the case may be. In this chapter we will learn some techniques to correct film photos and also how to deal with the latest craze—photos from digital cameras.

Discovering Hidden Treasure in Dark Backgrounds

Sometimes the camera records things that remain hidden until you use PHOTO-PAINT to locate what is hidden. The photograph shown in Figure 8-1 looks like the happy waitperson (I remember when I could call them waitresses) stepped out of a black hole. This is a common occurrence with flash photography. The foreground is picked up and the background is lost, or at least it seems lost. Here is a demonstration to show you how to detect and then restore the background.

1. My first step is to see if there is anything back there to recover. I choose Image | Histogram and the histogram, shown next, reveals some important information about the photograph.

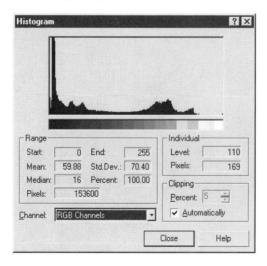

FIGURE 8-1   This woman can sure hold her beer

2. Don't let all of the numbers concern you; we are only interested in the left part of the graph, which shows the shadow region (sounds like the name of a daytime soap). If there were no recoverable information, there would be a thin line flat up against the left side. Instead, there is some space between the last major spike and the left side. Our histogram has told us that there is image detail in the darkness.

To see what we have got back there, we will use a *lens,* which is a handy feature that allows us to see an effect without applying it. I first choose

Object | Create | New Lens; and from the list that appears, shown next, I select Gamma and crank it up to 3.0.

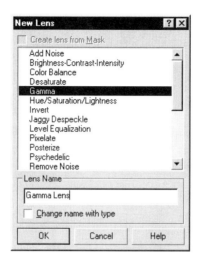

3. With the Gamma Lens applied, we can see what's in the background. It looks really washed out because the Gamma was set quite high. This was done because a mask must protect the foreground in order to apply effects that allow the recovery of the background. A high Gamma setting makes it possible to see where the foreground ends and the background begins. With the Freehand Mask tool, the beer lady and the man next to her are selected, as shown next.

4. The Gamma lens has served its purpose, so I right-click it and choose
Delete. The photograph looks like the original, except now it has a mask.

8

Using the Contrast Enhancement from the Image | Adjust menu, as shown next, I first uncheck Auto-Adjust in the Channel section of the dialog box. Normally, this would be left on; but since the changes being made are extreme, it is best to leave this feature off. To spread out the tonal range of the background, I move the White Input Value Clipping (the inverted triangle on the top-right side of the display) to 100 and move the Gamma Adjustment slider to around 1.6–1.7.

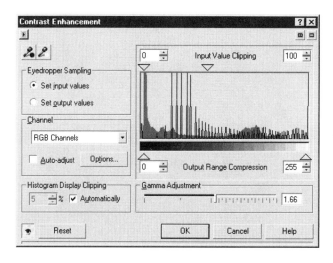

5. The histogram–style display in the dialog box shows the original tonal range of the background in the light gray, and the resulting tonal range with the darker black lines. The result of this adjustment is shown next.

NOTE   *Contrast Enhancement was called Levels Equalization in previous releases of PHOTO-PAINT. The new term is more descriptive of the action this filter performs.*

6. The background is still too soft (low contrast), so using the Brightness-Contrast-Intensity command, I apply a medium amount (10%) of both contrast and intensity.

7. To complete the background work, I next apply a small amount of Gaussian blur (about 1.5) to the background. A blur? Yes, for two reasons. First, as you can see, we have done some pretty drastic things to the background to recover it from the darkness, and it shows in the form of graininess. Second, we expect the background to be slightly out of focus. The result is shown next.

8. While it is not necessary for anything but my perfectionist nature, after removing the mask I use the Clone tool to remove the empty beer stein from the table (is anything sadder than an empty beer stein?) as well as the cigarette package. I also use the Clone tool (at a transparency of 80) to darken the poor individual behind the man in the foreground. His bald head and brightly colored clothes suffered greatly at the hands of our image correction. This mild darkening of head and clothes makes his fashion crimes less visible. Last of all, I select the Effect tools and choose the Blend tool, set to the Blend a Lot brush type. I use this tool to soften the transition between the foreground and the background. The before-and-after photographs are shown in Figure 8-2.

Beerhall lady before and after.tif (8-Bit Grayscale) @100% - Background

FIGURE 8-2 PHOTO-PAINT allows us to reveal the hidden portions of photographs

Now that you have learned a few things about image correction, let's learn
how to improve images made with digital cameras.

Fixing Digital Camera Photographs

"You can't make a silk purse out of a sow's ear." That phrase, a favorite in Texas,
seems fitting when working on photos created by the vast array of digital cameras
that have recently flooded the market. The pictures produced by digital cameras
tend to be grainy, and the colors may be completely different from those contained
in the original subject or the image may exhibit a bluish cast. Yet, for all that's

wrong with them, these new digital marvels represent the beginning of a new era. It seems that each day sees a newer and less expensive version of a digital camera that only six months ago represented the best of the best. I believe that digital photography will continue to expand, thereby making it imperative that we, as publishers of these digital gems, learn how to repair them. In other words, we are about to learn the basics of making silk purses out of sows' ears.

Some Digital Camera Basics

To understand the problem, it will help to understand just a little bit about digital cameras. Digital cameras are scanners. While that is an oversimplification, the basic premise is valid. Sensors in the digital camera, usually CCDs (charge-coupled devices), capture digital images. Photosensitive pixels within these sensors respond to light, and their response is recorded as digital information. Filters control the wavelengths of light recorded. In some digital cameras, the individual pixels are coated with color filters, while others use multiple CCDs to capture red, green, and blue values. The point to note is that CCDs, which are almost identical to the ones used in scanners, are used to record the image. Why is that important? Because from working with scanners, we know that CCDs have some limitations. The CCD in the camera is least sensitive to the color contained in the blue part of the spectrum, and it is more difficult for many digital cameras to interpret those colors. Also, when you capture an image with a digital camera, often as not, it is compressed with JPEG compression, which introduces distortion—usually in the form of little ugly splotches, that are called *artifacts*. The combination of these two factors introduces noise into an image that is already challenged. If all of that weren't bad enough, CCDs have little ability to record subtle tonal differences in the shadow region (darker portions) of an image. So it shouldn't come as a big surprise that some digital images don't look great when we first get them. The first step is to learn how to make general corrections. These steps apply to images produced with either a digital camera or a scanner.

Color Fundamentals

One of the greatest defects introduced by less expensive digital cameras is color shift. Sometimes the shift is subtle, and at other times it can be really gross. In order to understand how to correct it, you must first learn something about color balance and brightness. The brightness of a pixel in an image is expressed as the sum of its red, green, and blue values. If you increase the level of one or two colors, you will not only change the color balance of the image but also slightly increase its overall brightness. Likewise, decreasing the level of one or two colors will darken the picture. Here is a table to help you understand the color correction relationship.

If the Color	Then
Is too red	Decrease red, increase green and blue by half as much.
Is too green	Decrease green, increase red and blue by half as much.
Is too blue	Decrease blue, increase red and green by half as much.
Is too yellow	Decrease red and green, increase blue by twice as much.
Has flesh tones that look too orange	Convert to CMYK, and ensure that cyan is 20% greater than magenta and yellow.

The first photo we will look at is shown in Figure 8-3. If you want to take a try at adjusting this image, you can download the file Dogs uncorrected from the Osborne Web site. The photo was taken inside with the original HP PhotoSmart camera. I am using an image from this first-generation digital camera because it suffers from several problems that are common with less expensive digital cameras in the market today. You will find that images from most digital cameras that cost less than $500 suffer hue shifts (color casts) when taking photographs indoors. In the case of Figure 8-3, I can see by examining the pug in the image that the colors are off in the direction of green and, possibly, cyan. I know this for two reasons. First, you don't see many pugs with fur that has a greenish blue tinge. Second, that same said pug, Mr. Belvedere, is lying at my feet as I am writing this chapter and I assure you there definitely isn't any green—which leads to a brief philosophical discussion.

FIGURE 8-3   Two dogs who can't sleep because they're worried that the digital camera won't properly register the color of their fur

What Color Should We Make the Orange?

One of the major issues when dealing with correcting color—whether from film, scanned photos, or digital cameras—is this: to what standard are you trying to correct or adjust the color? In Figure 8-3, the color in the dogs, and the couch they have commandeered, is slightly wrong, but wrong to whom? If you don't have the original to compare with, the colors are within an acceptable perceived range of colors. If the dogs were purple, it would give us pause, but the colors in the photo are close enough—or are they?

Here is the crux of the issue: do you correct the color so that it is faithful to the colors in the original, or do you adjust the colors so they look good? For example, last year I visited the Musée d'Orsay in Paris, and like the tourist I am, I bought the book that contained high-quality prints of all of the paintings that were exhibited in the museum. I was actually a little surprised when I compared the reproductions of the art in the book to the original. The prints in the book looked better than the originals! The colors in the book were faithfully reproduced, but the printer had increased the saturation to make the paintings in the book look more vivid. Was this wrong? According to some, the prints should look exactly like the originals. For my personal taste, I appreciated the slightly more saturated version of the art in the book. My point is (yes, I do have a point in all of this) unless someone else is paying for the work (in which case, he or she sets the rules), you should always adjust the color so it looks good to you. That's one of the fun things about digital darkrooms: you can bend the color rules. When correcting color, don't be a slave to color accuracy.

Change the Color Hue

Fortunately, PHOTO-PAINT offers an easy interactive correction for minor shifts in color. Found under Image | Adjust, it is called Color Hue. (The dialog box follows.) Below the before-and-after style preview, the image shows the primary colors red, green, and blue; and below that, their complements, cyan, magenta, and yellow. Each time you click the Preview window of a color, that color is applied to the onscreen image and the preview thumbnails are updated. Since the primary tinge we want to remove is green, we need only apply the complement (magenta). The Preview windows each show the result of applying the amount shown in the Step setting. To this image I applied both magenta, to correct the green color cast, and red.

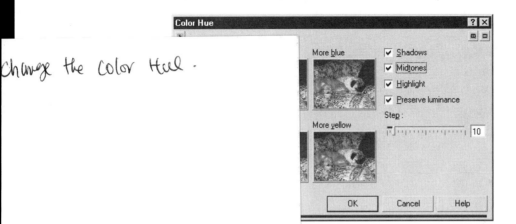

Change the color Hue.

8

...on, I did a few other things to emphasize the
...ading Dogscorrected.TIF. These changes have
...and are more along the line of composition

...logs are resting on is their favorite, it is
...Mask tool and made a crude outline of their
...ied to the mask so that the transition boundary
...e. After inverting the mask (so the dogs would
...(1) Gaussian Blur. The sofa is still in focus,
...the mask again (so that the background is
...tting of 10. Normally, I do not advise using
...rightness; but in the case of digital photographs,
...especially true if the camera has compressed
...image. My last step was to remove the mask
and apply the vignette filter to darken the edges, as shown in Figure 8-4.

An Exercise in Color Correction

Here is an exercise that will let you try your hand at removing a color cast from
a photograph, as well as applying the Clone tool to remove a few imperfections
in the photograph. The photograph is of Mr. Dakota Kleffner; and while the color
in the original was acceptable, when the local camera store made an enlargement,
they introduced a slight color cast. When the photograph was scanned, I decided
to correct the color cast with PHOTO-PAINT, rather than through multiple passes
with the scanner. After we correct the color, two other items require our attention.
If you will look carefully at Mr. Kleffner's cummerbund, you will see the fingertips

FIGURE 8-4   After improving this picture, I find that the dogs are still awake; maybe I need to feed them

of the hand that is holding him upright (we will need to remove that); and, finally, there is a little bit of drool that doesn't seem appropriate for someone in black tie—so we'll correct that as well.

1. Download the image Dakota.JPG, shown next, from the Osborne Web site, and open it in PHOTO-PAINT.

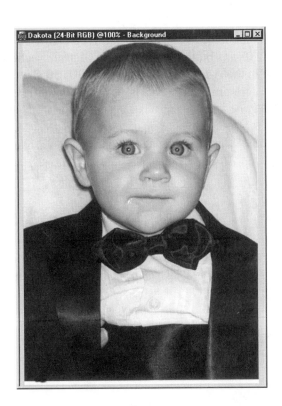

2. There are several different approaches to color correction with PHOTO-PAINT. With the dogs in the previous part of this section, I used Color Hue. Let's try another way to eliminate a color cast. Select Image |Adjust | Selective Color. When the dialog box opens, as shown next, change the

Adjustment Percentage to Absolute (not to be confused with the Vodka), and select the Cyans button in the Color Spectrum section. Change the Cyan setting in the Adjust section to a negative 10. To see the effect, click the Preview button in the lower-left corner on and off. Click OK and our bluish cast is gone.

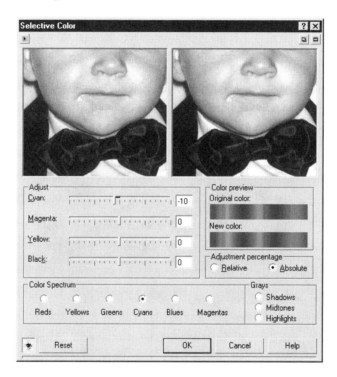

3. Next, the drool. Be aware that some moms may think the drool is cute and may not want it sent into the pixel bucket. We could use the Clone tool to dispatch the drool, but let's look at another method. What makes the drool stand out is the bright spots or highlights. PHOTO-PAINT has a filter that

removes highlights, among other things. First we need to mask the area we want to de-drool. Choose the Mask Brush tool (B) and paint the bright areas with a mask, shown next:

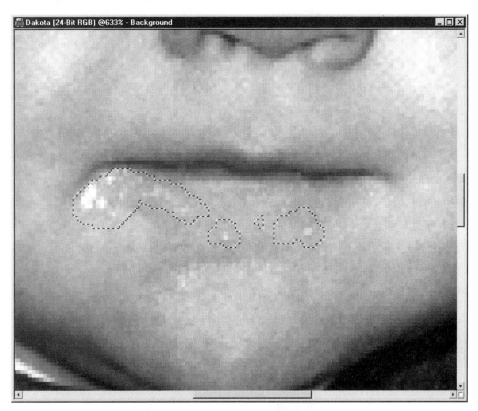

4. Once you have the brighter areas of the drool selected, choose Effects | Noise | Dust and Scratch. When the dialog box opens, as shown next, lower

the Threshold to negative 11 and change the Radius to 4. Click OK and the
drool is gone. Remove the mask (CTRL-SHIFT-R).

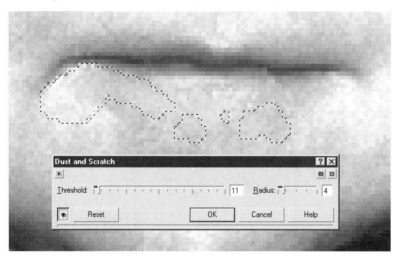

5. Removing the supporting fingers is done by selecting the Clone tool (C)
and cloning parts of the shirt and pants over the fingers. The finished
photograph should look like the one that follows.

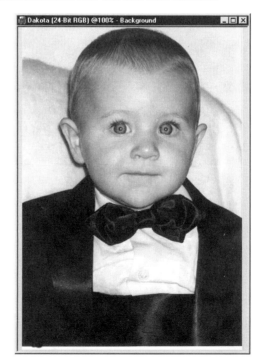

Now let's figure out how to deal with problems that aren't related to color.

Repairing Noncolor Photographic Problems

I cannot deny that I enjoy using PHOTO-PAINT to create tantalizing text textures (try saying that after two pints of Guinness) and other exotic effects. Yet, for every wild and wonderful image I create with PHOTO-PAINT, there are many more photographs that I manipulate so they can look good for publication.

Some of the material I cover in this section may be old hat for many of you, but I encourage you to review it nonetheless, as you still might find some little nugget you didn't know before.

Cropping—It's Quick and Easy

One of the most basic features of PHOTO-PAINT is its ability to crop and resample an image. Cropping is often overlooked, but it's an easy way to improve the composition of an image. Our subject for this topic is a photograph of a wine bottling facility in Argentina. In many ways, it is a classic of composition. The photographer, my son, included the cardboard boxes on the left, as well as most of the rear wall. All too often, a photo like the one in Figure 8-5 appears in some company newsletter.

8

Cropping in PHOTO-PAINT Reduces File Sizes

Although most page-layout programs allow an image to be cropped with the frame, the original image is not actually cropped. I was always puzzled about this, so I asked Kelly Fraiser, Ventura Product manager at Corel, who responded, "Because Ventura doesn't have any way of knowing if the image is being used in another part of the publication, the original image is left unaltered." While the image appears cropped in the publication, the file remains at its original size. This is true of the other major page-layout programs as well.

The advantage of cropping the image in PHOTO-PAINT is that after the photo is cropped, its file size is reduced. The original image in Figure 8-5 is over 2MB. After cropping, the file size is reduced to 1.01MB. In a publication with a lot of nonreoccurring photos, this can create a significant reduction in the size of a file sent to a service bureau.

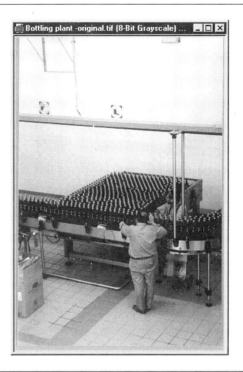

FIGURE 8-5 The problem with this digital photo is composition

Figure 8-6 shows the same image, after it has been cropped to center the viewer's attention on the subject. There have been several additional steps. For instance, florescent lamps produce a soft green cast, and this was corrected by the addition of a small amount of magenta, as was done earlier with the dogs using Color Hue. The dirty apron worn by the operator was cloned out and replaced with a tiled background, and then an Airbrush tool painted him a new pair of trousers. The Eyedropper tool was used to get a matching color from the cuff of the existing pants. Of course, I also made the number of bottles much larger. I don't recommend doing this with most clients. The white soft edges were produced using PHOTO-PAINT's Vignette filter.

FIGURE 8-6 A poorly composed photograph is easily corrected in PHOTO-PAINT

Keystone (Not the Cops) Magic

One of the problems of photography with wide-angle lenses is a phenomenon of distortion known as *keystoning*. (An example of this is shown next.) While this building may look familiar to you if you saw the movie *Men in Black*, the apartment building on the left looks like it is leaning over, and the street looks like it dips in the middle. This is not the type of image the local chamber of commerce wants to use in their brochures. We can correct this type of distortion with PHOTO-PAINT's Perspective transform capability. It takes a little work, but it's not complicated—

here's how. The following procedure is numbered, but it is not a step-by-step tutorial; it is a recipe for doing it.

1. Mask the entire image (CTRL-SHIFT-A), and make an object from the image (CTRL-SHIFT-UP ARROW).

2. Once it is an object, click it until the object handles appear as small circles, indicating it is in Perspective mode. Now, drag the lower-left handle in toward the center until the apartment building, or whatever subject in the image you wish to use for a reference point, appears vertical, shown next:

Keystoned bldg.tif (8-Bit Grayscale) @100% - Background

3. In this image, I used my genuine calibrated eyeball to determine when the apartment building was vertical and when it was just a tad off. (Note: tad is a Texas unit of measurement. 1 tad = 0.2837 mm plus or minus a foot.) A more accurate way to do this is to display the rulers (CTRL-R) and drag a vertical guideline for reference. Regardless of how you get there, when you get your reference point so that it appears to be vertical, double-click the object to apply the transform. Until you apply the transform, you will find hardly anything else in PHOTO-PAINT works.

4. The challenge we face now is that the border of the photograph is keystoned. The easy way to correct this is to crop the photo. The result is shown next:

5. While this is simple, it does remove part of the original image. A different approach to the one described in step 3 that maintains more of the original image requires the Clone tool to clone parts of the transformed image onto the original. Note that this may be the only cloning that can be accomplished without sheep or controversy. You need to make a copy of the original photograph (CTRL-UP ARROW) for the object to transform in step 1, leaving a copy of the original as the background.

6. Next, drag the transformed duplicate image off of the original so that it becomes a separate image—it's just easier that way. After that, align the Clone tool so that the source point on the transformed image is on the bottom-left corner, and then place the Clone tool on the bottom-left corner. From this point, you drag the Clone tool straight up, replacing the top half of the image, leaving the bottom half alone. You will end up with a white triangle on the right side. Use the Clone tool to fill in the white area with pixels from the adjoining area. The finished image is shown next:

In Summary

If the image is going to be converted to CMYK, make all of your adjustments in the normal RGB mode. When you are satisfied with the results, then make minor adjustments for the loss of image tone that is expected with a CMYK image. When working with an image in which color accuracy is important, make sure that your monitor is calibrated and the images that come out of your printer are close to the ones on your screen. For this chapter, I found it necessary to use the RGB adjustments that were part of my Matrox II card to tweak the display so that it matched my Epson Stylus Photo.

PART IV

Painting with PHOTO-PAINT 10

CHAPTER 9

Filling with Color or Patterns

227

Fill tools have been around as long as bitmap paint programs. Also known as flood tools, their sole purpose is to cover an image or a selected portion of an image with a different color, texture, or pattern. The icon for these tools is almost universally a tipping bucket, which is appropriate, since the tools act much like pouring a bucket of paint on an image. Fill tools have come a long way since the early days when programs like Microsoft Paint seemed sophisticated.

The fill and shape tools in PHOTO-PAINT 10 can apply an infinite number of different combinations of colors, textures, and patterns in hundreds of different ways. When it comes to color selection, the on-screen color palette is just the tip of the iceberg. PHOTO-PAINT offers many options concerning what to fill and what to fill it with. In this chapter, we will cover the Fill command of the Edit menu, the fill tools in the Toolbox, and even the shape tools, since even their property bars have fill controls. You will learn to choose from four basic fills—Uniform, Fountain, Bitmap, and Texture—and tweak the huge array of options available with each. We will learn everything there is to know about the subject of fills. Wow, I can hardly wait to read what I am going to say. That's it...I am definitely cutting back to no more than 12 cups of coffee a day.

The Fill Tools...So Many Choices

PHOTO-PAINT has the following four fill tools:

- Fill command
- Fill tool
- Interactive Fill tool
- Shape tools

The Fill command, located in the Edit menu (shown next), operates on the entire image or the selected (masked) parts of it.

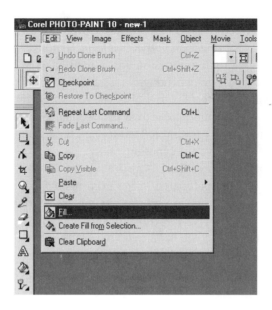

Staying true to its computer heritage, the Fill tool uses the cursor to position and initiate a fill, thereby allowing application of a fill to a selected area. In Figure 9-1 each character of the word is filled with a different fill.

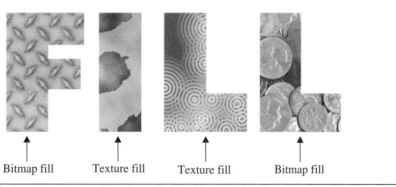

Bitmap fill   Texture fill   Texture fill   Bitmap fill

FIGURE 9-1   PHOTO-PAINT's fill tools can be applied to individual characters or objects

The Interactive Fill tool, found in the Fill Tool flyout in the Toolbox, is true to its name. It is a fill tool in which you control much of how the resulting fill is applied interactively by moving nodes on the actual image. While these three fill tools flood an area of an image depending on a mask boundary or the image content to determine its boundaries, the shape tools—the Rectangle tool, the Ellipse tool, and the Polygon tool—determine their own fill boundaries as they are created with the cursor. While they are not traditional fill tools, I have included them in the fill tool arsenal because they have fill capabilities.

Technically, it could be said there is a fifth type of fill tool, the Create Fill from Selection command, which is located in the Edit menu. This command creates a bitmap fill from an area of an image selected by a mask. I do not consider it a fill tool because it is really a tool for creating fills, not applying them.

Before we can apply a fill, we have to learn how to select the type of fill we want to apply. In PHOTO-PAINT there are three ways to select and control the fill that the fill tools apply:

- The Edit Fill & Transparency dialog box, which can be accessed by double-clicking the Fill tool in the Toolbox

- The Select Fill dialog box, which can be accessed by double-clicking the Fill swatch in the status bar

- Property bars of the selected tools

Although all three share common parts, they essentially offer different ways to control the fill tools.

Selecting the Right Fill

Located in the Edit menu, the Fill command opens the Edit Fill & Transparency dialog box, as shown in Figure 9-2. The Edit Fill & Transparency (EFT) dialog box is the Grand Central Station for all of the fills within PHOTO-PAINT. To paraphrase President Truman, "The fill starts here." While other dialog boxes and property bars offer some degree of selection and control, it is the EFT dialog box that offers enough controls and features to satisfy anyone. The EFT dialog box contains two pages—Fill Color and Transparency. Fill Color is used to set the type and color of the fill, and the Transparency page contains different transparency options that are possible with the fill.

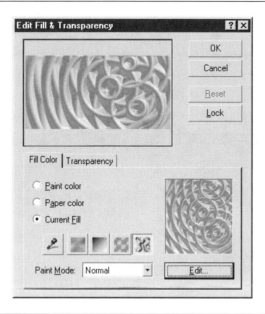

FIGURE 9-2   The Edit Fill & Transparency (EFT) dialog box is a good jumping-off point when you need to fill an entire image or a selected object

The Select Fill dialog box, shown next, is an abbreviated version of the EFT dialog box. It is accessed by double-clicking the Fill swatch in the status bar. While it is limited in the controls and features it offers, I use it every time I work on this book. Was that too subtle?

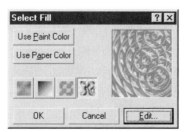

The property bars have replaced the fill tools Tool Settings roll-up. In case you haven't figured it out yet, all of the roll-ups are gone. They will be missed (by someone, but not me). Figure 9-3 is a dazzling display of all of the property bars for fill tools. Don't worry about them yet; I just wanted you to see them. We will learn about them as we go along.

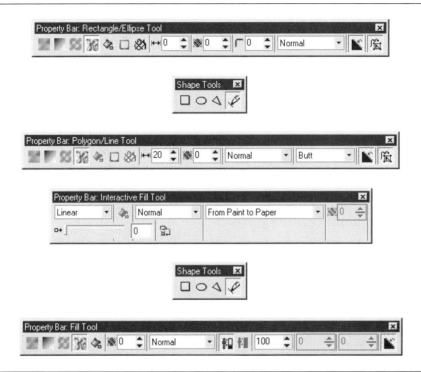

FIGURE 9-3   Here are the four property bars that control the fills. Learn them well as there may be an exam—a bar exam

More Fills Than You Could Have Thought Possible

Before going into detailed descriptions of the individual fill tools, let's see what fills are available. We will learn about the different fills by using the buttons of the EFT dialog box, as shown next.

Eyedropper tool   Fountain fill   Texture fill

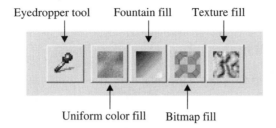

Uniform color fill   Bitmap fill

Meet the Fill Buttons

The first button—the one that looks like an eyedropper—selects the Eyedropper
tool (this button only appears in the EFT dialog box). Enabling this button activates
the Eyedropper tool. In this mode, when you place the cursor on the image and
click the desired color, it becomes the current uniform fill color, which happens
to be the next button—Uniform Fill. From Uniform fill mode, you can select any
solid (nongradient) color from a color palette or the Eyedropper. Solid colors are
boring, so Corel put in a Fountain Fill (middle button). Selecting this button uses
the last selected fountain fill. With fountain fills, you can select a nearly endless
combination of colors or shades. The next button is the Bitmap Fill, indicated by
the strange icon on the button (it used to be a checkerboard, I am not sure what it
is now). The Bitmap fill is a tiling engine. (Boy. That was clear as mud, wasn't it?)
If that didn't make sense, try this. Inside of PHOTO-PAINT is a collection of bitmap
fills. These are, in many cases, images that have been selected from photographs
and then modified so that when placed side-by-side the viewer cannot detect where
one begins and the other ends. These are called seamless tiles; the bitmap fill uses
the tile you select to fill the selected area. By the way, the Bitmap fill will flood
an area with just about any bitmap fill, seamless or not. The last button is the
Texture Fill, the most unique in the Fill palette. This mode does not use existing
tiles or patterns. Instead, it creates them at the time of use through a powerful
fractal generator. You can produce some unusual and exotic textures (or patterns)
with this fill.

Fill Status Line

Regardless of what fill you select you can see the currently selected fill color/pattern (sort of) by viewing the status bar, shown next. You will notice that there are three small rectangles located on the status bar indicating their fill colors or fill. The Paint color is the foreground color, the Paper color is the background color, and the Fill can be a color or a pattern. Because the swatch area is small, it is sometimes difficult to accurately determine the selected type of fill, but having worked with this program for over seven years, I know it is enough to get the job done, so I have no complaints.

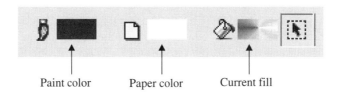

Paint color   Paper color   Current fill

The Uniform Color Fill Mode

Uniform Color fill is the simplest fill mode of all possible fills. It is used to select and apply solid (uniform) colors to an image or selected portions of it. There are several ways to select a fill color for this mode. The quickest way to select a uniform fill color is to right-click the desired color in the on-screen color palette.

If the color you want is not available in the on-screen color palette, you have a few other options open to you. From the EFT or Select Fill dialog box, you can choose to use either the current Paint color or Paper color. If none of those has that specific color you need, then your next step is to open the Uniform Fill dialog box, as shown in Figure 9-4. There are several ways to access this color-choosing monster. The quickest way is, with the fill tool or shape tool (excluding the line tool) selected, click the Edit Fill icon in the property bar. You can also go the long way and select Edit | Fill | Uniform Fill Button | Edit Button. Regardless of how you get there, from the Uniform Fill dialog box, you can select or create any color. Once you enter into the world of custom color selection, you may never get out. Because this color selection tool is so powerful, I have dedicated part of an entire chapter to using it—Chapter 11, "Getting the Right Color."

Once you have the color you want, click OK to return to the real world. The fill color you have selected floods all areas of the image not protected by a mask.

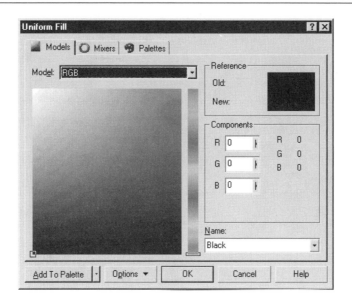

FIGURE 9-4   The Uniform Fill dialog box contains all of the colors in this world and possibly the next

This means that if you have an image without a mask and choose the Edit | Fill tool, you are going to have an image of a solid color. While this might sell in the pop art market, it isn't what you want. The preview window gives you a good visual of what is and is not going to be filled with a solid color.

The Fountain Fill Mode

Next to the Effect filters, the Fountain fill represents the greatest tool for creating cool backgrounds and fills. A fountain fill is a fill that changes gradually from one color to the next. This type of fill is also called a "gradient" or "graduated" fill. With the Fountain Fill button selected in either the EFT or the Select Fill dialog box, you click the Edit (fill) button, opening the Fountain Fill dialog box shown in Figure 9-5. From here you can create a vast array of fountains fills.

Fiddling with the Fountain Fill Dialog Box

The Fountain Fill dialog box may look scary, but in truth it is pretty simple once you figure out where the gas and brake pedals are located. It is laid out into five

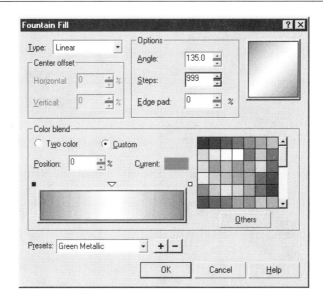

FIGURE 9-5   The Fountain Fill dialog box contains tools to create a large variety of gradient fills

sections: Type, Center Offset, Options, Color Blend, and Presets. The Preview window gives you an idea of what the finished product will look like. Let's check out each section.

Types

The Type list is located in the upper-left corner of the dialog box, shown next. Your selection of a fountain fill will, most of the time, begin in this area. It is from here that you determine how the fountain fill will move from one color to another. The Type section selects one of five types of fountain fills. Clicking the name of the type opens a list of the following choices:

- **Linear**   This selects a fountain fill that changes color in one direction.

- **Radial**   This selects a fountain fill that changes color in concentric circles from the center of the object outward.

- **Conical**   This selects a fountain fill that radiates from the center of the object like rays of light.

- **Square**   This selects a fountain fill that changes color in concentric squares from the center of the object outward.

- **Rectangular**   Same as square except it uniformly radiates to all corners of the rectangle.

In Figure 9-6, I have created a display of four of the five fills. There would have been five, but when I applied the Rectangular fill to a square it looked the same as the square—go figure.

Center Offset

The Center Offset settings, located directly below the Type selection, are used to reposition the center of a Radial, Conical, Square, or Rectangular fountain fill so

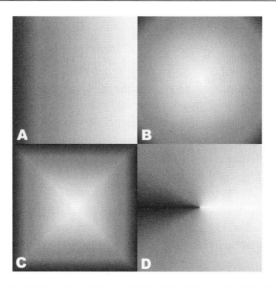

FIGURE 9-6   Four Fountain fill types: a) Linear b) Radial c) Square d) Conical

that it no longer coincides with the center of the object. Negative values shift the center down and to the left; positive values shift the center up and to the right. You can also click the mouse in the Preview window and drag the center to the desired position.

At first appearance this seems pointless. Why would anyone in their right mind waste the time to use a value system to determine where the offset is when you can move it with the cursor to the desired position in the Preview window in the upper-right portion of the dialog box? You did know that, didn't you? However, the Center Offset is necessary when you need to make several fills with exactly the same offset values. Hey—it could happen.

The Options Section

The Options section of the Fountain Fill dialog box, shown next, allows you to adjust any of the settings to customize the appearance of the fountain. The choices are described in the following paragraphs.

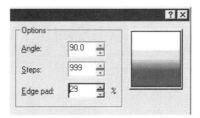

The Angle box determines the angle of either the Linear or Conical Fountain fill. You can also change the angle by dragging the line that appears when you click in the preview box with the mouse button. Holding down the CTRL key while dragging constrains the angle to multiples of 15 degrees.

The Steps value box determines the number of bands used to display and print the fountain. Unless you have some reason to want to see some degree of banding, you should always set this to its maximum value, which is 999.

The Edge Pad (0%–49%) controls the smoothness of the transition between the start and end colors in the fountain fill. A setting of 0% (default) creates the smoothest transition, while a maximum setting causes a very abrupt change, as shown in Figure 9-7. The Edge Pad option is not available for Conical Fountain fills and therefore is grayed out.

FIGURE 9-7   Edge Pad settings control the smoothness of a fountain fill's transition; the fill on the left has a setting of zero percent; the fill on the right has a maximum (49%) setting

Color Blend

The Color Blend section of the Fountain Fill dialog box, shown next, is where you select the colors you want to use in your fill. There are two modes of operation in the Color Blend area: Two Color (default) and Custom.

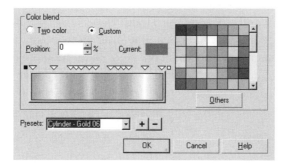

Two Color blends are fountain fills created using two colors—the From color and the To color. The operation of the Two Color blend is controlled by one of the three buttons to the right of the From and To colors. These buttons are

■ **Direct**   This option determines the intermediate fill colors from a straight line beginning at the From color and continuing across the color wheel to the To color.

- **Counter-Clockwise Color Path**   Selecting this option causes the fill's intermediate colors to be selected by traveling counter-clockwise around the color wheel between the From and To colors. If colors are very close to each other, the path travels almost completely around the wheel. This type of fill was applied to the image in Figure 9-8.

- **Clockwise Color Path**   This option determines the fill's intermediate colors by traveling clockwise around the color wheel between the From and To colors.

- **Mid-Point Slider**   This option is only available with Direct selected. It adjusts the midpoint between the From and To color. The Mid-Point slider allows the user to control the distribution of color/shading of the fountain fills.

Custom Blend   For all of the fancy stuff we have been doing with fountain fills up until this point, we have been controlling the fill with two colors. The Custom Blend setting allows you to add more than two colors in specific locations on the fill. When the Custom button is clicked, the dialog box changes, as shown in Figure 9-9. Now there is a color ribbon on which you can select up to 99 intermediate colors from the palette to its right. You specify where you want the color to appear on the color ribbon by adding markers, which look a lot like the tab markers on my word-processing program.

Referring to Figure 9-9, you notice that quite a few colors are involved in making this little example I've cooked up. As with all fountain fills, there must be end colors. They are the squares at each end of the color ribbon. To add additional

FIGURE 9-8   This image was made by applying a radial two-color direct fountain fill to the text

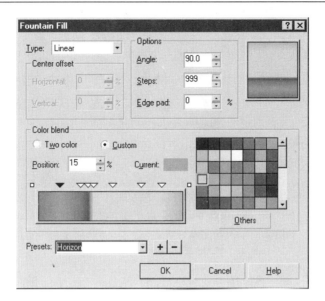

FIGURE 9-9 Custom blends allow you to make create backgrounds and horizons

colors, you must add markers. There are two ways to add markers. When you double-click just above the color ribbon, a black marker will appear. Another way to add a marker is to select the To or From color squares at either end of the preview ribbon and specify a new value in the Position box and then click the end color square again. (The first way works the best.)

To change the color of either the end colors or the markers, you only need select the marker or end square by clicking it and then clicking a color from the palette to the immediate right. The color ribbon and the preview window in the upper-right corner of the Fountain Fill dialog box will reflect the change. Is the color you want not in the palette? Click the Others button to open the Select Color dialog box. Every color in the universe is in this jewel.

> **TIP** *Want to find the name of the color you just selected? Many times we are following directions on how to make some project and the writer will specify a color like "Electric Blue." Select the color for which you need a name, click the Others button, and when the Select Color dialog box opens click the Palettes tab and the name of the color will be highlighted (assuming it has a name).*

To reposition a color on the color ribbon, select its marker and drag it to the desired spot, or edit the value in the Position box. To delete a color, double-click the marker.

More than one color marker can be selected at a time by holding down the SHIFT *key when selecting or deselecting.*

The Presets Area

The Presets area lets you save the fountain settings you specified so that you can apply them to other objects at a later time. It also contains over 100 predesigned fills that were installed with Corel PHOTO-PAINT.

If you want to browse through the list, just click the down arrow to the right of the preset text box and then click the first fill you wish to view. After that, each time you press DOWN ARROW or UP ARROW on your keyboard, the next preset will be selected and previewed. With one of the presets selected, you can type in the first letter of the preset's name and it will jump right to it. You might enjoy doing this if your cable TV is out and you are really bored.

To save a preset, type a name (up to 31 characters in length) in the Presets box, and then click the plus button. Clicking the minus button removes the selected Preset from the list.

Putting Fountain Fills to Work

While it is easy to use fountain fills to fill existing text or objects, the real power of the fountain fills in PHOTO-PAINT is the ability to use the custom blend to produce backdrops for other work.

Using the tools in PHOTO-PAINT, I was able to capture the peace and beauty of the mythical Lake Wobegon, as shown in Figure 9-10. (This figure also appears in the color insert.) The image began as a fountain fill horizon. By applying the clouds and trees with the Image Sprayer, I had the background I needed for a project. The water surface was created by applying darker areas with the Tint effect tool and applying noise before applying a very slight setting of the Gaussian blur filter.

In Figure 9-11 (which also appears in the color insert), the brass rod and everything else behind the gold lettering were created with a single fountain fill. To obtain a sharp cutoff of a color, place a different color very close to it (as in almost on top of it).

In Figure 9-12 (likewise shown in the color insert), the entire background for the magazine cover layout is a fountain fill. The gold rods are part of the fill

FIGURE 9-10   This photograph of the famous Lake Wobegon was created using a fountain fill for the water and sky to which the clouds and trees were added with the Image Sprayer tool

FIGURE 9-11   A single fountain fill created the brass rod and the black background

created by placing dark colors very close to the gold colors. Just as in the previous example, a lighter color was sandwiched in the gold/bronze colors to give the appearance of highlights. The cars were applied with a clone tool using one of the unusual nibs that ship with PHOTO-PAINT.

I hope this discussion leads you to see fountain fills in a different light; try your hand at a fill or two. Next on our tour of the fill tools is the Bitmap fill.

Bitmap Fill

The Bitmap Fill dialog box allows you to fill a selected area with a bitmap image. There are a large number of images in the Corel library (located in the TILES folder on your Corel PHOTO-PAINT CD-ROM). In addition to the bitmap images provided, you can import almost any bitmap that can be read by your PC.

NOTE   *PHOTO-PAINT can import vector-based images for use as bitmap fills.*

FIGURE 9-12   Again it is fountain fills that create everything but the cars and the chrome

Loading a Bitmap Image

When you invoke the Bitmap fill, you will see the currently selected image in the preview window. To change the image, you must click the Edit button. This will open the Bitmap Fill dialog box. The dialog box in the image that follows is shown with the bitmap selection palette open to the left so that you can see all of the buttons.

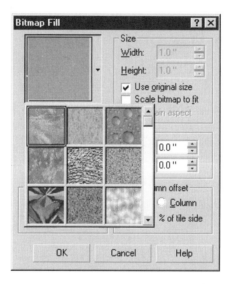

How the Bitmap Fill Operates

You have so much versatility when using bitmaps for fills that it is sometimes difficult to get a grip on all of it. Here are some pointers about using files for bitmap fills:

■   Remember that if you use the Fill tool (the bucket), the fill will be calculated to the boundaries of the mask or the edges of the image. If the bitmap image is larger than the mask or the image, Corel PHOTO-PAINT will put as much as will fit, beginning with the lower-left corner of the original image.

■   You can control what appears in a flood-filled area by using the many tile/offset controls in the Bitmap Fill dialog box.

■ The Rectangle, Ellipse, and Polygon tools, on the other hand, will fill to the perimeter of the defined area. If there is a mask, the masked area that falls within the area will be filled.

When using Corel Photo CDs as bitmap fills, make sure to crop them in the Import dialog box to get rid of any black film border. If you don't, the results can be really ugly.

Controlling the Size and Position of the Bitmap Tiles

If the bitmap that you import is too small to fill the area, the default settings will cause the bitmap to be tiled. If the bitmap is too large for the area being filled, only a portion of the bitmap will fill the area, beginning in the lower-left corner. But by changing the default settings, you can control the size, offset, and several other parameters of the bitmap fill. The following descriptions refer to the dialog box shown next.

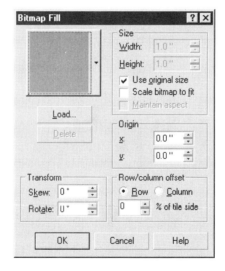

Size

The controls in this section allow you to set the size of your pattern tiles. You can choose one of the preset sizes or enter custom dimensions. When you select Use

Original Size, the bitmap file will not be scaled to a new size. If it is not checked, the bitmap will be scaled to the size set in the Width and Height settings. These settings are grayed-out if the Use Original Size option is enabled.

Scale Bitmap to Fit

When enabled, this option scales the tile pattern to fit entirely within the tile Preview window. It also disables the entire dialog box, except the Maintain Aspect option.

Origin

Controls in this section set the offset of the first tile (and therefore the rest of the pattern) relative to the top right-hand corner of the object. If you want the pattern to start flush with the corner, set the X and Y values to zero.

Row/Column Offset

These controls shift either the rows or columns of tiles so that the pattern is staggered rather than continuous. The % of Tile Side setting shifts alternating rows or columns by the amount specified. This feature helps break up repeating patterns.

Transform

The Transform setting specifies the angle on which the tile is rotated and skewed. You can set the rotation value in two ways: type a value in the Rotate box or use the scroll arrows to adjust an existing value.

Loading Bitmap Images

To the right of the Preview window in the Bitmap Fill dialog box is a Down-arrow button. Clicking the button or anywhere in the preview window opens a color preview of the first nine bitmaps that have been imported into Corel PHOTO-PAINT. If there are more bitmaps than can be displayed, scroll bars appear on the right side of the preview window that allow the user to see the remainder of the bitmap fills in Corel PHOTO-PAINT.

Clicking the Load button opens the Load Bitmap Fill dialog box, where you can import a graphic to use as your bitmap pattern. There is a large selection of existing bitmap fills available on the CD-ROM containing the TILES folder.

Putting Bitmap Fills to Work

There is no doubt I use bitmap fills more than any other fill. It is so much easier to make things appear photo-realistic when you can make the base images from photographs. Figure 9-13 was a project for a book. Obviously it wasn't for real life; after all, statistics show that over 99.95% of all chain smokers don't smoke chains. Bad jokes aside, the background is a bitmap fill. The text is also a bitmap fill that is a knotted wood. The reason it doesn't look like knotted wood is because I applied Gaussian noise to it and then used an Emboss with the original color setting.

The anchor chain began as a bitmap fill using the same fill that is in the text, as shown next.

FIGURE 9-13   Three different bitmap fills were necessary to make this unnecessary sign

Now I add Gaussian noise and then use the Emboss with Original color. The next image looks flat as a pancake.

Making a mask of the shape and applying an airbrush with the Stoke Mask command, we have depth and nearly a real link in an anchor chain.

9

The Texture Fills

Texture fills are the feature that makes Corel PHOTO-PAINT unique. I do not know of another package that can do the things that can be done with Texture fills. There are some tricks to using the fills effectively, but you will learn them here. The Texture Fill dialog box is used to select one of the 100-plus bitmap texture fills included in Corel PHOTO-PAINT. Each texture has a unique set of parameters that you can modify to create millions of variations. The results depend on your printer, your taste, and your willingness to experiment.

What's in a Name?

As with the filters, don't let the names of the fills confuse your thinking. As an example, I was once able to give some letters in a poster the effect of a cut metal edge by applying the Rain Drops, Hard Texture fill to each character individually. This approach kept the size of the "raindrop" from getting too large. Too large?

This leads to our first general rule regarding the texture fills. As in Boyle's law of expanding gases (gas expands to fit the volume of the container):

> **Rule of bitmap textures**   A texture fill expands to fit the volume of the available area.

In the following illustration, I have created squares of various sizes and filled them with the same texture fill. As you can see, as the squares increase in area, the size of the fill increases proportionally. While this can be used to create some unusual effects, it can also catch you by surprise, especially when working with a large image only to find that when it is applied, it looks nothing like the thumbnail preview.

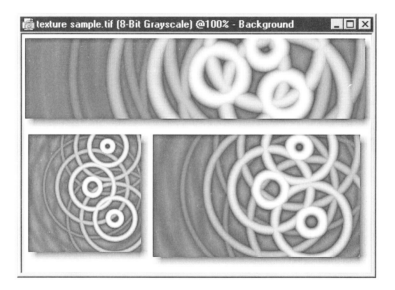

NOTE   *The fill size is calculated by creating a square that is determined by the greatest dimension of the mask. For example, if you made a mask that was 50 × 500 pixels, the resulting fill would be as if it were a 500 × 500 pixel square.*

Exploring the Texture Fill Dialog Box

When the Texture Bitmap mode of the Fill palette is selected, the currently selected fill is displayed in the preview window. The Edit button opens the Texture Fill dialog box, shown next. This dialog box allows you to edit and create an unlimited number of new texture fills from existing fills. Unlike when working with bitmap fills, you cannot import files for use as texture fills. The texture fills are actually fractals that are created as they are applied. This goes a long way to explain why some textures can take a long time to apply.

If you cannot find the exact file that you want in the 160+ preset textures that were shipped with Corel PHOTO-PAINT, you can edit the existing textures in the Texture Fill dialog box.

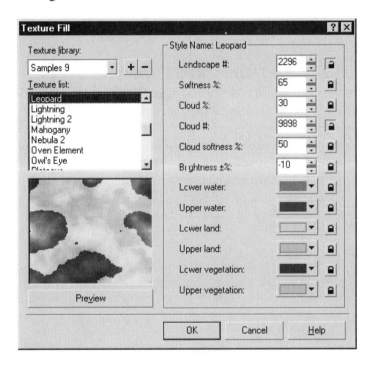

Texture Library

This list box displays the names of the texture libraries. Corel PHOTO-PAINT 10 ships with several libraries containing textures made with the Texture generator. The Styles library contains samples that are the building blocks of the bitmap texture fills. It is from the textures in this library that all other samples in the other libraries are made. This library is a read-only library. If you modify a texture and want to save it, you will not be allowed to save it in this library. You must either create a new library or save it in one of the Samples libraries. I find that I use the Night Sky and Planets textures in the Samples 5 library more than almost any other texture.

Texture List This window lists the texture fills available in the currently selected library. Clicking a texture in the Textures list will select it, and the default setting for the texture will display in the preview window.

 Each time a library is selected, the texture list returns to the default texture for that library. For example, if you were in Samples 5 and had been working with Night Sky and then you switched over to look at something in Styles, when you returned to Samples 5, it would have returned to the default texture.

Preview and Locked/Unlocked Parameters

Each time the Preview button is depressed, Corel PHOTO-PAINT varies the appearance of the selected texture by randomly changing all unlocked parameters. This button does more than is apparent at first. There are over 15,000 textures with several million possible combinations for each one. Rather than requiring you to wade through a sea of permutations, Corel PHOTO-PAINT textures have certain variables that are either locked or unlocked by default.

You can lock and unlock a parameter by clicking the Lock button next to it. You can also use the Preview button to update a texture after changing the parameters yourself.

 Until you get used to using a texture, I recommend using the default settings for the locks. They generally provide the best, quickest results.

Save As (Plus Button)

After changing the parameters of a texture in the library (or a new library you created), click the Plus button in the upper-right corner to overwrite the original. This opens a dialog box for naming (or renaming) a texture you have created. The texture name can be up to 31 characters (including spaces). The Library Name option allows you to create a new library in which to store the textures. You can type up to 31 characters (including spaces). The Library List displays libraries where you can store the modified texture.

 You must save any modified Style textures in a library other than the Styles library, because Styles is a read-only library.

Delete (Minus Button)

This deletes the selected texture. You cannot delete textures in the Styles library.

Style Name and Parameter Section

This part of the Texture Fill dialog box shows the names of the selected textures. Because each texture has different value assignments, methods, colors, and lights, it would take a separate book to list even a few of the combinations provided by the parameters. The value boxes in this area list parameters for the selected texture. Changing one or more of these parameters alters the appearance of the texture. The changes are displayed in the preview box whenever the Preview button is depressed. The Style Name fields list numeric parameters. All textures have texture numbers, which range from 0 to 32,767. The names of the other parameters vary with the texture selected and usually range from 0 to 100 or –100 to 100.

To change a numeric parameter, enter a value in the text box or use the cursor and click either the up or down arrow.

TIP	*If you are going to ascend or descend very far on the numeric list just described, you can use a speedup feature of the up and down arrows. Place the cursor between the up and down arrows. The cursor will change into a two-headed arrow cursor with a line between the two arrowheads. After the cursor changes, click and drag either up or down, and the selection list will move rapidly up or down the list (depending on which way you choose). To see the change entered, click the Preview button.*

The right side of the field lists up to six parameters, depending on the texture selected. To change a color, click the color button and select a new color from the pop-up palette. If you desire a specific color or named color that is not on the color palette, click the Other button. The Other button opens the Select Color dialog box. (See the Uniform Fill section for specific details regarding the use of this dialog box.) After you have made the desired changes, click the Preview button to see the effect the new color has on the selected texture.

Doing Something with Texture Fills

Next to the Bitmap fill tool, this fill tool is almost limitless in what you can do with it. Again, here are some projects I have done with the Texture fill tool. The purpose of these examples is to give your imagination a jump start.

The radio station letters in Figure 9-14 appear to be three-dimensional. The fill for the letters was made using the Texture fill tool. The shadowing on the letters was created by making a cutout from the white background and from that placing a drop shadow on the letters. It is difficult to think of the white being cut out and the letters behind the cutout because I have placed too many visual clues—like the perspective shadow.

FIGURE 9-14   3D Letters with a fill that would have been impossible without Texture fill

Did you ever wonder what happens when you apply The Boss filter to a texture fill? The answer is a pretty classy polished gemstone, as shown in Figure 9-15. Each of the letters was filled with a different texture fill.

NOTE   *This tool acts like the Gradient tool in Photoshop*

FIGURE 9-15   Application of The Boss filter to texture fill produces a slick polished gemstone

Interactive Fill Tool

This tool provides a way to apply a fountain fill interactively to an image without the necessity of figuring out the angles and percentages. Located on the Fill Tool flyout, the Interactive Fill tool applies a graduated color blend that changes the transparency from the start color to the end color.

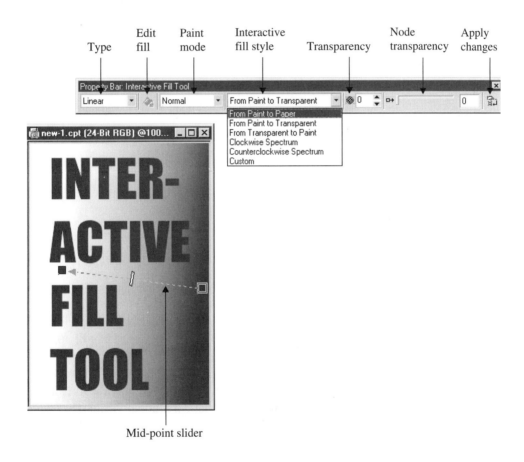

Mid-point slider

The Tool properties are controlled through the property bar shown here. There must be about a zillion possible combinations—I was never very good at math.

Many of the fill tools share common features with this property bar, so we will explore them a little more thoroughly in this section.

Type

Most of the fill tools in PHOTO-PAINT 10 offer the nine types of fill shown in the next illustration. With possibly one or two exceptions, their names describe the type of fill produced.

 One of the Types must be selected in order for the remaining parts of the property bar to be available.

Paint Mode

When you apply a fill in normal paint mode, the color of each pixel in the image is changed to the color/shade of the fill. For example, if a pixel is red and I apply a blue uniform fill, its color value will be changed. As simple as that sounds, it is an important concept with PHOTO-PAINT. The color is not "flowing" on top of the other color, it is replacing the underlying color. Now as you may recall from previous chapters, we have discussed that a mathematical number defines a color or shade. If I can replace one numeric value with another, I can also do mathematics with those color-defining numbers. That is exactly what the paint modes do—

all 27 of them. In the next image I have shown the Interactive Fill Tool property bar open, showing all of the paint modes. It is difficult if not impossible to predict the outcome of different paint modes, so most of the work with the Paint Mode setting involves creating a fill and experimenting with different paint modes.

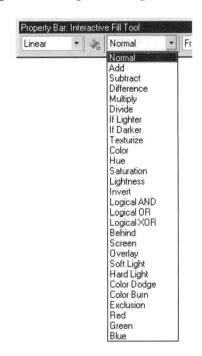

My favorite use of this tool is to create quick graduated masks in the Paint on Mask mode.

Interactive Fill Style

The Fill Style settings give you a choice of six different combinations. The fill that you create will begin and end with the color you specify.

9

Great, So How Does It Work?

That's the best part. Just click at a point in the image and drag a line. The selected
fill will be applied to the image. As you drag the cursor, the image shown next
appears. This is the interactive part. For example, if the fill style were set to From
Paint—to Paper, the top node would be the Paint color and the bottom node would
be the Paper color. The bar shown between the two nodes is used to slide the
transparency between the nodes. Once you have applied the fill and before you
apply it by clicking the Apply button in the property bar, you can change the colors
of each node and position it as well.

   This tool is a great device to put a quick fill on an object or to create a graduated
mask while in Paint on Mask mode.

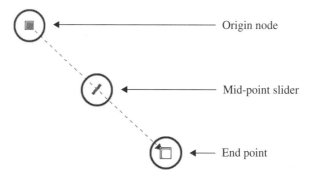

Origin node

Mid-point slider

End point

Transparency Controls

Until now we have been talking about controlling solid fills. The Edit Fill &
Transparency dialog box has two pages: Fill Color and Transparency. The first
page has the fill controls described earlier in this chapter. The second page, however,
offers the ability to control the transparency of the selected fill. There are eight
transparency options listed in the Type box. Choosing None (default) means there
is no transparency applied to the fill. This is the way fills are normally applied. The
other seven options can be used to create interesting effects.

Flat

Choosing Flat creates a transparency that is uniform throughout the fill. Because it is a uniform transparency, it only has a starting value. The default setting for the Start Transparency is zero. If this setting isn't changed, the Flat setting operates like the None setting. The photograph shown next had a bitmap fill applied to it at a Flat transparency setting of 50.

Linear

The Linear setting applies a fill beginning with the level of transparency specified in the Start Transparency value and ending with the level defined by the End Transparency. The beginning and ending points of the fill are determined by the starting and ending points placed in the Preview window. Using values of 0 to 100, the Linear fill was applied to the picture of the mask in the image. In the next image the cursor in the Preview window indicates the starting and ending points of the transparency.

Elliptical

The Elliptical setting provides the greatest control in the creation of irregularly shaped fills. The original photograph has a solid black background. By applying a white fill through an elliptical transparency as shown in the following dialog box, I was able to make a soft white blurred border of Grace (daddy's girl) that provided greater control than possible with the Vignette filter, which is described in chapters 13 and 14.

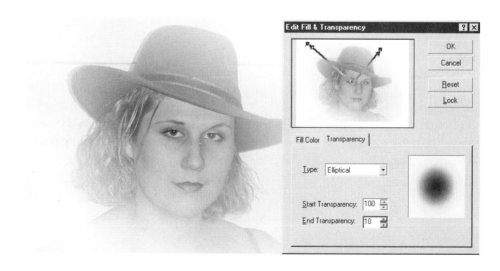

Radial

The Radial setting, like the Elliptical setting, produces transparency along circular lines. While any fill can be used with this setting, a circular transparency allows another image to be applied without straight lines, making the transition much more subtle.

Square, Rectangle, and Conical

The Square and Rectangle transparency settings are good for creating frame style effects. The Conical setting has limited use due to the nature of the effect. To produce the conical appearance, a small segment of a circle appears darker and gradually fades into the remainder of the circle.

The Disable Fill Button

I call this one the No Fill Fill button. Unfortunately Corel didn't agree with me. The Disable Fill button is only available on the property bars for the shape tools, which makes perfect sense once you understand the operation of the shape tools, which happens to be the next subject.

The Shape Tools

The Shape Tool flyout contains four tools: The Rectangle tool, the Ellipse tool, the Polygon tool, and the Line tool. The first three tools allow you to draw outlined or filled shapes on your image. If you want to create the shape as an object, enable the Render to Object check box in the property bar. This allows you to reposition or edit your object before you merge it into your image. If you do not create the shape as an object, it will instantly merge into the background, so ensure you set the color, fill, and outline before you begin. Another unique feature of the shape tools is the Disable Fill tool. When enabled, the shape tools create rectangles, circles, and polygons with borders but no fill.

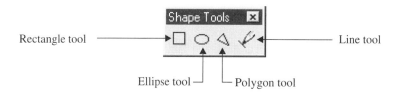

Rectangle tool — Shape Tools — Line tool

Ellipse tool — Polygon tool

The Render to Object option in the property bar creates shapes as objects that can be moved and transformed without affecting the underlying image. If you enable it on the Rectangle tool, for example, it is not automatically enabled on all of the other tools. This is true of all of the shape tool properties.

Width and Roundness of Borders

With the property bar, you can control the size and shape of the border made by the Rectangle, Ellipse, or Polygon tool.

Width

This determines the thickness of the border in points (remember, a point is 1/72 of an inch).

Transparency

The Transparency setting determines how transparent the fill will be when applied to the image. This setting can be of great benefit when you need to apply a fill for an effect. It can also be a real pain.

When you enable the transparency setting, it remains, and it is very easy to forget that you now have a transparency setting. If you apply a color like red and think it looks washed out, you may have a transparency setting enabled. This transparency setting only works for the Rectangle, Ellipse, or Polygon tool. It does not affect the transparency setting for the Fill tool.

Roundness (Rectangle Tool Only)

The "roundness" of the corners is determined by the Roundness settings. A rough representation of the rounded curve is continuously updated as the value of roundness is increased or decreased.

Joints (Polygon Tool Only)

This setting, available when the width value is at least 1, gives you three choices for how PHOTO-PAINT is to treat the joints of multiple line figures. Use the pop-up menu to select the type of joint. Choices are Butt, Filled, Round, and Point:

■ **Butt**   The joints are the squared ends of the lines where they meet and overlap.

■ **Filled**   The open areas caused by the overlap are filled.

■ **Round**   The corners are rounded.

■ **Point**   The corners end in points.

Paint Mode

The Paint mode pop-up menu lets you control the way Paint colors and Paper colors combine to create new colors and effects. With most paint tools, the Paint color simply replaces the Paper color (just as you would use a colored paint to paint a white wall). However, with the Paint modes, it is the combination of Paint colors and Paper colors that produces the new color.

Antialiasing

Antialiasing removes jagged edges from a mask, object, or image by adding duplicated pixels where the mask, object, or image edge contacts the background image.

The Rectangle Tool

The Rectangle tool is used to draw hollow or filled rectangles and rounded rectangles. Without the tools in this flyout, we wouldn't be able to control the fill of masked areas as well as we do.

Here are the facts for the Rectangle tool:

- F6 is the keyboard shortcut.

- If the CTRL key is held down while defining the shape, the rectangle is constrained to a square.

- Holding down the SHIFT key while creating a rectangle will cause the rectangle to shrink or grow (depending on the direction of the mouse movement) from the center.

- When the Rectangle is produced, it is filled with the current fill setting in the Fill palette.

- If the Disable Fill setting is selected, a hollow rectangle is created. It doesn't consume system resources; it doesn't do anything. Sounds Zen. Very good, Grasshopper.

To Draw a Rectangle or Rounded Rectangle

Here are some hints about drawing Rectangles or Rounded rectangles:

- Select the Rectangle tool and choose the border color by clicking the desired color on the Color palette and the Fill color by clicking the desired color. The Paint (background) color determines border color.

- Specify the width and roundness of the border in the property bar.

- Press the mouse button to anchor the rectangle and drag until you have achieved the desired size.

- The rectangle is filled with the current Fill color when the mouse button is released. The rectangle is hollow if the Disable Fill option is selected.

- If the rectangle is not what you desire, it can be erased by pressing the ESC key *before* releasing the mouse button.

The Ellipse Tool

The Ellipse tool draws hollow or filled ellipses. If the CTRL key is held down while defining the shape, the ellipse is constrained to a circle. Holding down the SHIFT key will shrink or grow the ellipse from the center.

To Draw an Ellipse

The following are some general guidelines for drawing ellipses with the Ellipse tool:

- F7 is the keyboard shortcut.

- Holding down the CTRL key produces a circle.

- Click the Ellipse tool and choose the border color by clicking the desired color in the Color palette with the mouse button.

- The Paint (background) color determines border color. The ellipse is filled with the current Fill color unless the Disable Fill is selected in the property bar.

- Specify the width of the border in the property bar.

- Press the mouse button to anchor the ellipse and drag until you have achieved the desired size.

- If the circle is not what you desire, it can be erased by pressing the ESC key *before* releasing the mouse button.

9

The Polygon Tool

The Polygon tool produces closed multisided figures. Of course, if you thought a polygon was a dead parrot, the fact this tool makes multisided images may have come as a surprise. By selecting different Joint (I understand they are no longer called joints – but that's what we called them back in the 60s) settings in the Tools Settings palette, the Polygon tool can provide a wide variety of images. For the record, I never inhaled.

To Draw a Polygon

The following are some procedural guides for using the Polygon tool:

- Y is the keyboard shortcut.

- Choose Color, Width, type of joints, and Transparency of the border and fill.

- Click where the polygon is to begin to anchor the starting point. Move the cursor where the first side of the polygon is to end. As the cursor is moved, the closed shape of the polygon is continually redrawn on the screen to assist the user in what the final shape will look like.

- Click the mouse button again to complete the first side. Continue moving the cursor to define the remaining sides.

- Double-clicking the end of the last line completes the polygon.

- Holding the CTRL key down while moving the cursor constrains the sides of the polygon vertically, horizontally, or at 45-degree angles.

The Line Tool

The last button on the Shape Tools flyout is the Line tool. Sometimes you just need to make a line. This tool draws single or joined straight-line segments using the Paint color. The Render to Object option in the property bar creates new lines as objects that can be moved and transformed without affecting the underlying image.

In Summary

Color on a computer may seem to be a daunting subject—because it is. (Not that mixing oil paints on a palette is any simpler.) In this chapter, we have only covered the basics of color selection and creation. If you were actually reading through the color selection section of the chapter from beginning to end, you just might be in a coma now. (I only hope you have friends who can revive you.) The Fills and Shape tools are much more interesting and—dare I say—more useful for creating cool stuff with PHOTO-PAINT. During the day (my day job) I create graphics for a Fortune 100 company and must work with color issues all day long, so I actually think they are pretty interesting. The next chapter deals with what is the most neglected feature in PHOTO-PAINT: Corel TEXTURE. We will also discover a little about a Corel program called KNOCKOUT.

9

CHAPTER 10

Corel TEXTURE
and Corel KnockOut™

269

This chapter explores two Corel applications: Corel TEXTURE and Corel KnockOut. Corel TEXTURE is a stand-alone graphics utility that ships as part of the CorelDRAW 10 suite and is used to create colorful, photo-realistic textures. The textures can be converted to seamless tiles for Web page backgrounds or used as texture fills in PHOTO-PAINT. Corel TEXTURE can also be used to make delicious 3D buttons, which will spiff up your Web page.

Corel KnockOut is a separate stand-alone application that provides the best and most powerful tools for automatically creating selections that would otherwise be next to impossible. While it does not ship with the CorelDRAW 10 suite, it is a powerful tool that anyone who must mask images as part of their daily photo-editing tasks should seriously consider adding to their software library. That said, let's start by looking at Corel TEXTURE.

What Is Corel TEXTURE?

Technically, Corel TEXTURE is a procedural texture rendering application (yawn). That was clear as mud, wasn't it? PHOTO-PAINT has its own texture creation engine, Texture bitmap fill. Unlike those you produce using the Texture bitmap fill (explored in Chapter 9), the textures produced using Corel TEXTURE can be so photo-realistic that viewers will believe they were created from photographs—no kidding!

An outfit called Three D Graphics created Corel TEXTURE, which was originally named Texture Creator. Even though it has been shipping with CorelDRAW and Corel PHOTO-PAINT since the release of CorelDRAW 7, many users have ignored this jewel—partially because it isn't installed during a typical installation and, even if you did make the extra effort to install it, Corel failed to provide any documentation about how to use it. We'll rectify that omission by telling you that you can download a PDF file of the user's manual for Texture Creator at www.threedgraphics.com. The manual provides a lot of information about the original product, which, apart from the name change, is identical to Corel TEXTURE.

In this chapter, we'll explore how to use the program to create textures using one of the many preset textures provided and learn how to create new ones from scratch. Let's get to it.

How Does It Work?

Quite simply, COREL TEXTURE combines a series of layers to create realistic textures. Each layer of a texture adds a different texture, lighting, or surface to the finished look and contributes a part to the finished texture. A preview feature allows you to see an accurate representation of the texture while you are working on it. Once the texture is just the way you want, it can be saved in its native format (*TEX), allowing the texture to be modified using TEXTURE at a later time. Mostly, you will be saving it in a format that allows its use as a fill in PHOTO-PAINT or any other graphic program that accepts bitmap fills. The size and type of the textures you create determines whether the texture is used as a seamless tile, a background, a Web button, or a fill. There is even another program called Corel TEXTURE Batcher that enables you to render many textures automatically. This can be handy if you have several large images to render; you can just set up the job and go to lunch or take a nap.

Now that we know what it can do, let's take a quick tour of Corel TEXTURE's interface so that we can become familiar with it.

Before You Can Launch It, You Must Find It

In case you are wondering just where this program is located, as I mentioned earlier, there is a slight chance it wasn't installed when you installed CorelDRAW. In previous versions, it wasn't installed as part of the "typical installation." During the beta testing cycle, it is installed. So, if it isn't installed, never fear. Just stick CD No. 1 into your trusty CD-ROM drive, and at some point the Corel installer will ask you if you want to install additional programs. The program is located under Graphic Utilities on the Corel installation CD, appropriately enough. Once it is installed, it appears under the same folder name in the CorelDRAW folder.

Once you launch it, you end up with a pretty uninteresting workspace. It isn't until you either open an existing texture or create a new texture that the program really begins to look interesting, as shown in Figure 10-1.

10

Title bar   Toolbar

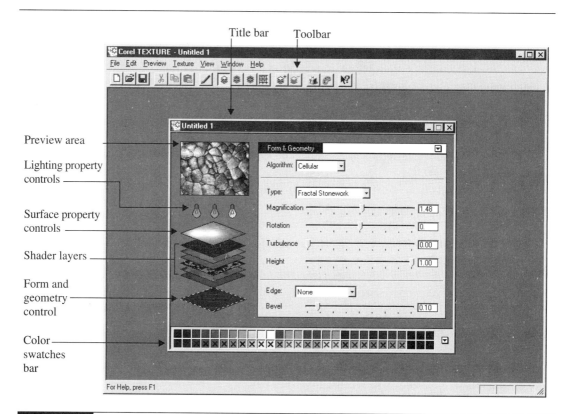

Preview area

Lighting property
controls

Surface property
controls

Shader layers

Form and
geometry
control

Color
swatches
bar

FIGURE 10-1   The Corel TEXTURE editing window

Menu, Window Title Bar, and Toolbar

This stuff is really basic, so I'll be brief. The menu bar is the bar you sit at while waiting for your table (sorry). Okay, the menu bar is where the drop-down menus are located. The title bar displays the name of the texture (if it has been saved). The toolbar contains icons representing 15 different tools (they are actually commands). The first six icons are Windows standard stuff—New, Open, and so on. The remaining nine are specific to Corel TEXTURE and will be described as we get to them.

Workspace and Preview Area

Below the title bar is the workspace containing the Preview area, among other items. The Preview area in the workspace only gives a rough approximation of how the texture appears. Depending on which of the Layers buttons in the toolbar is selected, the Preview area is limited to the display of a selected layer or all layers. There is a separate Preview window in Corel TEXTURE that is not in the workspace—it is a separate window. When enabled, it displays a rendered (accurate) version of the texture.

Layer-Specific Dialog Box (Work Area)

In the Texture Creator User's Manual, this area is labeled a work area. Since calling it Layer-Specific dialog box more accurately describes its function, and it's my book, we'll call it that. The appearance of this dialog box changes depending on which layer is selected.

Let There Be Light(ing Properties)

This layer adjusts the number and placement of light sources in the texture. It is used to create highlights and shadows in a texture. It is the interaction of the light sources and the surface properties of the layer that help produce the cool photo-realistic effects that are possible with this program.

Surface Properties

Mom always said that beauty was only skin deep. Well, when it comes to textures, everything is only skin deep. Surface properties are used to create a finish for the texture. Surface properties that can be adjusted include roughness, shading, and graininess. As I mentioned in the previous paragraph, these settings interact with the lighting properties.

Shader Layers

The Shader layers are used to apply patterns such as solids, woods, and marble. Each texture file can have up to seven different Shader layers. Most textures won't have this many, but some of the more complex presets that are provided with Corel TEXTURE (made by designers who don't date much) have many intricate Shader layers. Don't let the fact that there can be up to seven of these layers scare you; many times when using TEXTURE, you will only use one layer. Creating shades and patterns on a Shader layer uses a system similar to the one used for bitmap fills in PHOTO-PAINT.

Color Swatches and the Color Palette

The color swatches are used to select colors used in the Shader layers, while the Color palette (it is only open when creating textures) allows you to modify the brightness and the opacity of colors in the Color Swatches palette.

Form and Geometry

The name of this control layer reminds me of a class I hated in high school. Appearing on the bottom of the stack in the workspace, one of the tasks of this layer is to give the texture bumps, dents, and other bump map functions. Its other purpose is to define the edge of the texture with things like bevels; rounded corners; and, of course, my favorite—nothing at all. Now that you know where the major tools are located, let's learn how to put them to use.

How to Make a Texture

Unlike with PHOTO-PAINT, it is not necessary to select the dimensions and the resolution of the image before you start a new texture.

1. To start the process either click the New button or select New from the File menu on the menu bar. Either way opens the Start New Texture dialog box, shown next.

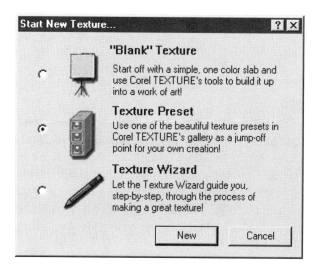

2. As you can see, you have three choices: "Blank" texture, Texture Preset, Texture Wizard.

3. Selecting Texture Preset (it is selected by default) opens a new dialog box called New Texture, which appears next. It provides a visual catalog of all of the 200 presets that are provided with Corel TEXTURE. The operation is pretty obvious. The tabs are used to select categories of textures: wood, marble, stone, and so on.

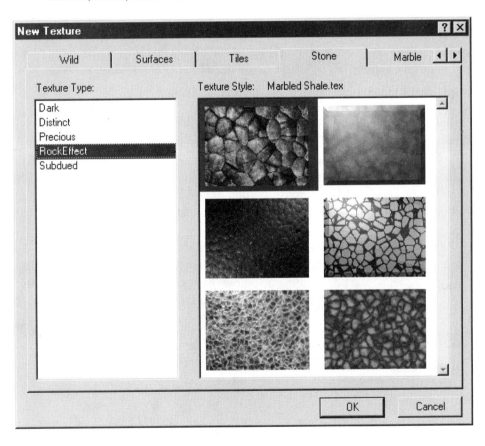

10

> **NOTE**   *Not all of the tabs are visible, and you must use the scroll arrows to see all of the tabs. Each category contains multiple texture types, and high-lighting a type displays thumbnails of the textures in that texture type.*

4. To make the texture usable in PHOTO-PAINT, you must render the texture to a file. Choose Texture | Render to File, which opens the Render to File dialog box. Name the new texture and click the Save button. That's all there is to it. You have created a texture file.

> **NOTE**   *When you render a texture, you can save it in one of five file formats through the Save As Type setting in the dialog box. If you are going to be using it in PHOTO-PAINT, use the default BMP setting.*

Making a Seamless Tile

Seamless tiles are great for Web pages and bitmap fills in PHOTO-PAINT. By their very nature, they enable you to cover a large area using a single seamless image. Corel TEXTURE does a good job of making textures into seamless tiles; but, as we are about to learn, the real burden of making them really seamless lies in our choice of textures. Here is a short procedure for making a seamless tile.

1. Choose File | New, and choose Texture Preset. When the New Texture dialog box opens, scroll over to the Wild tab and choose the Other texture type. Select the bright blue one below the basketball. When you select it, the Texture Style just below the tab will display the name of the texture file—BlueScales.TEX. Click OK.

2. Choose Texture | Generate Tiling Image; depending on the speed of your CPU, the preview will redraw the new tile image, as shown next.

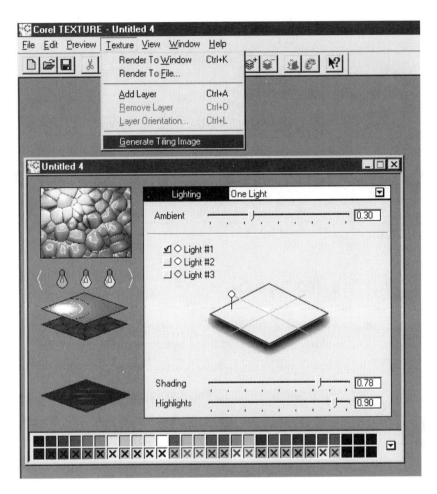

10

3. To see the effect of the conversion, select Preview | Test Tiling (CTRL-T). If you are satisfied with the result, choose Texture | Render to File. In Figure 10-2, I have put together a comparison between the seamless and the non-seamless versions of the texture. Pretty slick, right?

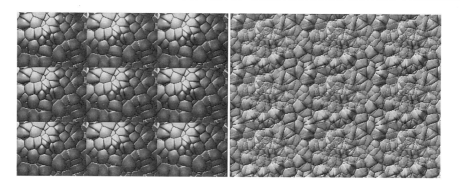

FIGURE 10-2   Original texture tiled (left) and seamless image tiled (right)

Changing the Texture Size

One of my favorite features of Corel TEXTURE is its capability to render the
texture image in almost any size for almost every graphic application. After you
have selected or created a texture, choose File | Image Setup to open the dialog
box shown next.

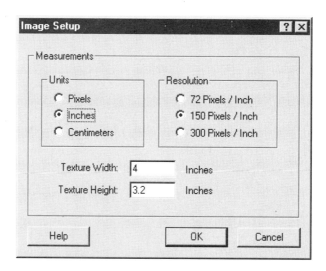

Corel TEXTURE uses the information in this dialog box when the file is rendered. Just a reminder: if you make the settings in this dialog box large, your CPU is going to take a long, long time to render the file.

Making a 3D Button

Here is how you can make a nice 3D button from scratch using Corel TEXTURE:

1. Choose File | New and select the "Blank" texture from the top of the dialog box. The new texture dialog box opens, as shown next.

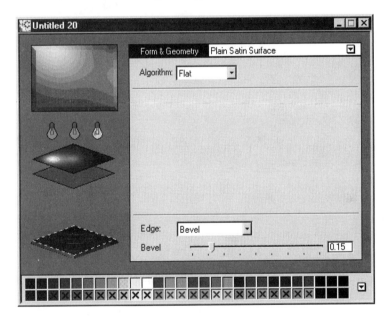

2. Click the Shader layer (the middle one), and then click a color you like from the Color Swatches bar (I chose red) and drag it onto the color pin on the gradient bar for the Shader layer, as shown next. To remove a color pin from the color gradient bar, select the pin and press the DELETE key.

NOTE *Colors marked with an "X" are transparent colors—solid colors with transparent bands that allow colors and other elements from lower layers to show through.*

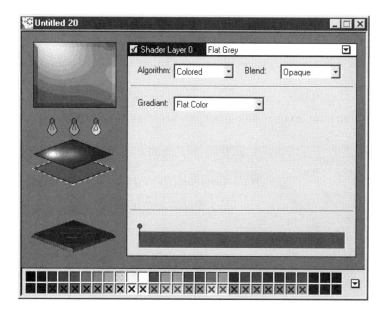

3. Now that we have a button with some color, it is way too dark. Click the Lighting layer (light bulbs). Change the Ambient light setting from 0.05 (very dark) to 0.30. But that makes the upper-left corner too bright. Change Highlights to 0.30 and ensure that Shading is at 0.50.

4. Select the Surface Properties layer. Our objective at this point is to make the button look less synthetic. The following settings were determined by experimentation: Roughness: 0.05, Brilliance: 0.35, Metallicity: 0.00, and Graininess: 0.05.

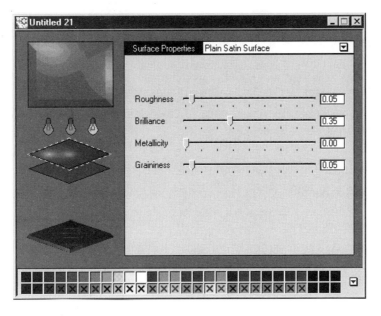

5. Now, as an optional step, select the Form and Geometry layer (bottom). From here you can change the size of the bevel. In the example shown next, the width was changed to 0.30. From this layer, you can also change the setting from Bevel to Round, Extruded, or even a picture frame. We'll keep the bevel and then choose Texture | Render to File. Save it as Red button.bmp. Please remember where you saved the file.

10

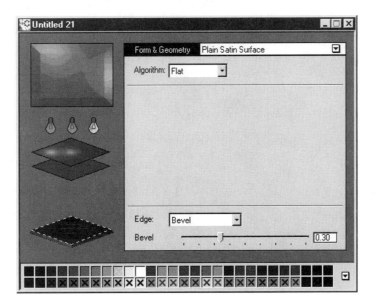

6. In PHOTO-PAINT 10, choose File | Open and open the file. That's all there is to it.

We have just touched on a few things that you can do with Corel TEXTURE. If you will get in the habit of experimenting with this program, you will get to the point that you will use it more and more to create some great textures and effects. Now, let's look at Corel KnockOut.

Corel KnockOut

If you're not familiar with the KnockOut filter, here is a recap of what it is and where it comes from. This is the best automatic selection filter on the planet. I know that sounds a little extreme; but once you learn to use this program, you will discover that I am correct. Ultimatte—a company that has won numerous film awards, including an Oscar, for their work in blue screen technology—created KnockOut. (Blue screening is what your favorite weatherman uses to make him appear to be in the middle of his weather graphics.) It is fair to say that Ultimatte has a lot of experience in the field of isolating foregrounds from their backgrounds, and so they applied what they knew to the creation of KnockOut, which was for the Mac (logical choice), cost $500.00 (questionable decision), and required a hardware copy protection device (terrible decision). To put it kindly, it wasn't a runaway success. Corel acquired the product in 1999, cut the price in half, removed the copy protection device, and released version 1.5 on both Windows and Mac platforms. Enough history, let's see how it works.

RAM Requirements for KnockOut

Before opening an image, we need to consider RAM requirements for this program. Why? Because this program likes RAM, lots of it. That shouldn't be too surprising, since the term "photo-editing" comes from the original Latin that means—buy RAM (I'm kidding). The minimum rule of RAM is that you need five times the amount of RAM as the size of your image. That is the minimum. For best performance, the amount of RAM in your system should be eight times the size of the image. With RAM prices what they are today, this isn't a big deal; but more than once I have talked to users who have scanned in their favorite photos at 1440 dpi (since their printer operates at 1440 dpi) and are amazed they are having difficulties working on 60MB images with 24MB of system RAM.

How KnockOut Works

The principle of operation of KnockOut is simple. You tell KnockOut what is inside and what is outside, and KnockOut makes the selection. Using the Inside Object tool (which works like a pencil or line tool), you select an area inside of the part of the photograph you want to keep, as shown next.

When selecting the inside of the subject, you should stay away from the edge of the subject matter, which contains both foreground and background information. Of course, this brings up a good question, which is, how close is close? You want to make sure that the inside selection goes through all of the colors that are near the edge of your subject. Our little teddy bear is almost all white, so the selection line can be pretty loose. If the bear had lots of different colors, that would be a bear of a different color . . . sorry. Where was I? If the subject has lots of colors, you need to make the inside selection closer to the edge—but not too close. Once the inside selection is finished, you can use the Inside Object tool to add to (SHIFT key) or subtract from (ALT key) the selection.

Next use the Outside Object tool to outline the subject. Again, you must ensure that you do not include any of the colors that make up the edge of your subject when making the outside selection, as shown next.

Your Next Stop—The Transition Zone

At this point, two lines of "marching ants" on the image define three zones—inner, outer, and transition. The outer defines the background; the inner zone, the object being selected; and the transition zone contains both the background and the foreground information. The "marching ants" of the inside or outside of the selection are black and white when the tool is active.

Once you've finished telling KnockOut what's in and what's out, you need to click the Process button. At this point, there are three possible views of your subject: the original (CTRL-1), the knocked-out version (CTRL-2, old background is replaced with a new and temporary one), and the alpha channel (CTRL-3, the mask image). You can use the key combinations to quickly move between these views. Because the subject you are isolating may be the same color as the default background color of the knockout view, you can easily select a different color from an onscreen palette.

Once the Mask Is finished

When you are happy with the selection, you can save it as a CKO file, which can only be read using Corel KnockOut. Of course, if that were all you had, you wouldn't have much. To be able to use this selection, you need to export it to either PHOTO-PAINT or (dare I say it?) Adobe Photoshop.

The Process button acts on the image according to the setting of the transition complexity setting. There are several choices available; the default setting is Med-High. Our teddy bear is hairy, but the background color is uniform (dull), as are the colors in the teddy bear. The bottom setting is Low; it is fast and good for backgrounds and subjects containing very few colors. If this setting is used on a complex image, background information will get included in the transition zone—not good. The setting of Low-Med is a good choice for the photo that appears when you first open the program, which is shown next.

Don't let all of the hair trick you into using a higher transition complexity. The background is only two basic colors, and the color of her hair is in sharp contrast to those background colors. You could almost do it with a Low setting, except for the transparency of the bubble. Speaking of transparency . . .

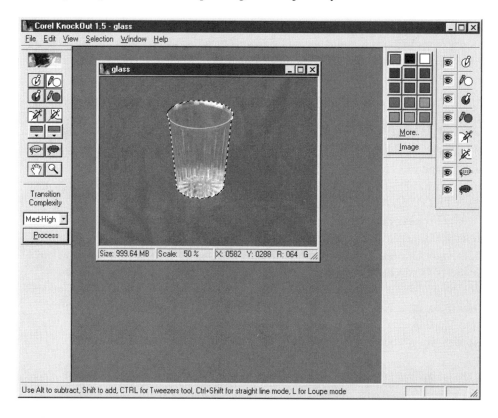

The glass just shown is tough because it (as Ultimatte was found of saying) isn't about edges, it is about transitions. The challenge is that the glass is transparent and the mask must allow that transparency to show through, requiring Med-High to sort it out. The background is textured, resulting in noise or details that must be removed.

The next image shows the glass after the original background was removed and a new one generated in PHOTO-PAINT. The High setting is reserved for subjects with many different colors or backgrounds with multiple colors.

In Summary

This is just a glimpse of what this application can do. Corel KnockOut has a separate set of tools for isolating shadows (although I like to make my own). Once you begin to use KnockOut, you'll wonder how you ever could make selections without it.

10

CHAPTER 11

Finding the Right Color

289

This chapter is a result of many e-mail messages I receive asking questions about the selection of colors in PHOTO-PAINT. I wanted to put together a short chapter on how to select, create, and save colors in PHOTO-PAINT 10. Although some of the material in this chapter is repeated throughout the book, I'd rather make sure you get the material.

The Trio of Colors—Paint, Paper, and Fill

There are three areas in PHOTO-PAINT—Paint, Paper, and Fill—for which we are always looking for "the right color." Of the three, only Fill can be something other than a solid (uniform) color. The quickest way to tell what color each area is currently set to is by checking the color swatches in the lower-right portion of the status bar, as shown in Figure 11-1. The two icons that appear to the left of the color swatches are Swap Paint/Paper Colors (left) and Reset Colors.

When you click the Reset Colors icon, the Paint and Fill colors become Black and the Paper becomes White. Not exactly exciting stuff, but a place to start.

Once you have established what colors are in these three swatches, the next question is, what do I do with them?

All of the paint tools (Paintbrush, Air Brush, and so on) apply the currently selected Paint color. The Paint color also controls the initial color of text created by the Text tool. The Paper color is used to determine the color of the background when you create a new image (unless you choose a different color in the dialog box). It also is the color used by the Eraser tool (X), which is, in truth, not an eraser but a paint brush that paints the current Paper color. The Color Replacer tool (Q) uses both the Paint and Paper colors. The Paint color determines the colors

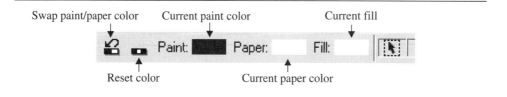

Swap paint/paper color   Current paint color   Current fill

Reset color   Current paper color

FIGURE 11-1   This part of the status bar contains a quick view of the current color settings

that are to be selected, and the Paper color is the color that replaces them. The Fill color is used by the Fill tool (obviously) and also by the Rectangle, Ellipse, and Polygon tools.

Now that we know what they are and what they are used for, the next question is, how do I change them?

Changing Colors—It's Easier Than You Think

So you want to change the Paint, Paper, or Fill colors? The quickest way is by using the onscreen color palette. I have shown a variation of it in the following illustration:

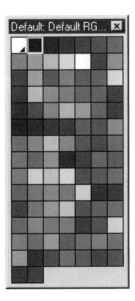

If you have used PHOTO-PAINT before, you may be saying, "Hey, the onscreen color palette is a long tall thing with the color swatches that docks against the right side of the screen." True, by default it is; but you can click and drag the top of the onscreen color palette onto the PHOTO-PAINT workspace, causing it to float. A palette is a collection of colors. PHOTO-PAINT contains both fixed palettes and custom palettes—which will be explained in greater detail later in the chapter. Unless it is changed, the default color palette is named "Default RGB" and contains 99 different colors that cover the spectrum. That's all we need to know about palettes for the moment.

Picking Colors from the Palette

The easiest way to change colors is by selecting them from a palette.

- **Paint color**   Picking a Paint color only requires placing the cursor on the desired color swatch in the onscreen palette and clicking the left mouse button. So far, so good.

- **Paper color**   Picking the Paper color is a little more complicated. Hold down the CTRL key and click the left mouse button on the desired color.

- **Fill color**   Click the right mouse button with the cursor over the desired color swatch.

Is that the only way to choose these colors? Not hardly. But for now, it's good enough; you'll learn more later.

Picking Palettes

So what happens when the color you want isn't one of the 99 colors on the default palette? Pick a different palette. Corel has provided a ton of palettes with PHOTO-PAINT 10. Okay, maybe it isn't a ton, but it's close. Earlier versions of PHOTO-PAINT could only have one palette open at a time, but now you can open all of the palettes at the same time—don't do it, I just wanted you to know you could. There are two ways to open the color palettes. Choose Window | Color Palettes and a list of fixed palettes appears, as shown next. Third-party manufacturers provide fixed color palettes. Some examples of these are HKS, Focoltone, Pantone, and TRUMATCH. It may be useful to have on hand a manufacturer's swatch book, which is a collection of color samples that shows exactly what each color looks like when printed.

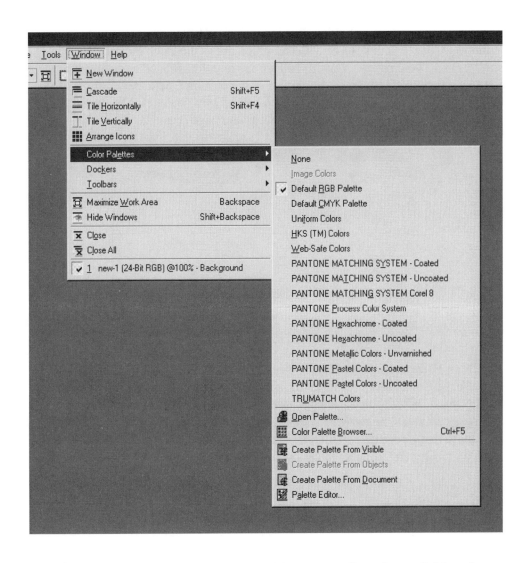

11

| TIP | *Some of the palette commands and functions will not be available unless an image is open.* |

To open the custom palettes that shipped with PHOTO-PAINT 10, choose
Window | Color Palettes | Open Palette, which opens the Open Palette dialog box
shown next. These palettes contain collections of colors related to subject matter
for which the palette is named. Examples of the custom palette names include
Autumn, Jungle, Fire, and Neon. The idea behind these palettes is to provide
users a ready-made palette of colors for original image creation.

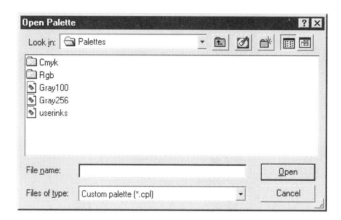

Although there are several other ways to open the color palettes, the best way
is to use the Color Palette Browser (CTRL-F5), shown in Figure 11-2. To open a
palette, you need only check the palettes that you want and they open instantly.
The nice part about the browser is that it remains open until you close it. There is
a lot more that can be done with the Color Palette Browser, which we will cover
later in this chapter. Now, let's learn about color names.

What's in a Name? A Rose by Any Other Name . . .

Many times when I write tutorials I ask readers to select a particular color. Now,
I could give them the RGB or CMYK numbers, but that is complicated and they
would probably never do the tutorial. Instead, I try to use named colors that exist

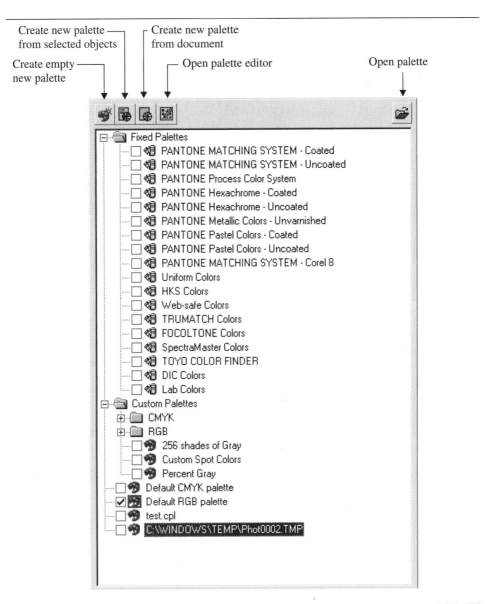

Create new palette
from selected objects

Create new palette
from document

Create empty
new palette

Open palette editor

Open palette

Fixed Palettes
- PANTONE MATCHING SYSTEM - Coated
- PANTONE MATCHING SYSTEM - Uncoated
- PANTONE Process Color System
- PANTONE Hexachrome - Coated
- PANTONE Hexachrome - Uncoated
- PANTONE Metallic Colors - Unvarnished
- PANTONE Pastel Colors - Coated
- PANTONE Pastel Colors - Uncoated
- PANTONE MATCHING SYSTEM - Corel 8
- Uniform Colors
- HKS Colors
- Web-safe Colors
- TRUMATCH Colors
- FOCOLTONE Colors
- SpectraMaster Colors
- TOYO COLOR FINDER
- DIC Colors
- Lab Colors

Custom Palettes
- CMYK
- RGB
- 256 shades of Gray
- Custom Spot Colors
- Percent Gray

Default CMYK palette
Default RGB palette
test.cpl
C:\WINDOWS\TEMP\Phot0002.TMP

11

FIGURE 11-2   The Color Palette Browser provides a fast and easy way to work with
color palettes

in the Default RGB palette. To find 80% Black, for example, place your cursor over the swatch of a likely candidate and wait a moment. The name of the color appears, as shown next.

Another way to find a color by name is to use the Find Color feature, which is hidden in the Palette dialog box. Click the icon at the top of the palette, choose Edit and Find Color, as shown next. When the Find Color dialog box appears, type in the name, click OK, and the color becomes selected. The names that can be searched are limited to the names in the currently selected palette. If you are not sure of the available names, you can click the down arrow in the Find Color by Name dialog box and a drop-down list of the available colors appears.

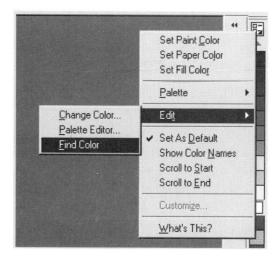

Getting the Right Color with the Eyedropper Tool

The chances of locating the exact shade of color you need for retouching a photograph from the onscreen palette are close to impossible, but you can do it with the Eyedropper tool.

The Eyedropper tool (E), located in the Toolbox, is used to pick a specific color from an image by clicking it. This tool has more uses than might first be apparent. Let's go through the basics of how to use the Eyedropper.

Eyedropper Tool Hot Key

To quickly select the Eyedropper tool, press the E key on your keyboard. This enables the Eyedropper tool. To return to the previously selected tool, click the SPACEBAR.

> **TIP**   *The E key shortcut is a quick way to get a numerical color value for a spot or area. This information can be very helpful when setting Color Tolerance values.*

11

Eyedropper Sample Size

The property bar is used to set the sample size of the Eyedropper tool. By default, the Eyedropper tool samples an area one pixel wide to determine a color value. Sometimes when selecting colors for the Color Replacer tool or retouching photographs, you want an average color from an area. This is why PHOTO-PAINT gives you the ability to select different sample sizes. If you want to select a specific color, you can click the last button, which opens up the Color docker window.

To change the sample size, click an alternate sample size on the property bar. The property bar, shown next, has a Selection setting, as well as three preset sample sizes:

- ■ **1 × 1 Area (1 pixel)**   Default setting
- ■ **3 × 3 Area (9 pixels)**

- **5 × 5 Area (25 pixels)**

- **Selection**   Enables you to click and drag the Eyedropper tool to define any size sample area

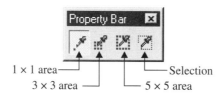

1 × 1 area ────   ──── Selection
3 × 3 area ────   ──── 5 × 5 area

With a click on a color, you can find the color value of the sampled color, which is very handy for retouching. With every sample size (except 1 × 1), the color selected when the mouse button is clicked represents the average of all the colors in the sample area. Obviously, with the 1 × 1 setting, it represents the color value of the single pixel underneath the cursor. When sampling areas of high contrast, be aware that the averaged color may be quite different than any individual color in the sampled area. The settings made in the property bar only affect the Eyedropper tool; they have no effect on other tools that may use an Eyedropper to define colors, such as the Color Mask tool.

Notes on Using the Eyedropper Tool

If there are multiple objects on the image, the Eyedropper tool can only read the colors on the top object, whether or not the object is active or selected. A good rule of thumb is that if you can't see it, the Eyedropper can't see it either.

When a large area is sampled and averaged, the result may be a color that, while representing the average color in the image, may not actually exist in the image. An example of this would be an area that had the same number of white and red pixels. The resulting color would be pink, even though there was no pink in the image.

Use the Eyedropper hot key (E) when you want to see what the color value(s) are for a part of the image to help set a tool's Color Similarity values. An example of using this is when determining where a Magic Wand mask in an image is to be created. I use the E hot key to see what the color value is of the starting area (where I click to start the mask).

TIP | *Use the E hot key when retouching images. It provides a fast and easy way to pick up adjoining colors, which is critical when touching up an imperfection on a picture.*

Yeah, but what if you want a lot of colors from an image? Well, Corel has included a tool that will extract all of the colors in an image into a new or existing palette. The buttons at the top of the Color Palette Browser shown in earlier Figure 11-2 can be selected to create a new palette of colors from either objects in an image or the entire image. The palette created by this tool is actually a color table that contains 256 colors. This means that PHOTO-PAINT reduces all of the colors in the image to 256 colors that are representative of the colors in the image. What if you need a color that doesn't exist in an existing image or in one of the color palettes? Then you will need to open the Paint Color dialog box.

Selecting a Paint Color

If the color you want is not available in the onscreen palette, then double-click the Paint color swatch. This action opens the Paint Color dialog box, as shown in Figure 11-3. From this dialog box, you can just about do anything that you can think of in regard to solid color.

TIP | *The only difference between the Uniform Fill dialog box and the Paint Color dialog box, besides the name, is that Uniform Fill controls the Fill color, and the Paint Color dialog box obviously controls Paint color.*

11

The Paint Color Dialog Box

The Paint Color dialog box is where you can literally pick any color in the universe. Although the appearance of this dialog box can intimidate the faint of heart, the Paint Color dialog box allows you to create colors using different color models and even mixing colors.

Pick Your Own Color Models Selection

The Paint Color dialog box has three modes of operation controlled by three tabs—Models, Mixers, and Palettes. When the dialog box first opens, the default mode is Models. It's called Models mode because you choose one of nine color

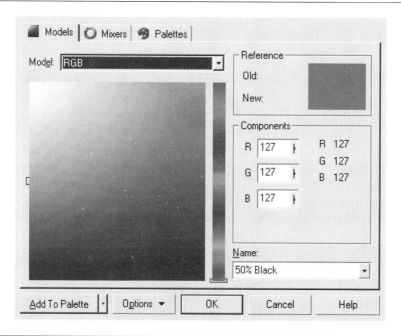

FIGURE 11-3   The Paint Color dialog box

models to view the color spectrum. The theory behind using different color models when selecting colors is that different types of color work require different models to display the color. For example, if you are color-correcting a photograph that has already been converted to CMYK for printing using the four-color printing process (CMYK), you should choose the CMYK or CMY color model.

> **TIP**   *Even if the image is to be a CMYK image, you should work on it in RGB mode, converting it to CMYK and performing final color correction as needed as your last step.*

The default color model of PHOTO-PAINT is RGB; and while you can select one of eight other color models by clicking the down arrow, I recommend keeping RGB selected for most applications unless you have a specific reason for using a different model.

Color Models

A color model is a method for representing colors, usually by their components, such as RGB or HSB. The Model pop-up list contains nine color models. As you change color models, the numerical value system on the right and the color model displayed below the model name change.

Color Model Options

- **CMY** This color model contains only cyan, magenta, and yellow. You should only select this if the final output will be done on a CMY device, such as a three-ink printer. The C, M, and Y values range between 0 and 255.

- **CMYK** This shows the CMYK model and lists value boxes for each of the components in percentages. Cyan, magenta, yellow, and black (CMYK) is the model used for the four-color printing process. *A note about CMYK:* When this model is selected, there may be some display irregularities if you are using blended colors. When blended colors are displayed on the monitor, they show up as banding. The printed output itself is unaffected, but the display may be banded.

- **RGB** This is the standard of monitor color models. All computer displays are RGB (red, green, and blue)—the same as your eyes. The RGB model is the default color model of Corel PHOTO-PAINT. This is the ground zero of all color models.

- **HSB** The popularity of HSB isn't what it used to be, although components of this model are still used when working with the filters. Hue, saturation, and brightness (HSB) is an alternative to the RGB model.

- **HLS** HLS (hue, lightness, saturation) is a variation on HSB and an alternative to RGB. Hue determines color (yellow, orange, red, and so on), lightness determines perceived intensity (lighter or darker color), and saturation determines color depth (from dull to intense). The visual selector defines the H value (0 to 360), the L value (0 to 100), and the S value (0 to 100).

- **Lab** This color model is becoming more and more popular. It was developed by Commission Internationale de l'Eclairage (CIE) based on three parameters: lightness (L*), green-to-red chromaticity (a*), and

11

blue-to-yellow chromaticity (b*). The rectangular two-dimensional visual selector defines the a* and b* coordinates from –60 to 60, and the L* value from 0 to 100. This model is device independent, meaning that it does not need to have information about the devices it is working with to operate correctly. For the prepress industry, it encompasses the color gamuts of both the CMYK and the RGB color models.

■ **YIQ**   The preferred model when working with video is YIQ, which is used in television broadcast systems (North American video standard: NTSC). Colors are split into a luminance value (Y) and two chromaticity values (I and Q). On a color monitor, all three components are visible; on a monochrome monitor, only the Y component is visible. All values are scaled from 0 to 255. In Corel PHOTO-PAINT, the Y component of the splitting process produces a grayscale image that is often superior to results obtained with a grayscale conversion using the Convert To command from the Image menu.

■ **Grayscale**   This is your basic plain-vanilla, 256-shades-of-gray color model. No, that's not a typo—gray is a color. The visual selector contains 255 levels of grayscale, with 255 being the lightest and 0 the darkest.

■ **Registration color**   The Registration color model consists of a single color in the CMYK color space, for which C, M, Y, and K are at 100 percent. You can use this color on any object that you want to appear on all separation plates. It is ideal for company logos, job numbers, or any other identifying marks that you may need for the job. This color cannot be added to the custom palette.

> **TIP**   *If the project you are working on is not going to an offset printer, select the RGB or Grayscale color model.*

How to Select or Create a Color Using Color Models Mode

As complicated as all of the buttons and graphs appear, the simplest way to select the color is to use the following general procedure:

1. The first step is to remember what color it was that you were working on to begin with. It is found in the upper-right corner in the Reference area and is labeled Old. This is the Paint color originally selected from the onscreen palette or in the Paint Color dialog box.

2. Select a color model. This step is easy: use RGB unless you have good reason to use another model.

3. If the only change you want is to make the Reference color darker or lighter, click and drag the small square in the color model display, moving it to make the selected color darker or lighter. The color of the area under the square is shown in the New box under the Old box in the upper-right corner of the dialog box.

4. If you want a completely different color, you can click any color that appears in the color model display area. To change the range of colors that appear in the display area, click a color on the rainbow-colored vertical spectrum on the right side of the color display area. For example, if you want a deep blue, you would first click on the shade of blue that was closest to the one you want on the vertical spectrum, and then pick the desired color in the color model display by clicking it. You can adjust the shade of the color in the color model display area by moving the vertical slider up and down the scale.

5. When the New Color is the desired color, update your Paint color by clicking OK.

Colors by the Numbers

Many times, the easiest way to specify a color is to define its RGB or CMYK values. For example, entering the values of 102, 153, 51 in the Components section of the dialog box produces a named color in the Default RGB palette: Avocado Green, which appears in the Name section. If the component values don't exactly match a named color on the palette you are using, the Name section remains blank.

Name That Color

The least used situation for selecting a color in the Models tab will be where you actually know the name of the color on the selected palette. Let's face it, being from Texas, I know my avocados, and I would have never thought of that color as being Avocado Green. When you begin to enter the name, a drop-down list appears with all of the names beginning with the first letter. Back to our Default RGB palette, entering the letter **A** produces Army Green. Before we move to the Mixers tab, let's talk about a few other doodads in this dialog box.

Checking Out the Options Button

When you open the Options button in the dialog box, you confront some options whose purpose is not obvious.

- ■ **Value 2**   This option allows you to select the color value displayed to the right of the Component value of the selected color. This feature is a handy way to see RGB values when looking at CMYK colors, or vice versa. From the list, you can select one of four component value displays: RGB, CMYK, HSB, and Lab.

- ■ **Swap Colors**   This option is a toggle. Each time you click it, the Old and the New Color values are swapped in the Reference part of the dialog box.

- ■ **Gamut Alarm**   When selected, the color preview area has all of the colors that are out of gamut covered with a bright (ugly) green, as shown next.

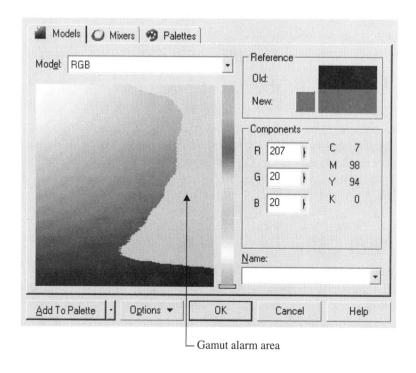

Gamut alarm area

- **Color Viewers** Allows you to choose which viewer to use to view the selected color model. The default viewer is HSB—Hue based. Unless you have serious reasons to change it, leave it alone.

That was the easy part. Let's take a brief look at the Mixers tab.

Saving a New Color to a Palette

Now that you have created that special color you wanted, you may want to save it. Colors are saved on palettes, which, like the original artist's palette, are files that store colors. Palette files have a .CPL extension. Clicking the little arrow on the right side of the Add to Palette button displays the list of palettes that are currently open. As you can see in the next image, I had four palettes open. Again referring to the dialog box shown next, if the Add to Palette button were clicked, the new color would be added to the bottom of the Shades of Spring palette.

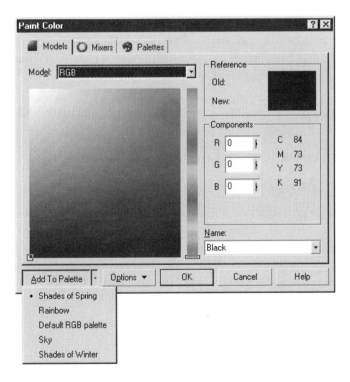

The Default RGB PHOTO-PAINT palette is named Corelpnt.cpl. The palettes discussed in this chapter can contain an almost limitless number of colors. You can use a special palette to keep all of the colors used in a particular project or painting. Some people like to keep a palette that contains all of their favorite colors. The choice is yours. Here is how to save a color you have created:

1. After you are satisfied with the new color, enter in a name for the new color in the Name box. Naming colors is not necessary, but it is recommended.

2. Click the Add to Palette button and the new color will be added to the end of the current palette.

If you accidentally add a color to a palette, you cannot remove it from the palette with this dialog box; you must use the Palette Editor.

When creating new colors, especially for company logos, be sure to give the new color a unique name. This can be critical when the job needs to be modified and you are trying to guess which color that you used out of a possible ten billion combinations.

Now that you have learned how to pick colors using Models mode, let's next learn how to use the Mixers mode to blend and mix colors together.

The Mixers Mode

The Mixers mode provides two unique mixers for selecting colors, Color Blend and Color Harmonies, which are selected through the Options button. The Mixers mode tab reveals a slightly different version of the Models mode we just left. The Model, Reference, Components, and Name sections of the dialog box remain the same as they did in the Models tab. What has changed is the part that replaced the color preview section: Color Harmonies and Color Blend. The one that appears first when you open the Mixers tab is Color Harmonies, as shown next.

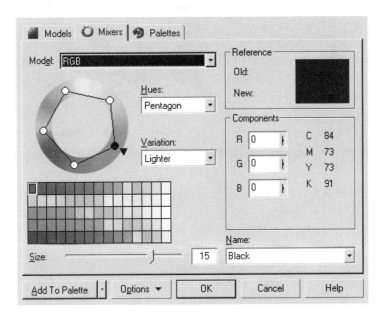

Color Harmonies

Color harmonies are most useful when you're selecting several colors for a project. By using color harmonies, you are guaranteed that the colors you choose look good together. Color harmonies work by superimposing a shape, such as a rectangle or a triangle, over a color wheel. You can also manipulate the superimposed shape (the rectangle, triangle, or pentagon). Now, these shapes appear to be leftovers from that geometry class you slept through in high school, but they actually serve a purpose. In Figure 11-4, we see the options available in the Hues section of the Color Harmonies mixer. As you move the black spot on the shape around the wheel, the colors displayed below the color wheel change.

While this looks really complicated, it's not. The colors at each corner are always complementary, contrasting, or harmonious, depending on the shape you select. As an example, the option selected in Figure 11-4 is Complement. This means the color selections that appear below the color wheel are the color under the black spot and its complement. The color selections that appear are controlled by the Variation tab, as shown in Figure 11-5. Between the Hues and the Variation settings, you can create a great assortment of colors that complement any project you are doing.

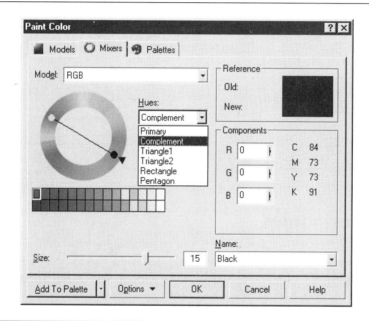

FIGURE 11-4 The Color Harmonies mixer provides several different options for creating different selections of color harmonies using its color wheel

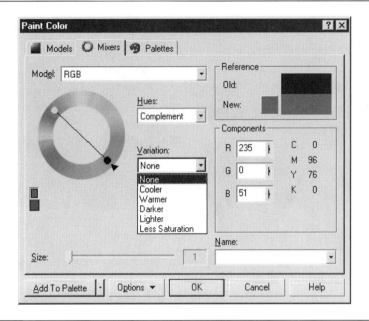

FIGURE 11-5 A number of variations are available to increase the number and type of colors created by the Color Harmonies mixer

Now that you have learned to harmonize your colors, let's blend them and see what happens.

11

Color Blend

The other mixer in the Options drop-down list, Color Blend, shown next, allows you to pick up to four different colors, and PHOTO-PAINT automatically generates all of the intermediate colors. It is from these intermediate colors that you can pick the color you want. Use the Color Blender to create a four-way blend of color and choose from the range of color variations. The grid ranges in size from 3 × 3 to 32 × 32, with smaller numbers producing larger grids having more distinct color squares; and larger settings producing tiny grids, and thereby almost continuous color variations.

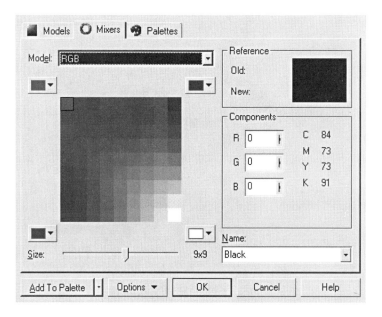

The operation Color Blend is relatively simple. Choose the basic colors that you want to use on a project from each of the four corners of the display box, as shown. What if you have only two or three colors instead of four? Either duplicate the dominate color or use white or black for the missing color.

Palettes Mode

The Palettes tab of the Paint Color dialog box, shown next, offers a collection of different color-matching-system palettes available to the Corel PHOTO-PAINT user. The number of colors or shades available in each palette is dependent on the color mode of the image. The different palettes are provided when you have projects that work with Spot or color process systems like Pantone, Toyo, and TRUMATCH. The palettes contain industry-standard colors that are essential for color-matching accuracy when the project is to be output to offset printing.

The tools in PHOTO-PAINT that allow the creation of photo-realistic images shown below are some of my favorite features.

Using a combination of PHOTO-PAINT masks and filter allows you to make cookies that appear real.

Creative use of drop shadows in a cookie-cutter fashion creates the illusion of a number shape cut out of a brass plate.

This image was a monthly winner in the 2000 Corel World Design contest. Using the same technique used to make the cutout brass plate shown above, it is possible to create the illusion of 3D characters sitting on a sheet of music.

Using a combination of masks and image sprayer gives PHOTO-PAINT users the ability to create photo-realistic weathered and corroded text.

In this book you will learn how to make text look corroded like the text of "Titanic."

Using the Image Sprayer brush, it is possible to create the illusion of rivets in metal.

Using the noise filter to create the rust and the Image Sprayer brush to create the rivets, it is possible to create this authenticate Texas barbeque.

Using both the Image Sprayer tool and Corel PHOTO-PAINT's wide selection of natural media brushes, it is possible to create a variety of graphic images from scratch.

The clouds and the grasses in the foreground were created using the Image Sprayer tool over a gradient fill. Adding a bitmap fill created this water image using several of PHOTO-PAINT's Artistic filters.

The ability to apply different image modes to the clouds was used to create the effect of moonlit clouds for this StarCore™ ad I created for Motorola.

The Image Sprayer tool was used to create everything but the floating balls. The balls are objects created at various sizes to give the illusion of vanishing into the distance.

Until now we have been showing images created from scratch. On this page and the next are photographs that have been made into art using PHOTO-PAINT's filters and object modes.

By using PHOTO-PAINT's merge modes and Edge Detect filter, it is possible to convert the photo into an impressionist image, as shown below.

Making an object of a copy of the image and applying the Edge Detect filter causes the photo to look like a pen and ink watercolor when different merge modes are applied, as shown below.

This page contains photo compositions that were created from combining all or parts of existing photographs to create the final result.

This grand prize winner in the 1997 Corel World Design Contest was created from eight different photographs that were imported as objects. Use of object transparency allowed the gradual blending between the objects.

This photograph of a swan wasn't very interesting until I removed it from the photo and placed it in another. Application of object transformations allowed the other duplicate swans to appear to be different birds.

Another common use of mixing different photographs together is replacing backgrounds.

This photograph of a magnificent monument appears drab and lifeless, which is easily corrected using Corel PHOTO-PAINT 10.

In the new composite image the empty sky was replaced with a photograph of the Austrian Alps, the trees and their reflections were removed, and the reflection of the Alps now appears in the reflecting pool. Oops! In the background the light is coming from the left side of the picture and in the foreground it is coming from the right side.

Sometimes it only takes a small amount of a real photograph to make images created with PHOTO-PAINT appear more realistic. The top two images on this page are examples of created images mixed with real photographs.

Most of the objects in this image were created using color bitmap fills. The glass ball was created using the Sphere filter, and the winter scene outside the window was from a photograph.

The Christmas ornaments were created using fountain fills; the addition of some holly that I scanned in makes the entire image look more realistic—as long as you don't look too close.

I began with a photograph of an owl and made two copies (each of which I made into a sphere). The original had the Zoom blur applied to it and served as a background.

Some of the most interesting effects are the subtle transformations possible using the Mesh Warp and the SQUIZZ filters. So, which one of the images is the original model? If you guessed the lower-left I am a little concerned about you. However, if you chose the upper-right you were correct.

Here is a stock photograph of a professional model. Sometimes it is just fun to make changes to these nearly perfectly proportioned people.

Using the SQUIZZ filter, I was able to make him look like he had given up being a male model and tried professional beer tasting instead.

After plumping him up, it was only fair to pump him up.

The power of the Image Sprayer tool is demonstrated in the images shown on this page.

The clouds and trees of this fictitious place were all painted into the scene using the Image Sprayer brush. The water was made using a bitmap fill, which is explored in Chapter 9. The text was made using a bitmap fill and applying the Plastic filter to it.

The anchor chains in this image were applied using the Image Sprayer brush; the background is a bitmap fill.

This wreath was created by applying the Image Sprayer tool to a circular mask using the Stroke to Mask feature.

PHOTO-PAINT 10 offers many tools for correcting and enhancing photographs. Some examples of this digital wizardry are shown below.

I was a little disappointed in the results obtained using my digital camera at the wedding of a close friend. In Chapter 5 you learn how to remove the color from all but the subject to draw attention to the subject and away from the fact that it was a grainy digital photograph.

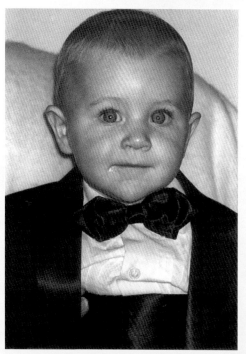 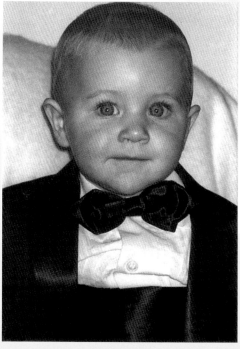

The photo of Dakota developed a light blue color cast when it was enlarged. In chapter 8 you learn how to remove the cast and also how to use the clone brush to remove the drool from his face and the fingertips of the hand supporting him.

Looking like a return to sixties, the butterflies shown are the final result of a workshop in Chapter 12 teaching you how to make custom brush nibs.

Using the Plastic filter, it is possible to create a star from one of the Wingbat fonts and then use the Tile filter to create a suitable background.

In Chapter 16 you will learn how to do selective color replacement, which you can use to change some of the colors in the lamp shown on the left to the (better) colors shown on the right.

In Chapter 8 we cover the correction of this image in some detail. As you can see, the dogs have a faint color cast.

After correcting the color cast, the Vignette filter was used to emphasize the dogs as the subject of the photograph.

The text was placed on top of the stone bitmap fill that ships with PHOTO-PAINT 10. The Zig Zag filter produced the ripples and the airbrush tool was applied to simulate the shading of an underwater object.

Filter Fun. This page contains images that have been fancifully modified or distorted with a few of the many filters in Corel PHOTO-PAINT 10.

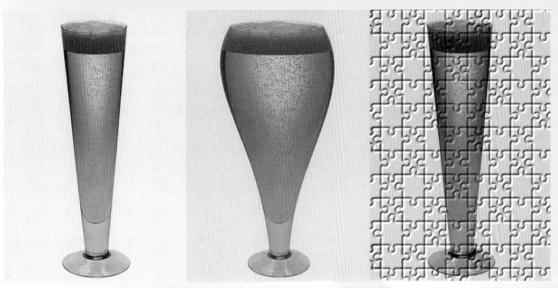

The enlarged beer in the middle was created using the Mesh Warp filter. The Puzzle beer at the right was created with the Bumpmap filter using the jigsaw preset.

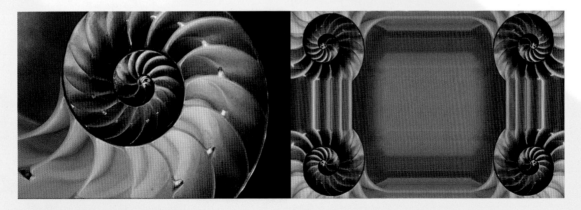

This photograph of a nautilus shell becomes a great background after application of the Offset filter and then dividing it into four equal parts using the tile filter.

The secret to this image is in the use of fountain fills. The word "CHEVY" was simple text to which the Emboss filter was applied. The background is a single fountain fill. The key to the effect of depth is created by placing darker colors close to brighter colors, which gives the appearance of an edge or rounded corner.

Each wire is created by making a narrow vertical rectangle with a fountain fill. Actually, it was only necessary to make one (rendered as an object) and then apply a hue shift to the duplicates to create different colors.

The background fill in the CHEVY image is used to create the center portion of the art for a magazine cover. The effects on the cars were created by cloning another photograph onto the cover. It was possible to keep the brush strokes of the clone brush straight by using the Constrain key.

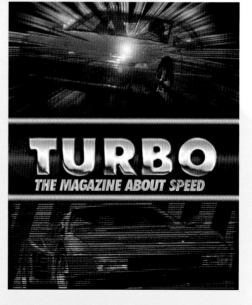

NOTE   *The Tint slider is only available when using the Fixed palettes.*

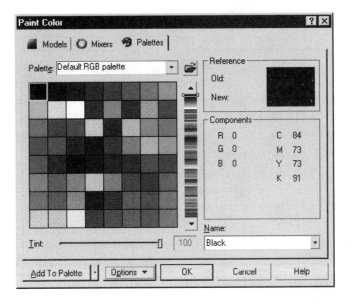

NOTE   *When using the Pantone color-matching system in Palettes mode, be aware that the colors cannot be changed. Only the percentage of Tint can be modified. This is because the ability of a system like Pantone to match the colors printed on the swatch (which you must buy from them) is based on the combination of inks that make up the color and do not change.*

11

Viewing Palette Selections by Name

Click the Options button and you will immediately notice some of the selections have changed. Most are self-explanatory; the ones that follow are not. Selecting Show Color Names will cause the currently selected palette to change to an alphabetical listing of all of the color names for the color system selected, as shown next. Each name is displayed on a color rectangle displaying a sample of the named color. Regarding the displayed colors, please remember that what you see is only a good approximation of what that actual color looks like, even when you are using a very expensive monitor and graphics card and even when you have done all of the calibration voodoo. When using color samples from a color-matching system, always trust the swatches provided by the manufacturer over the screen.

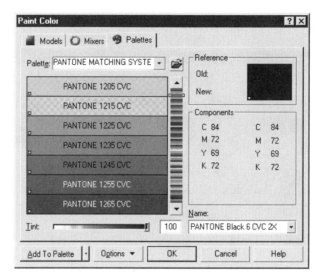

Clicking PostScript Options, which is available with the Fixed palettes, will open a dialog box in which you can modify the Halftone screen. The dialog box that appears is shown next.

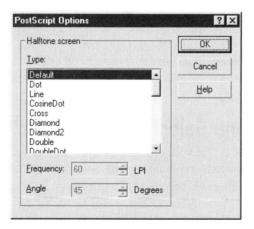

In Summary

Well, are you still awake? As complicated as this might appear, it was really basic in what it covered. The truth is, color is a complex science; and when we as humans declare that we understand it, we are only kidding ourselves. Whether we actually understand it or not, I hope you learned enough to find the color you want, when you want it.

Exploring Corel PHOTO-PAINT's Brush Tools

Corel PHOTO-PAINT provides several types of brush tools, which provide a rich assortment of tools and effects. The brush tools are divided into four different sets, which appear in the Brush Tools toolbar shown next.

Paint tools ——————→ 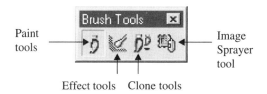 ←—————— Image Sprayer tool

Effect tools   Clone tools

The four different sets of tools are

- **Paint tools**   These tools are the "natural media" tools that act like paintbrushes, airbrushes, pens, and so on.

- **Effect tools**   These tools are used primarily for photo editing and retouching. They allow local application of sharpening, blurring, saturation, and contrast, just to name a few.

- **Clone tools**   These tools apply pixels copied from a different part of an image or even a different image.

- **Image Sprayer tool**   This tool paints multiple copies of bitmap images that are stored on an image sprayer list.

More Tools, Same Controls

In addition to the brush tools, there are other tools that share the same brush setting controls. They are the Local Undo, Mask Brush, and Object Transparency tools. In this chapter, we will explore the Paint and Effect tools and their variations, some of which you have already seen in other chapters. While the purpose of each tool differs, all of the tools can be customized using the property bars and Brush Settings docker. Before discussing individual types of brushes, we will look first at the common features.

The brush tools paint an area with pixels that represent the type of brush selected. For example, the Paint tools' brushes replace (not cover) pixels with the currently selected Paint (foreground) color in a pattern that mimics an airbrush, while the Mask Brush tool replaces pixels on an image's mask to modify a selection.

Selecting and Configuring Brush Tools

The hierarchy of brush tools is daunting. Each of the four sets of brush tools
(except Image Sprayer) contains groups of tools. For example, there are 15
different groups of Paint tools, which include airbrush, felt pen, art brush, and
so on. Selection of an individual group is accomplished by clicking its icon button
from the property bar, examples of which are shown next. Once you have selected
a tool, you're still not finished, because you can choose one of many preset
variations of the tool from the Brush Type list on the property bar. That's just
the preset brushes; you can also vary the effect of any tool by changing its mode
on the property bar or modifying one of the many settings from the Brush
Settings docker (CTRL-F8).

TIP	*Many, but not all, of the settings in the Brush Settings docker are duplicated in the property bar.*

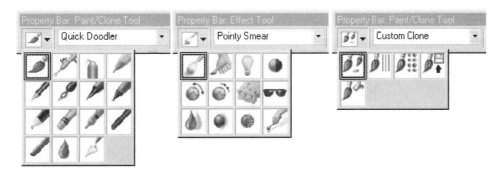

Quick Start Brushes—the Artistic Media Docker

The Corel PHOTO-PAINT developers knew that some users want a quick way to
visually select Paint tools or Image Sprayer lists, depending on what the resulting
brush stroke looks like, so, back in PHOTO-PAINT 9, they introduced the Artistic
Media docker (CTRL-F10), shown next. It provides a quick way to view and select
a paint tool by what its brush stroke looks like. A nice feature of the Artistic Media
docker when it is not docked along the side is the appearance of the icons on the
left side of the docker indicating which paint tool makes that brush stroke. Also
at the top of the docker is a visual list called Last Used tool. This is a very handy
way to let you jump around among several frequently used brush tool settings.
Previous versions didn't let you add your own brushes to this docker, but now

12

you can even display all of your own custom brushes. This leads us to the next subject: how to make your own brush tools.

Constraining and Automating the Brush Tools

Before you learn how to make the brushes, it is important to know a few barely documented features built into Corel PHOTO-PAINT to make using the brush tools more manageable. With a steady hand, it is theoretically possible to maintain a straight line with a brush tool, but it is very difficult. Fortunately, Corel provides some features that allow you to create straight lines with any of the brush tools:

- **Making a straight line**   Use the CTRL key to constrain a brush tool to a vertical or horizontal direction.

- **Changing stroke direction**   Pressing the SHIFT key changes the direction of constraint.

- **Automatic brush strokes**   You can automatically apply any brush tool along a straight line between two points by clicking the brush at

the beginning of a line, holding down the ALT key, and clicking at the end
of the line. The brush stroke is applied between the two points automatically.

Brush Nibs—Everything Else Is Details

Each brush tool is composed of a combination of up to 30 different settings.
Scary, right? That said, the most important part of the brush tool is the *nib*,
which is simply the tip of the brush. The size and shape of its nib determine
the size and shape of the brush stroke. So, once you know how to select a nib
and control its size and shape, you're about 90 percent done.

Corel has included almost 100 nibs in different shapes and sizes, a few examples
of which are shown Figure 12-1. You will notice that some of the screen shots include
numbers. These numbers are guaranteed lottery winners—eventually. Actually, each
number represents the size of the nib in pixels. The reason only some of the nibs have
numbers is that PHOTO-PAINT automatically inserts the pixel size for nibs whose
actual size is greater than the size of the display.

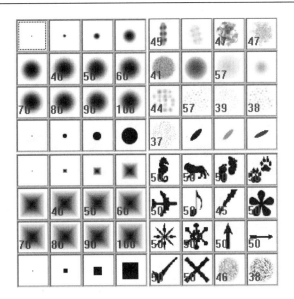

FIGURE 12-1   PHOTO-PAINT provides an extensive collection of brush nibs in many
shapes and sizes

Brush nibs can be viewed and selected from several different locations. Clicking the Nib Shape button on the property bar or the Brush Settings docker window shown in Figure 12-2 opens the nib display. The number of nibs displayed is fixed at 16. You can access any of the nibs by using the scroll bars on the nib display. To select a nib, just click its thumbnail.

The Brush Settings Docker

Each brush tool can be modified from either the property bar or the Brush Settings docker. There are a few settings that can only be changed in the property bar, for example, the Amount setting for the Airbrush tool. While you can make general changes to a brush tool that are most commonly applied using the property bar (like nib size, transparency, or soft edge), you need the Brush Settings docker to change the settings that control the "natural media" appearance of the brush tool. An example would be loading the bitmap file that produces a brush's texture.

The Brush Settings docker window, shown next, is opened several ways. You can select Dockers in the Window menu and choose Brush Settings, or you may press CTRL-F8 or double-click one of the brush tool buttons. If this is the first time you have opened the Brush Settings docker, shown next, you may be a little

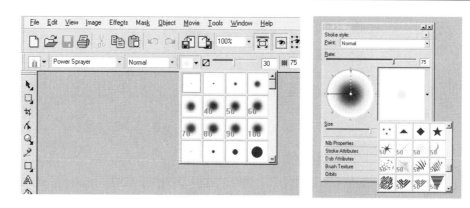

FIGURE 12-2   Brush nibs can be displayed and selected from either the property bar (left) or the Brush Settings docker (right)

intimidated. Don't let the number of settings overwhelm you. All of the settings have been neatly divided into seven groups. Each of the settings is described in some detail later in this chapter.

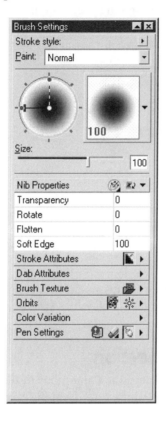

The Brush Settings docker contains over 100 different settings and adjustments. It is not the purpose of this book to either replace the user's manual/online help or put you to sleep. In this chapter, our goal is to learn about the most commonly used features and explain how to use them.

A Quick Tour of the Brush Settings Docker

The Brush Settings docker is divided into three general areas. The top is the Stroke Style section, from which you can control the Paint mode and manage the brush

12

tools. Below this section are the nib controls. From this part of the docker, you can interactively modify the shape of the nib using the Size slider and, using the interactive area on the left, control the shape by clicking and dragging the Flatten and Rotate handles. The resulting nib appears in the multipurpose preview on the right side of this section. Clicking the nib preview window opens a gallery of nibs. Below this interactive preview area are seven roll-ups that control the following brush attributes:

- Nib Properties
- Stroke Properties
- Dab Attributes
- Brush Texture
- Orbits
- Color Variation
- Pen Settings

Some of the names of the roll-ups sound strange, but we'll talk about each one as we get to it. That said, let's look at the Stroke Style section.

The Stroke Style Section

From this section you can change the Paint mode of the brush stroke and manage brushes. You can also select Paint modes from the property bar. The Paint mode setting determines the way the paint pixels are applied to an image. Be aware that Paint modes are called Merge modes when referring to how pixels in objects appear when applied to an image or another object. It is the same feature, with the same selections; they just call it a different name in the Objects docker. When you open the list, shown next, you are presented with a large number of different mode names that are a little confusing.

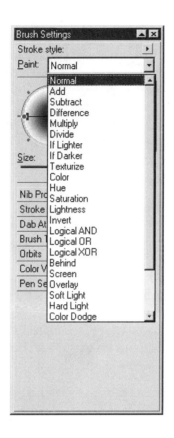

Paint Mode—A Primer

In Normal mode, a brush pixel replaces the pixel in the image to which it is applied. Simple, right? Change the Paint mode to Add, and PHOTO-PAINT takes the color value of the brush pixel and adds it to the color or brightness value of the existing pixel on the image, making a new color that is different from that of the brush or the original pixel. In this example, the two values being added together produce a brighter brush stroke than would have otherwise occurred. The rest of the Paint modes all do some kind of mathematical gymnastics or another to the pixels as they are applied. So, how do you figure out which Paint mode works best? The answer is, you don't figure it out. The key to using either Paint modes or Merge modes is experimentation. Corel has provided a nice explanation, with visuals, of how each of the different modes operates. It is located in the online help and can be found in the index under "Merge Modes." One last note before we leave this subject: the last modes at the bottom of the list represent the color model with which you are working, which means that they will be different for CMYK, and not there if any color model other than RGB or CMYK is used.

Managing Brush Tools

In the far-right corner of the Stroke Style section is a tiny arrow button that opens a pop-up box, shown next, from which you can save and delete brushes, as well as reset either an individual brush or all of the brushes. Clicking the Save Brush button opens the Save Brush dialog box. Entering a name and clicking the OK button saves all of the current brush's settings in the Type list for the currently selected tool. The newly named custom brush will only appear in the Type: box for the tool under which it was saved. For example, I created a brush I use a lot called Foam. I made it by modifying an existing art brush, so Foam only appears when I open the Type list for the art brush.

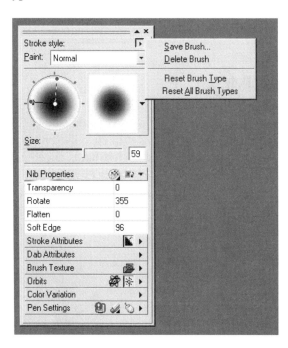

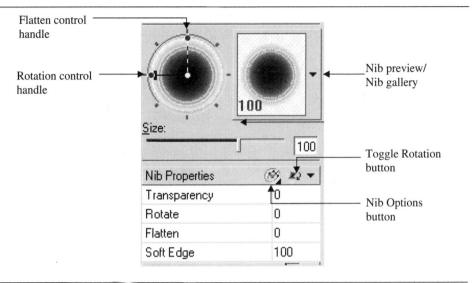

Flatten control handle

Rotation control handle

Nib preview/ Nib gallery

Toggle Rotation button

Nib Options button

FIGURE 12-3 The Nib Properties area of the Brush Settings docker provides control of the basic nib properties

Nib Properties Control and Selection

This section shares many settings of the Nib Properties roll-up. Figure 12-3 shows the Nib Properties Control/Preview section with the Nib Properties roll-up directly below it open.

Nib Size

The size of the nib is controlled either interactively or by using the slider, either on the Brush docker or the property bar. I recommend using the interactive method for size control of the brush's nib, holding down the SHIFT key and dragging the brush either up or down on the image. Nib sizes range from 1 to 999 pixels.

> **TIP** *You can adjust the nib size interactively on the image by holding down the SHIFT key and dragging the brush up or down.*

Transparency

The Transparency setting (range 0–99) sets the level of transparency of the brush stroke. The higher the setting, the more transparent the brush stroke. At a high setting, the color acts like a tint. A setting of 0 has no transparency, whereas a

12

setting of 99 makes the brush stroke almost invisible regardless of any other settings. The availability of the Transparency setting in the property bar is dependent upon the tool selected.

Rotation and Flatten

Rotation and Flatten attributes determine the shape of the nib. Although they can be controlled through numeric value settings, I recommend creating the shape interactively using the rotation and flatten handles shown in Figure 12-3. As you make changes to the nib properties, the preview of the nib shape appears in the Nib preview/gallery area.

Soft Edge

This determines the amount of transparency at the edges of the nib. Large settings produce soft edges, creating brush strokes that have soft edges and blend well. This is a desired setting when doing photo-retouching. Low settings produce hard edges that are dense up to the edge, with little to no softening, depending on the nib size and other brush settings. The preview box displays the softness of the nib selected.

Nib Options Button

The Nib Options button opens another pop-up menu, shown next, containing a selection of commands to manage nibs. From here you can load, save, delete, and create nibs. Later in this chapter, we will return to this pop-up menu when you learn how to create a custom nib.

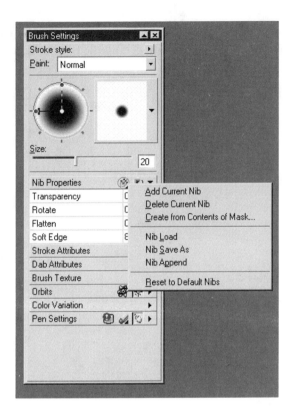

Toggle Nib Rotation

To the right of the Nib Options button is the Toggle Nib Rotation button. This is
a new feature in PHOTO-PAINT 10. When enabled, it causes the nib to be rotated

as the brush is applied to the image, as shown next. The top row was made with successive clicks with Nib Rotation enabled, and the bottom without.

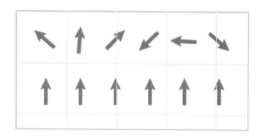

NOTE   *Nib Rotation does not operate with Stroke or Mask.*

Stroke Attributes

The second roll-up, shown next, is Stroke Attributes, which provides antialiasing, smoothing, and fade to give the brush stroke the appearance that it was produced by a brush.

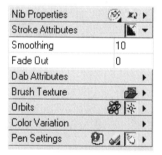

Anti-Aliasing and Smoothing

The Antialiasing button smoothes the edge of the stroke, giving it a smoother appearance. The Smoothing function attempts to smooth out the variations in a line. While this is important when attempting to draw with a mouse, it is less important when using a pressure-sensitive pen. The only negative side to a high smoothness setting is if you move your tool quickly, the display will lag behind and sharp changes in a line will be smoothed out.

Fading Away

As shown Figure 12-4, Fade Out controls the transparency of a brush stroke as it progresses—meaning with a higher setting, the stroke fades out more quickly. The range of this attribute is –100 to 100. Once you understand how it works, you will see that these numbers are very close to being meaningless. When you begin a brush stroke, PHOTO-PAINT counts the number of dabs in the stroke until it reaches the point set by the Fade Out setting. At this time, it will fade out. The length of the fade out is fixed; the control setting determines when the fade begins. A negative setting will begin with a fade and then become less transparent. In Figure 12-4, the top row was painted with an Image Sprayer at a Fade Out setting of –90. The middle row is the reference, and the bottom row was made with a Fade Out setting of 90.

Dab Attributes

The third roll-up, shown next, is Dab Attributes. This roll-up controls the number of dabs, as well as the spacing, spread, and HSL applied when any of the brush tools are applied.

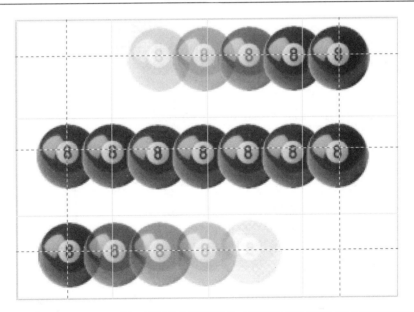

FIGURE 12-4   The Fade Out attribute makes brush strokes fade in or out depending on their settings

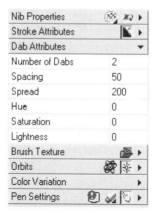

So, What's a Dab?

A *dab* is the area covered by the nib of a brush. When you drag the brush, you make a brush stroke; but even though a brush stroke looks like a solid swoosh of pixels, it is actually composed of a series of overlapping dabs. In Figure 12-5, a nib that is 40 pixels in diameter is applied as a brush stroke at four different settings for spacing. As the distance between the dabs becomes greater, it no longer appears as the smooth brush stroke at the top of the figure.

Number of Dabs

The Number of Dabs setting controls how many dabs are applied to the image with each single click of the pen or mouse. This attribute has a range of 1–25 dabs. Normally this value is set to 1, since applying the same nib to the same pixels multiple times doesn't accomplish anything except make your computer break into a sweat. An exception is when the brush stroke has a Spread value, which is described later in this section. Then, multiple dabs can be applied over a larger area.

Spacing

Spacing sets the distance, in pixels, between dabs. To create a brush stroke, the pointing device draws a line across the image and dabs are applied to the line at the frequency determined by the Spacing setting. For example, in Figure 12-5, the nib is 40 pixels across. If a brush stroke is made with a Spacing setting of 20 (pixels), Corel PHOTO-PAINT will produce the selected brush on the image area at a spacing of every 20 pixels. This means that each nib is overlapping the last one by 50 percent. As you can see, it produces a smooth line. While it may seem

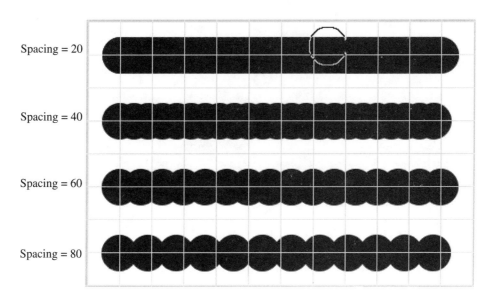

Spacing = 20

Spacing = 40

Spacing = 60

Spacing = 80

FIGURE 12-5　Changing the spacing of a brush stroke affects the smoothness of the stroke

that a setting of 1 would be desired, a lower setting slows down the generation of the brush stroke considerably. It can be really slow on some systems, especially when using a large nib (>70). When a large nib is used, the Spacing setting should be greater because of the overlap caused by the larger brush nib.

Spread

The Spread setting has nothing to do with the stuff you spread on your toast. As the brush stroke moves along a line, this setting controls how far (in pixels) each dab can be off the stroke centerline. Higher values mean the dabs can appear greater distances from the centerline of the brush stroke. A setting of zero means each dab will be placed on the line of the brush stroke. In the next illustration, the number of dabs for each brush stroke was set at 2. The top line was created with a Spread setting of zero, resulting in a straight line. The middle line had a Spread setting of 100, and the bottom brush stroke making a ragged line was made with the Spread value increased to 200. In case you were wondering why you would ever want to use this, it is great for creating random natural patterns like trees and shrubs, for instance.

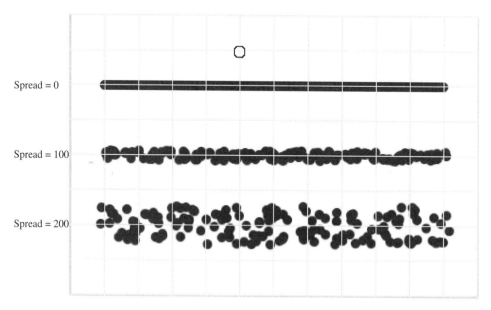

Brush Texture

The fourth roll-up is Brush Texture, as shown next. Essentially, you load a texture that acts a lot like a seamless bitmap. With the texture loaded, each brush stroke applied has the appearance that it was applied to a textured surface.

Loading a Preset Texture

To load one of the preset textures, click the Load Texture button, opening the Load Texture dialog box. By default, it should always go to the Program Files\Corel\ Graphics10\Photopnt\Brushtxr folder, which contains 10 texture presets. If you want, you can load almost any bitmap to use for a texture. Some of the bumpmap textures also make good brush textures. They are located in Program Files\Corel\ Graphic10\Custom\Bumpmap. My favorite is the Mesh.

Controlling the Texture

The Brush Texture setting controls how much texture is applied with each brush stroke. Lower settings result in less texture. The Edge Texture controls how much of the texture is applied to the nib's edge. The rationale behind this attribute's setting is a little strange. The value in the setting represents the transparency of the edge, so at a setting of 100, the edge of the nib is totally transparent and there is no texture applied to the edge of the stroke. Conversely, a setting of zero results in maximum texture at the edge of the nib. Be aware that your nib must have a soft edge for Edge Texture to work. The remaining attributes, Bleed and Sustain Color, control how the brush stroke reacts with the colors in the image. Bleed makes the brush seem to pick up colors from the image, as if you were dragging the brush across wet paint. Sustain Color determines how much of the Paint color is retained in the brush stroke when Bleed is being used. If Bleed is zero, then Sustain Color has no effect.

12

Orbits/Color Variation

The fifth and sixth roll-ups are Orbits and Color Variation. Although Color Variation appears as a separate roll-up, it is actually part of the Orbits roll-up. Why are they separate? To quote my favorite line from the movie *Shakespeare in Love,* "It's a mystery." Considering the appearance of the icon on the Orbits roll-up, you may have thought it to be a nuclear roll-up—never fear. Orbits creates incredible brush strokes by rotating a nib around a centerline as you drag the brush tool. The results are brush strokes that would be impossible any other way.

Nib Properties		⊗	🔣 ▸
Stroke Attributes			◤ ▸
Dab Attributes			▸
Brush Texture			🖌 ▸
Orbits		🔣	☼ ▾
Number of Orbits	10		
Radius	999		
Rotation Speed	1		
Grow Speed	10		
Grow Amount	65		
Color Variation			▾
Hue Range	100		
Hue Speed	0		
Saturation Range	180		
Saturation Speed	0		
Lightness Range	180		

Don't let all of the settings intimidate you. Most of the time you will be loading existing presets that some poor engineer on the development team spent hours creating, and you will either use it as is or modify it.

Toggle Orbits Button

The most important control in either of the two roll-ups is the Toggle Orbits button. When it is not selected, the Orbits feature is disabled. As with all of the other roll-up settings, if you save a brush with Orbits enabled, the orbits will be enabled any time the saved brush is selected.

Include Center Button

As you learned earlier, *orbits* are pixels painted by nibs around a centerline that you create with the Paint tool. Normally, you never see the centerline of the brush stroke that you create when using orbits. If this button is enabled, the centerline is also included.

■ **Number of Orbits**   This setting determines the number of orbits that are distributed around the center of a brush stroke. Use a value from 1 to 128. Use lower values for spirals and higher values for rings. In Figure 12-6, the Artbrush preset *Rings* was applied using the default setting of 60 on the top brush stroke. The middle brush stroke is the result of decreasing the Number of Orbits setting to 30; and for the bottom stroke, the setting was lowered to 15. Of course, the effect of changing the number depends on the preset selected. The image shown next is the Artbrush preset *Muscle Fiber*. As the Number of Orbits setting is increased, the fibrous portion becomes denser.

Number of orbits =16
(default)

Number of orbits = 32

Number of orbits = 64

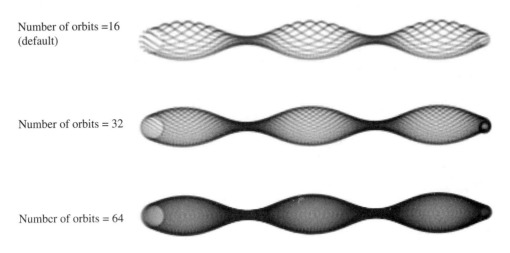

- ■ **Radius**   This setting has nothing to do with the size of the brush, but refers to the size of the orbits produced.

- ■ **Rotation Speed**   This setting can be thought of as how many times per brush stroke the orbit is going to cycle through its pattern.

- ■ **Grow Speed and Grow Amount**   These two settings control the overall amplitude and duration of the cycle.

- ■ **Color Variation Settings**   The settings in this roll-up control the colors (Hue Range and Speed), how vibrant the colors in the orbit brush stroke are (Saturation Range and Speed), and the overall Lightness.

NOTE   *For more detailed (and accurate) descriptions about each setting, go to the online help.*

What Can You Do with Orbits?

Let your imagination run wild. I recommend playing with the existing presets first, some of which are shown in Figure 12-7, before you begin rolling your own variations. To see some of the presets, select the Paint Tools and choose the Art Brush group. Click and open the Brush Type list, shown next, and scroll down the list to Blending Rag; and all of the presets below it, which use orbits, are displayed.

Number of
Orbits = 60

Number of
Orbits = 30

Number of
Orbits = 15

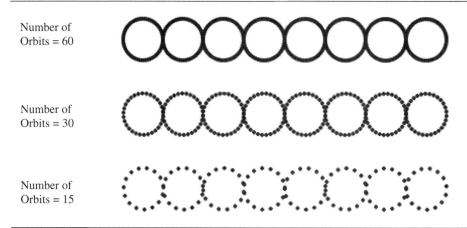

FIGURE 12-6   Changing the Number of Orbits settings changes the shapes of the
resulting brush strokes

While you are playing (sorry, experimenting), use the orbits in concert with other
PHOTO-PAINT features.

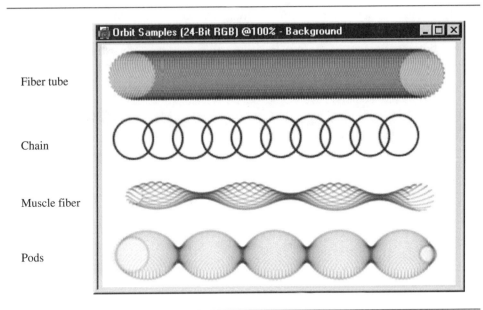

Fiber tube

Chain

Muscle fiber

Pods

FIGURE 12-7   Four of the Art Brush paint tool's presets show a little of what this versatile PHOTO-PAINT feature can do

The Pen Settings Roll-Up

The Pen Settings roll-up, shown next, is used to control brush strokes applied using a pressure-sensitive pen, as well as some settings to make a mouse act like a pressure-sensitive pen—assuming you are really coordinated and have a vivid imagination. The pressure applied with the pen on a pen tablet determines the size, opacity, and other attributes of the brush stroke. In addition to this, if your tablet supports multiple styluses, you can assign a different tool to each pressure-sensitive pen and eraser available with the pen tablet.

Over the past eight years of working with PHOTO-PAINT, I have received hundreds of questions from PHOTO-PAINT users asking if they need to use a pen tablet. Traditionally, pressure-sensitive pens have been expensive. In the last few years, the cost of tablets has dropped dramatically. Wacom, which is the undisputed leader in the field of pen tablets, introduced a small USB tablet called Graphire™ for about $100. So with pen tablets now being affordable, the answer to the question is yes. You will find that everything from making mask selections to retouching photographs is much easier with a pen tablet.

All options in the Pen Settings roll-up correspond to brush tool attributes on the property bar or those described previously in the section "The Brush Settings

12

Docker." You can customize the Pen Settings to change the response of the brush tool as you apply pressure to the pen. Most of the Pen Settings involve a range of values, both positive and negative. Positive values increase a brush tool attribute as you add pressure to the pen, resulting in a more pronounced effect. Negative values make a brush tool attribute less pronounced.

 The pressure-sensitive pen attributes can be saved for future use when you save a custom brush.

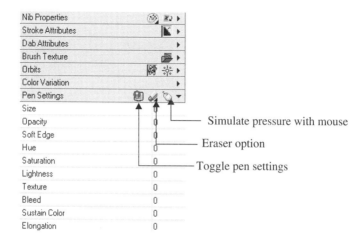

Configuring Your Pen

Before you start using a pressure-sensitive pen, I recommend configuring the pen tablet with the range of pressure that you typically apply to the pen. This configuration is used when you apply pressure effects to brush strokes. Corel PHOTO-PAINT automatically configures most pen tablets.

NOTE *To vary the shape of artistic nibs that do not support pressure-sensitive sizing, change the settings of circular and rectangular nibs.*

Auto Pen Tablet Configuration

You can configure the pen tablet using the amount of pressure that you typically apply to the pen. Each stroke that you apply as you configure determines the range of pressure of the pen.

1. Click Tools | Options (CTRL-J).

2. Under Workspace, click General.

3. Click the Pen Tablet Configuration button.

4. Apply five strokes using a full range of pressure. When the configuration is complete, the OK button will no longer be grayed out. Click OK and close the Options.

Pen Settings

All of the settings for the pressure-sensitive pens have been discussed earlier in this chapter, with the exception of Elongation, which represents the amount of tilt and rotation of the pen. It should be noted that the pen tablet must support the tilt function for this setting to work.

To Associate a Paint Tool to a Stylus

This feature may have puzzled you, since it seems logical that you have a single pen with a tablet. Actually, with the Wacom family of tablets, it is possible to have several different styluses. In my case, I use the standard stylus that came with my Intuos™ tablet for most of my paint tools, but I also have one that is shaped like a real airbrush. Speaking as one who grew up using airbrushes, it feels more "natural" to use the airbrush stylus when I am retouching photographs, so I have assigned the airbrush stylus to my custom Airbrush paint tools. Here is how to do it:

1. Click Tools | Options (CTRL-J).

2. From Workspace, click General.

3. Enable the Save Last Used Tool for Each Stylus check box.

4. Click OK.

Pen Settings Roll-Up Buttons

The PHOTO-PAINT development and QA teams are great, and I enjoy the things they do with the PHOTO-PAINT product. That said, when it came to the layout of

12

the Pen Settings roll-up, they were out to lunch. There are three buttons on the top of the Pen Settings roll-up:

- **Toggle Pen Settings**   When the button is enabled, PHOTO-PAINT does not respond to pressure information from a pen tablet. Logically, it would seem that when the button was enabled (pushed in), PHOTO-PAINT would read the stylus—it's a mystery.

- **Eraser Option**   The Eraser button at the top of a Wacom stylus is, by default, assigned as the Eraser tool in PHOTO-PAINT. Click the Eraser Option button and a huge list of tools opens up. Clicking any tool in the list automatically assigns the Eraser button to that tool.

- **Simulate Pressure with Mouse**   When this button is enabled, PHOTO-PAINT allows you to simulate pressure information from a pen when using a mouse. To use, while dragging the mouse use the UP ARROW and DOWN ARROW keys on the keyboard to change the settings that are enabled. Be aware that the changes that occur using this method are relatively slow. In other words, buy a pen tablet.

The Symmetry Toolbar

This feature was introduced back in PHOTO-PAINT 8 and was tucked away in the Brush Settings docker. Now, you can access it by choosing Window | Toolbars and picking Symmetry Bar, shown next.

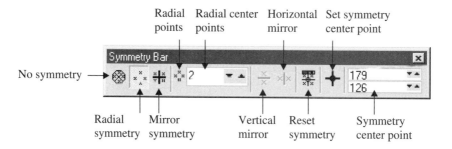

This feature is like an old Spirograph, but on steroids. The Symmetry bar has three modes of operation—No Symmetry, Radial Symmetry, and Mirror Symmetry. The first time the toolbar is selected, the No Symmetry button is enabled and most of the icons on the toolbar are grayed out. When you paint in Radial Symmetry mode, satellite brush nibs, called satellite points, create brush strokes around a center point. When you paint in Mirror Symmetry mode, an identical brush stroke is created on the horizontal plane, the vertical plane, or both, depending on which one you have selected on the toolbar. You can spend a lot of time playing with this tool. I regret I do not have the time or the space in this chapter to really get into this tool, but I can recommend a great resource for PHOTO-PAINT information, including information on making images like those made by Alex Link, shown in Figure 12-8. The site is called "The PHOTO-PAINT Place" and is run by a very knowledgeable lady named Debbie Cook. Her URL is www.cedesign.com/cefx/tppp.html.

NOTE	*After you have finished using the symmetry tools, be sure to select the No Symmetry button before you close the Symmetry toolbar. This is because the last-used Symmetry mode remains in effect regardless of whether the toolbar is open or not.*

The Paint Tools

The Paint tools are the virtual equivalent of a fully stocked artist's studio, but with the advantages of being able to work around things like the law of gravity and not having to clean your brushes to change colors. The Paint tools are selected by clicking their icons either on the property bar or on the Paint Tools toolbar, shown next.

12

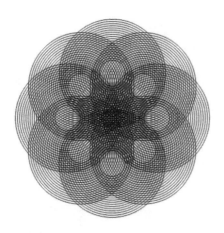 

FIGURE 12-8   Both of these figures were made using Radial Symmetry

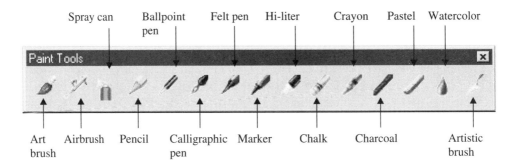

Spray can — Ballpoint pen — Felt pen — Hi-liter — Crayon — Pastel — Watercolor

Art brush — Airbrush — Pencil — Calligraphic pen — Marker — Chalk — Charcoal — Artistic brush

Creating Custom Nibs from Masks

Before you learn about the Effect tools, you must learn how to make custom nibs from mask contents. As we discussed near the beginning of the chapter, nibs are really tiny grayscale masks through which the brush applies color or effects to the image. Creation of a custom nib is pretty easy, but most users don't do it because how it's accomplished is less than obvious. Here is how to do it:

1. Create a new image (size and resolution isn't important). Select the Image Sprayer tool (I). On the property bar, click the Brush Type and choose Butterfly from the drop-down list.

2. Click the image one time to produce a single butterfly, as shown next. Do not be concerned if your butterfly is different.

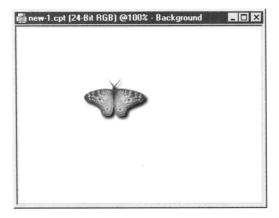

3. Select the Magic Wand tool (W) and, while holding down the CTRL key, click anywhere in the image background. A mask marquee, shown next, should now surround the butterfly.

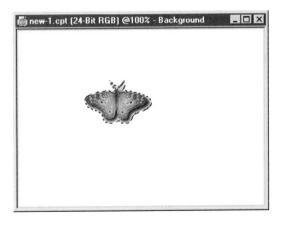

4. Select the Paint Tools (P) and from the Nib Properties roll-up in the Brush Settings docker. Click the Nib Options button, and choose Create from Contents of Mask, as shown next.

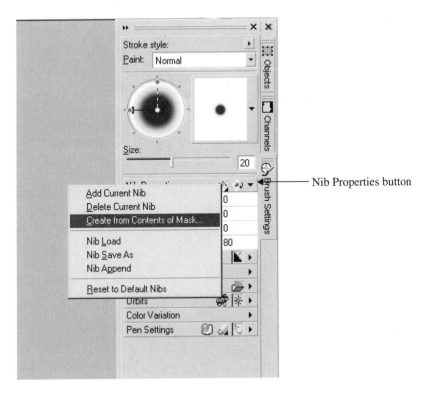

Nib Properties button

5. When the Create a Custom Brush dialog box opens, as shown next, click
   OK. Note that at this point you can change the finished size of the custom
   nib by changing the value in the dialog box. You now just created your
   own custom nib. The new nib is shown in the nib preview area of the
   Brush Settings docker, as shown in Figure 12-9.

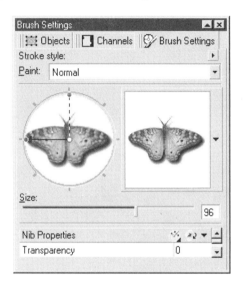

So, what can you do with this custom nib? Lots of stuff. Here are a few ideas.
After you remove the mask and butterfly from the original image (use CTRL-Z
several times), change the Spacing so that it is the same size as the butterfly, and
change the Hue settings in Dab Attributes to 100. Now use the auto brush feature
to make lines of butterflies. Click the brush in the upper-left corner and then,
holding down the ALT key, click in the upper-right corner of the image. You
should have a line of several butterflies in different colors. The result is shown
in Figure 12-10.

TIP   *Remember to use the Reset Brush Type options in the Brush Settings
           docker, Stroke Style section, if you don't want to save your custom brush.*

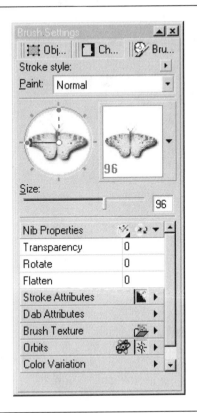

FIGURE 12-9   Making a custom nib from the contents of a masked area is simple to do

The Effect Tools

The Effect tools are accessed by clicking the Effect Tools button in the Brush Tools flyout of the Toolbox. Selection and configuration of the tools are via the Brush Settings docker. The Effect tools include tools to apply image adjustments found in the Image and Effects menus. Unlike their menu-based counterparts, the Effect tools can be applied selectively in small areas, sometimes without the necessity of creating a mask. Although the effects provided by many of the tools

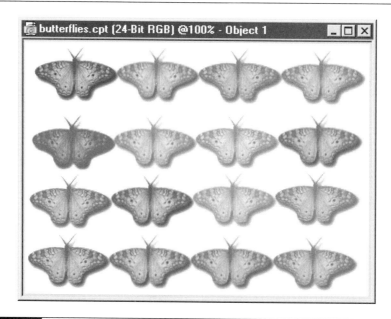

FIGURE 12-10   Using a custom nib we create, you can make rows of colorful butterflies

can also be achieved through various menu commands, others are unique to the
Effect tools and not available elsewhere in Corel PHOTO-PAINT. There are 12
different tools that constitute the Effect tools. Like the Paint tools, the Effect tools
offer multiple types for each tool. We will begin our exploration of the Effect tools
with the Smear tool.

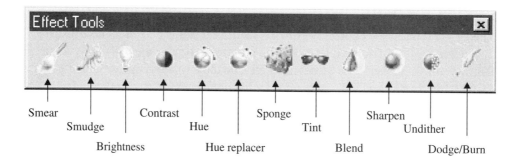

> **NOTE**   *The names of some of the Effect tools may seem, at times, inconsistent. For example, if you select the Smear tool, it will say Pointy Smear. That is the default Type setting. I have named each tool according to its overall description rather than the name associated with the default type setting.*

The Smear Tool

The Smear tool smears colors. The same tool in Adobe Photoshop is called the Smudge tool (which can get confusing, because there is a Smudge tool in Corel PHOTO-PAINT). The Smear tool spreads colors in a picture, producing an effect similar to dragging your finger through wet oil paint. The size and shape of the Smear tool is set from either the property bar or the Brush Settings docker.

Using the Smear Tool

The purpose of this tool is to smear colors. I know I said that before, but it's worth repeating, because many first-time users of Corel PHOTO-PAINT misuse the Smear tool. That is, they use it to soften color transitions. That is the purpose of the Blur tool. Think of it this way: the results of using the Smear tool are not that much different from finger painting (except you don't have to wash your hands after you're done). Blending an area causes the distinction between colors to become less pronounced. Setting the Amount to 0% in the Brush Settings docker causes no blending to occur, although it still smears existing pixels; while an amount of 100% will give you the maximum amount of blending possible. Adjacent pixels must be different colors for the effect to work correctly.

Have the property bar or Brush Settings docker open when you work with this tool. For retouching, the Soft Edge and Transparency settings should be adjusted to produce the greatest effect without being obvious. A higher Soft Edge setting causes the edges of the Smear tool to appear more feathered, which is desirable for most Smear tool applications. The effect of the Smear tool is additive. Every time you apply it to the image, it will smear the pixels, no matter how many times you apply it.

For retouching, you may end up "scrubbing" the area with the tool to get the effect desired. When retouching a photo, you do not want a solid color after you are done—you need to have texture for the subject to look real.

12

If you start the Smear tool well off of the image, it pulls the pixels (Paper color) onto the image. This can be used to give the brush-stroke effect on the edge.

If you are doing touch-up work with the Effect tools, never count on an image being small enough to cover the sins of sloppy touch-up. With all of the fancy equipment in the world today, it is too easy for people to get a photo blown up to poster size, and that is when they might get real ugly about your touch-up work.

The Smudge Tool

Maybe it is just me, but the first time I began exploring the freehand editing tools, I thought Smear and Smudge sounded like they did the same thing. The Smudge tool in Corel PHOTO-PAINT is different from the tool with the same name in Adobe Photoshop. As it turns out, the Smudge tool adds texture by randomly mixing pixels in a selected area. It is like a can of spray paint that sucks up color from the area that it is currently over and then sprays it back onto the subject. Technically, it acts like a local color noise filter. I am not aware of any equivalent of this tool in Photoshop.

The Smudge Tool Settings

All of the controls are identical to those shown for the Smear tool with one exception. The Rate setting determines how fast the noise (texture) is placed on the image. A rate of flow of 1 causes the noise texture to flow very slowly; therefore, to create a noticeable change, the tool has to be held at the same location for a longer period.

Using the Smudge Tool

The Smudge tool adds texture. It is really color noise. The effect of the Smudge tool is additive. As long as you hold the button down, the effect is being applied, *even if the brush is not moving.*

Always remember when working with the Smudge tool that it acts like the Airbrush or Spray Can brush. That means that you do not need to drag it across the image unless you have a high Rate of Flow setting. Just put it over the area you want and hold down the mouse button until you get the desired effect.

Thoughts About Retouching Photographs

While the Smudge tool removes highlights very well, it must be used with caution. When the bright highlights are removed, the image appears to be "flatter" than before. This is a drawback as we seek perfection in a photograph. Too many highlights may distract, but they also add contrast to the photograph, which deceives the human eye into thinking the image looks sharper. Another consideration when you are touching up photographs is whether what you are removing or modifying is necessary for the overall effect the photograph is trying to convey. Ultimately, you must make the call, but consider what you are changing before you change it. The only photographs that are digitally manipulated to perfection without regard to the original subject generally are the type that fold out of magazines.

The Brightness Tool

Brightness is the degree of light reflected from an image or transmitted through it. You can use the Brightness tool to both lighten and darken areas of the image by choosing different modes in the Brush Type drop-down list in the property bar.

Using the Brightness Tool

The Brightness brush can brighten or darken areas in an image. Choosing an Amount of 100 in the Brush Settings docker causes all the black to be removed from the affected area, resulting in a much lighter color. Conversely, an Amount of 0 has no effect on the image.

Using the Brighten Tool

When using this tool, remember that you want the changes to be subtle, so make them in small increments using a Brighten tool with a round shape unless you are working near straight lines, as in a geometric figure. The effect of the tool is additive. It will apply the effect at the level set in the Tool Setting dialog box each time it is applied.

　　To achieve any subtle effects in areas that have no naturally occurring visual boundaries, you must be prepared to apply the brush in several stages to reduce the sharp transition of the contrast effect.

12

The Contrast Tool

Contrast is the difference between the lightest and the darkest parts of an image. The Contrast tool intensifies the distinction between light and dark. It operates in the same manner as the Contrast filter, except that it can be applied to small areas without the need to create masks.

Using the Contrast Tool

Use the Contrast tool to bring out color in scanned photographs that appear dull or flat. Don't increase the contrast too much or the picture might appear overexposed. Some scanners have a tendency to darken the photographs when they are scanned, which causes them to lose contrast. Video images that are obtained through a frame grabber also tend to be dark. Both of these applications can benefit from the selective application of contrast.

Be careful not to overuse the Contrast tool, which can result in exaggerated white and dark areas. At the maximum Amount setting for Increase Contrast, highlights and shadows are blown out. That is, the areas that are lighter become white, and almost all shades are lost. It is as if the image were converted to *bi-level,* which means the image is composed of only black and white pixels.

The effect of the Contrast tool is additive. It will apply the effect at the level set by the Tool Setting dialog box the first time it is applied. After the mouse button is released, progressive applications add to the effect already applied.

The Hue Tool

There are two hue tools, the Hue tool and the Hue Replacer tool, that at first seem to do the same thing. I found their names to be especially confusing. The Hue tool shifts the pixels of the image the number of degrees specified in the Brush Settings docker. The Hue Replacer is used to replace the hue of pixels in the image with the hue of the selected Paint (foreground) color.

How the Hue Tool Works

The Hue tool actually changes the color of the pixels it touches by the amount of the setting.

TIP *The best way to get the most realistic color change is to experiment with the transparency settings for the Hue tool. I have found that the default setting has insufficient transparency.*

Limiting the Effect of the Hue Tool

The Hue tool is like using the tint control on your color TV. The difficulty with using this tool is that it will shift every pixel you paint with the tool. To prevent unwanted hue shifts, it is best to mask the area first. By using the Color Mask, you can create a mask that is limited to the colors that you want to change. The best part about this combination of Color Mask and Hue tools is that you need not concern yourself if the Color Mask exists in an unwanted portion of the image, since you will limit the application of the Hue shift by where you place the Hue tool.

TIP *Use the Hue brush to create interesting shifts in color within your image.*

The effects of the Hue brush tool are additive if the Cumulative option on the Stroke Attributes tab of the Brush Settings docker is selected. It will apply the effect at the level set by the Tool Setting dialog box the first time it is applied; progressive applications after the mouse button is released will then shift the hue of the pixels that much again.

The Hue Replacer Tool

The Hue Replacer tool replaces the hue of pixels in the image with the hue of the selected Paint (foreground) color. By changing the Hue, the color changes but the other two components (saturation and brightness) remain unchanged. The same considerations exist with the tool's masking and other settings, as mentioned with the Hue tool. The Hue Replacer brush changes the colors of pixels by the value set in the Amount value box.

Mixing Colors and Other Confusion

The amount of the original hue that remains is determined by the Amount setting in the Brush Settings docker or the property bar. All of the traditional rules of color you learned, like yellow + blue = green, do not apply with digital color.

12

To complicate matters further with regard to predicting the color outcome, the default color model of Corel PHOTO-PAINT is RGB. To accomplish the Hue mix, Corel PHOTO-PAINT must temporarily convert the model to HSB. This text is not here to discourage you, only to help you understand that predicting the color outcome is very difficult, and the best method I am aware of is experimentation.

 Use this Hue Replacer effect tool to replace the color of an object without removing its shading and highlights. For instance, you can change the color of a red dress to yellow, while still retaining the shading that distinguishes the folds in the skirt.

The Sponge (Saturation) Tool

The Sponge tool is used to increase the saturation or intensity of a color. When saturation is added to a color, the gray level of a color diminishes; thus, it becomes less neutral. The Sponge tool can also be used to desaturate or diminish the intensity of a color. When Saturation is reduced to –100 percent, the result is a grayscale image. The size, shape, and level of the Saturation tool is set from the Brush Settings docker.

 Also use the Sponge brush to make colors more vibrant. For the amount, select a low value (5, for example) and brush over the desired area. Nonessential colors that cause dullness are stripped away, leaving pure, vivid colors.

Using the Sponge Tool

The Sponge tool actually removes the color of the pixels it touches by the amount of the setting. The effect of the tool is additive. It will apply the effect at the level set by the Brush Settings docker the first time it is applied. Progressive applications will make any changes to the previously affected area unless the tool settings are changed.

The Tint Tool

The Tint tool tints an area in the current paint color. This may seem the same as painting with a high-transparency paintbrush, but it is not. The paintbrush is additive. That is, when the same area continues to have the brush applied to it, the paint builds up until it reaches 100 percent. The Tint tool will apply the paint color as specified by the Tint setting, regardless of how many times it is applied. The amount of tint set in the Brush Settings docker is the maximum level of the paint color that can be applied to the pixels in the image.

Using the Tint Tool

The first thing to remember with the Tint tool is that 100 percent tint is a solid color without any transparency. The Tint tool provides a way to highlight a selected area with a color. The same effect can also be achieved over larger areas by using the Rectangle, Ellipse, or Polygon Draw tool, and controlling the Transparency setting through the Tool Settings roll-up.

Another use of the Tint tool is for touching up an image. The technique is simple. When you have a discoloration to cover, pick an area of the image that is the desired color. Using the Eyedropper tool, select a large enough sample to get the average color that is needed to match the adjoining areas. Now apply the tint to the area with progressively larger percentage settings until the discolored areas disappear into the surrounding area. If the resulting tint application looks too smooth, use the Smudge effect tool to add texture. You can also use the Blend tool to reduce spots where there are large differences in the shades.

The Blend Tool

This is a better tool to use for some types of retouching than the Smear tool. The Blend tool enables you to blend colors in your picture. Blending is the mixing of different colors to cause less distinction among them. For example, if you have two areas of different colors and they overlap, it is possible to blend the two different colors so that the separation of the two areas is indistinct. You can use the Blend tool to soften hard edges in an image and to correct any pixelation caused by oversharpening.

TIP	*You could use this effect to blend the edges of a pasted object with the background to make it appear more natural.*

Blending an area causes the distinction between colors to become less pronounced. Choosing an Amount of 0 in the Brush Settings docker causes no blending to occur, while an amount of 100% will give you the maximum amount of blending possible. Adjacent pixels must be different colors for the effect to work.

12

Using the Blend Tool

The Blend tool acts like applying water to a watercolor. The effect of the tool is additive. It will apply the effect at the level set by the Brush Settings docker each time it is applied.

The Sharpen Tool

The Sharpen tool sharpens selected areas of the image by increasing the contrast between neighboring pixels. It operates in the same manner as the Sharpen filter, except that it can be applied without the need to create masks. The size and shape of the Sharpen tool are set from the Brush Settings docker.

Using the Sharpen Tool

Avoid overusing the Sharpen tool, which results in exaggerated white spots (pixelation) wherever the white component of the image approaches its maximum value. The effect of this tool is additive. It will apply the Sharpen effect to the Sharpen level set in the Brush Settings docker every time it is applied. Progressive applications intensify the changes. Any application of the tool can be removed with the Undo command (CTRL-Z), as long as it was applied with one continuous stroke without releasing the mouse button. If you must be zoomed in at great magnification to do your work, keep a duplicate window open to a lower zoom value so that you can see the effect in perspective.

The Undither Tool

This brush, introduced in PHOTO-PAINT 7, is described as "allow[ing] you to create a smooth transition between adjacent pixels of different colors or brightness levels." It works by adding intermediate pixels whose values are between those of the adjacent pixels. In other words, it really messes up an image. Maybe Corel will sponsor a contest to find a good use for this tool.

Dodge and Burn Tool

The Dodge and Burn tool has several modes of operation, and I will do my best to describe them to you. These modes selectively affect pixels in an image, depending on where in the tonal spectrum they exist. Clear as mud? The tonal range of an image is divided into shadows, midtones, and highlights. The Dodge and Burn tool will make pixels in one of these three regions either darker or lighter. It is an excellent retouching tool because you can darken (burn) or lighten (dodge) pixels in an area without affecting pixels that are adjacent to it. For example, you can lighten an area that is close to a shadow with the midtone or highlight setting without concern about affecting the shadow area.

The Power of the Clone Tool (C)

Many people assume that the primary use of the Clone tool is to duplicate people or things in an image. The process of cloning one object over another is commonly used both in still photography and motion pictures. In the movie *Forrest Gump*, the actor who played Lt. Dan had special blue socks on when they shot the scenes that showed his legs below the knees. During post-production, anywhere his blue socks appeared, a cloning tool was used to replace the blue with the background—one frame at a time. The result made it appear that his legs were missing. Figure 12-11(a) is an image I made when I wrote the PHOTO-PAINT 5 book; and I have enjoyed it so much, I still use it as the perfect example of the value of a clone tool. Using PHOTO-PAINT's Clone tool, it was a simple matter to replace the man in the image with pixels from the surrounding background, effectively removing the man from the image, as shown in Figure 12-11(b). The process is simple but time-consuming. It took me almost 40 minutes to get rid of the guy. Of course, the easiest method would have been for her to tell him to buzz off before the photographer took the picture.

While the Clone tool can be used to replicate images or portions of them for effect, it's more often used in photo-editing for repair and restoration. The principal role of the Clone tool is to copy (clone) a portion of an image and apply it to another part of an image. The resulting cloned area can be on the same image or even on a different one. The Clone tool is most handy when you are removing things from photos like dirt, fingerprints, or the original art your two-year old created with a felt marker on the only picture of your favorite aunt (the one you hope will remember you in her will).

How the Clone Tool Works

Once you select the Clone tool in the Toolbox, five modes are available in the property bar, the first of which is the Clone tool. The Clone tool is composed of two basic parts, as shown in Figure 12-12. It has a part that copies (called the source-point), which is represented by the crosshair cursor. The other part

12

(a)

(b)

(a) Breaking up may be hard to do—according to the song—(b) but not with PHOTO-PAINT's Clone tool

is the Clone brush that applies what the source-point copies. The brush tool appears as either a shape cursor (represented by a circle that depicts the size of the brush) or a tool icon cursor, depending on which mode the cursor is in. To toggle between the shape cursors, use the / key. I recommend always using the shape cursor, as it lets you see how much area the Clone brush is covering.

FIGURE 12-12   The two parts of the Clone tool are the source-point (indicated by the circle) and the Clone brush (indicated by square)

Cloning from What to Where

When Clone tool is first selected or reset, the two cursors are aligned with the source-point cursor blinking. Clicking the left mouse button anchors the origin. The Clone brush cursor continues to follow your mouse or stylus movement until you click it again, at which time the Clone brush begins to paint the pixels copied from the source-point. As you move the Clone tool, the origin moves, operating in what is called *aligned mode,* which will be described in greater detail in the next few pages.

The source-point and the Clone brush tool can be on the same image or on different images. It is also possible to clone from a selected object to another in the same image, or even an object in a different image.

Resetting the Clone Tool

There are two ways to reset the source-point: click the right mouse button or press the C key. Applying either of these actions resets the source-point of the Clone tool to the area of the image covered by the Clone brush cursor. Using the C key aligns both cursors without anchoring them at the new location; so you must click the left

12

mouse button to anchor the source-point, just as if you had opened the Clone tool for the first time.

Constraining the Clone Tool

As with the other brush tools, the constrain features allow the creation of straight lines. Holding down the CTRL key constrains the Clone tool to horizontal/vertical movements. The images shown next are part of a magazine cover I created using the Clone tool. Both of the cars were cloned onto a black background using one of the textured nibs on the Clone tool.

To clone a straight line in any direction with the Clone tool, click to establish a starting point, move to where you wish the line to end, hold down the ALT key, and click again to create the straight brush stroke between the two points. Applying the Clone brush in the center and then using the ALT key caused PHOTO-PAINT to create a straight diagonal line in an outward direction, creating the car shown next.

The car shown next was also cloned with a textured nib on a black background with the CTRL (constrain) key enabled to achieve the straight horizontal lines.

The size of the Clone brush nib can be set numerically either in the property bar or interactively. To change the size onscreen, hold down the SHIFT key, click, and then drag the mouse either up or down. As you do, the size of the Clone brush cursor will either expand or contract until you release the mouse button. If for some reason the shape cursor in the Option (CTRL-J) is not selected (and it should be), the change in size can be viewed in the property bar as the mouse is dragged.

| TIP | *The quickest and best way to select the Clone tool is to press the C key on your keyboard.* |

12

The Clone Tool Settings

Like the other brush tools, the Clone tool contains many different tool types. It can operate as the world's best Undo tool or let you paint patterns with a brush. You can make a pointillist painting with surprisingly good results, or copy a portion of an image with the resulting cloned image looking like it had been run over by a 16-wheeler—many times.

The Clone toolbar contains the entire set of Clone tool types. The five tool types and their icons as they appear on the property bar (top) and in the Clone toolbar (bottom) appear next.

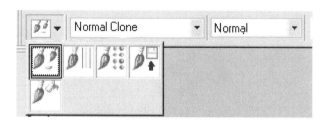

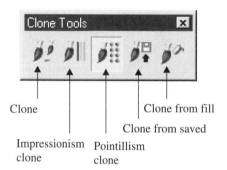

Clone

Impressionism
clone

Pointillism
clone

Clone from saved

Clone from fill

Aligned and Nonaligned Clone Modes

The Clone tool has two modes in which it can operate: aligned and nonaligned. Unlike in Photoshop, the Normal mode operates in aligned mode unless nonaligned mode is enabled by holding down the CTRL-ALT keys.

In aligned mode, once the origin is reset, the two cursors are locked in relation to one another. As the Clone brush cursor is moved, the origin moves and the only way to change the distance/position relationship of the two is to reset the point of origin.

While in nonaligned mode, the origin will follow the Clone brush until the mouse button is released, at which time it snaps back to its starting point. This mode is great for repeatedly cloning from a single portion of an image. To enable nonaligned mode, click the cursor on a point on the image you wish to clone. Next, while holding down the CTRL-ALT keys, drag the Clone brush and release the mouse button without releasing the CTRL-ALT keys. When the mouse button is released, the origin point jumps back to the previous starting point. This is what nonaligned mode is all about. As long as you hold down the CTRL-ALT keys, each time you release the mouse button, the origin will return to its previous (not the anchor) point. Use this mode when you want to make multiple clones of the contents of a single area.

Clone

In Clone mode, the Clone tool does not modify the pixels. As you drag the origin over an image, the pixels are copied and are simultaneously painted by the Clone brush.

 To make your cloning activities less evident, use a soft edge and a greater transparency setting.

Impressionism Clone

In this mode, the pixels from the source are modified using the Impressionist effect. This effect applies Clone brush strokes to the image, causing it to look like an Impressionist painting. If you look up Impressionist paintings in an art history book, it seems they are marked by the use of unmixed primary colors and small brush strokes to simulate reflected light. You can use that definition at your next party and make people think you are an art critic.

The results that can be obtained with the Impressionism clone fall into the what-where-they-thinking-about category of effects. I am still looking for a good use for this tool.

12

Pointillism Clone

The brush stroke made with the Pointillism Clone tool incorporates a selected number of dots in colors that are similar (e.g., eight shades of red). The size, shape, and qualities of the Pointillist Clone tool are set from the property bar or the Dab Attributes of the Brush Settings docker. In Pointillism mode, a dot-like appearance is added to the cloned image. Colors in the image are selected and then painted in a pointillist style. It does not reproduce areas in an image as does the Normal Clone tool; in other words, you may not recognize the image you have cloned. Nonetheless, I have discovered it can be used to create some nice effects. The secret is to make the clone brush size very small (like 1 or 2 pixels). Any larger and the results look pretty gruesome.

Clone from Saved

This is the ultimate Undo tool. It uses the last saved version of the image file as a source, allowing you to selectively remove any changes that had been made since the last time the file was saved. Obviously, you must be working on a saved version of a file; PHOTO-PAINT will give a warning to that effect if you are working with a new file. Cloned from Saved has three presets that are unique to it, each producing a different effect:

- Light Eraser
- Eraser
- Scrambler

After you have cloned a portion of an image, you may end up with cloned material that you do not want. The Eraser and the Light Eraser allow you to restore the original pixels from the last saved version of the image. The Light Eraser allows you to control how much of the changes you want to remove, requiring multiple passes to achieve the full restoration. The Eraser removes all of the cloned pixels. The Scrambler option is a pointillism version of Clone from Saved, so it allows you to distort the current image from a saved version. (What were they thinking?)

To restore background with the Clone from Saved feature, I recommend you use the Eraser setting with a soft edge setting of 60–80. This way, the transition is gradual and you won't need to go over the area later with a Smear or Blend tool.

You must have already saved a copy of the image to use this mode. If you attempt to use it with an unsaved image, you will get a warning message.

Rules of the Road for Clone from Saved, and a Workaround

There is a strict rule regarding the use of the Clone from Saved mode: the saved original and the current image must be the same size. If you have resized the current image (using either Paper Size or Resampling), Clone from Saved will prompt the warning message shown next.

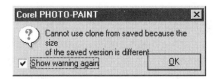

Here is a workaround for this particular Clone from Saved Rule:

1. Use Edit | Checkpoint to save a copy of the current image.

2. Select File | Revert to revert to the original image.

3. Select File | Document Info, make a note of the size of the original, and then click OK to close Info.

4. Choose Edit | Restore to Checkpoint.

5. Use either Image | Resample or Image | Paper Size to change the size of the current image to match that of the original.

6. Use the Clone from Saved tool.

Clone from Fill

The Clone from Fill tool uses the current fill as the source and applies the fill to the image with the clone brush. The advantage of Clone from Fill lies in its capability to selectively apply fills with a brush tool without the necessity of a mask.

 The equivalent of the Clone from Fill tool in Photoshop is called Clone from Snapshot.

Advanced Cloning Stuff

Most of the controls and settings for the Clone tool are common to the other brush tools. The exceptions follow:

- Cumulative
- Merged Objects

Cumulative/Merged Objects Operations

Clicking the Toggle Cumulative button on the Stroke Attributes roll-up of the Brush Settings docker, shown next, enables the Cumulative option. When enabled, the source-point copies all pixels that are on the current image, including not only the original pixels but also any cloned pixels that have been added to the original. The result is multiple copies, as shown in Figure 12-13. When this option is not enabled, the Clone tool makes a copy of the image contents and uses it as the source-point. Any changes made to the image by the Clone brush are not "seen" by the source-point. The Cumulative option is a nice feature that prevents accidental duplications and, in some ways, makes cloning work easier.

 The Cumulative button and the Merge Source button in the Brush Settings docker are mutually exclusive. When one of the buttons is enabled, the other one is no longer visible.

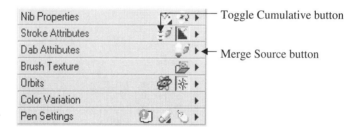

Toggle Cumulative button

Merge Source button

Merged Objects

Until now we have only considered cloning operations using a flat image (no objects). Normally, when the source-point of the Clone tool is on an image containing objects, only the selected object or background is visible to the source-point part of the Clone tool. For example, suppose an image were composed of a background, and several objects and the background were selected. Placing the source-point of the Clone tool on this image would only clone the background, and the objects (even though they were visible) would not be cloned. If the Merge source button on the Dab Attributes roll-up, shown previously, were enabled, all of the objects that have not been hidden and the background of the image would be cloned. If an object is hidden, it will not be cloned. The Lock Transparency option does not affect the ability of the origin to copy an object. It does limit the action of the Clone brush in the same manner as any brush tool.

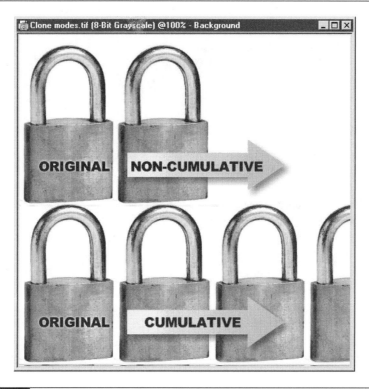

FIGURE 12-13   The results of cloning the lock with cumulative and noncumulative cloning enabled

This only scratches the surface of what you can do with the Clone tool. As you gain experience, you will begin to discover that it is one tool that can solve many photo-editing problems. While the Clone tool copies from one point on an image to another, the Image Sprayer tool, discussed next, actually paints with stored images.

The Image Sprayer Tool

The Image Sprayer tool is fantastic. Instead of painting with color, the Image Sprayer paints with images; and not just one or two images at a stroke, but a variety of changing images. By changing the direction of the stroke, you can change the rotation of the images being applied. Multiple application of images creates "natural" effects that would be otherwise difficult and time-consuming to create. Enough of the hype, now let's learn how to use the tool. The Image Sprayer tool can be found next to the Clone tool on the Brush Tools flyout.

 Pressing the I key is the quickest way to select this tool. Many of the controls are common to the brush tools.

How the Image Sprayer Works

The Image Sprayer is a brush tool—yes, really. To use it, you must first load it with images. The images are kept in special files called *image lists*, which may contain any number of images. Usually, the images are similar and form a logical series—that is, the images progress along some order. For example, the images might rotate about a point or increase in size.

As you paint with the Image Sprayer, you can control the order and size of the application of images with settings in the property bar or the Brush Settings docker. You can spray images sequentially, at random, or according to stroke direction. You control the images in an image file by opening the image list in PHOTO-PAINT and making changes. A normal installation of PHOTO-PAINT installs a small number of image lists on your hard drive. If you want more variety in the images, locate a folder labeled Imglists on the Corel CD-ROM or go to www.designer.com, where they are always posting new image lists.

How to Create Your Own Image List

If you don't like the image lists that ship with PHOTO-PAINT 10, it is quite simple to make your own. You can make an image list from a single object, from multiple objects in an image, or from selections (masks) on an image. The easiest image list is the one made from a single object, so let's look at it first.

Creating an Image List from a Single Object

If you make an image list from a single object, you will have the choice of using the single object or having PHOTO-PAINT create a Directional List. The Directional List is composed of a user-defined number of copies of the original object. Each copy is equally rotated. For example, if you type **4** when prompted for a Directional List, PHOTO-PAINT will make three copies of the original (3 + original = 4), each rotated 90 degrees. Here is the procedure:

1. Create an image and place one object in it. There are no size limitations (other than good sense) regarding the size of the object used for an image sprayer, but the object must be selected. In the example shown next, I used the Text tool to place an asterisk (Broadway BT at size 300) in a 2 × 2 inch image at 72 dpi.

2. Select the Image Sprayer (I) in the Brush Settings docker, click the flyout button, and choose Save Objects as Image List, as shown next.

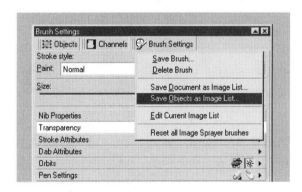

3. Because there is a single object, you will be asked if you want to make a Directional Image List. If you select Yes, you must enter the number of images and then name the new image file. Beware that if you make the number for the Directional List huge (>60), or if the size of the object is large, or both, the program will spend the next two weeks processing it.

12

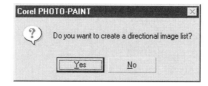

4. Choose the drive and folder where you want to save the image list.

5. Type a filename in the File name box, and you're done.

So, what can you do with an image list composed of a single asterisk? I created the image shown next with the steps that follow.

1. I used the Text tool and made an "8" in the middle of an image (font: Impact at 150). It seemed only right, since an asterisk is an "uppercase" 8.

2. Next I created a mask of the character (CTRL-M) and used the Image Sprayer brush to fill it in. I had to play with the Spacing adjustments to make it look right.

3. I selected the Airbrush Paint tool using Wide Cover and clicked the Stork Mask button in the property bar.

4. After applying the brush stroke to the middle of the mask, I ended up with an unwanted glow outside of the mask. No problem, I inverted the mask (CTRL-I) and double-clicked the Eraser tool.

Creating an Image List from an Image Containing Multiple Objects

Creating a list from an image containing more than one object is the same as previously described with a few exceptions. All of the objects in the image that are to be included in the image list must be selected. The order or position of the objects isn't important. If the objects have drop shadows, ensure that the shadows are grouped to the object casting the shadow. If you don't do this, each shadow will appear as a separate object in the image list.

TIP *Looking for objects with which to make an image list? There is a large collection of objects located in the folder labeled "objects" on the Corel CD-ROM.*

Creating an Image List from an Image Containing No Objects

This method is a little trickier than the previous methods. Since there are no objects for PHOTO-PAINT to select, it divides the image into equal parts based on the information provided by the user. The procedure is as follows:

1. Select an image containing the images you want made into an image list. I have provided an example, shown next. From the flyout option in the Brush Settings docker, click Save Document as an Image List.

12

2. You will next be prompted to input the number of images that are in each column and row. If there is only one image, leave the setting at the default of 1 and 1. In the case of the example, there are four images, so I changed both the row and column settings to 2, as shown next.

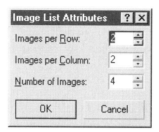

3. Officially, that's it. The new image file is loaded in the Image Sprayer.

The problem with this approach is that PHOTO-PAINT neatly divided the image into the number of squares you entered. In other words, instead of painting numbers, you are actually painting squares that are the color of the background with numbers on them. To illustrate the point, using the Image Sprayer, I painted the list from the example on a black background.

The solution is to use the Mask tools to select portions of the image you want to be included in the image list before converting it into an image list. Only the areas inside the mask will be in the resulting image list.

1. In the example, I have used the Magic Wand mask tool (W) to select the numbers, as shown next.

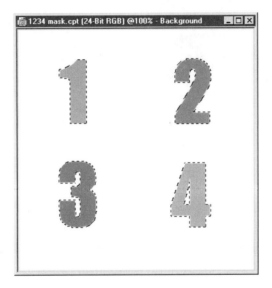

2. The resulting numbers, shown next, don't have the white rectangles that the previous one had. While this example isn't very interesting, it does prove that this approach works. Have you figured out how I got shadows behind the numbers yet? Since the Image Sprayer doesn't paint "objects," the easiest thing to do is to create a new object and apply the Image Sprayer on it. When it is complete, the object layer on which the numbers were painted can have a shadow attached using the Interactive Drop Shadow tool.

12

When you are masking an image for the creation of an image list, there is a good chance that part of the background will form a slight fringe around the edges of the object in your image list. The solution is to paint the images on a new object layer, as described in the preceding text, and select Object | Matting | Remove White Matte. That should do the trick—if the original background was white.

CAUTION *When you load a new image list, the property bar settings (spacing, Orbits, and so on) from the previous brush remain.*

Image Sprayer Presets

The Image Sprayer tool also has presets found on the property bar. These presets change the settings of the Brush Settings docker and property bar. Of special note is the Orbits tab. This applies the powerful Orbits engine to control the application of the Image Sprayer. If the image list only contains one object, the best effects are achieved with Orbits enabled. When a list containing multiple objects is selected, the effect is diminished, if not lost altogether.

Painting with the Image Sprayer

When you are painting with the Image Sprayer, it will apply the images from the image list in a manner determined by the Image Choice list on the property bar. The choices are Randomly, Sequentially, and by Direction. The first is obvious; the second refers to the order in which the images appear in the image list. To manipulate the order or contents of an image list, click the Create Spraylist button on the Image Sprayer property bar shown next.

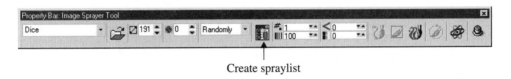

Create spraylist

This opens the Create Spraylist dialog box, shown next. Once an image list is loaded into the image sprayer. it is called a Spraylist. From this dialog box, you can add, remove, and change the order of items in a Spraylist. The selected item in the image list is previewed in the center.

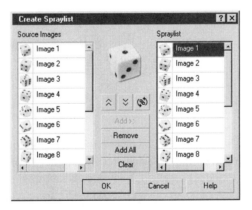

Real Art with the Image Sprayer

Figure 12-14 shows a watercolor I made while demonstrating PHOTO-PAINT at a trade show. The background was a gradient fill, while the clouds and the plants on

FIGURE 12-14 A beach scene created using the Image Sprayer brush (see also color insert)

the beach were created using the Image Sprayer tool. The watercolor effect was created using eight different PHOTO-PAINT filters.

In Summary

This chapter has given you some of the basics for working with the brush tools. While it would take several hundred pages to thoroughly explore all of the basic combinations of techniques and setting for using these tools, I hope you have learned enough to want to pick up the tools and begin to explore their possibilities.

PART V

Those Incredible Filters

CHAPTER 13

Exploring PHOTO-PAINT Enhancement Filters

Filters are the magic stuff of photo-editing programs like PHOTO-PAINT. Whether you need to create images like those from Andromeda Software, shown next (something I have an urge to do every day), or automatically mask an image or enhance a photograph, there is probably someone that makes a filter that does it. PHOTO-PAINT 10 offers a vast array of different filters. We'll begin this chapter by exploring how to enable the filters that are included in PHOTO-PAINT 10, how to install filters from other vendors, and some tips about the use of filters in general. After that we will explore the basic filters used for image enhancement—sharpening, blurring, and noise.

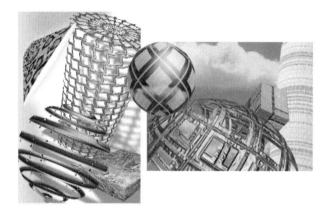

Understanding Plug-In Filters

The concept of plug-in filters is simple. A company (like Corel) provides an access that can be used by programmers to control parts of PHOTO-PAINT. These programs (known as plug-in filters) can be called from within an application (like PHOTO-PAINT) to provide a wide variety of functions and effects. The plug-in concept first appeared in Adobe Photoshop many moons ago, and the concept is now being used in other applications, including page-layout and vector-drawing programs.

Installation of Filters

When you initially open the Effects hierarchical menu, the list of filters appears, as shown next. The filters in PHOTO-PAINT are either internal or installed. Internal filters are built into PHOTO-PAINT, making them faster and inaccessible to other programs. Installed filters—including the ones shipped with PHOTO-PAINT 10—are connected to PHOTO-PAINT in the same way as third-party plug-ins. Installed filters either appear below the line of the Effects menu or in one of several categories under the File menu, such as Import.

Repeat	▶
3D Effects	▶
Art Strokes	▶
Blur	▶
Color Transform	▶
Contour	▶
Creative	▶
Custom	▶
Distort	▶
Noise	▶
Render	▶
Sharpen	▶
Texture	▶
Digimarc	▶
Fancy	▶
HSoft	▶
KPT5	▶

NOTE *Some plug-ins when installed also appear in the Input Plug-Ins and Export Plug-Ins of the File menu. There are also Mask plug-ins that appear in the Mask menu under Selection Plug-Ins.*

The procedure for installing plug-in filters is a breeze. First, follow the manufacturer's directions to install the filter. To make plug-ins appear in the list in the Effects menu, press CTRL-J to open the Options dialog box shown in Figure 13-1. Under Workspace, click Plug-Ins to select it. If all it says in the left column is Workspace, click the Plus symbol to open it up.

Once Plug-Ins is selected, the area on the right side of the dialog box displays the filters that are already installed in PHOTO-PAINT.

TIP *You may find that some of the filters give you a choice of automatically installing them for Corel PHOTO-PAINT. If this choice is offered, make note of the location where the program will install them, since they may be loaded in an unexpected area.*

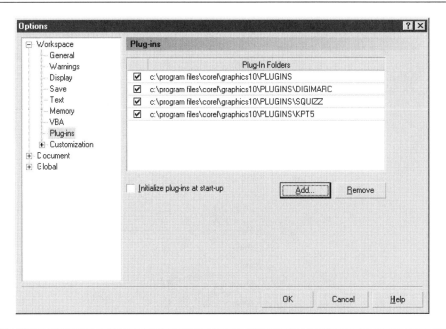

FIGURE 13-1 This is where your plug-in filters are managed

Managing Your Plug-Ins

The Plug-Ins area of Options is a nice plug-in manager. Note the close-up of the four installed filters shown next. Each line is composed of two parts. There is a check box on the left side, and on the right side is a path describing the location of the filter. By either checking or unchecking the check box, you can turn filters on or off without the need to restart PHOTO-PAINT. This means you can have a large number of filters installed and, through plug-ins, you can select the ones you want to make active.

Plug-ins

	Plug-In Folders
☑	C:\Program Files\Corel\Graphics10\PLUGINS
☑	C:\Program Files\Corel\Graphics10\PLUGINS\DIGIMARC
☑	C:\Program Files\Corel\Graphics10\PLUGINS\SQUIZZ
☑	C:\Program Files\Corel\Graphics10\PLUGINS\KPT5

☐ Initialize plug-ins at start-up   Add...   Remove

To add an installed filter to the set of filters, you must first tell PHOTO-PAINT where the filter has been installed. Do this by clicking the Add button to open the dialog box. The operation is pretty much self-explanatory at this point. Just select the location where the plug-ins have been installed and click OK.

> **TIP** *PHOTO-PAINT recognizes newly installed filters when it is restarted only if the Initialize Plug-Ins at Start-Up check box is checked.*

To remove a filter, highlight it and click the Remove button. No thoughtful message box will appear asking you if you are sure you want to banish the filter. It is gone, and there is no Undo. It isn't a big deal, because you haven't removed the file from your system but only removed its link from the plug-in manager. You can click the Add button and add it right back again, or you can also click Cancel on the Options dialog box. When you open Options again, any changes you made from the time you opened Options will not be there.

So that's the built-in plug-in manager. Isn't it sweet? My favorite part about it is that unlike when using other photo-editing programs (which shall remain nameless), you don't have to have all of your filters in the same location.

13

Introducing the Filter Dialog Box

Since a majority of the controls for the filters share a common dialog box, we are going to take a quick look at one and see what options it offers. Although the portion of the dialog box containing the sliders, check boxes, and number boxes changes to accommodate the different filter controls, the view options remain generally the same.

Preview Options

In the image next is a dialog box for Edge Detect—a pretty basic filter. There are four buttons in the upper-right corner. The top two are standard Windows fare— the X closes the dialog box and the question mark enables a help function. The two below them determine which of the three preview options are used. The button with the eye icon in the lower left of the dialog box determines whether the preview is updated with each change in the dialog box.

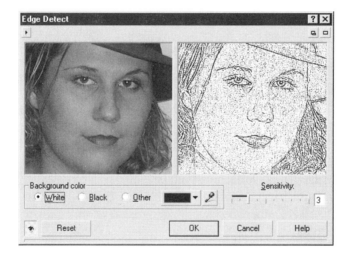

The dialog box shown next is currently in onscreen preview mode —hence, no Preview windows. The lower two buttons in the upper-right corner of the dialog box determine whether the preview is a large single window, or a split window in a traditional before and after format.

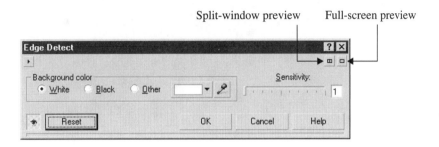

A different filter dialog box is shown in the next section in split-window Preview mode. Notice that the icon on the left button has changed. Split screens show preview thumbnails of the original image as well as what the image will look like after application of the filter. The advantage to using this approach is that you can see and compare the result against the original. The disadvantage is that the Preview windows are smaller than the single-screen preview.

Panning and Zooming

You will notice a hand in the left preview screen shown next. This is a combination zoom and grabber tool. Whenever the cursor is placed over the left preview, it becomes a hand, which is very handy (groan). Left-clicking the preview zooms in, and right-clicking zooms out. If you click and drag in the left preview, you will drag the image— it's called *panning*. The results of this panning and zooming happen

13

in real time in the left preview, and follow in the right preview after the filter has processed the filter and generated the preview.

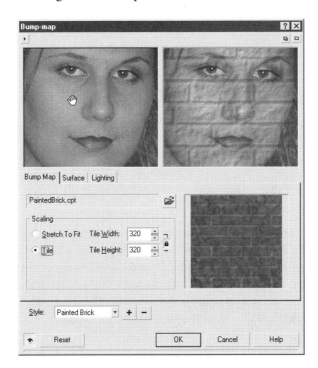

In the single-pane preview, shown next, the pan and zoom hand works in the entire Preview window. If the filter is complex, like the Watercolor filter that is shown, there will be a delay as the computer tries to update the display as quickly as possible. You would be best advised to turn off the preview (button in lower-left corner), while fine-tuning the zoom and position of your Preview window.

Onscreen preview, some will say, is the best way to preview filter actions. Using the actual image to preview the effects gives the most accurate possible form of preview. For what it's worth, I use PHOTO-PAINT about 6–8 hours a day, and I find I use all three preview modes.

13

Other Effects

Corel has left a shortcut to other effects without having to cancel the current filter and go back through the Effects menu. The button located in the upper-left corner opens a combined list of both the Effects and Image menus. In the illustration that follows, from the Smart Blur filter dialog box, I have opened the menu of items from the Effects menu and am about to select Impressionist filter from the Art Strokes. Please get in the habit of using this feature. In the long run, it will save you a lot of time.

I believe that you can figure out the remainder of the buttons—Reset, OK, and so on—without my help.

Repeat and Fade Last Commands

There will be times when you want to reapply a filter's effect one or more times. You could reopen the filter dialog box and apply the effect again, but there's a better way. PHOTO-PAINT has several commands that allow you to repeat a command or reapply the last command at a reduced level. These commands are not limited to filters.

The Last Effect and Repeat Effect Commands

You can repeat an Effect by choosing Effects | Repeat | Last Effect. The last effect will be applied just like the last time it was applied. A shortcut for repeating the last effect is CTRL-F. You could also repeat the effect or any other command with the Repeat command in the Edit menu or CTRL-L. The name of the Repeat command varies according to the last operation you performed. For example, if you want to repeat a brush stroke that you just applied to an image using the Paint tool, the Repeat command is called Repeat Tool Stroke.

Fade Last Command

While the Fade command can be used with other effects, it adds a special dimension to filter applications. With the Fade Last Command item in the Edit menu, you can reapply a filter using one of the merge modes. When filters are initially applied using their regular filter dialog box, it is done in Normal merge mode; there are no options to use the different merge modes. When the Fade Last Command choice is used, however, the last effect is undone and reapplied using the percentage and merge mode selected in the dialog box shown next. The onscreen preview can be turned on and off by clicking the eye icon in the upper-left corner. The Percent slider controls the amount of fade to apply to the last effect application. Therefore, if I set it for 99% (max) in Normal mode, the effect will be completely faded. In other words, the last effect is not applied. At a 50% setting, the last effect is faded by 50%. Don't get bogged down with this; you can't sit down with a calculator and predict the outcome. Play with different settings. Fade Last Command is very powerful, and I have discovered many unusual effects using it in combination with existing filters.

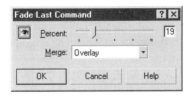

> NOTE   *Onscreen preview is the only preview option available with this filter.*

Now that you know the principles of operation for the filters, let's begin to explore the vast array of filters included in PHOTO-PAINT. Our filter odyssey continues as we will look at the filters that are used for image correction.

The Sharpen Filters

While blur filters reduce differences between adjacent pixels, thereby softening the image, sharpen filters do the opposite: they increase the differences, giving an apparent sharpness to the image. No matter how crisp your original photograph and how great your scanner is, you will always lose some sharpness when any

13

image is digitized. An image also loses sharpness when it is sent to an output device or when it is compressed. As a result, most images will appear "soft" when printed unless some degree of sharpening is applied. Corel PHOTO-PAINT contains several sharpening filers that can help make your images as sharp as possible. The Sharpen category of the Effects menu contains six filters that provide a wide range of sharpening effects that can be used to both improve image quality and create special effects.

The Sharpen subgroup of the Effects menu has the following filters:

- Tune Sharpen

- Adaptive Unsharp

- Directional Sharpen

- High Pass

- Sharpen

- Unsharp Mask

Three of these filters—Adaptive Unsharp, Unsharp Mask, and Directional Sharpen—act in roughly the same manner, introducing small amounts of distortion to the image to reduce noise enhancement. The Sharpen filter is a true sharpen filter that sharpens both the image and its noise equally. The High Pass filter removes low-frequency detail and shading, while emphasizing highlights and lighter areas of an image. The Tune filter allows you to apply all but the High Pass filter to an image from the same dialog box.

Please notice that in the group of filters called the *sharpening filters*, there is an individual filter called the Sharpen filter. As a point of clarification, when I talk about the Sharpen filter, I am referring to the specific filter and not to a general type of filter. If you find that confusing, wait until you learn that the best sharpening filter is called the Unsharp filter. Before we learn more about the individual filters, let's look at what happens when we sharpen an image.

What Is Sharpening?

Edges are what sharpening is all about. The human eye is influenced by the presence of edges in an image. Without edges, an image appears dull. By increasing the difference (contrast) between neighboring pixels, PHOTO-PAINT can enhance the edges, thus making the image appear to be sharper to the viewer, whether it is or not. While sharpening filters help compensate for images or image elements that

FIGURE 13-2 The original photograph lacks detail

are out of focus, don't expect sharpening to bring a blurred photograph into sharp focus. Figure 13-2 shows a photograph before sharpening was applied; Figure 13-3

FIGURE 13-3 Application of sharpening brings out detail in the ancient building

shows the result of selective application using one of the filters in the sharpening group. In this example, a mask protected the background and the sharpening was applied to the architecture.

When to Apply Sharpening

Some argue that the best time to apply sharpening is when an image is scanned. I have seen several comparisons between images that were sharpened during scanning and those done with sharpening filters after the scan; believe me, the sharpening on the scanned images was visibly sharper. In fairness, the scanner was a $500,000 drum scanner and the operator was an experienced professional. Once the image is in electronic form, the decision to apply sharpening during the scanning process has already been made for you. If your image didn't have sharpening applied during the scan, then to sharpen it, you will need to use one of the filters included with Corel PHOTO-PAINT.

TIP   *Sharpening is one of the last effects you should apply. Apply it after tonal and color correction, as it will affect the results of both.*

How Sharpening Affects Noise

All computer images include noise. Noise consists of pixels that may produce a grainy pattern, or the odd dark or light spot. Images from photographs will always have noise. Actually, any image, including those captured with digital cameras, will have noise of some sort. The most pristine photo in your stock photo collection that was scanned on a ten-zillion-dollar drum scanner will exhibit some noise. The only exception to this concept of universal noise is the Uniform color fill, which has no noise—or detail.

What does noise have to do with the sharpening filters? When we sharpen an image, we "sharpen" the noise as well. In fact, the noise generally sharpens up much better and faster than the rest of the image, because noise pixels (like the tiny white specks in a black background) contain the one component that sharpening filters look for—namely, the differences between adjoining pixels. Since the act of sharpening seeks out the differences (edges) and increases the contrast, the edges of the noise are enhanced and enlarged more than the rest of the pixels in the image.

Unsharp Masking Filters (USM)

In the trade, there is a group of filters generically referred to as *unsharp masking filters (USMs)*. The word *unsharping* is confusing to first-time users of photo-editing programs. Unsharping is named after a traditional film compositing technique that highlights the edges in an image by combining a blurred film negative with the original film positive, which results in a sharper image without enhancing the noise. In PHOTO-PAINT, the Adaptive Unsharp, Directional Sharpen, and Unsharp Mask filters fall into this category.

The Unsharp Mask filter can minimize the effect of the noise by distorting the image. Don't panic—when I say *distorting,* I am referring to the effect of toning down the sharp borders of noise while providing general sharpening of the other pixels in the image. The result is an overall sharpening of the image without enhancing the noise.

The Unsharp Mask Filter

The Unsharp Mask filter, like the Sharpen filter, compares each pixel in the image to its neighboring pixels. It then looks for amounts of contrast between adjacent pixels. PHOTO-PAINT assumes that a certain amount of contrast between adjoining pixels represents an edge. After it has found pixels that appear to be an edge, it creates a light corona around those pixels. USM can also produce an undesired effect by creating halos around detected edges when applied in excessive amounts. The Unsharp Mask filter (and any other filter in the Sharpen group) is best used selectively.

13

The Adaptive Unsharp Filter

With the Adaptive Unsharp filter, you have local control over the sharpening process around each pixel, rather than a global sharpening amount applied to the image in general. Adaptive Unsharp uses a process that evaluates statistical differences (Adaptive) between adjacent pixels to determine the sharpening amount for each pixel. The Adaptive Unsharp filter is very similar in its effects to the other two Unsharp filters, Directional Sharpen and Unsharp Mask. Testing done while writing the book has shown some subtle differences, mainly that Adaptive Unsharp appears to produce slightly less contrast than the other two.

The Directional Sharpen Filter

This is another sharpening filter with local sharpening control. With this filter, sharpening amounts for each pixel are computed for several compass directions, and the greatest amount of these will be used as the final sharpening amount for that pixel. In other words, the Directional Sharpen filter analyzes values of pixels of similar color shades to determine the direction in which to apply the greatest amount of sharpening. I have found that the Directional Sharpen filter usually increases the contrast of the image more than the Unsharp Mask filter does. The Directional Sharpen filter also produces good sharpening, but with higher contrast than either the Unsharp Mask or Adaptive Unsharp filter. I prefer to use the Directional Sharpening for any image that contains lots of strong diagonals.

The Sharpen Filter

The most important thing to remember about sharpening an image is that the Sharpen filter is rarely the best filter to use. Use one of the three USM filters discussed in the previous paragraphs. Why? Because the Sharpen filter doesn't care about noise; it just sharpens everything in the photograph. It is a powerful filter that will blow the socks off your image if you are not careful. The Sharpen filter sharpens the appearance of the image or a masked area by intensifying the contrast of neighboring pixels. There are times when this filter may be preferred over any of the previously described filters, but they are rare.

The Sharpen Filter dialog box contains three controls. The Edge Level (%) slider controls the amount of sharpening applied to the image. Use this filter at higher settings with some degree of caution. Higher values usually produce blowouts. The Threshold slider determines the level of contrast between adjoining pixels that is necessary for the filter action to occur. For example, if the Threshold value is set high, more pixels meet the minimum requirement and the sharpening effect will be applied to more of the image. If the Threshold is set low, only the high-contrast elements of the image will be affected. The Preserve Colors check box, when enabled, prevents dramatic shifts in hue when applying a sharpening effect.

The High Pass Filter

I placed this filter last because it is unique. Officially, the High Pass filter removes low-frequency detail and shading, while emphasizing highlights and luminous areas of an image. This filter enables you to isolate high-contrast image areas from their low-contrast counterparts. The action of the filter makes a high-contrast image into a murky gray one. Now you may rightly wonder why you would ever want a filter to do something like that. The answer is that this filter is best used as preparatory to other filter actions.

The Tune Sharpen Filter

Now that you know what all of the sharpening filters do, you can see them all (except High Pass) at once with Tune Sharpen, shown next. While having the filters grouped together facilitates multiple applications of different filters, there is a loss of control. The Edge Level (%), Preserve Colors, and Threshold controls found in the Sharpen Filter dialog box are missing in the Tune Sharpen filter, as are the Radius and Threshold controls of the Unsharp Mask filter.

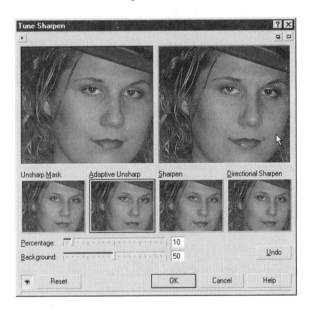

Now you know a lot more about the sharpening filters. Please, if you remember nothing else from this section, remember that excessive sharpening brings out noise, lots of noise. Now, let's look into the opposite of sharpening—the blur filters.

The Blur Filters

The blur filters represent a fundamental category of filters that is essential to photo-editing. Blur filters accomplish what their name implies: they make selected portions of an image blurred, in other words, out of focus. They accomplish this magic by softening the transitions between adjacent pixels. If you are new to photo-editing, it may seem that blurring an image is the last thing you would want to do. In fact, there are many reasons to blur an image, ranging from creating the illusion of depth of field to creating special effects.

Here is some factual information about blur filters that is about as interesting as cold coffee. The Blur category in the Effects menu, shown next, contains a collection of ten filters that produce a wide variety of blur effects. The last filter on the list is also the newest: Smart Blur. There is also a Tune Blur filter, which allows you to apply four of the Blur filters from one dialog box. The type of blur filter you select is chiefly determined by the type of image you are working with and by the effect you want to obtain. None of the blur filters will work with paletted (8-bit) or line art (images composed of only black and white pixels). When working with Grayscale 16-bit or RGB Color (48-bit), Jaggy Despeckle is the only blur filter available. For you to access all of the blur filters, the image must be either grayscale or color (24-bit, CMYK, or multichannel). Of all of the filters in this bunch, the Gaussian Blur filter is undoubtedly the most used, so we will begin there.

The Gaussian Blur Filter

This filter, although deceptively simple, is used every day to make shadows, produce glows, diffuse backgrounds, and aid in many of the special effects created with PHOTO-PAINT. At its lower settings, the Gaussian Blur filter can give an image a slightly out-of-focus look; while at higher settings, it can make the image into fog. I have heard it said that this filter can be used to improve the quality of images containing jaggies, with some loss of detail. In practice, I have found that once there is enough blur to make jaggies acceptable, the picture looks as though it were shot in London on a very foggy morning.

Subtle Emphasis by Creating a Depth of Field

Creation of a pseudo-depth of field by slightly blurring an area of the image is a good way to subtly emphasize a subject without making a big show of it. While it is easy to define edges of buildings and other straight-line objects, in day-to-day photo-editing work, you have edges that require a more subtle approach. In this session, you will learn how to define the edges of the subject using a path.

Depth of Field

When working on photographs (digital or film), it is important to become acquainted with some of the terms. Any serious photographer knows about the phenomena named *depth of field.* If you're not familiar with the term, read on to find out more.

Unlike the brain, which has two "lenses" (the eyes) to produce three dimensions, most cameras have only one lens, which produces two dimensions on the film plane. Again unlike the eyes, a camera lens records a scene in a split moment of time. We humans believe we see sharply over large areas, but this is an illusion. The reason everything within our vision appears sharp (assuming I am wearing my glasses) is that our eyes are constantly refocusing on whatever has our attention. Most of these refocusing movements are so tiny that we aren't even aware of them. The camera lens cannot re-create what our stereoscopic and constantly refocusing eyes view naturally. Instead, it focuses on one object. The amount of the picture in front of and behind the object that is also in focus is determined by the size of the lens opening (aperture), called the *f-stop setting.* The smaller the f-stop, the wider the plane of focus (or depth of field) and the more the image is in focus. The wider the f-stop, the shallower the depth of field and the less the image is in focus.

13

The viewer who doesn't know anything about depth of field still unconsciously makes use of its principles. When shown the image in Figure 13-4, a viewer knows that all of the globes are grouped together. When shown the image in Figure 13-5, the viewer assumes the two globes that are slightly out of focus are much farther behind the three globes in the foreground.

Removal of Banding Using the Gaussian Blur Filter

The Gaussian Blur filter can also be used to diminish the effect of banding in a fountain fill. The text shown in Figure 13-6(a) contain a six-step fountain fill to make the banding apparent. After the application of the Gaussian Blur filter, there is no evidence of the original banding (see Figure 13-6(b)). Be careful not to set the amount of Gaussian Blur too high. At very high settings, you will turn the entire image into fog.

FIGURE 13-4   With all the globes in focus, it appears they are all grouped closely together

FIGURE 13-5   Blurring two of the globes causes them to appear more distant from the others

FIGURE 13-6   (a) The original text has serious banding problems; (b) The Gaussian Blur filter removes the banding

13

The Motion Blur Filter

The Motion Blur filter is designed to create the impression of movement in an image. It achieves this effect by determining the edges of the image for the direction selected, and smearing them back and forth across the adjacent pixels. There are several issues to consider before using the Motion Blur filter. First, the ideal subject is something—people, events, or things—associated with speed. After all, it looks wrong to see a photograph of two chess players in Central Park with speed blurs coming off of them. Not only does the subject need to be associated with movement, but the direction the subject is facing is also important. For instance, the photograph of a racing car shown in Figure 13-7 is a good choice because it appears to be traveling across the field of view. If it were coming directly at or away from the viewer, it would be more difficult to achieve the effect.

High-speed films can freeze the action so that the subject in the photograph appears to be standing still. In fact, there isn't any indication in this photo that there is movement. It looks as if the vehicle is parked on the raceway. When using a photograph like this in an ad or brochure, you want to convey a sense of action to the viewer. You can achieve apparent motion using the Motion Blur filter.

FIGURE 13-7   The photograph, taken with high-speed film, makes the car look parked

There are two ways to approach the application of motion. You can blur the subject or blur the background. Blurring the subject makes it appear to be moving fast but has the drawback of making the subject blurred. A popular technique used in car advertisements these days is to blur the background. This approach is most effective, since it conveys the sense of speed and keeps the product (car) in focus.

A mask is necessary to limit the areas being blurred. If you apply the Motion Blur filter to the entire image, it will just appear to be an out-of-focus picture. To limit the effect to just the background, a mask was placed around the car and then inverted. A mask with hard edges will produce areas of transition where the blur begins and ends abruptly, which looks very strange. To eliminate this, the mask must be feathered.

In Figure 13-8, the background had a large amount (70 pixels) of Motion Blur applied. This amount made the background unrecognizable; but since the subject is the car, it heightens the effect of apparent motion. The Motion Blur filter created a faint halo around some of the car edges because the mask had been feathered. Doing this also helps convey the sense of motion to the viewer and is done more in recognition of perceptions we humans have regarding things in motion than of the laws of physics.

13

FIGURE 13-8   Blurring the background while leaving the car in focus is one way to give the impression of speed

Figure 13-9 shows the result of applying the Motion Blur filter directly to the subject, and then using the Local Undo tool from the Eraser tool's flyout to remove the effect on the front, top, and sides of the cars. Not wishing to remove all of the effect, I set the Transparency value of the Local Undo tool (on the property bar) to a moderate-to-high value. Remember that double-clicking the Local Undo tool removes the entire application of the effect. I did this more than once myself, so learn from my mistakes.

The Jaggy Despeckle Filter

The Jaggy Despeckle filter scatters colors in an image to create a soft, blurred effect with very little distortion. It also smoothes out jagged edges *(jaggies)* on images. There are a few techniques that benefit from the Jaggy Despeckle filter. When applied to a photograph, it has a tendency to blur the image slightly. Jaggy Despeckle operates by performing edge detection on the image. After the filter thinks it knows where all the hard edges are, it applies antialiasing to the edges to give a smoother appearance.

FIGURE 13-9   A more subtle way to show speed is to blur the subject

> **NOTE** *Photoshop refers to this filter by its last name—Despeckle—and it is found in the Noise category rather than the Blur category.*

Using the Jaggy Despeckle Filter

My favorite use of this filter is for descreening a scanned image. When halftone images are scanned, the halftone patterns have this nasty tendency to make their presence known. Here is my recipe for removing halftone screens from scanned images.

1. Scan the image at 200% of the size of the desired finished image. For example, if the final image is going to be 3 × 4 inches, scan the image in at a size of 6 × 8 inches.

2. Apply the Jaggy Despeckle filter at a low setting. This will break up the halftone pattern.

3. Resample the image to its desired size and apply the Unsharp mask filter to restore the image sharpness.

Another application of the Jaggy Despeckle filter is to correct an individual color channel that has a lot of noise or areas that are exhibiting jaggies. This happens a lot with the images you get from digital cameras and occurs mainly with the blue channel. If you use this approach to reduce noise in an image, check each channel in the image to see which one exhibits the greatest amount of noise (it's always blue, trust me). Next, with a mask tool, select the area of the channel image needing the Jaggy Despeckle filter. Be aware that applying a large setting to an individual channel or applying the filter to the entire image may cause multicolored artifacts to appear when the channels are viewed together.

The Radial Blur Filter

The Radial Blur filter creates a blurring effect by rotating the image outward from a central point. The area immediately surrounding the center point is relatively unaffected, while the degree of the effect increases as it moves away from the center point. The crosshair button is used to set the center point of this effect. Setting the Center Point involves clicking the button and then clicking the image, either on the screen or in the preview window, to place the center point of the effect.

13

As with most of the filters, the key to using the Radial Blur filter effectively is either to use it with images whose subject matter has a symmetry that naturally flows with the flow of the filter or to control affected areas with masks.

Zoom Filter

This filter acts in the same way as the previously discussed Radial filter, except the Zoom filter smears pixels outward from the center point. It is meant to duplicate the effect a photographer gets when moving a zoom lens in or out while taking a picture. This is a great filter for creating dynamic attention-getting effects with sports and action photos.

The Directional Smooth Filter

The Directional Smooth filter analyzes values of pixels of similar color shades to determine in which direction to apply the greatest amount of smoothing. You adjust the Percentage. Sounds great, right? Remember, this is a blur filter. The Directional Smooth is nearly identical in operation to the Smooth and Soften filters, although the results obtained are slightly different.

The Smooth Filter

The Smooth filter tones down differences in adjacent pixels, resulting in only a slight loss of detail while smoothing the image of the selected area. The differences between the effects of the Smooth and Soften filters are subtle and may only be apparent on a high-resolution display, and sometimes not even then.

The Soften Filter

The Soften filter smoothes and tones down harshness without losing detail. The differences between the effects of the Smooth and Soften filters are subtle and may only be apparent on a high-resolution display or in the mind of the person who programmed this filter.

Getting It All Together—The Tune Blur

The Tune Blur feature, which used to be called "Control," was of limited value in releases prior to PHOTO-PAINT 9, because you could only see the effects in a small preview window. In PHOTO-PAINT 10, it is possible to view the results onscreen. Choosing Effects | Blur | Tune opens the dialog box called Tune Blur, shown in the following illustration. Four blur filters—Gaussian, Smooth, Directional Smooth, and Soften—can be applied to the current image. The Smart Blur filter, discussed next, is not available in Tune Blur. When you adjust the number of Steps, the thumbnail of each filter reflects the changes. Clicking the thumbnail of the desired filter applies the filter to the image in the Result window. To Undo the last filter application, you can click the Undo button. Repeatedly clicking this button lets you step back through a group of effects applied. To return to ground zero, press the Reset button. Different filters can be applied multiple times using the Tune Blur dialog box.

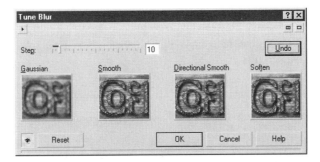

Smart Blur Filter

The newest addition to the PHOTO-PAINT Blur family is the Smart Blur filter. The purpose of the Smart Blur filter is to blur the low-contrast portion of an image while retaining the edges. This way, you can de-emphasize photo grain, blemishes, and artifacts without blurring the real edges in the image. The filter has a single Amount slider control with a range of 0–100. This slider controls both the amount of blur and the threshold together. As the Amount slider is increased, the blur begins to blur the edges. Figure 13-10 is an image that contains high-contrast edges in the text and only medium-contrast background. Figure 13-11 is the result of applying the Smart Blur filter.

13

The Original image has high-contrast letters and a medium-contrast background

Application of the Smart Blur filter preserves the letters and smoothes out everything else

The Low Pass Filter

The Low Pass filter is not a traditional blur filter. What makes this filter unique is that it selectively blurs. It does this by detecting and removing high-frequency (highlight) portions of the photograph, leaving shadows and low-frequency detail. The dialog box contains two Slider bars, one for Percentage (0–100) and the other for Radius (1–20). The Percentage value controls the intensity of the effect, and Radius controls the range of pixels that are affected. At higher settings, the Low Pass filter creates a blurring effect, which is why it is in the blur filter section. This action erases much of the image's detail. If you need only to de-emphasize (smooth) highlights, use a lower percentage setting.

Next, we explore the exciting world of noise. Noise—not the kind that comes from a boom box—is a fact of life in digital imagery and these filters help create, remove, and control it.

Noise Filters

Noise, those random pixels that appear in your digital images, is unavoidable. However, you can control it, get rid of it, and even add it to your images. It can be used to add an apparent sharpness to a soft image or "grit" to an otherwise smooth surface. Yet naturally occurring noise, which can result from poorly scanned images or from the film grain of certain film types, can be distracting. Whether noise needs to be removed or added, Corel PHOTO-PAINT provides the necessary filters. The Noise subgroup in the Effects menu has the following eight filters:

- Add Noise
- Diffuse
- Dust & Scratch
- Maximum
- Median
- Minimum
- Remove Moiré
- Remove Noise

13

The Tune Noise dialog box has a group of nine filters: More Spike, More Gaussian, More Uniform, Diffuse, Minimum, Median, Maximum, Jaggy Despeckle, and Remove Noise.

Noise in digital images is normally a bad thing, akin to visual static. Like an uninvited guest at a party, noise seems to show up in the worst possible places in an image. During scanning, for example, it is difficult for the scanner elements to pick out detail in the darker (shadow) regions of a photograph. As a result, these areas will contain more than their fair share of noise. All those ugly little specks on the faxes you receive are caused by noise. Because of the physical composition of noise, it tends to stand out and make itself known in a photograph, especially when you sharpen an image. In this chapter, you will learn how to minimize noise; but first, let's see how useful noise can be when added to digital images.

The Add Noise Filter

Why would you want to add noise? Actually, adding noise has more uses than you might first imagine. Noise can give the effect of grit and texture to a picture. With images containing fountain fills or uniform colors, the addition of noise can make them appear more realistic. Adding noise can be helpful in softening the look of stark image areas. When you are retouching photographs that have unwanted film-grain texture, it can be helpful to add noise so that the blending is less apparent.

The Add Noise filter creates a granular effect that adds texture to a flat or overly blended image. There are several neat tricks that can be done with this filter. Let's begin with a description of how it operates.

The Add Noise Filter Dialog Box

As with the other filter dialog boxes, there are three possible preview modes on the Add Noise dialog box: Onscreen, Original/Result, and Single Result preview. The application of noise is determined by the level, density, noise type, and color mode.

Two different settings, the Level and the Density sliders, determine the amount of noise applied to an image. The Level slider controls the intensity of the noise pixels. In other words, the white component of the noise becomes much more apparent. The slider operates on a percentage scale of 0–100. A lower setting makes the noise barely visible; a higher setting moves right into dandruff. The default setting of 50 for this slider is much too high for most applications. A Level setting of 6 is recommended as a starting point.

The Density slider, operating on a percentage scale of 0–100, controls the number of noise pixels added to the image. A lower setting adds very few noise pixels; a higher setting produces something so dense you can't see the original without squinting.

This dialog box, just shown, also has the Color Mode options. Intensity produces black specks, Random produces multicolored specks, Single allows you to choose a color from the pop-up color swatch, and the Eyedropper allows you to choose a color from the image. Color noise looks like someone put a rainbow into a blender and then pressed the frappé button. I think selecting a specific color is a neat idea, but at this point, I haven't made much use of it. This doesn't mean there isn't one, it's just I haven't thought of one yet.

Color noise is a horse of a different color. Applying color noise to a color photograph is a great way to give a negative or distressed feeling to a photograph. A few years back, a mother drowned her two children and *Time* magazine put her on the cover. The only photograph they had was less than their usual high quality. The solution was simple—they applied color noise. Defects in the photograph were no longer apparent, and the color-speckled graininess added a strong emotional impact to an already grievous crime. Regardless of the color you pick, you must also choose what type of noise. Corel offers three choices: Heavy Metal, Grunge Rock, and Yodeling. Just kidding—no e-mails, please.

13

Types of Noise

Three types of noise are available: Gaussian, Spike, and Uniform. The difference between the Gaussian and Uniform noise is slight. The Spike noise appears as tiny speckles on the image.

- **Gaussian**   This is the noise of choice. The other two noise options are included only because Corel is an equal opportunity employer. Technically, the filter prioritizes shades or colors (if color noise is selected) of the image pixels along a Gaussian distribution curve.

- **Spike**   This filter uses shades or colors, if color noise is selected, that are distributed around a narrow curve (spike). A thinner, lighter-colored grain that looks like black-and-white specks is produced. In fact, it is almost impossible to see, unless you use a very high setting.

- **Uniform**   This filter provides an overall grainy appearance that is not evenly dispersed like the Gaussian noise. Use this option to apply noise in an absolutely random fashion. You will discover that this is a good choice when combined with the Emboss filter to create rough textures.

Noise Filter Effects

The noise filters are used to create a wide variety of effects, from creating textures to adding dramatic touches to an image.

Removing Banding from a Radial Fill

Many times, if a radial fill (or any gradient fill, for that matter) is applied to a large area, some banding occurs. *Banding* is the phenomenon wherein the changes of color or shades appear as bands in the image. This effect is more pronounced in low-resolution output than in higher-resolution output. It is also more apparent in grayscale or 256-color fills than in 24-bit color. In Chapter 22, you will learn that while a Gaussian Blur filter could reduce or remove banding, it also blurs the subject matter. In some cases, it is better to remove the effect of banding with noise. In Figure 13-12, an eight-step fountain fill was applied to some text to simulate banding (top). Next, a Gaussian noise with a Level setting of 29 and a Density setting of 100 was applied to disguise it (bottom).

FIGURE 13-12   A little noise can hide banding in fills

Noise and Focus

Because the human eye believes images are in sharper focus when it sees areas of higher contrast, the viewer can be tricked into seeing an image as being in sharper focus by introducing a very small amount of Gaussian noise onto a soft image. This process is often referred to as *dusting* the image. When you see the results, you may think at first that nothing was accomplished. In fact, to the operator, the image appears noisier. That's because (1) it does have more noise, and (2) you know what the original looked like before you added the noise. To a first-time viewer of the photograph, it will appear sharp.

Removing Noise Without Buying Earplugs

Up until now we have been adding noise. The remaining filters in this chapter are dedicated to removing noise. While names like Diffuse, Maximum, and Minimum don't sound like the names of filters that remove noise, you will learn that removing noise is what they were designed to do. I'm not saying that all these filters actually remove noise, just that removal of noise is what they were *designed* to do.

13

The Diffuse Filter

The Diffuse filter scatters pixels in an image or a selected area, creating a smooth appearance. Like the Gaussian Blur, the Diffuse filter scatters the pixels, producing a blurred effect. So why is the filter listed in the Noise section of Effects? Because its operation is to reduce noise, which is correct. When an image is blurry, you can't see the noise very well, or anything else for that matter.

This filter is a no-brainer. The Level slider in the Diffuse Filter dialog box controls the amount of diffusion in the image. The Level slider in the dialog box can be set to a value between 1 and 100. The important question is what to do with the Diffuse filter. In the illustration shown next, the character in the middle is the original. One of the characters had the Diffuse filter applied three times at 100%, and the other had a Gaussian Blur applied once at a setting of three pixels. Can you see the difference? Neither can I. Okay, just to save the e-mails, the one on the right had the Diffuse filter applied, or . . . was it the other one?

The Dust & Scratch Filter

The Dust & Scratch filter does a fantastic job of removing noise. It removes or reduces image noise at areas of high contrast, softening the appearance. The Dust & Scratch filter is not a magic cure-all, but it is quite effective in removing garbage from an image that would take too long to manually remove with a brush. To clean up problem areas without affecting the rest of the image, you may wish to mask the dirty area before applying the filter. Make sure you feather the edge of the mask before applying the filter so that there are no visual indications that you have been playing with the image.

Most of your adjustment to this filter should be done with the Threshold slider (0–255). By setting Threshold low, you are telling the filter that all levels of contrast above the Threshold setting are considered noise. The Radius slider (1–20) determines the number of pixels surrounding the noise that will be included in the removal process. Be advised that increasing the Radius setting dramatically increases the area affected. In almost all cases, you should be using settings at or near 1.

Using the Dust & Scratch Filter

The best way to remove the dust and debris is to take the photograph (or negative, in this case), clean it, and rescan it. This option is usually not available, so the second-best solution is to use the Dust & Scratch filter. When an image has a lot of debris on it, I recommend a two-stage approach. First, use the Mask Brush tool (in Additive mode) to select all the worst areas.

To clean up the general noise, remove the mask and apply a milder setting of the Dust & Scratch filter. The easiest way to determine the optimum setting is to set the filter to operate in Onscreen Preview mode and adjust the Threshold slider until the image looks right. The best setting will be a compromise between noise reduction and loss of image detail. To correct for the loss of image detail, you can apply a small amount of the Effects | Sharpen | Unsharp Mask filter.

Messing with Masks

The next three filters—Maximum, Minimum, and Median—are in the Noise category because they theoretically remove noise. Just because I've never seen the noise removal concept actually work using these filters doesn't mean they don't remove noise. They just don't remove noise for me. So are they useless? Not in the least. They are the principal tools for a category of techniques that involved extensive operations with the individual channels in Photoshop. They were known as *channel ops (CHOPs)*. Before Photoshop got sophisticated, most of the effects we take for granted were created using CHOPs. Now that we have fancy filters, the need for CHOPs has diminished; but the Maximum, Median, and Minimum filters still have important roles to play in the area of mask manipulation. To give you some idea what these filters can do, the illustration shown next will serve as a reference image. This mask, which was made from text that was then deleted, is shown in

13

Paint on Mask mode. As we discuss these three filters, we will see just what the filters can, and cannot, do.

Maximum Filter

The Maximum filter makes the lighter pixels larger and shrinks the darker ones. With the Percentage slider (1–100), you can control the amount of filtering applied to the affected pixels. The greater the value, the darker the affected pixels become. The Radius slider (1–20 pixels) determines the number of pixels that are successively selected and affected. In the next image, the Radius was set to 10 pixels and the Percentage set to 50. The result visually demonstrates the filter action. The white area expands by 10 pixels in all directions, while the black area shrinks. However, the percentage setting dictates that the 10-pixel expansion be only 50 percent affected, so the expanded area is 50 percent gray. Now, what is the difference between applying the Maximum filter to a mask and using Mask | Shape | Expand? Other than the ability to control the percentage, the results are identical.

The Minimum Filter

Quite simply, the Minimum filter is the evil twin of the Maximum filter. It makes the lighter pixels smaller and the darker ones larger. When applied to a mask in Paint on Mask mode, the white portion of the mask shrinks. Applying the Minimum filter to a mask is equivalent to choosing Mask | Shape | Reduce, except for the ability to modify the percentage of effect. In the illustration shown next, we have applied the Minimum filter to the original mask at a Percentage of 50% and a Radius of 10 pixels. Notice that with both filters, the expansion or reduction of the mask does not follow the shape of the original very well. That is because the greater the increase, the greater the amount of distortion that is introduced into the resulting shape.

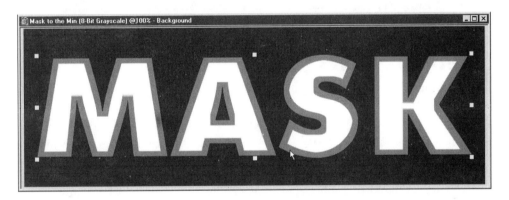

TIP   *The best way to expand or contract the mask of a single object or single character of text is to use the Mask Transform tool and drag the corner handles. This technique will not work on a string of text because the kerning (spacing between the characters) goes out the window.*

13

What can you do with an expanded or reduced mask? Here is a suggestion for something you can experiment with. Type some text (use a thick sans-serif text, because on thin text the effect is lost). Create a mask from the text. Next select Paint on Mask mode and apply the Minimum filter with a percentage of 50% and a Radius of 15. You now have a nice border surrounding your text. While still in

Paint on Mask mode, select Edit | Fill and choose a different fill. Invert the mask and apply The Boss filter to the edge. The result is shown in the following image:

The Median Filter

This filter simplifies the colors or shades in an image by reading the brightness of adjacent pixels of noise and averaging out the differences. Its ability to remove noise is dependent on the type of noise (sharp and high-contrast or blurred and low-contrast) in the image. One use is to smooth the rough areas in scanned images that have a grainy appearance. It does remove noise, but at the expense of making the image much softer (which sounds better than "blurry"). In Figure 13-13, the original image (left) has the Median filter applied at a radius of 5 (right). As you can see, the noise, along with about everything else, has been removed.

This filter uses a Radius slider to set the percentage of noise removal that is applied. The filter looks for pixels that are isolated and, based on the Radius setting in the dialog box, removes them. The Median filter tends to blur the image if it is set too high. What's too high? It has been my experience that if you are working on an image smaller than a billboard, you don't want to use a setting higher than 2.

Unleashing the Real Power of Median

Based on what we have learned so far, the Median filter appears to be about as useful as a screen door in a submarine. The secret is to use it with the Paint on Mask mode. Here is a quick session that will prove my point.

1. Create a new image that is 4.2 inches × 2 inches at 150 dpi. Make sure the Paint is set to black, select the Text tool, and change the font to GoudyOlSt

FIGURE 13-13 The original (on the left) and the image after the application of the
Median filter

BT at a size of 72. Select Bold. Type **Antique**. Select the Object Picker
tool, and center the text on the image (CTRL-A).

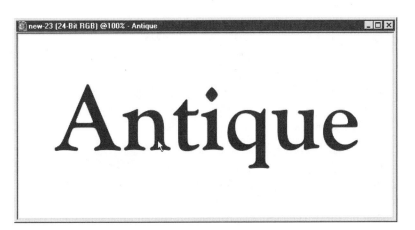

2. Create a mask (CTRL-M) and select Paint on Mask (CTRL-K). Choose Effects | Distort | Displace. Select Rusty.PCX as the displacement map. Change the Horizontal and Vertical settings to 20. Click OK.

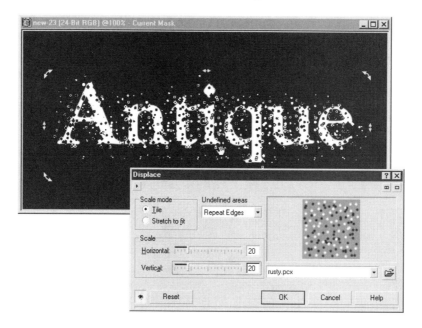

3. Choose Effects | Noise | Median. Change the Radius setting to 4 and click OK. The amount of Radius used depends on the size of the object. When I originally created this tutorial, I used a font size of 150, and the resulting Radius setting needed to be 6.

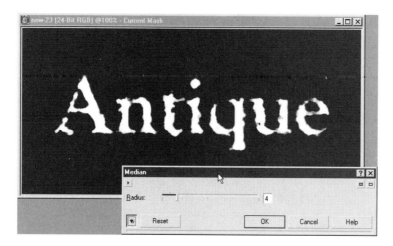

4. Exit Paint on Mask (CTRL-K) and choose Object | Crop to Mask.

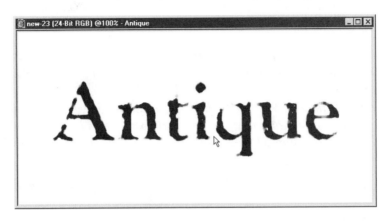

That's all there is to it. Didn't I tell you this filter was useful? I also use this filter to create corroded and perforated metal effects. Here are some additional ideas. You can use the Fill tool to add a background that looks a little like parchment or old paper.

The Remove Moiré Filter

Moiré patterns are nasty patterns that sometimes appear when you scan halftone or screened images. You rarely see the moiré patterns in PHOTO-PAINT, because the images are resampled when you change the size of an image. These unsightly patterns can also originate when you're resizing a dithered image. As the pixels in the image are moved around, their proximity to other pixels causes patterns to develop. Removal of these patterns is also called *descreening*.

Internally, the Remove Moiré filter uses a two-stage process to break up the patterns that cause the moiré effect. First, the equivalent of a Jaggy Despeckle filter is applied to soften the entire image. Second, the filter applies some sharpening to reduce the softening produced by the first step.

NOTE   *This filter is also known as a "descreening" filter in other scanning or photo-editing applications.*

The Remove Moiré filter provides an Amount slider, ranging from 0 to 10, to determine the amount of offset applied to the image. As the Amount is increased, the shift applied to the pixels is increased. Larger amounts produce greater softness and loss of detail. The two Optimize buttons—Speed and Quality—allow you to experiment if you have a really slow machine or a very large photograph (billboard). The output resolution of the filter provides the option of decreasing the resolution

13

(downsampling). If you select to downsample the final output, it will make the image smaller and increase its apparent sharpness. It's a Yin-Yang thing; one softens, the other sharpens.

> **TIP** *Okay, before we leave this exciting topic, let me give you my easy recipe for descreening a scanned image. Scan the original at 200% of what will be the final size. If the image has a lot of flat colors, apply the Jaggy Despeckle filter. If not, skip to the next step. Resample at 50%. Resampling the image applies antialiasing, which almost always breaks up any patterns in an image. Finally, apply Effects | Sharpen | Directional Sharpen at 50%. That's it.*

Moiré Patterns

Moiré patterns are one of most annoying things that happen when you're working with scanned bitmap images. You see them every now and then, especially when you scan printed originals—you know the ones I'm talking about—those copyrighted pages that we aren't supposed to scan.

The physical nature of moiré lies in the interference of two or more regular structures with different halftone frequencies. You can see this effect in real life if you watch a video of a computer display. The video is recording the image of the display that is slightly different from the one used by the computer display. It is the difference between the frequency that produces a third frequency, called a *beat* frequency, as illustrated in the next image The original photograph is of yours truly wearing a striped shirt. The striped patterned creates a moiré.

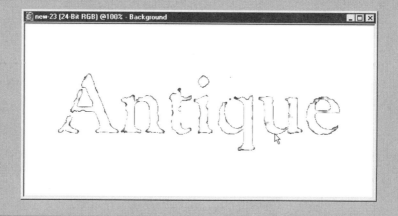

When an image is converted to a halftone (screened) to be printed, the two linear patterns of the screen have different frequencies; and being superimposed, they will show a frequency pattern, as can be easily seen in the illustration.

Want to get more technical? When you scan an image, a line of *CCD* (photosensitive elements) digitizes it. The optical resolution of the scanner and the size of an image determine the number of elements. For example, if you scan with the 600-dpi scanner and the image is 3 inches wide, then 1,800 CCDs will take part in digitizing the image. Each CCD is a discrete unit.

When the image has a pattern (such as plaid), it is superimposed with the scanner grid (the line of CCDs), possibly causing interference and resulting in moiré patterns. This is especially true if you scan printed originals, because usually a photograph (continuous-tone image) is printed with halftone screens. The screen frequency and a scanner resolution may mismatch, producing those dreaded moiré patterns. A misaligned or rotated original produces them, too.

Obviously the best way to remove the moiré patterns is to avoid scanning printed originals. Always choose the photographs and slides when possible.

The Remove Noise Filter

The Remove Noise filter acts as if you had combined the Jaggy Despeckle filter with the Median filter. This filter softens edges and reduces the speckled effect created by the scanning process or from line noise in faxes. Each pixel is compared with surrounding pixels, and an average value is computed. The pixels that exceed the value of the Threshold setting in the dialog box are removed. This operates in the same manner as the Jaggy Despeckle does on objects (reducing jaggies by softening edges); but unlike Jaggy Despeckle, it also removes random pixels (noise) in the image.

The operation of this filter is similar to the Remove Dust & Scratch filter described earlier. The most important setting in this dialog box is the Auto check box. Use it! The Auto check box, when enabled, automatically analyzes the image and determines the best Threshold setting for it. The Threshold setting cannot be changed when Auto is selected. The Threshold slider controls the amount of threshold (0–255) the program uses to differentiate between noise and non-noise. Use the Preview window to see the effects of different slider settings. While this slider can be set manually, I don't recommend it.

13

TIP
You can improve the performance of this filter on really trashy scans by masking the worst areas and applying the Remove Noise filter to them first. This speeds up the operation (because the area is smaller) and also keeps the filter from modifying areas that do not need to have any noise removed.

Tuning Up the Noise

As with many of the filters in PHOTO-PAINT, there is a Tune function that allows you to apply and combine many different types of noise in a single spot. It's kind of one-stop shopping for noise. Using this jewel is pretty straightforward. As you can see in Figure 13-14, you are given thumbnail previews of the effect that the application of each type of noise will produce. Clicking the thumbnail applies the noise and updates all of the thumbnails and the preview display. Because the

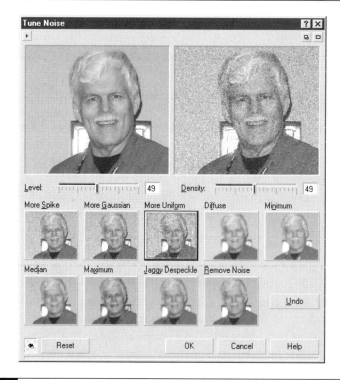

FIGURE 13-14 The Tune Noise dialog box allows previewing combinations of noise, and yet it is silent

thumbnail displays are quite small, you should view the effects of the application on the larger preview display and use the Undo button to remove effects if they are not satisfactory.

In Summary

This discussion of the noise filters concludes the noisiest part of this chapter. Of all the features in a photo-editing program, I use the noise filters almost as much as the blur filters, and I use them a lot. Now that we understand what the photo-enhancement filters do, let's see what effect filters Corel has put into PHOTO-PAINT 10.

13

CHAPTER 14

Exploring the PHOTO-PAINT Effect Filters

Unlike the filters in the previous chapter, which were used to correct or enhance images, the filters in this chapter are there to add all kinds of wild and crazy effects. All of these filters are located in the Effects menu, where they are divided into 16 different categories. In the previous chapter, we already looked at three of these categories: Sharpen, Blur, and Noise. This chapter will focus on the other 13 categories, beginning with the 3D Effect filters.

3D Effect Filters

Corel PHOTO-PAINT has a rich collection of ten filters that can be loosely grouped under the 3D category. Most give effects that appear to be 3D, but none are true 3D filters. All ten filters, shown next, are available with grayscale, duotone, 24-bit, and 32-bit color images. You can use 3D Rotate, Sphere, Cylinder, Perspective, Pinch/Punch, and Zig Zag filters with paletted (256-color) images. I put this stuff about what filters work with what at the beginning, so every section that describes a filter doesn't begin with "This filter works with blah, blah, blah." The bottom line is, this category contains filters I can't imagine working without and others that I can't imagine a useful purpose for. We will be looking at filters in their order of appearance; so, leading off the lineup is 3D Rotate.

The 3D Rotate Filter

The 3D Rotate filter rotates the image according to the horizontal and vertical limits set in the 3D Rotate dialog box. The rotation is applied as if the image were one side of a 3D box.

The 3D Rotate Dialog Box

The dialog box is shown next. The operation of filter is pretty obvious. The preview (either Preview window or onscreen) shows the perspective of the image with the current Vertical and Horizontal settings. The plane of the little box in the Preview window that is shaded represents the image. By changing the Vertical and Horizontal values, you can orient the preview box into the correct position. If the Best Fit check box is checked, the resulting effect will be made large enough to fit inside the image window borders. If it is not checked, it will be smaller as the program tries to calculate a size of the proper scale for the rotation selected.

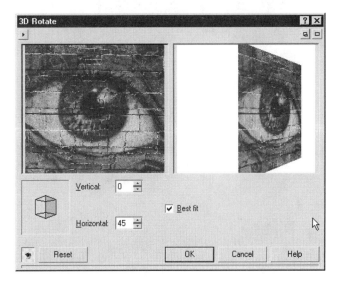

Using the 3D Rotate Filter

The 3D Rotate filter may be applied to the background or to objects, although the Lock Transparency option should not be enabled, as the results may be unpredictable. The basic problem is that while the rotation of the image occurs within the object, the object retains the same shape.

There are a few limitations to this filter. Although you can apply rotation to both the horizontal and vertical axes simultaneously, it is not recommended. The resulting image loses varying degrees of perspective. Also note that the preview doesn't always display the 3D perspective correctly.

Now that I have told you the bad news, that doesn't prevent us from applying the 3D Perspective filter to a photograph and making a box out of it, as shown in Figure 14-1.

14

FIGURE 14-1   A cool floating box that takes less than three minutes to create

The Cylinder Filter

This filter used to be one of the variations of the Sphere filter. Now it is out on its own. The purpose of the filter is to distort an image along either a horizontal or a vertical plane to give the appearance of a cylinder. It provides a good start for making a cylinder, but I find shading and highlights much more effective to create the effect.

The Emboss Filter

Embossing creates a 3D relief effect. Directional arrows point to the location of the light source and determine the angle of the highlights and shadows. The Emboss filter has its most dramatic effect on medium- to high-contrast images. Several filters can be used in combination with the Emboss filter to produce photorealistic effects.

The Emboss Dialog Box

The Emboss dialog box, shown next, provides all the controls necessary to produce a wide variety of embossing effects.

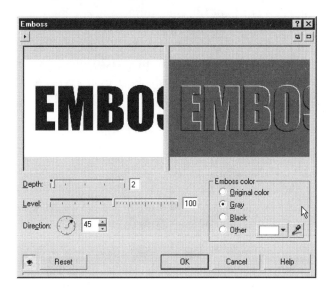

The Emboss Color section determines the color of the embossed image. When Original Color is selected, the Emboss filter uses the colors of the image to simulate the relief effect. When Black or Gray is selected, the entire image fills with that color. Maybe I spent too many years in the canoe club (Navy), but I have never had a desire to see something embossed in battleship gray. Now that I have said that, Gray is the preferred color to see the effect of the embossing before switching to Original Color. To select a solid color other than black or gray, you must click the Other button and choose from the Color palette.

The Depth slider sets the intensity of the embossing effect. Take care not to use an excessive value (greater than 5), since it can cause enough image displacement to make you think you need to schedule an eye appointment. The Level slider controls the radius of the effect. The effect on the image is that the white offset appears to be whiter. You can use a larger amount of Depth without distorting the image. Direction specifies the location of the light source. Light direction is important because it determines whether the image has a raised or a sunken surface. The best way to use these two sliders is when one is at a high value, make the other low. Follow that rule and you'll stay out of trouble.

14

The Glass Filter

The Glass filter creates the effect of a layer of glass on top of the image. Keep in mind that the sheet of glass is the 3D part, while the image remains flat. By adjusting the combination of light filtering, refraction, and highlights, you can achieve some striking effects with this filter.

The Glass filter requires a mask to do its job. The shape of the mask controls the shape of the glass sheet. The top edge of the glass bevel occurs along the mask. Feathering the mask has no effect on this filter's operation.

The Glass Dialog Box

The Glass dialog box, shown next, is a little complicated, just like organic chemistry is a little complicated. I'm just kidding; organic chemistry is much easier. In fairness, the dialog box has a certain logic to it, and it works pretty well even if you don't read what I have written next. But if you really want to get the most out of this filter, you should at least skim over the material.

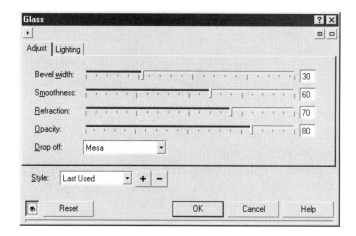

The dialog box is divided into two pages: Adjust and Lighting. Clicking its respective tab accesses each page. The Style portion of the dialog box, shown next, is common to both pages. It contains a drop-down list of presets that are provided with the Glass filter. Choosing any of them changes the controls in the dialog box for the selected presets. Custom settings are also saved in the Style area by changing the controls to the desired settings and clicking the plus button to the right of the

style name. Another dialog box opens that allows you to name the new style.
The minus button is used to remove a saved style.

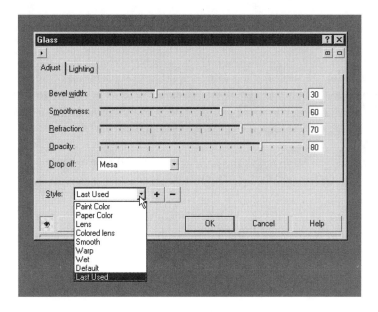

The Adjust Tab

This page contains all the controls for determining the width, breadth, and depth
of the effect, as well as the type of effect that is applied.

The Bevel Width Slider   The Bevel Width slider is used to set the width of the
bevel. In most cases, getting the bevel width to a small value produces the most
dramatic effect. The *bevel* is the area around a masked object that is slanted to
produce that glassy 3D look.

The Smoothness Slider   The Smoothness slider is used to set the sharpness of the
edges of the bevel. A low-level smoothness produces sharper edges, but may also
display the steps used to create the embossed look. A higher smoothness level
removes the jagged edges and makes for rounded edges.

The Refraction Slider   The most striking 3D effect of the Glass filter is *refraction,*
which occurs when the direction of light rays is changed (bent) as a result of passing
through a material such as glass or water. Since we are looking directly at the glass

14

sheet, refraction only occurs at the beveled edges. The Refraction slider sets the angle at which the light is to be bent at the bevel.

To make the refraction effect more noticeable, try using a wider bevel. This will increase the area of glass that does not directly face the viewer.

The Opacity Slider   Colored glass affects light, and it affects it more where the material (the glass) is thicker. The Opacity slider is used to set the transparency level of the glass sheet. The more opaque you make the glass, the stronger the underlying image will be tinted to look like the glass color.

Drop-Off Type   The *drop-off* is the area adjacent to the bevel effect and has a value that is selected from a list. The following choices are available:

- **Gaussian**   Use the Gaussian drop-off when you want a very subtle effect. On a complex image, it gives a wet appearance to the masked area edge. The Gaussian drop-off has an "S" shape; it starts and ends with a round and gradual slope that becomes steep in between. It results in a smooth and less noticeable transition between the bevel and the rest of the image.

- **Flat**   Because the Flat drop-off produces a sharp drop-off bevel, the areas around the edges are sharp. The effect on text with dark colors may not even be noticeable. This effect works best with objects that have smooth, rounded edges. The Flat drop-off is a straight diagonal line starting at the bevel area and ending on the image. The transition is not as smooth as a rounded bevel, but the slope of the bevel is less steep.

- **Mesa**   This drop-off style probably gives the best overall glass effect of the three. The Mesa drop-off is a curve that begins abruptly (almost a 90-degree angle) and ends with a rounded gradual slope.

The Lighting Tab

The controls on this page, as shown next, control the highlights and reflections of the effect, as well as the angle and direction of the light source and the color of the glass.

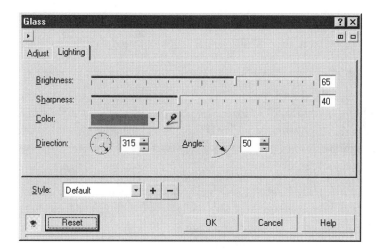

The Brightness Slider   The Brightness slider in the Adjust Lighting section controls the intensity of the highlights in the glass. A higher setting produces more highlights on the glass.

The Sharpness Slider   Theoretically, the Sharpness slider controls the sharpness of the light striking the edges of the bevel. That is, this setting controls the amount of reflections off the bevel. Here's the best part: the lower the setting, the greater the amount of reflections, which creates very realistic effects.

Color   The glass can be any color you choose. You can click the color swatch, opening a color palette, or use the Eyedropper button to select the color from the image. Dark glass will color the underlying image more strongly than light glass; so if you are experiencing difficulty in getting a noticeable glass effect, try darkening the glass color.

Direction and Angle Controls   You can control the direction that the light comes by using the Direction and Angle controls. High light-angle values illuminate the selection from directly above the surface, which tends to cause lighting that is bright and even. Low light-angle values tend to make shadows stronger, accentuating

14

the 3D effect. The angles are referenced to the horizon. High angle (90°) is similar to the sun being directly overhead, whereas low angle (0°) is like the sun sitting on the horizon.

- **Direction Dial and Value Box** The Direction dial controls the direction of the light striking the bevel. The bevel is the area around a masked object that is slanted to produce the 3D look. You can drag the dial to point toward the light source, or you can enter a value directly in the value box.

- **Angle Dial and Value Box** The Angle dial controls the angle at which the light is to be bent at the bevel. This distorts the image at the bevel location, which is the most striking effect of the Glass filter.

You get better effects with the Glass filter if you have a textured or high-contrast background to accentuate the glass effect.

Glass Raised Text Using the Glass Filter

The Glass filter is an excellent filter, but it takes some practice to get the hang of how and where to apply it. The following hands-on exercise will give you some experience using the Glass filter, and you will learn some of the tricks to make it work better for you. We are going to make text that looks like it is composed of raised glass.

1. Create a new 24-bit RGB image. From the dialog box, select Inches for Units of Measure. From the Size pop-up menu, select the Photo 5 × 7 option, and then click the Landscape button. The resolution should be 72 dpi. Click the OK button.

2. The glass effect looks better when there is high-contrast content in the background. Select Edit | Fill. From the Edit Fill & Transparency dialog box, click the Bitmap Fill button and click Edit, opening the Bitmap Fill dialog box. Open the preview palette of fills in the upper-left corner. Scroll down until you find a light-colored wood near the bottom. Click it to select it, and then click OK. Click OK again to apply the fill. The resulting image is shown next.

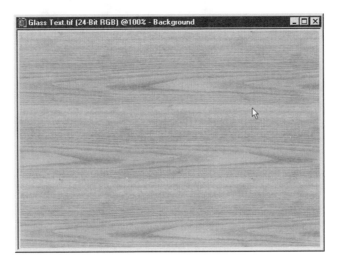

3. Click the Text button on the Toolbar. Change the Font to Times New Roman at a size of 150. Ensure the intercharacter spacing is at zero. Click inside the image and type **GLASS**. Press ENTER and type **GLASS** again. Click the Object Picker tool. Open the Align dialog box (CTRL-A), and select To Center of Document. Click OK.

14

4. Click the Create Mask button on the Toolbar (CTRL-M). Open the Objects docker window (CTRL-F7), and select the background by clicking it. Select Effects | 3D Effects | Glass. When the Glass dialog box opens, select Wet from the Style pop-up menu. Click the OK button.

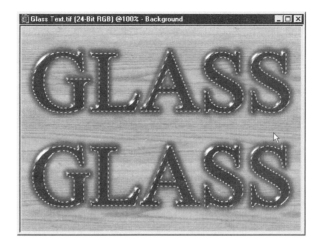

5. For the final touch, use the Object Picker and select the text object. Choose Edit | Fill and apply the wood fill used to flood the background. Change the Merge mode at the top of the Objects docker window to Exclusion. This lets the highlights created on the background text by the Glass filter appear through the text. The result is shown in Figure 14-2.

The important issue to remember when working with this filter is that it tends to make the image darker. We worked around that in the previous exercise by placing a copy of the original object on top of the background.

FIGURE 14-2   The Glass filter makes the text look like it is on embossed glass

Page Curl

This is a really superior filter. Its only drawback is that when it first came out, it was overused. I've seen a lot of flyers that have used the Page Curl filter, but its popularity has begun to wane. (I'm just warning you in case your clients seem less than enthusiastic when you show them something with the Page Curl filter.) Page Curl simulates the effect of a page being peeled back, with a highlight running along the center of the curl and a shadow being thrown from beneath the image (if your image is light enough to contrast with a shadow). The area behind the image, re-vealed by the page curl, is filled with the current paper color. An example is shown next:

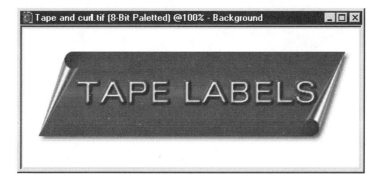

The Page Curl Dialog Box

The Page Curl dialog box is shown next, with a curled edge that I added to the image we just created with the Glass filter. The curl effect begins in one corner of your selection and follows a diagonal line to the opposite corner. You also may notice a slight transparency to the curl if there is any pattern or texture in the selected portion of your image.

14

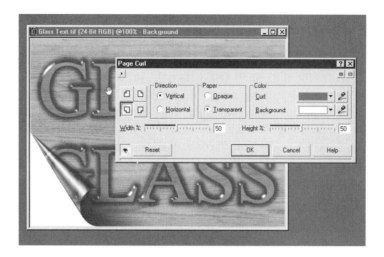

The origination point of the curl is controlled by use of the four keys in the Page Curl dialog box. The Vertical button creates a vertically oriented page curl, which curls the page across the image (from left to right or right to left). Experiment with this setting to achieve the effect you want. The buttons are mutually exclusive; that is, selecting one deselects the other. The Horizontal button creates a horizontally oriented page curl, which curls the page upward or downward through the image (from top to bottom or bottom to top). The Width % slider controls the vertical component of the page curl, regardless of whether it is a vertical or horizontal page curl. The Height % slider controls the horizontal component of the page curl, regardless of whether it is a vertical or horizontal curl.

The Opaque and Transparent options for Paper determine whether the underside of the curled page is opaque or transparent. Choose the Opaque option if you want the curl to be filled with a blend of gray and white to simulate a highlight. Choose the Transparent option if you want the underlying image to be displayed through the curled paper.

To apply the effect to a portion of the image, select an area using a mask before you choose the effect. The page will only curl inside the masked area.

The Perspective Filter

This filter has been around for a long time and fell into disuse when the Perspective transformation feature became available back in PHOTO-PAINT 7. Still, there are a few things we can do with it, and you should be aware of this filter.

The Perspective filter gives the impression of 3D perspective to an image. In the dialog box, shown next, there are two types in the Perspective filter: Perspective and Shear. Perspective applies the look of 3D perspective to the image according to the movement of the four nodes in the preview box. The nodes are moved by clicking them with the mouse and dragging them to the desired location. Shear also applies perspective, but it holds the original size and shape, similar to skewing.

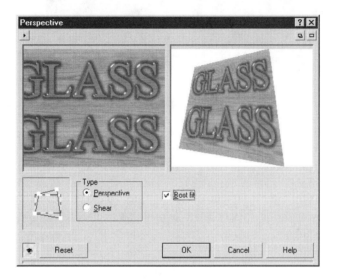

The Pinch/Punch Filter

The Pinch/Punch filter either squeezes the image so that the center appears to come forward *(pinch)* or depresses the image so that the center appears to be sunken *(punch)*. The results make the image look as if it has been either pulled out or pushed in from the center. The primary use for this filter is distorting people's faces so that they will consider suing you.

The Pinch/Punch Dialog Box

This filter reminds me of the house of mirrors in the amusement park near where I grew up. They had mirrors that distorted your features. This filter does the same thing. The Pinch/Punch dialog box, shown next, lets you set the distortion effect attribute. In the dialog box, moving the slider in a positive (+) direction applies a Pinch effect, and moving it in a negative direction (–) produces a Punch effect.

14

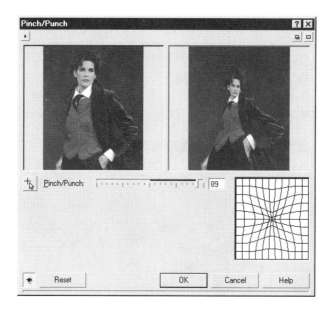

When using this filter, you can apply the filter to the entire image, as I have done to our poor model in Figure 14-3, or you can restrict the application to a

FIGURE 14-3   The Pinch effect when applied to the entire image has an interesting effect

small area defined by a mask—like her nose (see Figure 14-4). The effect is more pronounced and effective if the object has horizontal and vertical lines. The most important thing with this filter is to check the image and make sure the person you are profoundly distorting isn't a lawyer.

The Sphere Filter

The funny part about the name change is that in PHOTO-PAINT 5 the name of this filter was Map to Sphere. The Sphere filter creates the impression that the image has been wrapped around a sphere. The sphere is easy to work with.

The Sphere Dialog Box

The Sphere dialog box, shown next, is as simple as it gets. There is a button that allows you to choose the center of the effect and a slider to determine how much

FIGURE 14-4 The Punch effect, when restricted to a small area with a mask, can result in an inexpensive nose job

14

of an effect to apply. While there is a cute mesh model to show you the strength of the effect, the actual preview is still the best.

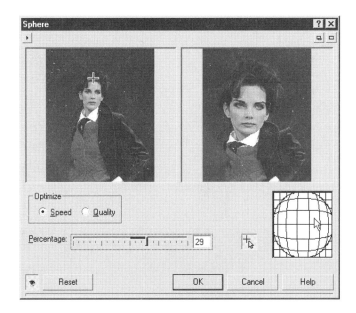

The filter can be applied to the entire image, but some of the most dramatic effects are achieved by applying it to a smaller area of the image that has been defined by a circle mask. The effect is more pronounced and successful if the object has horizontal and vertical lines. Almost all uses of the Sphere filter will require the application of highlights and shadows with an airbrush to enhance their appearance, as shown in the image I created in Figure 14-5.

The Boss (Emboss) Filter

The only thing I don't like about this filter is its name. After all, if I use correct grammar (and who does these days?) I would call this filter The Boss filter. Corel PHOTO-PAINT has two emboss filters: Emboss and The Boss. The Boss filter makes the selected area look as if it is pushed out of the image. The big difference between these two filters is that The Boss can be used to create some exciting 3D effects. The Boss filter effect is achieved by putting what appears to be a slanted bevel around the selected area. It is called The Boss to avoid confusion with the original Emboss filter.

FIGURE 14-5   The Sphere filter and a little airbrushing make a nice glass sphere from a field of daisies

The Boss Dialog Box

The Boss filter and the Glass filter operate similarly. This is because they use the same filter engine (program) internally. This is not an uncommon practice. I only mention it because if you have already read about the Glass filter, you may experience a feeling expressed by Yogi Berra, "It's déjà vu all over again." The major difference between the two filters is that The Boss filter has a check box that causes the filter to invert the mask. Other than that and the Refraction setting on the Glass filter, these filters operate identically.

The Zig Zag Filter

This filter creates paper for rolling cigarettes. Not really. It is a great filter for creating wavelike distortions that appear to be ripples in water. The dialog box

14

for the Zig Zag filter, shown here, has three controls that give you many options in using the filter's effects:

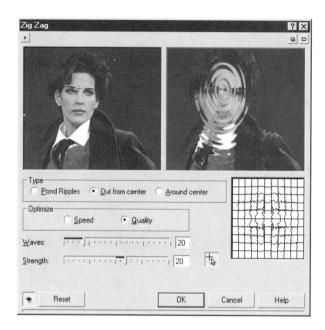

The Type settings control the direction and overall effect of the distortion. The Waves slider controls the distance between each cycle in the wave. Using larger values creates greater distances between each wave, resulting in a minimal number of waves. Smaller values create so many waves that it almost looks like a Fresnel lens. The Strength slider is used to control the intensity of the zigzag distortion. Keeping this value low helps most when you're trying to imitate the effect of ripples in the water. With the Around Center option, an additional Adjust option, Damping, becomes available.

To create Figure 14-6, I applied the Stone Bitmap fill to an empty image. Next, the Zig Zag filter with Pond Ripples was applied. The clock is an object (which Corel calls a "watch") that was placed in the center by use of the Paste from File command.

In Figure 14-7, some blurry shadows were added to the text before the Zig Zag filter was applied. I made this image for a German magazine, so that is why "underwater" is spelled that way. Still, I do want a spelling checker for PHOTO-PAINT.

FIGURE 14-6   *Ripples in Time* was easy to create with the Zig Zag filter

We have seen that while the 3D Effect filters are not true 3D, the variety of effects give the viewer the impression that they are. Next we'll learn about filters that can turn photographs into paintings.

FIGURE 14-7   The Zig Zag filter and some shadows make objects appear under water—or *Unterwasser*, as the case may be

14

The Creative and Art Stroke Filters

In a sense, the filters contained in these two separate categories of the Effects menu have been around for a long time. The Creative category is a mixture of old and new filters, while Art Stroke contains filters that use Paint Alchemy (internally) to achieve their effects—which are pretty fantastic. Let's begin our visual tour de force with the Creative Filters dialog box.

Creative Filters

These filters cover a wide gamut of effects. They produce everything from weather to fabric, and more. In this section, we will look through the effects that these filters produce, and I will offer suggestions on how to use them. We'll go through the list from top to bottom, so our first stop will be Crafts.

The Crafts Filter

The Crafts filter provides a unique collection of presets that create a wide variety of repeating effects. When you open the filter, the first place in the dialog box you should go is the Style drop-down list. It is from this list that you can choose the repeating pattern that produces the desired effect. The names of the styles are quite descriptive.

The image shown next is made with the Ceramic Tile style. While I think it looks more like needlepoint or mosaic tile, the effect is terrific.

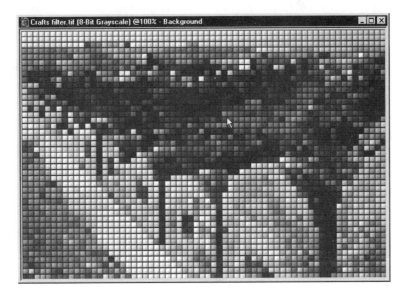

The Crystalize Filter

This filter is simple to use and produces interesting, although not tremendously useful, effects. It breaks down the image into blocks that are like the facets of a crystal. The only choice on this filter is the size of the blocks that the filter breaks the image into.

The image shown in Figure 14-8(a) is our glass of beer after the Crystalize filter has been applied at the default Size setting of 20. The image in Figure 14-8(b) was made at a Size setting of 1. As with the Crafts filter, the smaller the size, the more recognizable the resulting image. Let's move on to the Fabric filter.

The Fabric Filter

This filter can produce images that appear as if they were creations from a local handicraft store. The dialog box acts identically to that for the Crafts filter, except that the choices of styles are different. As with other filters in this category, after you have settled on a Style, the Size becomes the critical issue.

14

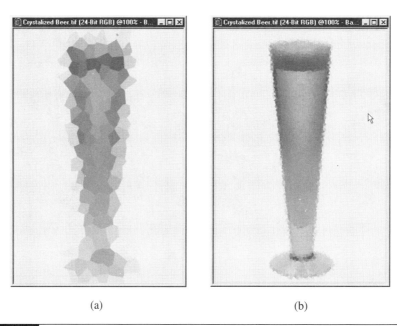

(a)   (b)

FIGURE 14-8 (a) Somewhere under those size-20 crystals is a beer. (b) Using the smallest setting, 1, produces a frosty effect

Figure 14-9 shows an image I put together to demonstrate the filter. The image is text placed on and combined with a bitmap fill background. An important issue has to do with the way the filter creates its effect and the seamless tile background. Certain tile sizes produce moiré patterns. The moiré patterns resulted from the interaction of the filter effect and the pattern inherent in seamless tiles (even when a human eye doesn't notice the pattern in the seamless tile).

The Frame Filter

The Frame filter puts an artistic edge on the border of an image. The Frame filter dialog box offers a large degree of control over the result. On the Select page, you select the frame you want to use from a list of frame files included in PHOTO-PAINT 10. You can make your own frames as well, since the program uses native PHOTO-PAINT files. Once you have selected your frame, you switch to the Modify page, where you can specify almost any conceivable aspect of the frame.

FIGURE 14-9   The Fabric filter makes this look like a handcrafted project

The Glass Block Filter

This filter, which is only available with duotone, paletted (8-bit), 24-bit, 32-bit, and grayscale images, creates the effect of viewing the image through thick transparent blocks of glass. The dialog box is very simple. The two sliders, Block Width and Block Height, can be set independently of each other. The setting range is 1 through 100. The lowest setting (1 Width, 1 Height) produces glass blocks that are 1 × 1 pixel in the image area.

Some Things to Do with the Glass Block Filter

Figure 14-10 is a standard studio photograph that has had the Glass Block filter applied as square blocks. I used this photograph to show that the filter appears to have little effect on the background. That's because of the lack of contrast in the background. Even though there is a difference in shading, there aren't any lines of hard contrast for the filter to act upon. Knowing this about the filter, we can take advantage of it.

14

This is either an example of the Glass Block filter or the result of one drink too many

Figure 14-11 is a glass ball I made using the Sphere filter. The background has hard horizontal lines but no areas of contrast in the vertical. By applying the Glass Block filter to the background, we can make the wood on which the ball is laying change shape to appear to be much smaller pieces, as shown in Figure 14-12.

Enough of the Glass Block filter. The next filter, Kids Play, is identical in operation to the Crafts and Fabric filters except for the style selections. The one style it offers that is clever is Building Blocks, which produces a look for all the world like the Lego® blocks our kids grew up with. On to the Mosaic filter.

The Mosaic Filter

This filter does a fantastic job of making images look as if they were constructed with actual tiles. The choices in the dialog box are the usual. You control the size and the background color. The one twist is, you can enable a built-in vignette. The mosaic image shown was Lithograph (a great choice for mosaic tiles) text on a white background. Again, you can find the best size by starting with a size

FIGURE 14-11 Glass ball on large wood poles

14

FIGURE 14-12 The Glass Block filter changes the poles into sticks

and then increasing or decreasing it until you get the desired effect. While the filter does work on photographs, the best effects are achieved with high-contrast images or images that have been posterized.

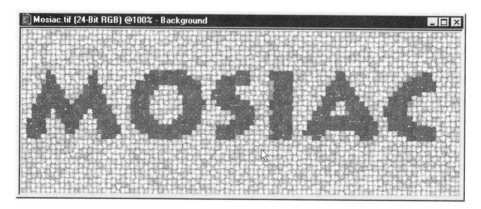

Keep a dictionary handy—PHOTO-PAINT doesn't have a spell checker, and you will avoid spelling mistakes like the one in the preceding illustration.

The Particles Filter

The next filter on the menu is Particles, with which you can create some respectable bubbles or random particles. This is one of those filters of which I will someday say, "Wow, look what I can do with this!" Until that day, I will leave you with one hint on the use of this filter for making bubbles—create a new object (layer) in the Objects docker, and apply the bubbles to that. This way, you can control the ultimate placement of the bubbles and also their merge mode.

The Scatter Filter

Like the Glass Block filter, the Scatter filter is only available with duotone, Paletted (8-bit), 24-bit, 32-bit, and grayscale images. This filter gives an image the appearance of an impressionist brush. Not really, but that's the official description. The amount of Scatter effect can be applied independently as Horizontal or Vertical values. The range is 1–100 and is measured in the amount of scatter (displacement) in pixels. For example, a Vertical setting of 10 will diffuse the image over a 10-pixel region in the vertical. Using a setting larger than the default (or 10) will scatter the pixels in the original image to the point that it becomes unrecognizable. In the previous edition of this book, I referred to this filter as "one of those 'what-were-they-thinking-about?'–type filters that ends up in every photo-editing package." I have since changed my mind. This filter has taken on a new life.

The Smoked Glass Filter

The Smoked Glass filter applies a transparent mask over the image to give the appearance of smoked glass. You can determine the color of the tint, the percentage of transparency, and the degree of blurring.

You can also set the Tint color in the dialog box. The Tint slider controls the opacity of the tint being applied. Larger values mean greater amounts of color tint applied to the image. A value of 100 fills the area with a solid color. The Blurring slider controls the amount of blurring applied to the image to give the appearance of the distortion caused by glass. A value of 100 percent produces the greatest amount of blurring, while 0 percent produces no blurring of the image.

The Stained Glass Filter

We finally have a Stained Glass filter. I would love to tell you that this filter takes a photographic image and converts it into a beautiful stained glass image—but it doesn't. The Stained Glass filter in Adobe Photoshop doesn't do it, either. The filter offers a lot of controls to determine the size of the random stained glass panes, the width of the leading, and its color. The end result is a nice montage of colored squares. This is still a great tool, and I look forward to exploring the possibilities of what can be done with it.

The Vignette Filter

The Vignette filter applies a mask to the image through the creation of a transparent shape in the center. The remainder of the mask is opaque. It is designed to appear as an old-style photograph when the image is placed in an oval or other shape.

A vignette can be applied to the entire image or just to a masked area. By clicking and dragging the Offset slider, you can control how large the selected shape appears around the center of the image. The larger the percentage, the larger the transparent oval. The Fade slider controls the fade (feathering) at the edge of the oval. Using the Vignette dialog box, you can determine the color of the mask by selecting Black, White, or a color from the pop-up Color palette.

14

The Vortex Filter

This filter applies brushstrokes in a semicircular pattern—one inside and the other outside, like the vortex of a tornado. The result is quite slick. The dialog box offers preset styles and several additional controls that determine the direction of the inner and outer vortexes.

This filter is best explained by showing you some of its effects. In Figure 14-13 is an excellent photograph of a surfer dude.

In Figure 14-14, we have applied the default setting of the Vortex filter and used the Local Undo tool (at a transparency of 90) to partially recover his face from the Vortex effect. After all, if you were in the photo, wouldn't you want people to be able to recognize you?

Figure 14-15 uses the Style named Thick, changing the Size from 1 to 17. Again, afterward, a thoughtful application of the Local Undo tool allowed our surfer dude to remain recognizable.

The Weather Channel, er, Filter

This filter is also cool, wet, or foggy, depending on what you select. The dialog box, shown next, is quite simple to use. The Strength slider range names change depending on the weather that you select. In the example shown next, Rain has

FIGURE 14-13   Nice curl, nice ride, nice photograph—let's use the Vortex filter and change it

FIGURE 14-14   With the help of the Vortex filter, our surfer is riding a wave of impressionism

FIGURE 14-15   With the help of the Vortex filter, he is ready to be sponsored by a surfboard company

14

been selected, so the range is Drizzle to Downpour. The other ranges are Snow: Flurry to Storm (I would have used "blizzard") and Fog: Mist to Peasoup.

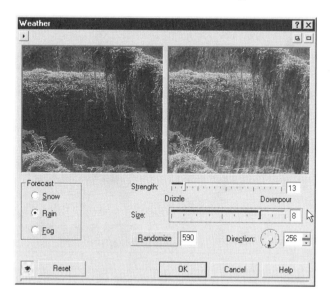

You can change the pattern used by all the styles by clicking the Randomize button (also good for generating state lottery numbers).

My favorite is Fog. My other favorite is Rain, because it looks so real. You can control the direction of the rain using, what else, the Direction dial. The snow needs some work—it looks more like a scene from the movie *The Attack of the Killer Cottonballs*. Next we are going to look at what the Art Stroke filters can do.

The Art Stroke Filters

As I said earlier in the chapter, these filters are like finely tuned presets of the Alchemy filter. You never see the Alchemy dialog box, but the engine is used for most, if not all, of these filters. The best way to look at these filters is to show the results they produce.

Charcoal

This filter does a good job of converting high-contrast subjects against a light solid background into charcoal renderings, as shown in Figure 14-16. Avoid dark or low-contrast images. In such cases, you will end up with a black snowstorm.

FIGURE 14-16   The Charcoal filter is applied to our serious fashion model with pretty good results

Conté Crayon

The Conté Crayon effect (pronounced con-tay) renders an image to appear as though drawn with conté crayon on a variety of rough, textured backgrounds. This style is characterized by dense darks, highly textured midtones, and pure whites.

Crayon

The effect of this Art Stroke filter looks less like crayon and more like a hard pastel. The darker low-contrast areas of the image will "plug up" with this filter, so keep an eye on these areas when working with the adjustments for this filter.

Cubist

This art stroke really trashes the photograph. That doesn't make it a bad filter. I have used the Cubist preset in Alchemy for years to produce backgrounds.

14

Dabble

This art stroke contains five Styles that really run the gamut of effects. The two styles to remember are Sponge and Ice Cube. Both are great ways to make backgrounds for other work.

The Impressionist Filter

This filter is one of those designed to turn your photograph into an impressionist painting. The problem is that your subject matter is not necessarily recognizable when the filter has finished its job.

The Palette Knife

The Palette Knife art strokes are quite abstract and so produce textured versions of what we saw in Dabble. Really nice backgrounds.

The Sketchpad

This filter is the first one I have seen that can automatically do a good job of making a photograph look like a graphite pencil drawing, as shown next:

It also has a respectable color pencil capability. I worked with the settings on this one, and I'm pleased with the results.

Watercolor

The Watercolor filter is a good filter for some types of images. On the model (with her high contrast and white background), it looked pretty poor. On a photograph of some ruins, it looked much better, although a little too abstract for my taste. When I applied it to the photograph of a crab, the result was outstanding.

The last two art strokes in PHOTO-PAINT 10 are Watermarker and Wave Paper. While both filters produce interesting effects, I can't think of what I could do with them.

Now that your mind is completely awash with the dizzying array of painterly effects, let's move on to the next section and see if understanding how the Contour and Custom filters work will clear your head.

Contour and Custom are two categories in the Effects menu in PHOTO-PAINT 10 that together contain seven filters. You may find some of these effects irresistible. Even though most of the filters existed in previous releases of PHOTO-PAINT, I think you will discover some really clever things you can do with them. In addition to learning about the seven filters, we will also be delving into the Paint modes to gain some understanding about not only how they work, but also what we can do with them. Our first stop will be the Contour category.

The Contour Filters

The three filters contained in this category are Edge Detect, Find Edges, and Trace Contour, as shown next. All three filters in one fashion or another detect and accentuate the edges of objects, items, and selections in your image.

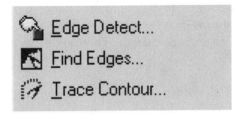

14

The Contour filters are equipped with controls that let you adjust the level of edge detection, the type of edges that are selected, and the color of the edges that you define.

The contour filters are

- **Edge Detect**   This detects the edges of items in your image and converts them to lines on a single-color background.

- **Find Edges**   Like Edge Detect, this determines the edges in your image and lets you convert these edges to soft or solid lines.

- **Trace Contour**   This is very similar to Edge Detect, except that it uses a 16-color palette rather than a single-color background.

The Edge Detect Filter

The operation of the Edge Detect filter is extremely simple. The Edge Detect filter dialog box has only two areas in which to make a choice. One allows you to choose the Background Color. This color will replace every part of the image that doesn't have a line in it. The other is the Sensitivity slider (1–10), which determines the intensity of edge detection. As you move the slider to the right, more of the original area surrounding the edges is included. A large sensitivity value can create the appearance of noise in the finished image. When this happens, use the Eraser tool to remove the noise from the image.

I used to recommend using this filter to convert photographs for reproduction on a photocopier.

The Edge Detect filter can work with both color and grayscale images. When used on a color image, it will generally produce lightly multicolored lines. To make all of the lines black, convert the image to a grayscale. Be aware that some images, especially low-contrast photographs, really look ugly after having this filter applied. If that happens, another alternative is to use the Band Pass filter, discussed later in this chapter, and then the Threshold filter.

TIP   *An application of contrast or equalization before applying the Edge Detect filter improves the resulting effect in most photographs.*

Find Edges

I love this filter; it kind of makes a colored pencil drawing. Find Edges is unlike any other filter in this chapter. Even though it is not a general image-enhancement tool, it allows you to obtain some effects that would not otherwise be possible.

The Trace Contour Filter

With the Trace Contour filter, you can highlight the edges of the objects in an image just as you can with the first two filters in this category. What makes this filter different from the previous two is that you can specify which pixels are highlighted by setting a Threshold Level. You can then choose an Edge Type. If you choose the Lower Edge Type, pixels with a brightness value below the threshold level are highlighted. If you choose the Upper Edge Type, pixels with a brightness value above the threshold are highlighted. The Trace Contour filter supports all color modes except 48-bit RGB, 16-bit grayscale, paletted, and black and white.

Now let's move on to the other category of filters, the Custom filters.

The Custom Filters

As I said earlier, all of the filters in this category, shown next, are old veterans, except for the Bump map filter. Let's look first at the three old timers: Alchemy, Band Pass, and User Defined; and then we'll look at the new kid on the block. All Custom filters are available with Grayscale and 24-bit RGB image files.

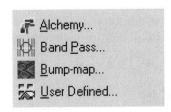

Alchemy Effects

The Alchemy Effects filter applies brush strokes to selected areas of your image in a precisely controlled manner. As with all filters, you can use masks to apply Alchemy Effects to part or all of an image. You can use one of the many brushes provided with the filter or create your own brushes. It's not hard to create effects with Alchemy Effects; the key to using and enjoying it is experimentation.

 As you learn how to make changes to the Alchemy Effects filter styles, I recommend limiting your changes to one at a time so that you can keep track of the effects.

Starting Alchemy Effects

In earlier releases of PHOTO-PAINT, the Alchemy filter was located with the other installed filters, and it had its own unique UI. Now, it is an integrated filter, and the filter dialog box is like all of the other Corel filters, just a little more complicated. Choosing Effects | Custom | Alchemy opens the Alchemy Effects dialog box.

 Alchemy Effects is only available with grayscale and 24-bit color images.

The Alchemy Effects Dialog Box

The Alchemy Effects dialog box is divided into two sections: control tabs and style controls. While the overall shape has changed, as well as the location of the controls, the functions of the controls haven't changed since it first appeared in PHOTO-PAINT 5. This is a very complex filter that applies brushstrokes to an existing image. Most of the effects that can be created with this filter are available as presets in the Art Stroke category. In previous editions of this book, I had an entire chapter devoted to the operation of this filter; but now that we have access to this filter through presets, I will cut this short and get on to the Band Pass filter.

The Band Pass Filter

While the operation of this filter is a little difficult to comprehend, it does have some uses—I think. The Band Pass filter lets you adjust the balance of sharp and smooth areas in an image. Sharp areas are areas where abrupt changes take place (for example, color changes, edges, or noise). Smooth areas are areas in which gradual changes take place. Smooth areas of the frequency plot represent low frequencies, while sharp areas represent high frequencies. The Frequency slider sets the fre- quency levels that determine the threshold. The Bandwidth slider sets the bandwidth or, in other words, the width of the frequency that components are going to pass. The filter in PHOTO-PAINT 10 works faster than any previous implementation of this filter. The previous ones were so slow it took minutes to see a preview. So, maybe between now and PHOTO-PAINT 11, I can figure out a use for this filter.

The User Defined Filter

The User Defined effect lets you "roll your own." Yes, you can make your own filters. The User Defined filter enables you to design your own *convolution kernel,* which is a type of filter in which adjacent pixels get mixed together. The filter that you make can be a variation on sharpening, embossing, blurring, or almost any other effect you can name.

The dialog box displays a matrix that represents a single pixel of the image at the center and 24 of its adjacent pixels. The values you enter into the matrix determine the type of effect you create. You can enter positive or negative values. The range of the effect is determined by the number of the values you enter into the matrix. The more boxes you give values to, the more pixels are affected.

This filter is not for the faint of heart. To understand the operation of this filter would take a chapter in itself. So that you can see what the filter does, Corel has provided several sample user-defined effects. Use the Load button for this. These effects have been provided to help you determine what values to enter into the matrix.

For more information about User Defined filters, in PHOTO-PAINT depress the F1 function key, select the Index tab, type **User**, and select User Defined Filters | Using. Finally, click the Display button.

14

Bump Map

The folks that make up the Corel PHOTO-PAINT development team were really excited about this jewel. Here is a filter you can get lost in. I am still trying to find all of the things that are possible with this filter, but I will share with you what I have already learned.

The quick and simple way to use this filter is to open the dialog box, shown next; pick a preset in the Style pop-up menu; and click OK.

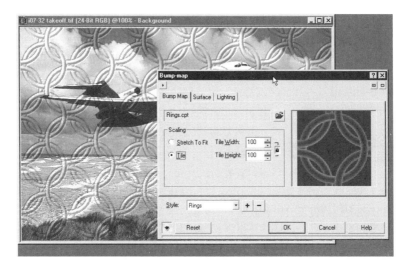

The principle underlying the operation is that there is something similar to a displacement map called a *bump map*. It is called a bump map because it bumps or displaces pixels on the basis of the values of the pixels in the bump map. The size of the bump map on the image is controlled by the Tile Height and Width values.

The key to using this filter is to either select one of the predefined styles near the bottom of the dialog box, or select one of the Bump maps and create your own effects. Once you have created something exciting, you can save it as a style.

Well, that wraps up another filter category; now it's time for a filter that is appropriate, since we just finished an election year—the Distort filters.

The Distort Filters

This group of 12 filters, shown next, comprises some of the most unusual and complex filters in Corel PHOTO-PAINT. In case you thought you had just come upon a whole new set of filters in PHOTO-PAINT 10, I need to inform you that the Distort filters were called 2D filters in the previous versions of PHOTO-PAINT. On top of that, several of the filters have had name changes as well.

Many of the Distort filters are not needed for day-to-day photo-editing work, but they can be genuine lifesavers in some situations.

The Blocks Filter (Formerly Known as the Puzzle Filter)

The Blocks filter lets you break down an image into small blocks—which I admit doesn't sound very interesting, but let's see exactly what that means. The filter is pretty simple to use. In the filter dialog box, the Block width and Block height sliders (1–100) control the width and height of the blocks created by the filter. If the Lock icon at the other end of the dialog box is enabled, these two controls will have identical values.

The Max offset (%) slider controls the offsetting, or shifting, of blocks. It is important to note that the offset is a percentage of the Block size. For example, if the Block size is set to a width of 50 pixels and the Max offset % slider is set to 10, the offset will have a maximum shift of 5 pixels (10 percent of 50). Therefore, increasing or decreasing block size changes the effect the maximum amount of offset has, even though the numbers don't change.

14

The Displace Filter

The Displace filter distorts an image by moving individual pixels and not moving others. The direction and distance that the chosen pixels move are determined by a separate image that is called a *displacement map*. What happens is that the Displace filter reads the color value of every pixel in the image and every pixel in the displacement map—hey! those speed-reading courses really do help. After all of that reading, the filter then shifts the image pixels on the basis of the values of the corresponding pixels in the displacement map. Clear as mud, right? A visual demonstration may help.

Figure 14-17 is an illustration of how a displacement map works (the Grid has been added to help show the effect). While the Displace filter uses both color value and brightness to determine displacement, we need only be concerned about brightness. The top of the figure shows a displacement map going from 70 percent Black to 30 percent Black in 12 steps. The map was applied to the original image (middle), and the result appears at the bottom. Notice that the 70 percent Black end on the left was pushed (offset) down, the 30 percent Black end on the right was

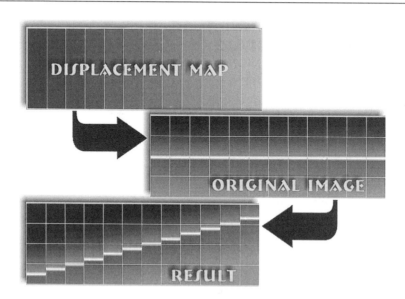

FIGURE 14-17   The graduated scale in the displacement map causes the original image to be displaced accordingly

pushed upward, and the 50 percent gray point in the middle is unaffected. Sound boring? Wait until you see what we can do with this little jewel.

More Technical Information About Displacement Maps

Were you wondering what PHOTO-PAINT was reading when I told you it read each pixel? It reads the brightness values of the pixels in the displacement map. Their values tell PHOTO-PAINT which pixels to move and how far to move them. It is important to remember that brightness values apply to grayscale and color images. The three determining brightness values are

■ **Black**   Areas in the displacement map that contain black will move the corresponding pixels in an image being affected to the right and/or down by the maximum amount defined by the Scale settings in the Displace dialog box. Values between black and 50 percent gray move pixels a shorter distance.

■ **White**   Areas in the displacement map that contain white will move the corresponding pixels to the left and/or up by the maximum amount defined by the Scale settings in the Displace dialog box. Values between white and 50 percent gray move pixels a shorter distance.

■ **Middle gray**   Areas in the displacement map that are composed of gray with a brightness of 50 percent cause the pixels to remain unmoved.

The Mesh Warp Filter

14

The Mesh Warp filter distorts an image according to positioning of grids in the dialog box. The user, through the dialog box, determines the number of gridlines positioned over the Grid using the No. Gridlines slider bar. Technically, the greater the number of nodes selected, the smoother the Mesh Warp distortion. In actual use, I find that choosing fewer nodes allows you to control larger areas more smoothly. Each node can be moved by clicking it with a mouse and dragging it to a new position. Each node moves independently and can be positioned anywhere in the Preview window. There is no way to group-select and move the nodes. I wish there were.

The Mesh Warp effect can be a little tricky to use at first; but once you get the hang of it, it's . . . still tricky, but fun. Use the Preview button to view the effects of a Mesh Warp transformation to ensure that it is acceptable before applying it to your entire image.

The Mesh Warp Filter Dialog Box

When the Mesh Warp dialog box opens, click and drag the No. Gridlines slider to determine the number of gridlines that will appear on the image. The first horizontal gridline lies along the top, and the first vertical gridline is on the left. Be aware that they can be hard to see, depending on your display. At each point where a horizontal gridline and a vertical gridline intersect, a node is positioned. To move the node, click it and drag it. The gridlines in the Preview window will twist and bend accordingly; and after a few moments, the image will change to preview the distortion. While it doesn't offer onscreen preview, the Preview window is large enough so you can see a good-sized representation of the finished result.

So . . . What Can You Do with It?

From a practical day-to-day standpoint, not very much. You can use the selective distortion capability to distort people and places. While this can be cute, it isn't particularly useful. It does allow you to distort or "morph" images or photos with some interesting results. Figure 14-18(a) shows the original photograph of an owl, looking curious. After the application of the Warp Mesh filter in Figure 14-18(b), he looks mad enough to start a fight.

(a)   (b)

FIGURE 14-18 With a little help from Mesh Warp, (a) a curious-looking owl becomes (b) an owl with attitude

The SQUIZZ! Filter

The SQUIZZ! 1.5 filter made its first appearance in the PHOTO-PAINT 7 Plus package. Located in the plug-in portion of the Effects menu under HSoft, this filter opens with the splash screen shown next:

What can you do with this filter? Well . . . you could use it to distort images much as we demonstrated with the Mesh Warp filter. I like to think of this filter as Super Mesh Warp. When the SQUIZZ! splash screen opens, you are presented with two possible options: Brush and Grid.

14

Grid Warping

Selecting Grid opens the Grid Warping screen shown next:

Although it looks like the grid in the Mesh Warp filter, the operation of this filter is somewhat different. Applying Grid Warping effects is a two-step process. The first step is to click the Select button in the Grid Action section. In the Preview screen, marquee-select the nodes that you want to be included. Once the nodes are selected, choose the action that you want to apply. If you use the Move action, click inside the selected nodes and drag them in the desired direction. For the other actions, click inside of the selected area and drag. Each time you click the mouse, all of the selected nodes move in the direction indicated by the selected action. Multiple effects can be selected and applied to the image, but there is no preview. Click the Apply button to apply the SQUIZZ effect to the image.

Brush Warping

Choosing the Brush opens the Brush Warping screen shown next. This mode applies the distortion using a brush stoke. As with Grid Warping, you can create multiple effects on the image before clicking the Apply button. One of the unique settings is the Undo mode, which acts like the Local Undo command and is used to remove an action that was applied before the Apply button is clicked. The PHOTO-PAINT Undo command does not work while working in the SQUIZZ! filter.

What Can You Do with SQUIZZ!?

While surrealistic distortions are okay, I love using SQUIZZ! to mess with images so that the viewer is not immediately aware that the image has been distorted. The advantage of the SQUIZZ! filter is the ability to apply effects in localized areas using a brush-style tool. There is also a Grid format tool that acts very much like the Mesh Warp filter.

The Offset Filter

The Offset filter is a pixel mover. Much like those hand games you play where you must move little tiles around to form a word, the Offset filter moves pixels in an image according to either a specified number of pixels or as a percentage of image size. The filter will shift the entire image unless there is an area enclosed by a mask.

14

If a mask exists, none of the pixels in the image being shifted will shift outside of the mask. When there is a shift, an empty area is created.

 The Offset filter is a favorite of those Photoshop users who were heavily involved in channel operations (called CHOPS). This filter remains critical to many techniques described in many Photoshop books. Most of the techniques involving the Offset filter were developed before the advent of objects and layers. It allowed you to create an image, save it to a channel, and offset the duplicate to create highlights and shadows. Today, it is easier to do that by creating objects and positioning the objects.

The Pixelate Filter

The Pixelate filter gives a block-like appearance to the entire image, the area enclosed by a mask, or the selected object. You have seen the effect many times before on newscasts, where certain persons had their features pixelated to prevent viewers from seeing the face of the person talking. Because the pixelation was done on a frame-by-frame basis, the boundaries of the pixelation varied from frame to frame, producing an apparent movement around the edges.

You can control the pixelate effect by selecting Square, Rectangular, or Radial mode and changing the size and opacity of the blocks. This filter can be used to create backgrounds that have the appearance of mosaic tiles.

Width and Height values (1–100 pixels) for the size of the pixel blocks can be entered independently. The effects of pixel block size are dependent on the image size. A value of 10 in a small image will create large pixel blocks. A value of 10 in a very large image will produce small pixel blocks. Use the Opacity % slider (range is 1–100) to control the transparency of the pixel blocks. Lower values are more transparent. The shape of the blocks of pixels is controlled with the Pixelate mode buttons. Square and Rectangular modes arrange the pixel blocks on horizontal lines. The Radial mode bends the blocks of pixels, and arranges them on concentric circles beginning at the center of the image or the masked area.

Using the Pixelate Filter

Since Corel PHOTO-PAINT can import and work on video files (if you have a video capture board), the most obvious use for the Pixelate filter is to pixelate the faces of key witnesses to gangland murders for the local news station. If that opportunity is not readily available, the Pixelate filter is very handy for creating unusual backdrops or converting background into something akin to mosaic tile. When working with backgrounds, remember that the best effects occur when there are contrasts in the image that is being pixelated.

The Ripple Filter

The Ripple filter is one of the "fun" filters. There is just *so* much you can do with it. While it is of little use in the day-to-day work of photo-editing, when it comes to photo-composition tasks, it is a very powerful tool. The Ripple filter creates vertical and/or horizontal rippled wavelengths through the image.

Controlling the Ripple Filter

The Ripple dialog box provides control over the amount and direction of the ripple effect. The Primary wave (by default, running horizontally) has two controls, Period and Amplitude. The Period slider (1–100) controls the distance in between each cycle of waves. A value of 100 creates the greatest distance between each wave, resulting in the fewest number of waves. The Period setting works on a percentage basis of image size: the larger the image, the larger the number of waves created. The Amplitude slider (1–100) determines how big the ripples (amount of distortion) are. In the diagram, the straight vertical line is the Perpendicular wave. Selecting this option on the left allows you to change its Amplitude.

The Angle value (0–180) determines the angle of the ripple effect. Enabling the Distort Ripple option causes the ripple produced by the filter to be distorted by placing a ripple in both directions.

The Shear Filter

Here is another distortion filter that is lots of fun—a real time waster. The Shear filter distorts an image, or the masked portion of it, along a path known as a Shear map. You can load and save maps with the options in the Shear dialog box and edit the Shear Map preview by dragging points with your mouse. The Undefined

Areas options are the same as with the Offset filter. In a nutshell, the Shear filter twists the image to the shape defined by the Shear map path. The actual amount of displacement caused by this filter is set with the Scale slider. As the amount of Scale increases, the amount of displacement increases.

The image shown next shows a good action photograph. By using the Shear filter with the Tilt preset, we add more energy to the photograph, as well as create space to add a short banner under the motorcycle, if desired.

As I said, this is a fun filter and easy to use. There are more things you can do with it, so I suggest that you experiment with it to see what the limits are. Try applying it to objects; the result might surprise you.

The Swirl Filter

The Swirl filter is the original no-brainer. It rotates the center of the image or masked area while leaving the sides fixed. The direction of the movement is determined by the Clockwise or Counter-Clockwise option. The angle is set with the Whole Rotations slider (0–10) and the Additional Degrees slider (0–359). Multiple applications produce a more pronounced effect. Clearly, this filter is also a time saver. Isn't science amazing?

Here is some food for thought when using this filter. In the next illustration, I created a 200 × 200 file and filled it with a simple conical fill. Next, I applied the

Swirl filter set to 360. Using the CTRL-F keyboard shortcut, I applied the Swirl filter twice more. The next image shows the application a total of six times. By using the Swirl filter, you can make excellent ornaments and effects for your desktop publishing projects.

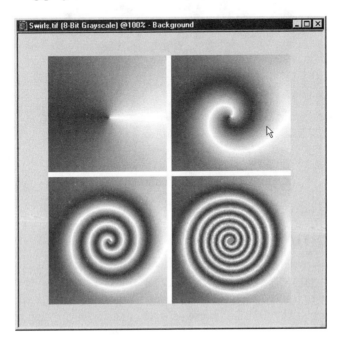

The Tile Filter

This is a very simple and quite useful filter. The Tile filter creates blocks of a selected image in a grid. You can adjust the width and height of the tiles using the Horizontal and Vertical Tiles sliders in the dialog box. The values entered represent the number of images duplicated on each axis. So what can you do with it? The Tile effect can be used in combination with flood fills to create backgrounds, as well as make wallpaper for Windows. Just remember that the Tile filter does not produce seamless tiles. The best effects are achieved when the number of tiles in relation to the original image is small. If you have a large number, then the original subject becomes so small as to be unrecognizable. The background shown in the next image was created using the Tile filter:

14

The Wet Paint Filter

This filter can quickly create some neat effects. It isn't necessary for you to think of images that need wet paint. In the image that follows, it makes the brandy glasses look like someone left them outside too long. The two controls for the Wet Paint filter are Percent and Wetness. Percent refers to the depth to which the wet paint look is applied; in other words, it determines the length of the drip. For example, if you set low percentages, the amount of wetness appears to affect only the surface of the image.

The Wetness values determine which colors drip, as shown in the next illustration. Negative (–) wetness values cause the dark colors to drip. Positive (+) wetness values cause light colors to drip. The magnitude of the wetness values determines the range of colors that will drip. Maximum values are +/–50 percent.

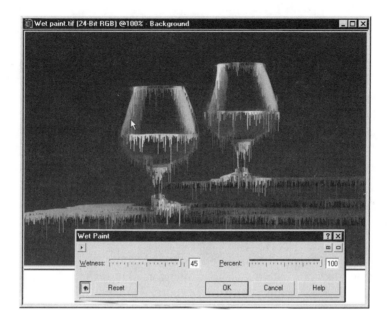

The Whirlpool Filter

I have referred to the Whirlpool filter as a "Smear tool on Steroids" to describe the blender operation it performs on poor unsuspecting pixels in an image. Jeff Butterworth of Alien Skin Software, the original creator of the filter, states, "We just couldn't resist throwing in something fun, which is why we developed it. Whirlpool uses state-of-the-art scientific visualization techniques for examining complex fluid simulations. This technique smears the image along artificial fluid streamlines." By selecting Effects | Distort | Whirlpool, you open the Whirlpool filter dialog box. This filter, unlike its cousins, The Boss and Glass, does not require a mask to operate.

The Wind Filter

The Wind filter is described as creating the effect of wind blowing on the objects in the image. This filter is normally ignored by most PHOTO-PAINT users because they rarely desire to put wind into their images. But the Wind filter does more than create wind: it can be used to create some artistic effects with objects and masks.

14

The Wind filter smears pixels as a function of their brightness. The brighter the pixel, the more it gets smeared. Click and drag the Opacity slider (1–100) to determine the visibility of the wind effect. Higher values make the effect more visible, while lower values make the effect more subtle. The Strength slider (0–100) controls the amount of distortion. The direction of the smearing can be entered numerically or by clicking the direction compass in the dialog box.

There are a few things to know about the operation of this filter when working with objects. It needs to have a source for the pixels it is "blowing" across the image. If you apply the Wind filter to an object, it will not work unless the background is unlocked or there is some unlocked object behind it.

Before We Leave Distort

I hope this chapter stirs your imagination a little. Always remember not to let the name of a filter dictate what you use that filter for. I know the original designer of the Wind filter didn't think, "Boy, this would be great for making textures and other stuff." Now that you understand the Distort filters, let's prepare to move on to the Render and Fancy filters.

The Render and Fancy Filters

The Render and Fancy filters run the gamut of effects from the fantastic to the patently useless. It's your job to figure out which is which. Enough already, let's see what we can see in the Render filter.

The Render Filters

Render filters are used to produce special effects, backgrounds, and novelty images. All three are available with 24-bit RGB images. Other exceptions are noted as each filter is discussed. The Render category of the Effects menu contains three filters:

- 3D Stereo Noise
- Lens Flare
- Lighting Effects

3D Stereo Noise

This filter (originally from the Kai Power Tools 2.0 collection) is my least favorite because it has become such a fad. The 3D Stereo Noise filter takes a perfectly good image and converts it to something akin to a printer failure all over your paper. By staring at the paper, you can see the original image with depth effect, similar to those stereogram posters that have gained such popularity at suburban shopping malls in recent seasons. (It's rumored that if you can stare at it for over an hour, just before the onset of a migraine, you can see Elvis.) See the online help for information about using this filter.

Lens Flare

The Lens Flare filter has controls in its dialog box, shown in Figure 14-19, that produce a spot of light resembling a reflection within an optical system. In photography, lenses of different focal lengths produce different lens flare effects. Photographers work very hard to make sure the effects added by this filter do not occur. With Lens Flare, you can add what they try to get out of a photograph.

TIP	*The Lens Flare filter works only with 24-bit color images. To apply this effect to a grayscale image, convert the grayscale to a 24-bit color image, apply the Lens Flare filter, and then convert it back to grayscale.*

When you first open the dialog box, it will immediately render and provide a preview of the selected image. Choose from three lens types to produce the type of lens flare you want. You can also adjust the brightness (1 to 200 percent) of the lens flare with the slider bar. To change the position of the "flare," select the "plus and arrow" icon, and click the Preview window at the point where you want the flare to be; you cannot "drag" it to the new location. With the Preview button enabled, the image update is automatic.

TIP	*Set the zoom before making any changes in the dialog box. To return to the "hand" cursor after making changes, click the "plus and arrow" button in the dialog box.*

14

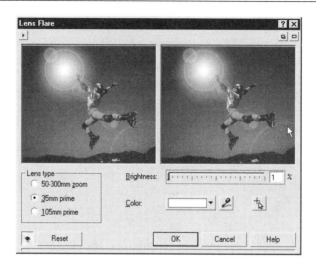

FIGURE 14-19 With the Lens Flare dialog box, you can produce a broad range of lighting effects

Lighting Effects Filter

The Lighting Effects filter lets you add one or more light sources to your image. Choose from a list of presets or create your own customized lights using the controls in the dialog box shown in Figure 14-20. You can add multiple lights and individually control the attributes of each. This is a rather intimidating dialog box. Using it is not quite intuitive. After opening the filter, the Preview window displays what the lighting effect will look like with the default or the last used setting.

This filter is available with grayscale (8-bit), 24-bit RGB, and multichannel images.

Setting Up the Lighting Effects Filter

The first step in using this filter is to choose one of the two Type settings: Spotlight or Directional. The Spotlight gives the appearance of a beam light source (like a spotlight?) with clearly defined edges and a hot spot. The other choice, Directional, uses a light source that is very close to being omnidirectional. It provides even lighting—unlike our spotlight. You can also add and remove your own styles. Each light source has been assigned appropriate settings to achieve a unique effect.

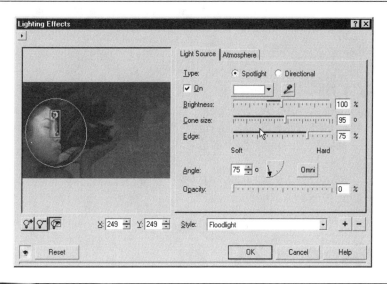

FIGURE 14-20 The Lighting Effects dialog box

For the purposes of illustrating the use of the various controls, we will use the Spotlight type. After selecting Spotlight, choose a color for the light; white provides a good starting point. Remember that colors add a color cast to an image. For example, I recently changed the background of a brightly lit photograph to that of a sunset. I applied an orange tint using the Lighting Effects filter to make the foreground look like it belonged in the same picture as the background.

The barbell icon representing the light consists of a large node indicating the focus of the light, and a smaller node indicating the direction and height of the light. Click the large node and drag the light source to a desired position. As you adjust the position of the light, the X and Y settings on the Position page indicate the horizontal and vertical position. You can adjust the direction of the light by dragging the smaller node. The Brightness slider changes the color of the light. The Cone Size slider changes the range of light. The Edge slider determines how to spread the light in relation to the cone—that is, a 100 percent setting spreads the light all the way to the cone.

This filter allows you to add up to 18 additional lights. Of course, with 19 lights, the rendering time will drastically increase. Clicking the Plus button below the Preview window adds another light; clicking the Minus button removes the currently selected light.

14

The texture controls of the filter are located on the Atmosphere page. You can create pseudo-shadows on surfaces that enhance the effect of the filter in some cases.

The Fancy Filters

The two Fancy filters, Julia Set Explorer 2.0 and Terrazzo, are two popular third-party plug-in filters in their own right. They are available with grayscale, 24-bit RGB, CMYK, and multichannel images.

 Are you looking for the Paint Alchemy filter? It's moved to the Custom category.

Julia Set Explorer 2.0

This is the one of the original filters from Metacreation Corporation (formerly Metatools, and before that, HSC). Just to eliminate a point of confusion, the filter is called Julia Set Explorer in the Fancy menu, but when the dialog box opens, it is called Fractal Explorer 2.0. The reason for this is simple. This filter is a hybrid of the Julia I Explorer from Kai Power Tools (KPT) 1.0 and the interface from KPT 2.0. Now you won't lie awake worrying about it.

If this is your first time with the Kai Power Tools (KPT) user interface, welcome to the jungle! Just kidding. I have heard this user interface (UI) described as everything from the best UI on the planet to a Klingon Control Panel. I personally opt for the latter. A friend of mine who is a big fan of KPT insists that it is really easy to learn to use. On the other hand, he believes that Neil Armstrong's moonwalk was a fake and that wrestling is real, so judge accordingly. Whether you hate it or love it, you have to use it. So, to get the most out of this very powerful fractal generator, you need to spend some time learning your way around.

Help

Clicking the Help button (to the immediate left of the title bar) brings up the Help menu for Fractal Explorer Kai Power Tools 2.0. Be sure to take the Guided Tour of the product, which is one of your choices from the Help menu. You can also get help by pressing the F1 key, which turns the cursor into a question mark. Clicking any part of the UI brings up context-sensitive help. No matter what you click, you are going to get the opening Help screen.

TIP	*Once you launch the F1 context-sensitive Help, you may be wondering how to turn it off. Use the ESC key.*

The Terrazzo Filter

The other plug-in filter in Corel PHOTO-PAINT's Fancy Filters group is called "Terrazzo." (The name comes from the Italian word for "terrace," and originally referred to a kind of mosaic floor covering.) I again acknowledge my gratitude to the fine folks at Xaos, who have let me borrow heavily from their manual so that the material in this chapter would be accurate.

Terrazzo enables you to create beautiful, regular patterns taken from elements in existing source images. With Terrazzo, the patterns are very easy to create and infinitely repeatable. The best part is that Terrazzo is simple to use. Xaos Tools ships a wonderful manual with their product that covers Terrazzo in incredible detail. Since detailed information about Terrazzo is not generally available, I have done my best to give you a condensed version of the major features and functions of this filter.

An Overview of Terrazzo

The regular patterns you can create with Terrazzo are based on 17 symmetry groups, which are known in the math and design worlds by several names, including "planar," "ornamental," and "wallpaper" symmetry groups. You choose the symmetry you want to use from a Symmetry selection box in the Terrazzo dialog box.

The 17 symmetries in the Terrazzo filter are named after common American patchwork quilt patterns. Each of these symmetries also has a mathematical name. Because these mathematical names (such as p-4m) aren't very exciting or as easy to remember as the quilt names (such as Sunflower), Xaos has only used the quilt names in the interface.

Tiles, Motifs, and Patterns

Each Terrazzo-generated pattern is made from a *motif*, which is the shape that builds a *tile* when a *symmetry* is applied to it. The tile, in turn, repeats to build a regular pattern. (These three terms will be used throughout this discussion.)

14

The motif in Terrazzo is very similar to the masks in Corel PHOTO-PAINT. The area that is enclosed by the motif is the foundation of the tile. There are eight different motif shapes. Different symmetries use different motifs.

Although the 17 individual symmetries produce different results, all of the symmetries perform one or more of the following operations:

- **Translations** Move the motif up, down, right, left, or diagonally without changing the orientation.

- **Rotations** Turn the motif one or more times around a center at a specific angle.

- **Mirror Reflections** Create one or more mirror images of the motif.

- **Glide Reflections** Create one or more mirror images of a motif and move the motif up, down, right, left, or diagonally.

The Terrazzo Filter Dialog Box

Terrazzo works on grayscale, duotone, 24-bit, and 32-bit color images, but not on black-and-white (1-bit) images. As with Paint Alchemy and all of the other filters, you must have an image open before you can access the filter.

When you first open Terrazzo, you will see the opening screen, as shown in Figure 14-21. Let's take a closer look at it.

The Original preview on the left side of the Terrazzo dialog box displays the masked area, or the entire source image if you haven't selected any areas with a mask. (Color masks don't count.) The motif is located here.

The large image on the right of the dialog box displays the source image with the current symmetry applied to it, which is referred to as the *Result image*.

> **NOTE** *The Result image is the one to which you are applying a pattern. You can open a new source image (a noncompressed BMP file) from within Terrazzo, but you cannot open a new Result image without closing Terrazzo and returning to Corel PHOTO-PAINT's main screen.*

The Continuous Preview Option

When the Continuous Preview check box is checked, the destination image is continuously updated as you change any of the settings in the Terrazzo dialog

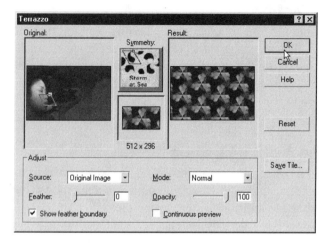

FIGURE 14-21   The Terrazzo filter dialog box

box. This allows you to see the effects of your adjustments in real time as you are making them.

> **TIP**   *Leaving the Continuous Preview option selected may slow down some older systems. This is especially true if you are using a large motif, a triangular motif like Sunflower, or a kite-shaped motif such as Whirlpool. If you experience system slow-down, you may want to consider deselecting the Continuous Preview option. That said, I find that having it on really helps in finding some nice patterns quickly.*

By default, Continuous Preview is turned off in the Terrazzo dialog box. When the Continuous Preview check box is not selected, the destination image is updated only when you release the mouse button after making an adjustment to one of the controls in the Terrazzo dialog box.

The Terrazzo Motifs

Every time you open the Terrazzo dialog box, the motif is positioned in the center of the source image.

14

Adjusting a Motif

You can change the tile you are creating by moving the motif to a new position on the source image, thus selecting a different part of the image to make into a tile.

In addition to moving the motif, you can adjust the size and, in the case of the Gold Brick symmetry, the shape of the motif. Each motif has a handle on it that enables you to resize it.

To Adjust the Motif's Position

Place the cursor anywhere inside the motif and hold down the left mouse button. The cursor becomes a hand; and while you hold down the mouse button, you can use the hand to drag the motif anywhere inside the source image.

If the Continuous Preview option is enabled, the Result image on the right side is constantly updated to show the results of repositioning the motif on the source image.

To Adjust the Motif's Size

Place the cursor over the motif control handle and drag it to increase or decrease the size. The only exception to this procedure occurs with the Gold Brick, which has two handles. The handle in the upper-right corner of the motif resizes the width, and the handle in the lower left lets you resize the height of the motif and skew its shape.

 To constrain the Gold Brick motif to a rectangular shape, or to return to a rectangular motif after you have skewed the motif, hold down the SHIFT *key as you drag the lower-left handle. The motif automatically becomes rectangular as long as you hold down the* SHIFT *key.*

Selecting a Symmetry

Every time you open Terrazzo, the active symmetry is Pinwheel. This symmetry is displayed between the Original and Result images in the Terrazzo dialog box. Each symmetry swatch displays a simple representation of the selected symmetry.

To select a different symmetry, click the currently displayed symmetry swatch and the Symmetry selection box opens, as shown next. Clicking the desired symmetry causes it to be highlighted with a blue border. Click the OK button when you are satisfied with your selection, and the selected symmetry appears between the Original and Result images.

Creating Seamless Patterns

With most of the Terrazzo symmetries, you may notice a visible edge or seam between the tiles. The feather option in the Terrazzo dialog box allows you to feather the edge of a motif so that the seams between tiles fade away.

Feathering in Terrazzo is produced in an area outside the motif (called the *feather boundary*), and the pixels inside the feather boundary are dispersed, thus creating a gradual transition between motifs.

> **TIP** *Sometimes there is such a thing as too much of a good thing. With certain patterns, using too large a feathering value causes faint black seams to develop on certain patterns.*

Using the Feather Option

You use the Feather option in the Terrazzo dialog box to set the width of the feather edge around the motif. The feather option is not available if you have selected the Sunflower, Prickly Pear, Turnstile, or Winding Ways symmetry. The option is not available because these four symmetries are kaleidoscopic and, therefore, always seamless.

To adjust a motif's feather edge, drag the slider to increase or decrease the feather edge around the motif, or enter a value directly into the data box to the right of the slider. The value is a percentage based upon the size of the image. For example, setting the Feather value to 25 creates a feather with a width of 25 percent of the distance from the edge of the motif to its center.

14

When you set the feather value above 0, you will notice that a second border appears around the motif in the source image. This border represents the area included in the feather edge of the motif.

 You cannot move the motif by clicking and dragging inside the feather border. You must be inside the motif itself to move a feathered motif. (This little jewel drove me crazy until I figured it out.)

If you don't want to see the feather boundary around the motif, you can turn it off by clearing the Show Feather Boundary check box in the Terrazzo dialog box. This turns off only the visible border; if you have feathering selected, the feathering is still applied.

You may notice that setting a Feather value slows down your system a wee bit. The folks at Corel have done a wonderful job of speeding up these filters in comparison to the Mac versions. However, if you noticed that the feathering is slowing your system down, keep it off until you are ready to fine-tune your image.

 Some symmetries create mirror lines as they reflect a motif to create a pattern. Feathering does not occur on mirror lines, because these are "seamless" lines; the effect only appears on edges with visible seams.

Feather Boundary Constraints

If the Show Feather boundary is off and you have some value of feathering entered, you will discover that you cannot position the motif any closer to the edge of the source image than the feather boundary.

If the motif is already positioned near the edge of the source image and you attempt to enter a value for Feather, you will be creating a boundary that goes beyond the image edge. You will then receive a warning, and the maximum allowable value will automatically be entered in the Feather value box. The slider or values will not exceed that value unless the motif is moved.

One last feathering note: if you have a very small motif, you may not be able to see the feather boundary, even if you have the Show Feather Boundary option turned on. Although you can't see it, the feather will still appear when you apply the pattern.

The Mode Settings

The Mode drop-down list in the Terrazzo dialog box lets you control the way a pattern is applied to a selection. This operates in the same manner as the Merge/Paint mode throughout the rest of PHOTO-PAINT.

The Opacity Slider

The Opacity slider in the Terrazzo dialog box lets you adjust the opacity of the pattern when you apply it to a selection. You may want the effect of an almost invisible pattern (low opacity), or you may want a bold application of a pattern, covering the destination image entirely (high opacity). An opacity value of 100 (100 percent) means that the pattern is completely opaque; an opacity value of 1 means that the pattern is almost invisible (which is not very useful).

Previewing Tiles

A preview of the current tile appears below the symmetry swatch. The pixel dimensions of the current tile are also displayed below the tile. You are provided with a constant preview of the tile you are creating.

Saving a Tile

One of the benefits of having the Terrazzo filter integrated into Corel PHOTO-PAINT is that the Save Tile button becomes a real time-saver. The Save Tile feature saves the tile created by Terrazzo as a BMP file. With this feature, you can use Terrazzo to make a tile quickly; and after saving the tile, you can use it immediately as a bitmap fill.

To save a Terrazzo tile:

1. Choose the symmetry, then position the motif where you want it in the source image.

2. Click the Save Tile button in the Terrazzo dialog box; the Save Tile dialog box opens.

3. Name the file and confirm where you want it saved. Click the OK button. When you return to the Terrazzo dialog box, click Cancel if you do not want any pattern applied to the image.

14

> **TIP** *Make note of where the seamless tile is saved (or be prepared to spend some time looking for it).*

In Summary

Considering all of the techniques you have learned so far, it is high time to put then into use. In the next chapter, you will discover how to use the creations made in PHOTO-PAINT in other Corel applications, as well as in non-Corel applications.

PART VI

Advanced PHOTO-PAINT Topics

CHAPTER 15

Scanners, Digital Cameras, and the Web

Five years ago, there were very few options for bringing images into Corel PHOTO-PAINT. Grayscale flatbed scanners were selling for over $1,000, and there were no consumer color flatbeds. The only digital cameras available were prototypes costing upward of $50,000, and the Internet was a text-based engine that was only understood by people who didn't get invited to many social events. The changes that have occurred in this relatively short time span are mind-boggling. Now, a decent color flatbed scanner costs around a hundred dollars, while good digital cameras (digicams) cost between $800 and $1,000. Digicams that can take acceptable photographs can be found around $150–$200, and there is even a Barbie digital camera for under $70 that takes recognizable photos—meaning you can recognize the subject being photographed. The Internet holds a wealth of both legal and illegal images covering every subject imaginable, including some that would have shocked the Marquis de Sade.

In this chapter, you will learn how to set up and use a scanner to bring printed material into PHOTO-PAINT. You will likewise discover how to bring in images from digital cameras (which, in truth, are just portable scanners) and capture video. We will briefly look at how PHOTO-PAINT's Scrapbook docker window is used to bring in images from Corel CDs; and, finally, we will explore how to use Corel CAPTURE—a very powerful screen capture utility that ships with Corel PHOTO-PAINT.

Scanners and Scanning

In previous editions of this book, I spent a few paragraphs explaining the economic justifications for the cost of a scanner; but now that they are so inexpensive, it isn't necessary to eat beans for a month to be able to afford one. Aside from cost, scanners are now much easier to install thanks to effective parallel port and Universal Serial Bus (USB) interfaces. These days, just about anyone can own and use a scanner to bring photos, images, and even food (nothing better than a scan of chocolate cookies) into PHOTO-PAINT. Let's review a few scanner fundamentals and then learn how to scan.

What Your Mother Never Told You About Scanners

Go into a computer or electronics superstore and you will find more scanners there than you even knew existed. The choice of a scanner isn't limited to choosing between manufacturers; once you decide on a brand you like, you may find as many as six different scanners made by the same company. It is almost a given that the salespeople selling the scanners aren't there because of their knowledge of scanners or computers in general. They are probably there because they didn't like the hours at the local fast-food eatery. So, advice from the salesperson—although liberally seasoned with technical-sounding terms—is questionable, making it all the more difficult to decide which scanner is right for you. If you haven't yet made the plunge and bought a scanner or you are considering giving away your old scanner, here are some basics that might help you in getting the most for your scanning buck.

All Scanners Are Not Created Equal

While all flatbed scanners look alike, they offer a wide range of features and capabilities. Worse, they all provide you with a dizzying array of specifications that makes your choice even more confusing. To make it a little simpler, let's begin by dividing scanners into one of three groups based on their interfaces— parallel port, SCSI (pronounced *scuzzy*), and the newest scanner interface: USB.

Parallel Port Scanners—Slow but Sure

The least expensive scanners are parallel port scanners, which almost always are indicated by the letter "P" after the model number. On the plus side, they attach to the printer port of your computer, which means relatively easy installation. The major drawback of this interface is that the speed is relatively slow. The slower the bits move to the computer, the longer it takes to scan an image, which only is a problem if you are spending several hours each day scanning. If you are not, it is not a major issue. Another possible issue is conflicts with other devices that might also be attached to the parallel port, such as Zip™ drives and printers. Problems can arise when the other devices and the scanner attempt to use the same parallel port at the same time. Although it is a minor issue, it is one to be aware of when choosing a scanner.

SCSI—Expensive, Fast, and a Wee Bit Complicated

The interface choice of professionals is SCSI (small computer system interface). High-end scanners have always used a SCSI interface for the speed improvement it offers over the other two interfaces. Because this interface is usually only found on high-end scanners, SCSI interface scanners are the most expensive of the three interfaces. Other than cost, the main challenge to using a SCSI interface is that it

15

nearly always requires the installation of a SCSI card in the computer, the thought of which can frighten even your computer-savvy neighbor. Still, there is nothing faster than SCSI once installed, although I think that USB will eventually replace SCSI on all high-end consumer scanners in the next few years.

USB—The New Kid on the Block

In the last year or so, USB scanners have been gaining in popularity because they offer lots of benefits and few drawbacks. USB offers speed and performance close enough to that provided by SCSI that it is even starting to show up on high-end consumer and business scanners. Installation with USB is simple, with many of the USB scanners being hot swappable (meaning you don't have to restart the computer to have the computer recognize the scanner after it is plugged into the computer). The two drawbacks to USB scanners relate to the computer you are using. If your computer doesn't have a USB slot built in, you will need to install a USB card. Second, your computer must be running at least Windows 98 to use any USB device—Windows 95 or Windows NT won't cut it.

What Resolution and Bit Depth Actually Mean to You

Now that we have reviewed the available scanner interfaces, our next daunting hurdle is the sea of numbers that we find displayed all around the scanners in the store. Again, I am going to condense and grossly oversimplify some information, but I think you will find it helpful.

Resolution—Other Than New Year's

Resolution is the most grossly misunderstood and misrepresented term when it comes to scanners. There are always two kinds of resolution advertised: *optical* (this is the real resolution of the scanner) and *interpolated* (think of this as the resolution that the scanner makes up as it goes along). The only resolution to be concerned about is the optical resolution, which is always the lower number. It used to be that all scanners had roughly the same optical resolution—300 dots per inch (dpi). With advances in scanner technology, some consumer scanners are offering optical resolutions of 1,200–1,600 dpi, which is pretty impressive. The question is, how much resolution do you need?

The quick (and incomplete) answer to this question is determined by what you're going to do with the image you are scanning. If you are scanning for a Web site, a scanner with an optical resolution of 300 dpi is more than sufficient. If you are scanning material that is to be printed by a commercial printer, you should have a scanner with at least a 600-dpi optical resolution. Now, let's talk about color depth.

How Deep Is Your Color?

As with resolution, your choice of color depth for a color flatbed was once also simple. All color scanners supported 24-bit and nothing else unless you were getting a drum scanner, which is a scanner the size of a Buick that costs more than your house. Today, scanners offer a range of color depths starting with 24-bit going all the way up to 48-bit. Since the final image will only be 24-bit (RGB), you might be wondering why they are offering so much depth only to throw the extra bits away. It is not all marketing hype; there is actually a reason for all those "spare" bits. It seems that flatbed scanners aren't very good at picking up detail in the shadow areas, and by scanning at a greater color depth (in the world of scanning, grayscale is color), it is possible to capture more detail in the shadow regions. Then, using a process that is too complicated to explain, the image is reduced to 24-bit color while preserving that detail information.

So, how much color depth do you need? The rule of thumb is pretty much the same as with resolution: If you are scanning for the Web, almost any color depth will do. For critical or prepress work, the additional color depth will most certainly help in getting the most information out of the image you are scanning.

Final Musings on Choosing a Scanner

Some final thoughts to consider when picking a scanner have to do with the scanner's pedigree—in other words, the company who made it. If you buy a scanner made by an unknown company like the Happy-Lucky Computer Company, odds are that you are buying a disposable scanner. When you need new drivers for the next version of the Windows operating system (and there are always new versions of Windows on the horizon) or if you require technical assistance when everything you scan comes out blue (it happens), it is nice to know that there is someone to call. Of course, you might wait on hold for 45 minutes listening to a voice tell you how important your call is to them; but, at least with the major scanner manufacturers, there is someone to call.

15

If you are going to be scanning a lot of negatives or color slides, you should consider a film scanner. While most midrange to high-end flatbed scanners come with an optional transparency scanner, these cannot offer anything like the ease of use and quality that can be obtained using a film scanner. These film scanners scan at much higher resolutions than the flatbed scanners (2,700- to 4,000-dpi optical) and, therefore, cost more than their flatbed cousins. Still, you can get a consumer film scanner like the HP-S-20 scanner shown here for around $400, or get a good used film scanner from Polaroid or Nikon for around $600 through the online auctions.

Scanners, PHOTO-PAINT, and TWAIN

Once the scanner is out of the box and you have installed the software that came with it, it is time to learn how to access it in PHOTO-PAINT and scan something with it. In early versions of PHOTO-PAINT, you had to install Corel drivers for the scanner being used. This is no longer necessary, since PHOTO-PAINT uses the TWAIN drivers (software) that were installed when you set up the scanner. TWAIN is the name of the software driver used by every scanner manufacturer to communicate with Windows applications like PHOTO-PAINT. Were you wondering what TWAIN stands for? See the "Story of TWAIN" sidebar in this chapter. Each TWAIN driver is unique to the device for which it was installed; and the TWAIN interfaces provided by scanner manufacturers range in functionality from the bare essentials to very sophisticated interfaces like the one shown in Figure 15-1, which provides many presets and automatic scanning functions. Next, let's learn how to use the scanner.

Where the TWAIN Meets

Scanning with PHOTO-PAINT involves two steps: select and acquire. Before you can scan the first time, or when you change scanners, you need to tell PHOTO-PAINT which scanner (TWAIN driver) you want to use. Select File | Acquire Image | Select Source (CTRL-SHIFT-Q) to open the Select Source dialog box, as shown next. Pick the TWAIN source that you want to use and click the Select button to open the UI (user interface) for the scanner. In the next illustration, you will notice that

15

FIGURE 15-1   Every scanner manufacturer provides its own unique TWAIN user interface

several TWAIN devices are installed. Although several TWAIN drivers are shown in the dialog box, only one scanner was actually installed when the screen capture of the dialog box was made. Just because the TWAIN driver is installed, that doesn't mean the scanner is available.

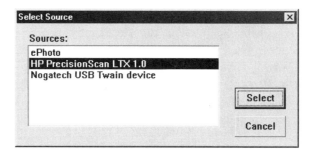

Previewing the Scan

When you begin to scan something, the scanner first performs a low-resolution scan that appears in the Preview window of the UI. I must emphasize that the preview is a low-quality scan for purposes of selecting the area of the image to be scanned (cropping) and making other adjustments. During the preview scan, most scanners do their best to figure out what kind of original (black-and-white, 256-color, and so on) they are scanning; still, they don't always get it right, so at this point you may have to manually adjust the color mode of the scanner. Also at this point, you can select the final size and resolution of the scanned image. Generally, the higher-end scanners have a lot more features and controls than the scanner that sells in your local supermarket for $39.99.

When you're satisfied that the image in the preview window is what you want, you are ready to scan. Click the button in the UI that scans the image. Since the scanner manufacturer, not PHOTO-PAINT, provides the scanner UI, the name of the button that initiates the final scan varies. The UI shown in Figure 15-1 actually is very clear that it will send the image to PHOTO-PAINT. Not all of them are this clear. Once the scan is complete, the UI closes and the scanned image appears in a new image window.

TIP *If you are scanning a lot of images and don't want the scanner UI closing after every scan, open Options (CTRL-J); and in the Workspace area, choose General and uncheck Close Scan Dialog After Acquire.*

The Story of TWAIN (Not Mark)

Not so long ago, it was the responsibility of every company that wrote paint (bitmap) programs to provide the software necessary to communicate with the scanner. However, every scanner spoke its own language, so to speak, and the result was that unless you owned one of the more popular scanners, you could not access the scanner from within your paint or drawing program. Most of the time, it was necessary to run a separate scanning program (provided with your scanner) to scan in an image. After the image was scanned, you could load it into your favorite paint or OCR program. That may seem like a lot of work, and let me assure you, it was.

Then one day all of the scanner people got together and said, "Let us all make our scanners speak one language" (sort of a Tower of Babel in reverse). So, they came up with an interface specification called TWAIN.

Why is the interface specification called "TWAIN"? This is one of those mysteries that might puzzle computer historians for decades to come. I have never received a straight answer to the question, only intriguing possibilities. My favorite explanation is credited to Aldus (now Adobe) Corporation. They say TWAIN means "Specification Without An Interesting Name." Logitech, one of the driving forces behind the specification, gives a different answer: "It was a unique interface that brings together two entities, application and input devices, in a meeting of the "twain."

Whatever the origin of the name, the TWAIN interface allows Corel PHOTO-PAINT (or any other program that supports TWAIN) to talk to the scanner directly through a common interface, and for that we should all be thankful.

More Ways to Scan

15

Although nearly every scanner uses TWAIN drivers to communicate with PHOTO-PAINT, there are other ways to control the scanner. One way is to choose the import plug-ins, which use PHOTO-PAINT's plug-in filter architecture to open the scanner UI. Import plug-ins allow third-party programs to be used to control—and at times, automate—the scanning process. Import plug-ins are located in the File menu. To use an import plug-in to scan, select File | Import |Import Plug-ins. If one is installed, it will launch and operate like the TWAIN scanners described in the previous paragraphs.

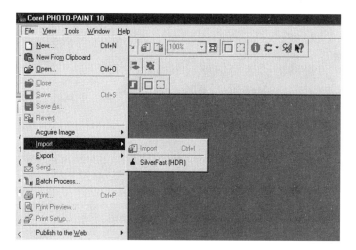

In the preceding illustration, I have installed the SilverFast™ program. If other import plug-ins were installed, they would also appear on the list. Examples of such programs are the PhotoPerfect program shipped with UMAX professional scanners and the SilverFlash program shipped with Epson's Expression series of scanners. Both of these programs, and others like them, are specifically configured to the scanner they are bundled with to offer many automated features, providing the user with the best possible scans while requiring the least amount of experience or effort. Figure 15-2 shows the very complex UI for the SilverFast plug-in. While it looks more complicated than the federal budget, it provides tools that allow you to get the most out of your high-end scanner.

Installing the import plug-in is simply a matter of installing the software per the manufacturer's instructions and then configuring PHOTO-PAINT to use it, as you would install one of the filter effect plug-ins described in Chapter 13. Before you start looking for the import plug-in for your scanner, you should know that these import plug-ins are usually found only on high-end scanners. Even if the scanner has an import plug-in, it will also have TWAIN drivers that can be selected as well. Before TWAIN became the standard interface for scanners, all scanners communicated with photo-editing programs through the use of plug-ins, and Mac computers still use this method.

FIGURE 15-2   The user interface for the SilverFast plug-in provides a wealth of tools to get the most out of your scanner

The other way scanners can be used to scan an image is by using the software that came with the scanner to operate stand-alone. The popular method for using a scanner in this manner is to press a "Scan" button located somewhere on the scanner that launches its own program to scan an image and save it without ever opening PHOTO-PAINT.

Customizing PHOTO-PAINT for Scanning Lots of Images

If you do a lot of scanning, you are going to get tired of opening up a multilevel file menu every time you want to scan. To make this operation easier, open Options (CTRL-J), select Workspace | Customization | Commands, choose Acquire

Image from the list shown next, and drag the image to an open command bar. Now you can begin the scanning process with a single click of the Acquire Scan button.

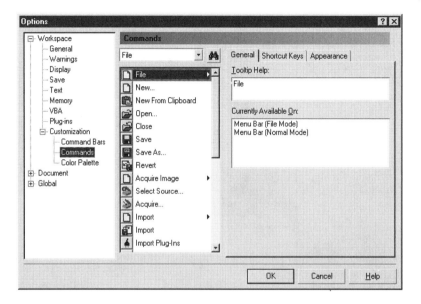

Some Facts About Scanning

Scanning is not difficult—we aren't talking brain surgery here. It is simply knowing a little and working a little to extract the most out of a printed image. Sadly, many users, including graphics professionals, do not understand some of the basics necessary to get the best-quality image from a scanner into Corel PHOTO-PAINT and out to a printer.

Scanning and Resolution . . . Making It Work for You

It seems logical that the resolution of a scan should be the same, or nearly the same, as that of the printer. The problem is that when we talk about the resolution of the scanner in dots per inch (dpi), we are not talking about the same dots per inch used when describing printer resolution. In Chapter 2, we learned about pixels. Scanners scan pixels, which are square, and printers make dots, which are round. The resolution of the scanner is measured in dots per inch, which is incorrect because its resolution is more accurately described in samples per inch. Each sample represents a pixel.

The resolution of the printer dot is measured in dots per inch. The resolution of the printer determines the size of the dot it makes. For example, each dot made by a 600-dpi printer is 1/600 of an inch in diameter. These printer dots come in only two flavors: black and white. To produce the 256 shades of gray that exist between black and white on a printer, these tiny dots are grouped together to form halftone cells. For example, let's assume, for the sake of illustration, that each halftone cell made by our printer is 10×10 dots in size. Each halftone cell can hold a maximum of 100 dots. To print the shade 50 percent gray, the printer turns half of the dots on in each halftone cell and leaves half off. This gives the appearance to the eye of being 50 percent gray.

When we talk about scanner resolution, we are actually talking about samples per inch. Each sample of a scan at 600 dpi is 1/600 of an inch square (remember that pixels are square). Unlike the printer's dot, which can have only two possible values, each scanner pixel can have one of 256 possible values (for simplicity, we are assuming grayscale). The relationship between scanner pixels and printer dots is shown in the photograph taken during a conversation between the two of them, as shown next:

At this point, we can see that a scanned pixel is much more like a printer halftone cell than the original printer dot. So how do you determine how many halftone cells per inch your printer is capable of producing? If you look in the back of your printer manual, you won't find a setting for halftone cells per inch, but you may (I emphasize the *may* part) find a setting for either screen or line frequency. Line frequency is measured in lines per inch (lpi). An old rule of thumb for scanning used to be to scan at twice the line frequency of the final output device. This rule has become pretty outdated. You should scan at roughly 1.5 times the line frequency of your final output device.

There is some serious math we could use to calculate the ideal resolution to match the scan to the output device, but there is a simpler way. The following sections give some basic recommended resolutions and tips for scanning different types of images. These recommendations are compiled from information provided by various scanner manufacturers and service bureau operators.

A Trick Question About Resolution

During a recent 51-city Corel WordPerfect roadshow, I had the opportunity to ask literally hundreds of attendees the following question: *"If you are going to print a photograph on a 600 dot per inch (dpi) laser printer, at what resolution should you scan the image for the best output?"* More than half answered that they would use a resolution of 600. Was that your answer? If so, read on. If you answered with any resolution from 100 to 150 dpi, you are correct. Take two compliments out of petty cash. If you answered 600 dpi, I recommend reading the sidebar "Scanning and Resolution . . . Making It Work for You" on the previous two pages. The good news is that most scanner software doesn't ask you for the resolution, but only to select what output type you are scanning for; the software selects the resolution for you, most often correctly.

Why You Shouldn't Scan at Excessively High Resolutions

Even after going through all of the explanations about the best settings to get a good scan, some still believe that scanning at a higher-than-necessary resolution somehow gives their image extra detail or makes it look sharper. In fact, doing this rarely improves image quality, but it always produces very large file sizes. Remember that each time resolution is doubled, the file size quadruples. Large image files take a long time to process, and time is money at your local neighborhood service bureau. Also, scanning at a resolution higher than the output device can reproduce tends to cause detail in the shadow area to be lost; and if the resolution is high enough and the image small enough, the final result may actually be a blurry picture.

Scanning Printed Material, or the Dangers of Moiré

Before photographs are printed, they are first *screened,* which is a process that makes it possible for the printing press to reproduce them. Scanning such material generally produces unwanted patterns called *moiré patterns.* The moiré patterns in Figure 15-3 were produced when the frequency of the lines in my shirt approached the frequency of the zoom factor in the display. When you scan a halftone image, for another example, you will likely see moiré patterns because the dots per inch (dpi) frequency of the original halftone screen differs from that of the scanned image. Doing this also produces potential legal problems involving copyrights, but that isn't what we are talking about here. There are several ways to either reduce or eliminate these moiré patterns; all of them slightly degrade the image to one degree or another, proving there is no such thing as a free lunch.

The stripes on the shirt produce moiré patterns

Using the Scanner's Descreening Filter

Most of the scanners in today's market offer some sort of descreening feature that in one fashion or another breaks up the screening pattern of the image to reduce or eliminate the dreaded moiré patterns. My experience with these scanner tools is that their effectiveness runs the entire range from very good to pathetic. If your scanner doesn't have one or it doesn't seem to work very well, you can try PHOTO-PAINT's own descreening filter.

PHOTO-PAINT's Remove Moiré Filter

The Remove Moiré filter, shown in Figure 15-4, offers two different controls for removing patterned noise that can occur in a scanned halftone image. The primary technique involves the application of the Amount slider, which applies a mild blurring to the image to break up the screen patterns. Operation is simple: move

FIGURE 15-4 PHOTO-PAINT's Remove Moiré filter removes the pattern that results from scanning printed images

the Amount slider, while viewing the image, until the screen pattern just begins to disappear.

Your Zoom level must be set to 100% to accurately view the effects of this filter. Try this at any other zoom level, and you may actually be viewing moiré patterns caused by the zoom level.

To use the Remove Moiré filter, click Effects | Noise | Remove Moiré. You have two choices for the preview quality: Speed and Quality. You need only use the Speed (faster) setting on very large images. As you increase the Amount, you will notice the image becoming softer. This is the image degradation I spoke about

15

earlier. The other control, Decrease Resolution, downsamples the image to a lower resolution, which will reduce the size of your image.

Things You Should Know About Using the Remove Moiré Filter

The Decrease Resolution feature is only available if you merge all objects with the image background (a situation that doesn't arise when you are applying this filter to freshly scanned images, as you usually will be doing).

For best results, scan the original image at 200 percent of the final desired size and then change the output resolution to half of that amount. This is one occasion when using a resolution of 300 (dpi) is advisable. I recommend that, after using the Remove Moiré filter, you apply a mild sharpening filter like Adaptive Unsharp to compensate for the softness introduced by the filter.

Now, let's explore the instant camera of the new millennium, the digital camera. In my day, it was the Polaroid™—times have changed.

Working with Digital Cameras

With the increasing popularity of digital cameras, more and more people are taking photos with these little wonders. As the owners begin to view and share these photographs on the Internet, it becomes important to use PHOTO-PAINT to improve both the composition (by cropping) and the tonal quality of the image.

Digital cameras come with a variety of internal storage media for keeping the photographs you take, including removable disks, microdrives, and memory cards—there is even one that actually records on a CD. Memory cards (either CompactFlash™ or SmartMedia™) are still the media of choice among camera manufacturers. As I write this, both of these media are about equally common; but it is clear that, as new models are introduced, the CompactFlash medium is going to become the standard. Regardless of the medium in the camera, the first step is getting the photograph from the camera to PHOTO-PAINT.

Getting from the Digicam into Your Computer

As in the case of scanners, there are several ways to get the image from the camera into PHOTO-PAINT, including

- Serial interface cable

- Flashpath™

- Clik™ drive

- USB adapter or direct

For the longest time, the only way to get information from a digital camera to the computer was to use the serial cable that came with the camera. The first time you tried to do this, you were probably amazed at how long an image took to download. USB is slowly becoming the interface of choice for newer digital cameras because it is nearly 100 times faster than a serial connection.

In a country that offers photographs and prescription glasses in an hour, it is not surprising that there are several alternatives for speeding up the digicam-to-computer connection.

The device that is offered by many camera manufacturers using SmartMedia cards is the FlashPath floppy adapter. You slip the SmartMedia card into the device and insert the device into the floppy drive. While it isn't the speediest thing in the world, it is still many times faster than a serial interface. Other third-party solutions include memory card readers that attach to the parallel port, USB port, or PCMCIA (PC card) slot of your computer. These products are significantly faster than serial transfers or even the FlashPath adapter. The Clik drive by Iomega is a little handheld 40MB drive that, when attached to a card reader, transfers the contents of the camera medium to the Clik disk very quickly. From there you can attach the drive to your computer. This approach has its advantages, but has seen limited acceptance in the marketplace.

15

Loading Images Directly into PHOTO-PAINT

Regardless of the media used or the interface device, getting the images into PHOTO-PAINT is done the same way we scan images: via the TWAIN interface. You select File | Acquire Image | Select Source and choose the TWAIN driver for your digital camera.

> **NOTE** *If you were wondering where they moved the digital camera interface feature that first appeared in PHOTO-PAINT 9, it is gone. As all of the digicams communicate with the computer using a TWAIN interface, it didn't make sense to continue to have a dedicated feature that duplicated the existing TWAIN support.*

Most of the digital cameras on the market today compress their images to get more pictures into the media. Several of the cameras apply some form of postprocessing to the compressed image when it is transferred from the camera to your computer using their software. For example, I use an old Agfa ePhoto 1280 that processes the photos with a program called PhotoGenie™ as they are downloaded from the camera to the computer. Close examination of an image both with the processing applied and without does not reveal any significant differences between the photographs. Still, you may want to make sure that using PHOTO-PAINT's TWAIN feature to load the images from your camera does not bypass a necessary post-processing step.

Video Capture—It's Easier Than You Might Imagine

There are more than a dozen devices you can buy that enable you to bring video into your computer; and even though PHOTO-PAINT is not a video editor, it does provide a few tools to clean up and modify video screen captures. The source of your video screen capture will determine how much and what kind of work it needs. For example, Figure 15-5 is a video capture of Spencer Tracy in a personal favorite, *Desk Set.* The source material was recorded from the local TV station onto videotape and then captured using a Belkin™ Video Bus. One of several problems with the image is that video capture tends to be low resolution. This lack of resolution is not apparent when the subjects are moving; but when a video frame is captured and no longer moving, all of its shortcomings become painfully obvious. Another issue with captured video is the presence of interlace lines that result from the way TV signals are broadcast.

FIGURE 15-5   This video capture needs work before it can be used

Improving Video Captures with Deinterlace

Unlike images on your monitor, the image on the TV screen is displayed through a process called *interlacing,* in which all of the odd lines of the image are displayed, followed by all of the even lines. When an interlaced video image is captured, the even and odd lines do not perfectly align, so it is necessary to correct this. The Deinterlace filter removes either even or odd horizontal lines from scanned or interlaced video images, and then fills in the resulting empty space by duplication or interpolation. *Duplication* fills the space with copies of adjacent scan lines. *Interpolation* fills the space with colors created by averaging the surrounding pixels. You will see the greatest difference when you choose even or odd horizontal lines. In all of the work that I have done, I have yet to see any significant difference between duplication and interpolation. You can use the Deinterlace filter to remove horizontal lines from scanned images or to remove interlace lines from video images. To use the Deinterlace filter, choose | Image | Transform Deinterlace. Since interlacing doesn't degrade video images that much, do not expect to see dramatic improvement when using this filter.

Corel Scrapbook Docker Window

This docker is a combination visual search engine and repository for images on the Web, on your system, and on the Corel CD-ROM. To open the Scrapbook, choose Window | Dockers | Scrapbook. Another drop-down list will appear, offering choices Browse, Content on Web, and Search. For the image shown next, I selected the Objects folder in the CorelDRAW 10 CD, Disc 3, and chose the Fruit folder, from which I dragged the tiny thumbnail of the pears into an image. The Scrapbook docker offers several options to customize the display, including whether or not thumbnails of the images are displayed and, if so, at what size. Also shown in the next image is the rather convoluted path that allows you to change the size of the thumbnails. Be aware that larger thumbnails give a better look at the image, but take longer to load and also let you see fewer images at a time in the docker window.

The Scrapbook offers a quick and very visual way to preview and grab images. For serious image management, you should use the Canto Cumulus 5image database that ships with CorelDRAW 10.

Getting Great Screen Shots Using Corel CAPTURE

Sometimes we need to capture screen shots of images on the screen. Every image in this book, with the exception of the screen shots of the CAPTURE program, was captured in one way or another by Corel CAPTURE 10.

Using CAPTURE is a four-step process. Launch the program; adjust the settings; click the Capture (not the Close) button; and when you are ready to capture, click the Activation key.

CAPTURE works with any image that can be displayed on your monitor. The images don't even have to be in Corel. The operation of CAPTURE is very simple. You can launch Corel CAPTURE using Start | Programs | Corel | Graphic Utilities | Corel CAPTURE; but an easier way to launch it, from within Corel PHOTO-PAINT, is to use the Corel Application Launcher, as shown next.

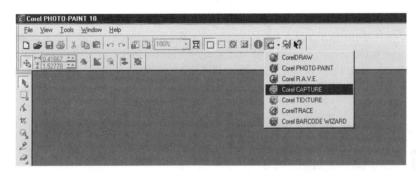

After launching the program, the Corel CAPTURE dialog box appears. It is divided into five pages: Source, Activation, Image, Destination, and Options. The first time you launch CAPTURE, the Source page is selected, as shown next.

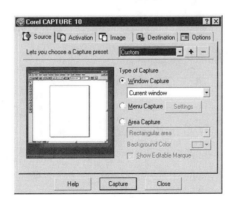

Selecting the Source

You can specify which part of the image you want to capture in the Type of Capture drop-down list on the Source page just shown. Most of the selections are self-explanatory. New in PHOTO-PAINT 10 is the ability to create and name a preset of Capture settings. This is a real time saver when you have to use CAPTURE for different jobs, each with different settings.

In the Type of Capture area, you can select what part of the image will be captured. Both Window and Area Capture have been around for a while, but Menu Capture allows the capture of just a menu with most applications.

 Not all applications allow the Menu to be captured. A warning dialog box will appear when a capture is attempted if it doesn't work. In such cases, use a Full Screen capture and crop away the unwanted part.

Here are some tips I learned while working with this page. If the Current Object with Border option is selected, the title bar on the image window will be included. The Elliptical Area and Rectangular Area features do not have a constrain key, so you must create your circle and square capture areas by using a steady hand on the mouse and your calibrated eyeball. If you use any setting that captures an area that is nonrectangular, the resulting capture will be in a rectangular image area.

Choosing the Hot Key

From the Activation page, shown next, you can pick the hot key you want to use for activation of the program. By default, it should be set to the function key F7. If User Defined is chosen, another dialog box opens that allows you to choose almost any combination of keystrokes you want just by typing them in. If the keystroke combination you select is already in use by a program, you will receive a warning message; you can then click OK and try a different combination.

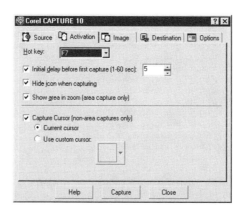

> **TIP**   *I wouldn't advise long, complicated keystroke combinations to activate the capture feature, since they can be difficult to remember and cumbersome to enter.*

Among the other features worthy of note on this page is Initial Delay Before First Capture. The default setting is 5 seconds. The delay is helpful when capturing areas of the screen that are shy—meaning that touching the activation key makes them go away. Most of the time you will want this unchecked. The other feature that deserves a little explanation is Capture Cursor. When checked (default), it will capture the cursor that is currently enabled. You can also select a cursor from another application. I recommend leaving it unchecked normally so that no cursor is captured.

Image Tab Page

The Image page is shown next. From the Image page, you define the color mode and resolution of the captured image. A few points about using this page: keep the Maintain Aspect Ratio check box is checked so that, regardless of the Resolution selected, the number of screen pixels captured will remain the same as in the original, and the resulting image will appear to be the same size.

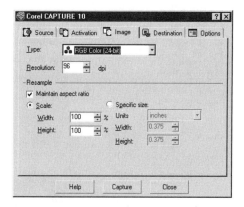

Selecting the Destination

The next tab is the Destination page, which allows you to choose where to send the screen capture you create. There are four choices: File, Clipboard, Printer, and OLE Automated Application. Since I must make a lot of screen captures for books and articles, I often save the image to the clipboard and then use the New from Clipboard command in the File menu in PHOTO-PAINT to make it into an image. The only caveat is to remember that the clipboard can only hold one object at a time. More than once, I have saved a screen capture in the clipboard and then, before unloading it in PHOTO-PAINT, proceeded to copy some text to the clipboard while in another

15

application, thus wiping out my screen shot. Other than this small consideration, the clipboard works best for me.

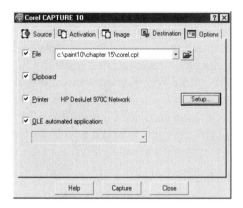

The Options Page

This page used to be a little crowded; but since Corel added an additional page to the Corel CAPTURE filter dialog box, there are only a few settings here worth noting. The Notify End of Capture setting is handy when capturing a large image such as a full screen shot; otherwise, it is a nuisance—leave it unchecked. Definitely uncheck Show Ready to Capture Dialog. When enabled, it displays a message box notifying you that CAPTURE is ready and waiting to capture your images.

Just a few notes of interest. The default file format is BMP. I recommend not using any lossy compression format (JPEG, Wavelet, and so on) for images that you may later want to modify.

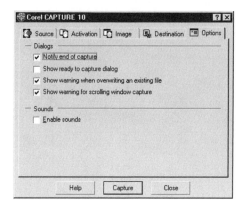

In Summary

In the short span of a few pages, we have covered just about every conceivable way to get an image from the outside world into PHOTO-PAINT . We have only skimmed the subject of scanning. To give the subject the treatment it is due would take an entire book, which I am in the process of writing—look for it. In the next chapter, we are going to explore some of the more advanced tools and techniques for working with objects.

CHAPTER 16

Using PHOTO-PAINT to Create Web Graphics

In this chapter, you are going to learn as much as possible about creating graphics for the Web using PHOTO-PAINT 10. You will discover that Corel has included a number of tools that enable you to create some great objects for the Web. Before you can begin making these cool objects, you need to understand a little more about color as it applies to graphics used on the Web.

The World of Internet Colors

One of the great dilemmas facing us when we want to make graphics for the Web is the need to make great graphics and still keep the file size as small as possible, so that the person visiting the Web page doesn't have to wait long for the image to download. As you may know, visitors probably won't wait; they will skip on to another Web site.

Converting color images for use on the Web is a two-step process: First, the colors in the image are converted to the narrow range of colors that display correctly on the Web. The second step of the conversion is accomplished when the image is loaded by a browser, which may cause your beautiful creation to be modified (read: corrupted) even further. The bottom line is that you want to make your graphic files as small as possible, consistent with the least amount of distortion or loss. That said, let's look at the first stage: converting the image from 24-bit to 8-bit with the least amount of loss.

Two Paths to Smaller File Sizes

There are two ways to initially reduce the size of a graphic image. The original method, used by the pioneers during the gold rush—okay, maybe it wasn't that long ago—is to convert the image to 8-bit color, which means a palette of 256 colors, and to save the image using the GIF file format. The other way, which is becoming increasingly popular, is to save the image using JPEG compression. The good news is, JPEG permits you to keep a large palette of colors and still keep the file size relatively small. The bad news is, JPEG is a format that degrades the graphic in direct relationship to the amount of compression used. For example, if I squeeze the 229K graphic file down to 5K, the image quality suffers. The good news is that if you don't go overboard compressing the image, you won't be able to see the loss of image quality, but you will still see a significant reduction of file size.

To GIF or Not to GIF, That Is the Question

When preparing to export your images to the Web, you must decide whether to use the GIF or JPEG file format. Here is a general rule of thumb. If the image is a vector drawing or text, use GIF; if it is a photograph, use JPEG. The reason GIF works well with vector images and text is that its inherently limited range of colors works well when reduced to a palette of 256 colors—most of the time. If you want to really explore this subject in greater detail, I recommend an excellent article entitled "Graphic File Formats for the Web," by Anthony Celeste, at www.designer.com. Enough about color, let's learn how to make some cool objects.

Button, Button, Who Made the Button

Here is a popular technique to create a 3D gradient button. If this is your first button, you may feel that this image is too small, but when was the last time you saw a large 3D button on a Web page?

1. Create a new 24-bit RGB image that is 72 × 72 pixels at a resolution of 72 dpi.

2. Select the Ellipse tool (F7); and on the property bar, ensure that the Fountain Fill and the Render to Object buttons are enabled, as shown next.

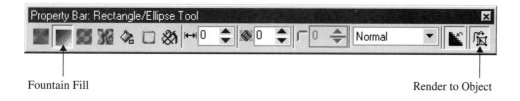

Fountain Fill   Render to Object

3. Hold down CTRL and drag a circle, and then click the Object Picker tool to select it. Ensure that the Lock Transparency button on the bottom of the Objects docker is enabled.

4. Choose Edit | Fill; and when the dialog box opens, click the Edit button. At this point, you are creating the outer rim of the button and it is necessary to make the light appear to come from the upper left. Change the settings of the Fountain Fill dialog box to match those shown in the next illustration. The colors are black and 10 percent black. When finished, click OK to return to the previous dialog box, and click OK again to apply the fill.

16

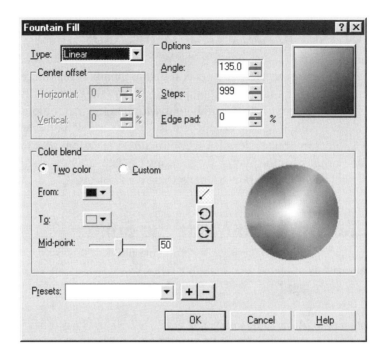

5. Open the Align & Distribute dialog box (CTRL-A), and check To Center of Document. The circle should look like the one shown next.

6. Create a mask from the object (CTRL-M). Choose Mask | Shape | Reduce and change the settings to 2 pixels. Don't use a setting greater than 2 pixels, or the mask shape will distort.

7. Disable Lock Object Transparency by clicking the button again. Choose Edit | Fill; and after clicking the Edit button, change the Preset to Circular—Orange 01, and change both the Center Offset and Steps as shown next. Click OK twice.

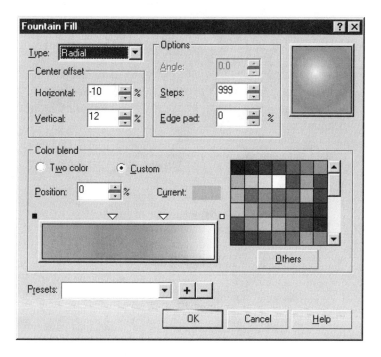

8. Remove the mask (CTRL-SHIFT-R) and Choose Effects | Texture | Plastic. When the dialog box opens, click the Reset button and then change the Smoothness setting to 100. Click OK.

9. Next, select the Drop Shadow tool (S) and click the button that has just been created. From the property bar, choose the Flat Bottom Right. You now have a tiny button, as shown.

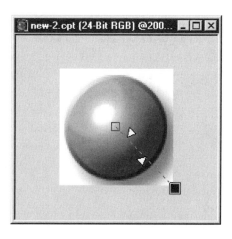

10. Now, crop your image (to get rid of unwanted background), resample to the size you require, and then choose Image | Mode | Paletted (8 Bit).

11. You can make more buttons from this object by using the Duplicate command (CTRL-D). You can also change the colors of the duplicate buttons by using the Hue controls in the Image menu. I have provided a modest example I was going to submit for a Florida Web page.

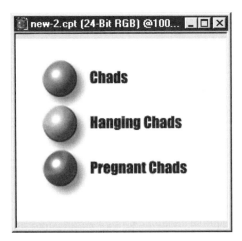

12. Needless to say, this button will look great on a white background; but what if you are using a different color or tiled background, and you want to avoid color fringing due to the anti-aliasing? Just change the color of the button's background to a similar one.

Beyond What the Designer Had in Mind

When Jeff Butterworth of Alien Skin Software originally created The Boss filter, he wanted it to be the best embossing filter available on the market. He put so many controls on it, it can be used to go beyond just plain old embossing. Here are some other things to try with it that even Jeff may not have thought of yet. I really enjoy all of the interesting 3D effects that can be created with CorelDRAW. Here is a technique to produce 3D objects for a Web page using The Boss filter.

Making a 3D Web Page Button

In this hands-on exercise, we will create a basic 3D object that can be used on a Web page or made part of a control panel illustration. Once you have made the basic button, before you add the text, you can duplicate the object and make as many as you want.

1. Create a new image, selecting 24-bit color, Paper Color: White; Size: 4 × 4 inches; and Resolution: 72 dpi.

2. From the View menu, select Grid & Ruler Setup. On the Grid page, enable Show Grid and Snap to Grid. Click the OK button.

3. Select the Circle Mask tool (J) from the Toolbox. Click the cursor in the image area and drag a circle mask in the central four squares of the image. Disable Snap to Grid (CTRL-Y).

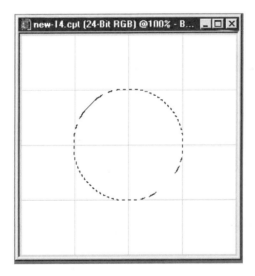

4. Click the color blue in the onscreen palette with the right mouse button. Select the Fill tool from the Toolbox, and click inside the circle mask.

16

5. From the Effects menu, select 3D Effects, choose The Boss from the drop-down list, and change the settings as shown in the following images.

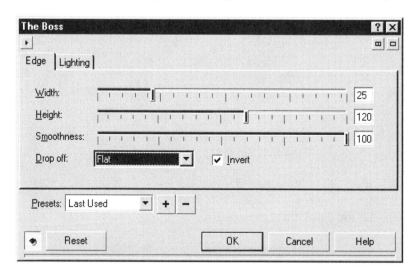

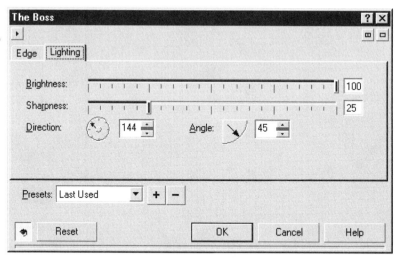

6. At this point, a blank button has been created, shown next, and I would save it as a blank if I were going to make more of them. In the next part of this session, I'll add a symbol to make our blank into a button that can be used to move to the next page on a Web site.

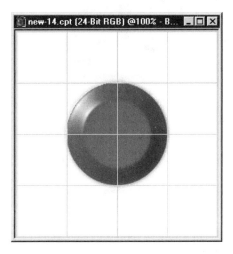

7. Change the Paint color to yellow by clicking it in the onscreen color palette. Click the Text tool and select the Impact font at a size of 150. Place the cursor on the button and insert a "+" sign. Select the Object Picker tool and use the arrow keys to line up the letter in the center of the image, as shown next. After you have it in position, select Create from Object(s) in the Mask menu (CTRL-M).

16

8. Use the Object Picker tool and select both the button and the "+" character. Choose Object | Combine | Combine Objects Together.

9. Open The Boss filter again. Change the settings as shown in the following two dialog boxes. Click OK. The button is finished, as shown in the illustration after the dialog boxes. All we need do now is make it into an object so that we can place it. Click the Remove Mask button.

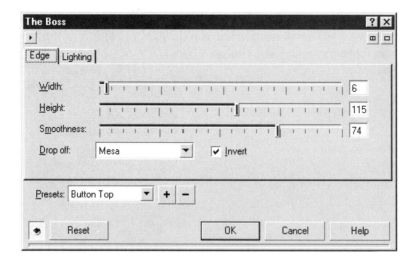

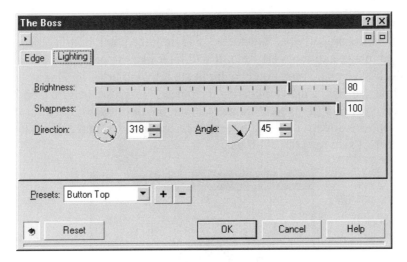

10. Our next step is to make the button into an object. We now need to make a mask that is roughly the same shape as our button. Select the Circle Mask tool from the Toolbox. In the middle of the upper-left grid square, click and hold the left mouse button, and then hold down the CTRL key. This action constrains the mask to a circle. Drag a circle that pretty much covers the entire button.

16

11. With the button masked, select the Create | Object: Copy Selection option from the property bar. Next, click and drag the blank button object out of the image into the work area. It will look like the one shown next. Once you have made one, you can duplicate it by either using Duplicate in the Image menu or just duplicating the object. Next, use the Flip | Horizontally command in the Object menu to make the duplicate object point the opposite direction. Use the Resample command to make the button the correct size for your Web page.

Making Green French Fries for Your Web Page

These "French fries" are actually ornaments that are easily made and placed as mappable objects on your Web page. In this session, we are going to make a simple green worm. The first step, setting up the grid, is probably the hardest part.

1. Create a new image that is 6 × 2 inches at 72 dpi.

2. From the View menu, select Grid & Ruler Setup. On the Grid page, enable Show Grid and Snap to Grid. Enable Frequency and make it 2.0 per inch in both directions. Click the OK button.

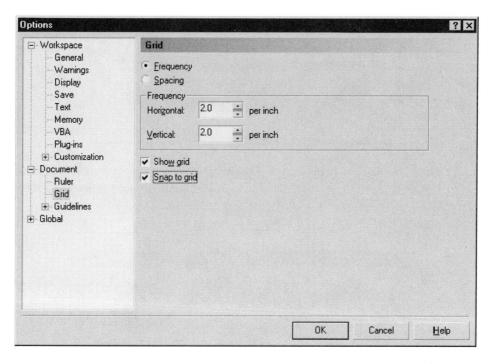

3. Select the Rectangle Shape tool from the Toolbox (F6). Double-click the Fill swatch on the status bar. When the Select Fill dialog box opens, click the Fountain Fill button (second from the left) and click the Edit button. In the Fountain Fill dialog box, choose Preset Cylinder—Green 04. Change the Angle to 270 and the Steps to 999. Click OK to accept the settings and OK again to close the dialog box.

4. Ensure that the Render to Object button is enabled.

5. Change the Rectangle Roundness setting in the property bar to 100. In the image, click and drag a rectangle in the center, leaving unfilled a width of one square all around, as shown next.

16

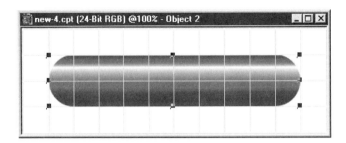

6. Open the Effects menu, choose Distort, and select Ripple. When the dialog box opens, click the Reset button and change the Amplitude setting to 10. Click OK. The result is an object that looks like a green French fry, as shown next.

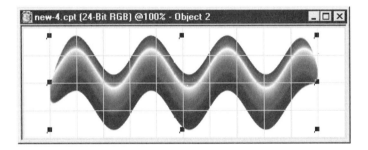

So, what can you do with this little fellow, other than serve it with green eggs and ham? By adding a drop shadow, you can make a nice ornament for a retro Web page.

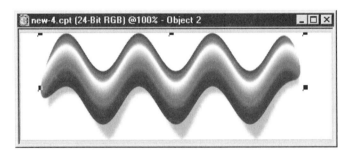

Using the Glass Block Filter to Make a Multimedia Background

This filter is good for distorting an image for use in backgrounds. Here is a quick hands-on exercise to make a background that would be a nice addition to a multimedia presentation.

1. Open a new file that is 6 × 6 inches, 72 dpi, and 24-bit color.

2. From the Edit menu, select Fill . . . . Click the Fountain Fill button and then the Edit button. Change Presets: to Cylinder—11, Angle: 45.0, and Steps: 999. Click the OK button to close the Edit Fill & Transparency dialog box.

3. From the Effects menu, choose Creative and select Glass Block . . . . Change both sliders to 30. Click the OK button.

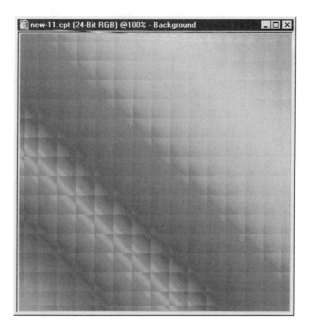

4. From the Effects menu, choose 3D and select Emboss. Click Reset and enable Original Color. Click OK.

5. From the 3D Effects category in the Effects menu, select Pinch/Punch. Set the slider to 100 and click OK. Choose Effects | Texture and Plastic and click OK. The resulting image is shown next.

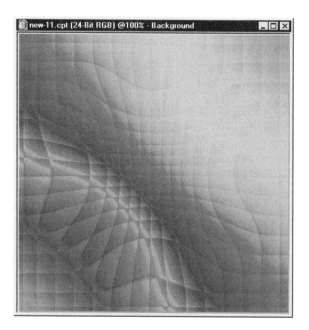

6. Close the file and do not save the changes.

That's all there is to it. The "glass blocks" made by this filter also make good borders for masks if you click them with a Magic Wand mask tool. The blocks cause the masks to align with the grid formed by the blocks.

 Due to the size of the background, you should slice the image up into smaller segments so that it loads in pieces.

In Summary

There are about a thousand more things you can do with PHOTO-PAINT 10 when it comes to Web creation. I recommend you check in the Help files for the section on Publishing to the Web. Now that you can create Web graphics, you'll learn how to use some of the automation features to make your life with PHOTO-PAINT a little simpler, or at least easier.

C H A P T E R   1 7

Using Advanced Masks and Channels

533

A s you learned in Chapter 6, simple masks are easy to make. Complex masks, on the other hand, can sometimes take hours to create, so saving a mask becomes almost as important as saving the image. This chapter begins with the all-important topic of mask management. We will also learn how to use Paint on Mask, the Color Mask tools, and several PHOTO-PAINT mask commands buried in the Mask menu that are real gems. We will also take a brief look at the Path Node Edit tool.

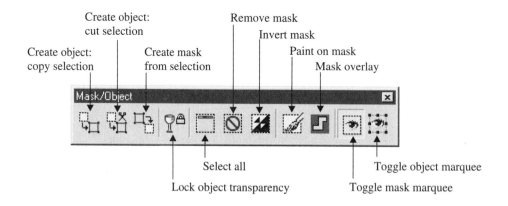

<table>
<tr><td></td></tr>
</table>

NOTE *Throughout this chapter, we will be referring to the Mask/Object toolbar (just shown); if it is disabled, I advise that you enable it—Window | Toolbars | Mask/Object.*

NOTE *If your Mask/Object toolbar looks different, it is because the default toolbar button size is small. The one just shown is set to a medium-sized button.*

Saving a Mask

All masks created in Corel PHOTO-PAINT can be saved and reloaded. This ability to save masks is essential because

- Only one regular mask can exist on an image at a time; so to use multiple masks during a project, it becomes necessary to store them. (Using Additive mode, you can create several mask outlines, but the result will be one regular mask.)

■ Masks are valuable. If you spent several hours creating a mask, it is essential to have a copy.

■ A mask is a great way to copy the same size image area out of several different images.

Saving a Mask with the Image

There are two ways that a mask can be saved: it can be saved to disk or saved with an image in a temporary storage called a *channel.* An image containing a regular mask that is saved in Corel PHOTO-PAINT format will have its mask saved with the image automatically. In addition to Corel PHOTO-PAINT format, masks can be saved in TIFF (.tif) formats. They are also saved as alpha channel information when an image is saved as an Adobe Photoshop™ (.psd) image.

Saving masks to disk is just like saving image files. Assuming you have a mask you want to save, choose Mask | Save, and the drop-down menu shown next opens. Choose Save Mask to Disk and, when prompted, select a drive and folder from the dialog box, name the mask file, and select the file type (CPT is strongly recommended).

	Save Mask To Disk...
	Save As Channel...
	Alpha Channel Save List

> **TIP** *Do not use a unique extension such as .msk for the mask. This three-character extension is used by Corel PHOTO-PAINT and other applications to determine the correct import filter to use. Although the mask can be saved in any bitmap format (PCX, TIFF, BMP, and so on), it is recommended to save masks in Corel PHOTO-PAINT's native CPT format.*

The ability to save a mask apart from the image allows a mask created in one image to be loaded and applied to other images for special effects or accurate placement of objects. How a different application uses the saved mask information depends on the application. For example, the mask information in a .tif or .tga file is interpreted by Photoshop as an alpha channel.

17

Loading a Mask

The Load Mask function allows a wide variety of image file formats to be loaded as masks. Any image file can be used for a mask. Using photographs or other non-mask files may give unpredictable, although not necessarily undesirable, results. A non-mask file is any image file that was not created using the mask tools in Corel PHOTO-PAINT.

When loading a mask, it is important to be aware that Corel PHOTO-PAINT *will resize the mask to fit the image!*

> **TIP** *If you have several images open on your screen, make sure that the one you want to load the mask into is active. If you load the mask into another image, the mask may replace any existing mask in that image, depending on the mask mode.*

Loading a mask into an image involves the following procedure:

1. Select the image to which the mask being loaded will be applied.

2. Choose Mask | Load | Load from Disk. The Load a Mask from Disk dialog box opens.

3. Select the file to be used for a mask. While any image can be used, the mask will become a black-and-white or grayscale image.

4. Click the Open button, and a thumbnail of the mask you are loading will appear on the cursor, as shown next. The mask being loaded in this illustration is a mask of the word "mask."

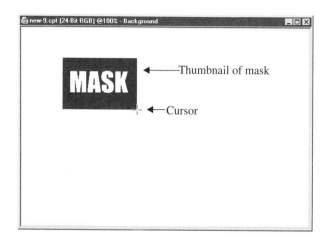

At this point you have two options:

■ You can click the cursor anywhere on the image and the mask will be applied to the entire image, as shown with the Mask Overlay enabled in Figure 17-1(a).

■ You can click and drag a rectangle and the mask will be resized to the shape you dragged. Figure 17-1(b) shows a mask that was made much smaller; and in Figure 17-1(c), the mask was made larger than the original, which caused some deterioration of the edges. Although you can change the size (I don't recommend it, but you can), you cannot change the aspect ratio of the mask (the ratio of the height to the width).

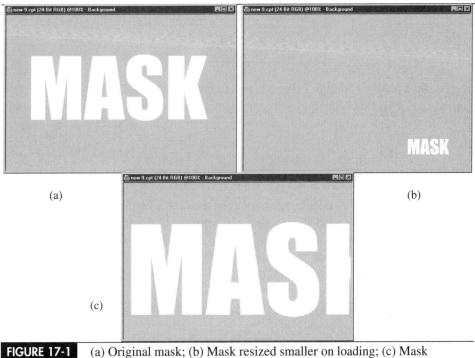

(a)

(b)

(c)

FIGURE 17-1   (a) Original mask; (b) Mask resized smaller on loading; (c) Mask enlarged on loading

17

Saving a Mask As an Alpha Channel

Since only one mask can be active in an image, each new mask you create replaces the current mask. When creating special effects, it is possible to use three or more masks. While we could save each of these to disk, as previously described, we also have the option to save the current mask to an alpha channel in the image so that it can be reused. When you save an image to a file format that supports mask information, such as Corel PHOTO-PAINT (.cpt) or TIFF bitmap (.tif), the current mask and all alpha channels are saved with the image.

You can also save the current mask or an alpha channel to disk as a separate file. Saving a mask or an alpha channel lets you use masks in other images. This is especially useful if you want to save an image to a file format that doesn't support mask information, but you want to keep copies of the masks used to edit that image.

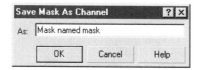

Saving a mask to an alpha channel is also very easy. Choose Mask | Save |Save As Channel. This opens the preceding dialog box that asks you to name the channel in which the mask will be stored, as shown. The mask is now safely stored as an alpha channel.

Managing Masks and Channels

The alpha channel can hold a large number of masks. How many? More than you could ever conceivably need. To load a mask from the alpha channel, choose Mask | Load; and the drop-down menu that appears, shown next, displays all of the alpha channels that have currently been assigned. As you can see in the illustration, I have already saved four alpha channels with appropriate names for masks.

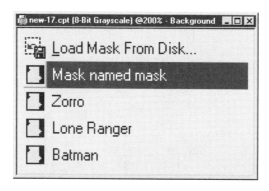

As long as you have a good memory, you could perform all of your alpha channel/mask operations from the Mask menu. For a more versatile tool for managing alpha channels, we need to open the Channels docker (CTRL-F9), as shown in Figure 17-2.

The Channels Docker

The Channel docker shown in Figure 17-2 has four masks stored as alpha channels; one of those is also the current mask. Whenever you click a channel, its contents appear in the current image window. Using the buttons at the bottom of the docker, you can make any selected channel into the current mask.

| NOTE | *You cannot delete any of the color channels using the Delete icon.* |

The size of the thumbnails in the docker is controlled by the flyout option in the upper-right corner of the docker. The thumbnails shown in the figure are large.

Exploring Channels

The top entries are the composite (RGB, in the example) and individual channels. Whenever a mask is created, the Current Mask appears below the individual color channels. That's simple so far, right? Although an image can have only one mask at a time, you can store many different masks with an image in the form of channels.

| TIP | *You can create a new channel without a mask by clicking the Create New Channel button at the bottom of the docker.* |

Removing a Mask

For all of this talk about saving masks, now and again you just want to get rid of them. How may I remove a mask? Let me count the ways:

■ Click the Remove Mask button located on the Mask/Object toolbar. A mask must exist on the active image for the mask button in the toolbar to be available.

■ Use a keyboard shortcut: CTRL-SHIFT-R.

■ Select Remove in the Mask menu.

17

■ Use the DEL key. A mask may also be removed with the DEL key if the mask is selected, as indicated by the control handles. (The mask is selected whenever the Mask Transform tool is selected.) If the mask is not selected, *the DEL key will clear the contents of the mask.* Therefore, use the DEL key with caution.

Inverting a Mask

One of the more useful mask functions is the Invert Mask command (CTRL-SHIFT-I). When a mask is created, the area inside the mask can be modified while the area outside the mask is protected. The Invert Mask command reverses the mask so that the area that was inside the mask now becomes protected and the area outside can be modified. The Invert Mask command can be accessed through the Mask menu on the Mask/Object toolbar by clicking the Invert Mask button or with the keyboard combination CTRL-I.

TIP	*Some masks are so complex it is difficult to determine what part of the image lies inside or outside of the mask. A quick way to check is to select the Mask Overlay button on the Mask/Object toolbar. Only the tinted area (red, by default) is protected. The Mask Overlay is a display function and does not affect the operation of PHOTO-PAINT.*

Select All

To mask the entire image, click the Select All button from the Mask/Object toolbar or choose the Select All command in the Mask menu. You can select the entire image by double-clicking any of the Mask selection tools in the Toolbox except the Mask Brush tool. The mask will encompass the entire image inside of the image window. If the image is only partially visible because you have zoomed into an area, the entire image is still masked. In this situation, you will not be able to see the entire mask.

Manipulating Masks

After a mask has been created, we often need to modify it. Corel has provided several mask manipulation tools to help us do this. Probably the most often used mask manipulation tool is the Feather Mask command.

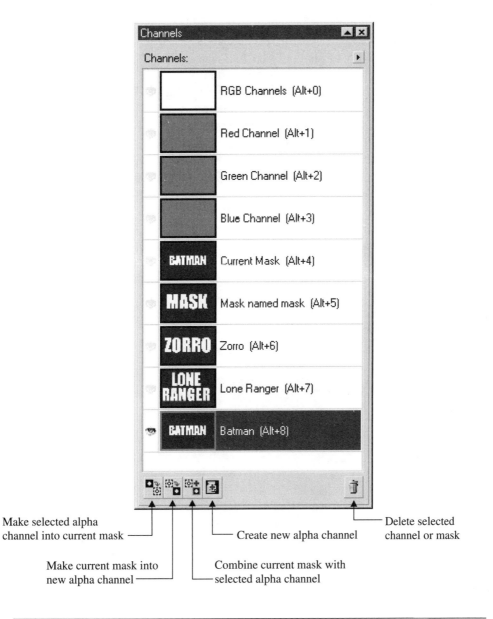

Make selected alpha channel into current mask

Make current mask into new alpha channel

Combine current mask with selected alpha channel

Create new alpha channel

Delete selected channel or mask

17

FIGURE 17-2   The Channels docker provides a visual method of managing alpha channels

Feather Mask

Feathered masks are the means by which we can add or subtract images or effects without the viewer being aware of it. Technically speaking, feathering a mask changes the transparency of the pixels located near the mask boundary. Any effect or command applied to the selection fades gradually as you get near the protected area. Feathering can be applied to a mask during or after its creation.

It is particularly useful if you want to apply an effect to the masked area but not the surrounding area. Feathering a mask makes the transition between the two areas gradual and, therefore, less noticeable. Figure 17-3 shows an example of an object created from a photograph using a nonfeathered mask and one from a feathered mask. See if you can figure out which one was made with the feathered mask.

FIGURE 17-3   Which object was created with a feathered mask? (Answer: the one on the right)

Whether you select Mask | Shape | Feather from the Mask menu or click the Feather Mask button on the property bar (shown next), a dialog box opens enabling you to set the direction, amount, and type of feathering to be applied to the current mask.

The Width setting determines how wide a feather to apply to the mask edge. The Average Direction effectively applies a Gaussian Blur to all of the pixels directly inside and outside of the mask; this provides the smoothest mask of the choices. Selecting any other Direction—Inside, Middle, or Outside—enables a choice of two different Edges: Linear and Curved.

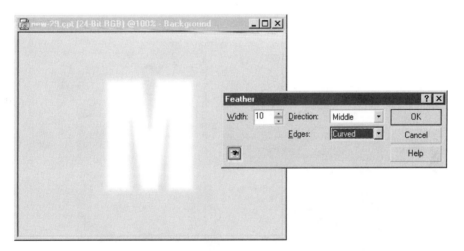

In Figure 17-4, the Feather Mask command was applied to three identical masks using Average direction, and Middle direction with Linear and Curved Edge settings. The masked area was filled with 100 percent black fill and zoomed to 300 percent. The Average mask (left) has the greatest amount of blurring. Linear (middle) has a tendency to produce points at perpendicular intersections of a straight-sided mask. The Curved feather (right) doesn't spread out as much as the other two, despite identical Width settings.

17

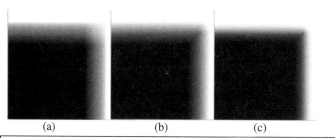

(a)   (b)   (c)

FIGURE 17-4 (a) Average; (b) Middle Linear; (c) Middle Curved

The Shape Category Mask Commands

Some of the other mask commands you may have occasion to work with are
located in the Shape category of the Mask menu, as shown next. These commands
are Border, Remove Holes, Smooth, Threshold, Expand, and Reduce.

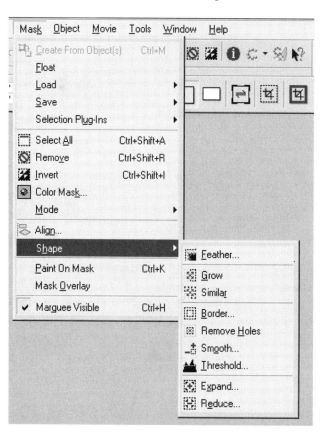

Border

The Border command removes a portion of an existing mask to a border according to the setting in the Border dialog box. It offers the option of three different Edges settings: Hard, Medium, and Soft. Borders only move outward from the mask regardless of the Mask Mode setting. Be careful when applying this command to circles; it tends to degrade the general shape of the circle. In the next illustration, the mask created from the letter "M" has a 20-pixel border applied, creating a diffuse glow. The preview feature of the mask is shown.

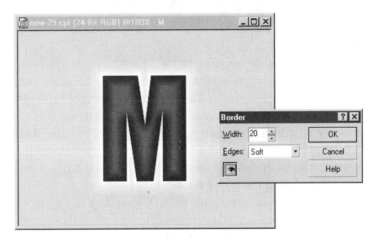

| TIP | *For a creative effect, try applying the Border command to a square or rectangular mask multiple times.* |

Remove Holes

Remove Holes is supposed to remove those nasty little mask fragments that tend to be left when using the color-sensitive masks.

Once enabled, Remove Holes goes on a merry hole hunt. As a result, there aren't many situations in which you can use it; but for the few times when the conditions of the mask and image are suitable, it works great. It has no adjustable settings; it will either work or not work for what you want to use it for. Keep the old faithful Undo command (CTRL-Z) handy and give it a try.

17

Smooth

The Smooth command creates a more fluid mask boundary by smoothing out sharp bends (jaggies) in the mask that occur especially when creating color-sensitive masks. Some pixels that are not in the selection before smoothing will become part of the selection after smoothing, and some pixels that are currently in the selection will no longer be included in it. The Smooth command, like the Remove Holes command, can sometimes eliminate entire portions of a mask. The amount of smoothing this command does is dependent upon the Radius setting you enter in the dialog box. Large values tend to completely change the shape of the mask. I have created a sample of a ragged mask edge in Figure 17-5(a). In Figure 17-5(b), at a setting of 10, the edges are smoother but the shape is changing. In Figure 17-5(c) and Figure 17-5(d), the Radius setting of the Smooth mask command has significantly altered the shape of the mask.

Threshold

The Threshold command is the opposite of the Smooth command. When you have a mask with an indefinite edge, as with a feathered mask, this command makes it into a binary (black-and-white) mask by applying a Threshold function to it. If you do the hands-on exercises in Chapter 18, you will get to use this filter. Oddly enough, this is one of my favorite filters in the category, because it allows me to make the edges of masks more distinct. The only setting, Level (1–255), determines which grayscale values in the mask become white (below the Level setting) and which become black (above the Level setting).

Expand and Reduce mask commands do just what they say they do. Use them to make masks larger or smaller. Like the Border command, these commands tend to degrade shapes with large values or multiple applications.

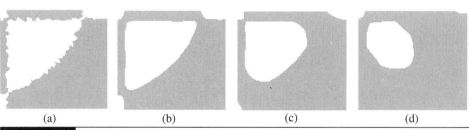

(a)   (b)   (c)   (d)

FIGURE 17-5   (a) Original mask edge; (b) Smooth applied at a setting of 10; (c) Smooth at 30; (d) Smooth at 50 (maximum)

Using Masks to Create Deteriorated Metal

Water and metal don't mix, period. When water, especially salt water, comes in contact with metal for prolonged periods of time, a chemical reaction occurs that we call just plain rust. After time, the edges begin to perforate, and tiny holes develop in the metal as it is slowly dissolved. The Deteriorated Metal technique (which works with most typefaces) may seem complicated, but I believe the finished product is worth the effort. In addition, you will see it has several variations.

1. Create a 24-bit RGB image. The sample shown in this exercise is 4.5 inches wide × 2 inches height @ 150 dpi.

2. Select the Text tool in the Toolbox. On the property bar, select the font Impact at a size of 96. Type in the word **TITANIC**, and select the Object Picker tool in the Toolbox. The text becomes an object and is selected. Center the text (CTRL-A) in the image window.

3. In the Objects docker window, ensure the Lock Transparency icon is enabled. Choose Edit | Fill, and choose Bitmap fill. Click the Edit button, and then click the Swatch button. Choose the reddish-colored burled wood on the right side of the bitmap preview second from the bottom. Click OK to select, and OK again to apply the fill.

17

4. Choose Image | Adjust | Auto Equalize. Next, select Effects | Noise | Add Noise. Select Gaussian, and change the Level and the Density to 100. Click OK.

5. Turn off the Lock transparency button. Choose Effects | 3D Effects | Emboss. Change the settings as follows: Original color; Depth, 2; Level, 200; and Direction, 135. Click OK. Congratulations, you have made rust.

6. Create a Mask from the text object (CTRL-M). Enable Paint on Mask (POM) mode (CTRL-K). While in POM, we modify the mask created from the text.

7. Choose Effects | Distort | Displace. Click the Reset button. Leave the Scale mode and Undefined areas settings unchanged. From under the preview window, open the displacement map named Square.pcx. Click OK.

8. Click the POM button (or CTRL-K) to return to Normal mode. Choose Effects | 3D Effects | The Boss. Change the settings on the Edge tab as follows: Width, 3; Height, 35; and Smoothness, 35. Select the Invert Mask box, and choose Gaussian Drop Off. Change the settings on the Lighting tab: Brightness, 50; Sharpness, 20; Direction, 135; and Angle, 12. Click OK. The result is shown next.

What Is POM?

This feature was introduced back in PHOTO-PAINT 7. In short, POM is a mode that temporarily replaces the image with a grayscale representation of the mask. In POM mode, the protected areas of your image are black, while the fully editable areas are white. Pixels included in the selection that are partially protected are displayed in varying degrees of gray.

17

Holy Corrosion, Batman!

Now our image appears rusty and worn, and we can use it this way. Let's now see some options that are possible with this effect. When metal objects become sufficiently rusted or corroded, they eventually are eaten away. PHOTO-PAINT allows us to re-create that effect.

1. With the mask still in place from the last tutorial, select Object | Crop to Mask. This produces holes the viewer can see through in the text, as shown next.

2. With so many holes, we need a shadow to restore some of the appearance of original text. For a final touch, with the text still selected, choose the Interactive Dropshadow tool from the property bar and use the preset Pers. top left. You will need to adjust this preset value by dragging its handle until it fits the image (mostly), as shown next.

Variations on a Theme

Several factors control both the sizes and shapes of holes. The physical size of the holes in the displacement map is fixed, so the only way to make the holes larger or smaller is to increase or decrease the size of the image. Figure 17-6 shows a sample of three different Boss filter settings used on a different text object and a different displacement map (rusty.pcx). The resolution of the image is 300 dpi. This makes the number of pixels in the image twice as large as in the exercise we just finished. Since the spots (holes) in the displacement map are a fixed size, the holes in the image appear smaller.

The shape of the holes is determined by the Smoothness setting of The Boss filter. The greater the setting, the fewer the holes that appear. The sample at the top had a Smoothness of 100 (maximum), while the one in the middle had the same setting we did in the exercise. The bottom of the three samples had the same Smoothness setting, but the height was reduced to only 30 pixels.

FIGURE 17-6   By changing the size (resolution) of the text, we can effectively change
the size of the signs of decay

17

The Color Mask

Most of the color-sensitive masks we have discussed until now could only include colors that were connected to the original sampled color. The Color mask, like the Similar command, selects pixels by their color content, regardless of the position of the selected pixels in relation to the original sample point.

The Color Mask

Selecting Color Mask, located in the Mask menu, opens the dialog box shown in Figure 17-7. The dialog box is quite simple to use. Use the eyedropper to select colors in the image that you want masked. If you don't like the result of one of the color selections, remove the checkmark from its box. Use the Preview option to determine how successful the color selection process has been, and click the OK button. Really simple stuff, right?

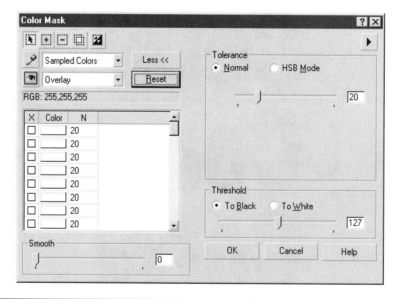

FIGURE 17-7   Sure, it looks complicated, but the Color Mask dialog box is quite simple to use

I have included some handy tips to help you get up to speed quickly:

- The Color mask uses a dialog box, so you must complete the selection of the mask and apply the mask before you can do any other operation.

- The Color mask command does not create a Color mask. It creates regular masks. When you save a Color mask, you are saving the settings of the Color Mask dialog box.

- Preview of the mask made by the Color Mask tool is done on the actual image.

The best way to learn how to use this jewel is to take it for a test ride, which is what we are going to do in the next exercise.

Replacing a Background Using the Color Mask

I am often asked to change colors in a photograph—not all of the colors, mind you, just certain ones. This is especially true with colors that are no longer in fashion. Selecting individual colors in a complex image can take time, even with the Color mask. In this case, we have a photograph I took of a great (although overpriced) stained glass lamp at a little shop in San Francisco. Let's assume that the client's art director wants to use the photo for a catalog cover but doesn't like the blue in the lamp. So, we need to select all of the blue and change it to the color that he wants—green.

The first step is to mask all of the blue glass. We could use the Magic Wand mask tool if we were being paid by the hour. Unfortunately, it is a piece job, so we need to finish the job as soon as possible. Let's get started.

1. Download the image dragonfly lamp.jpg.

2. Select Mask | Color Mask to open the dialog box . If you have room on your display, I recommend positioning the Color Mask dialog box, as

17

shown next, so that you can see the parts of the image we are masking. Click the Reset button to clear any previous settings.

3. Click the Eyedropper button and place the cursor in the image, and it will become an eyedropper. Click the image at a lighter blue portion of the lamp shade, as indicated in this image, and then click the other darker blue one, as shown next:

4. Click the Preview button (it looks like an eye) and the image in the
    Preview shows masked (protected) areas in a red tint. Please notice that
    similar colors in the room were also selected. This is normal, and we'll
    fix it in the next step. Click the OK button.

5. From the Mask/Object toolbar, click the Mask Overlay button. All of the
    area outside of the lamp that was selected will have blue shining through.
    Select the Mask brush, and change the mode to Subtractive by clicking the
    minus button on the property bar. Now paint all of the areas outside of the
    lamp. Technically, you could use the mask marquee to find the areas to
    remove, but it is much better to use Mask Overlay. When you have finished
    with the mask, turn off the mask overlay.

6. Choose Image | Adjust | Hue/Saturation/Lightness. Change the Saturation
    setting to −100 and click OK. That's all there is to it.

17

Additional Information About the Color Mask

There are other controls in the Color mask dialog box that deserve some explanation.
For example, across the top are the four Mask Mode buttons and the Invert Mask
button, as shown next. The Mask Mode buttons control how the mask you make
with the Color mask tool reacts to an existing mask. The Invert mask is a nice
feature that allows you to either protect or select the sampled colors.

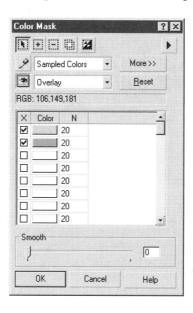

> **TIP**   *When you click the Reset button in the Color Mask dialog box, it resets
> the mask mode to whichever mask mode PHOTO-PAINT is in.*

Clicking the More >>| button on the Color Mask dialog box opens the rest of
the dialog box, shown next, containing a few additional settings that modify how
this mask tool operates.

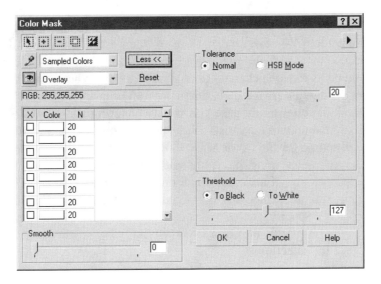

From the expanded dialog box, you can determine what criteria the Color mask uses to select its color. You can use HSB instead of Normal mode. For most applications, the Normal setting (default) will do the job. HSB uses a combination of hue, saturation, and brightness to make its selection of colors. You can also select to use the HSB components individually to determine which colors are selected. The Threshold settings act just like the Threshold filter. They use the value of the Threshold slider to cause the created mask to move toward either white or black.

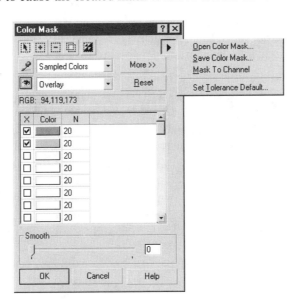

Click the flyout option arrow to get even more options, as shown in the preceding illustration. You can save all of the settings as a Color mask file. This file can be loaded into the Color mask and used at a later time. The Color mask can also be saved to an alpha channel through this option. When saved as an alpha channel, it is a grayscale image that can be used as a mask but cannot be loaded as a Color mask file later on. In case you were wondering about Set Tolerance Default, this sets the default tolerance value that is used when colors are sampled.

The default setting for the Color Mask tool creates a mask in Sampled Colors mode. In this mode, everything that is not selected is protected.

If you right-click one of the color selections, the Delete Color and Edit Color options become available. Choosing Edit Color opens the Color Palette dialog box, from which you can specify a color to select. If, for example, you wanted to select every place in the image that the color PANTONE CV742 was used, this is where you would make the selection.

At the top of the Color mask (next to the Eyedropper icon) is a large list of preset settings that allows you to quickly select a type, or range of colors or shades. I strongly recommend that you use Sampled Colors.

The Preview button changes the image so that you can see the parts of the image that are currently masked. There are several options available for viewing the Color mask. The default setting is Overlay, which places a tint over the masked area. The advantage is that you can see the mask in relation to the image. Another way to preview the mask is the Grayscale setting, in which you cannot see the image, just the grayscale image that is the mask. The Black Matte or White Matte preview options display protected areas covered by a black-tinted transparent sheet or by a white-tinted transparent sheet. Marquee displays a dotted line around the editable area, just like the mask marquee normally displayed for masks.

Using the Color Mask More Productively

The following are suggestions that may help you when using the Color mask:

If you are attempting to mask a narrow range of colors, like the blue in a sky, use multiple samples, or take a single sample and increase the Numerical setting for it. Many times when selecting a color or range of colors, you end up with parts of the image selected that you didn't want selected. Rather than waste time trying to balance the color and Numerical settings to get the "perfect" mask, use the Color mask dialog box to create most of the selection and then use the mask tools to fine tune the mask to its final shape.

When changing the Numerical value, the Preview window won't reflect the changes until you press the ENTER key or click another color.

Paths

What are paths? *Paths* are vectors that are living in a world of pixels. In other words, they are line and curve segments, connected by square endpoints called *nodes*. If you work with CorelDRAW, the paths will be familiar to you. Masks and paths share some common characteristics. A mask is created from a bitmap image. A path, on the other hand, is a vector drawing that exists on a layer above the image and is independent of the image resolution. A closed path completely encloses an area, as a mask would. An open path has start and end nodes that are not connected; this is something that a mask cannot do.

> **TIP** *In PHOTO-PAINT 10, you can now align text to a path (see Chapter 7).*

The advantage of the path over the mask is, in a word, precision. A path, being a vector image, can be precisely edited; a mask, being a bitmap image, is adjusted by adding or subtracting from it with a Brush tool or something similar. With a path, you have full Bézier-level control over the points and nodes, just as you have in CorelDRAW. When you need to make accurate masks, you will want to create a path using the Path Node Edit tool.

New paths can be created using the Path Node Edit tool, or existing masks can be converted to paths. When the path is exactly the shape you want, you can save the path or convert it to a mask, or both. A mask can be converted to a path, edited as a path, and converted back to a mask.

If you export a mask as a part of an encapsulated PostScript (EPS) image, the mask is converted to a path.

Corel has produced a large volume of material on paths. In the interest of saving space, I refer you to either the PHOTO-PAINT User's Manual or the extensive online help. With the online help, I recommend opening the index and entering the word **Path**. You will find a large amount of material on the subject.

Stroke Mask/Path Command

This command is used to automatically apply brush strokes along a path defined by either a mask or a path. You can use it to apply many of the brushes. Operation of this puppy is simple. Select the brush/tool you want to apply. Make any changes to the size or shape of the nib, and then click the appropriate button on the property bar.

To make the Stroke Mask or Stroke Path options available, there must be a mask or path on the image, and one of the following tools must be selected: the Paint tool, the Effect tool, the Color Replacer tool, the Eraser tool, or the Image Sprayer tool.

17

Here is an exercise that exhibits one of the best uses for the Stroke Mask command:

1. Create a new image using the size Photo 3.5 × 5 at a resolution of 72 dpi.

2. Using the Text tool with the Font set to Impact at a Size of 300, click in the image, type an **8**, and select the Object Picker tool to position the character, as shown next.

3. Create a mask from the object (CTRL-M). Ensure that the Lock Transparency button on either the property bar or the bottom of the Objects docker is enabled.

4. Choose Edit | Fill, choose the Fountain Fill, and click the Edit button. Change the Presets setting to Gold Plated and the Steps setting to 999. Click OK, and then click OK again to apply the fill as shown here:

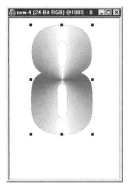

5. Select the Paint tools and choose the Airbrush. Select the Soft Wide Cover, and click the Stroke Mask button on the property bar, which opens a dialog box from which you should choose Middle of Mask Border. After applying the command, repeat it. When it is complete, Remove the mask. Use the Interactive Dropshadow tool, and use the Flat Bottom Right preset. The result is shown next.

In Figure 17-8 is a wreath I created with the stroke Mask option.

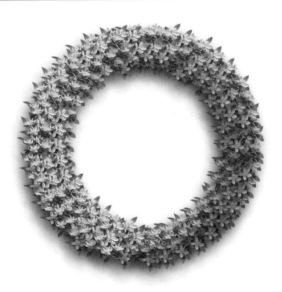

FIGURE 17-8 Here is a wreath I created using Stroke Mask and the Image Sprayer tool

17

In Summary

This chapter and Chapter 16 have only scratched the surface of the things you can do with masks. Now we need to move on to the daunting subject of image and color correction.

CHAPTER 18

Automating PHOTO-PAINT
Tools and Features

563

In this chapter, we will look at a few of the automation tools included with PHOTO-PAINT that are indispensable for production work. These are Batch Process, the Recorder docker, and Scripts docker. We will begin with Batch Process.

Batch Process (Formerly Known as Batch Playback)

This is one of those useful utilities that, if you do any amount of production work, you will find indispensable. Batch Process has been around since PHOTO-PAINT 6. It used to be located in a different place and had a different name. That was before the let's-change-the-name-and-location committee found it, around the time of PHOTO-PAINT 9. Regardless of the name change and the new address (it's now in the File menu), Batch Process works just as well as before. That's because the let's-improve-the-command committee hasn't found it yet. Many users think this is just for running scripts. Not true. I use Batch Process all the time, and I can only think of a few times that I have used it with a script.

Have you ever had a group of files that needed to be changed from one format to another? With Batch Process, it's simple as pie.

You do not have to have a file open to use this command. Choose File | Batch Process, opening the dialog box shown in Figure 18-1.

Add the files you want to process by clicking the Add File button. Unlike with certain Internet browsers, you can SHIFT-click to select all the contiguous files between two points, or use CTRL with the mouse to individually select multiple files.

After you have all the files you want, you can add scripts—it's your choice. These scripts can be something simple, like "add 10 percent contrast to every image." We will discuss scripts a little when we talk about the Recorder docker in the next section.

With the files selected and scripts optionally selected, we need to select what we want the Batch Process to do with the files after the scripts (or no scripts) are run. The On Completion pop-up menu contains the following choices: Don't Save, Save Over Original, Save to New Folder, Save As New Type.

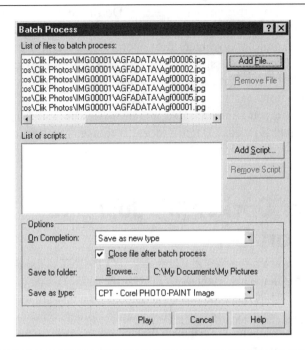

FIGURE 18-1   The Batch Process dialog box is simple to use but still powerful

When you select Save As New Type, you have the option of saving the files in any graphics format supported by PHOTO-PAINT. There are a lot more choices available from the drop-down list in the examples shown next.

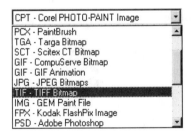

All the choices are self-explanatory except Don't Save. It allows you to apply a script to multiple images (both open and not) and keep them open. I would be careful about having too many image files open, which leads to the next option: Close Files After Batch Process. If you are processing a lot of files, you should make sure this is enabled. If it isn't and too many files are open, your system may throw a hairball.

So the next time you have a large number of files on which to do something repetitive, remember how easy Batch Process is to use. The Recorder is also pretty easy to use, and it's next.

The Recorder Docker (It's Just Like Your VCR, Sort Of)

One of the features often ignored in Corel PHOTO-PAINT is the Recorder docker. It is a powerful tool that allows you to produce some effects using repetitive steps that might otherwise be considered too labor intensive. If you haven't used the Recorder before, it may have been because the documentation borders on being vague. I had a different reason for not using it. I believed that the gains made by using the Recorder were outweighed by the time it took to use it. Was I ever wrong.

You open the Recorder by choosing Window | Dockers | Recorder, or by using the keyboard combination CTRL-F3. The Window menu is not available unless there is an image open. The Recorder acts like a macro recorder (think VCR). You click the Record button and go through the steps of the task that you want to accomplish. The Recorder records each step until you click the Stop button, as shown next. I have already recorded some steps in the following image so that all the buttons would be available.

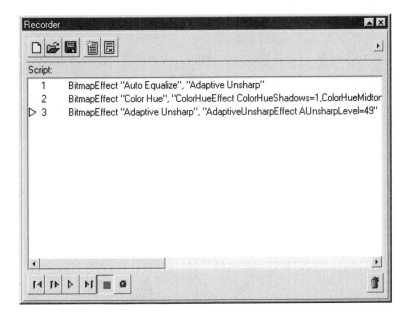

The buttons at the top of the Recorder docker window (shown next) from left to right are standard Windows buttons: New will erase the current recording and start a new one; Open will open the Load Script dialog box; and Save will open the Save Recording dialog box. The next two buttons are for editing the command contents of the script. Insert New Command inserts newly recorded commands in a recording or script, or overwrites the existing commands. Newly recorded commands are inserted when the button appears pressed. The other button has, I think, the longest name in PHOTO-PAINT. It is the Enable/Disable Selected Command(s) button. As its name says, it enables or disables selected commands in the command list so that only enabled commands are played. When a command is disabled, it appears grayed out in the list. It is a toggle operation, meaning that the same button that disables the command can be used to enable it.

18

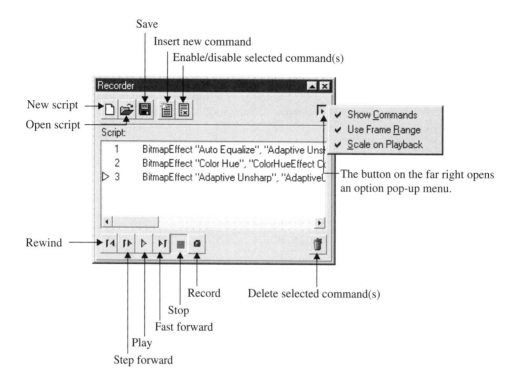

Show Commands / Use Frame Range

Show Commands toggles the display of the commands in the docker on and off. Use Frame Range, when enabled, allows the Recorder actions to be restricted to a range of frames in a movie. If you're not working with animation or video, the setting doesn't affect anything.

Scale on Playback

When this is enabled, the commands that are applied to images are scaled as a function of the image size. For example, using the Resample command with Scale on Playback enabled will produce the same final image size each time it is played, regardless of the original image size. I discovered this when making all the illustrations for the buttons in this book. I created a script with the Recorder that would resample the screen shot to a size of 0.75 inch. Yet, because many of the buttons are different sizes, running the script without enabling the Scale on Playback feature produced buttons of varying sizes. Therefore, if the button was a smaller size than the one I used for the original script, it would produce a button smaller than 0.75 inch. This feature is important because there are many operations that require the user to ensure that the image to which the script is applied is the same size as the original when the action was recorded.

The VCR-style buttons at the bottom of the Recorder docker provide the following functions (from left to right): Rewind, which returns the marker to the first command; Step Forward, which plays one command at a time; Play; Fast Forward, which advances to the last command; Stop; and Record. The docker operates like a VCR. When you have a sequence of events you want to record, you click the Record button, perform the steps, and then click the Stop button. The resulting list of commands is a script, which can be saved, reloaded, and replayed at a later date.

To save your recorded commands as a script file, click the Save Recording button at the top of the docker, which opens a Save Recording dialog box, shown next:

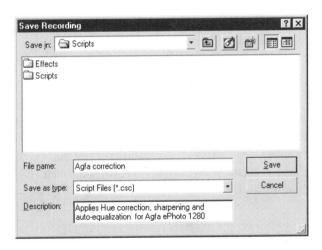

The commands are saved as Corel Scripts. The Script file (CSC) is the native format. If you made scripts with Corel PHOTO-PAINT before this release, you may need to rerecord them, as they will most likely not work on this version. The CSC file you created with the Recorder can be run from the Recorder or from the Scripts docker (CTRL-F6) shown next, which is where all the other scripts hang out.

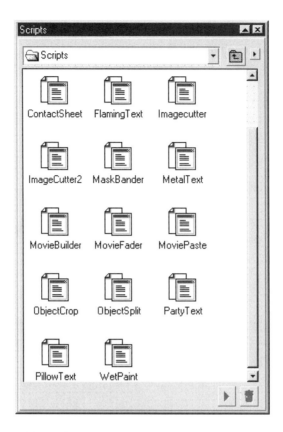

What got me working with this Recorder to begin with was a need to apply a tonal adjustment to over 100 digital photos. With a script and the Batch Process feature, this was a snap. Now, follow along and we will enter the world of PHOTO-PAINT automation.

 While Photoshop Actions resemble Corel Scripts, the two are completely different and not interchangeable.

Creating a Script

This is a simple text effect in which the automation is helpful when it is necessary to evaluate the effect on many different fills. Don't begin recording until instructed.

1. Create a new image that is 24-bit RGB color, 6 × 2 inches at 100 dpi. Open the Recorder docker (CTRL-F3).

2. Select the Text tool from the Toolbox, and change the Font to Lithograph at a size of 96. Click inside the image window and type **SCRIPTS**. Select the Object Picker tool, and align the text to the center of the document (CTRL-A), as shown next.

3. Ensure that Lock Object Transparency in the Object docker is enabled, and apply a fill to the text. For the example, I chose Edit | Fill | Bitmap Fill and selected a light-colored wood, as shown next.

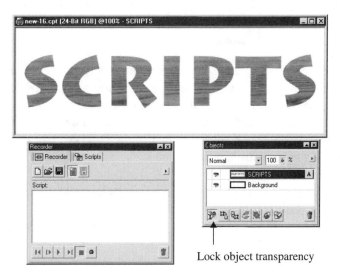

Lock object transparency

18

4. Now we begin to record by clicking the little red button at the bottom of the Recorder docker.

5. Create a mask (CTRL-M).

6. Choose Effects | 3D Effects | The Boss, and change the settings as follows: Width, 3; Height, 200; Smoothness, 60; Drop Off, Mesa; and Invert check box, enabled. On the Lighting page, set the parameters as follows: Brightness, 100; Sharpness, 3; Direction, 135; and Angle, 64; and click OK.

7. Remove the mask (CTRL-SHIFT-R) and click the Stop button (to the left of the Record button). The result is shown next.

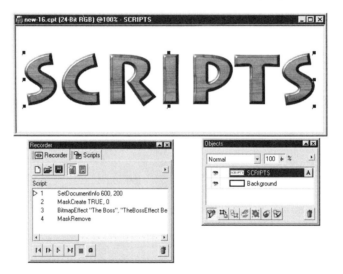

8. Now comes the fun part. Click the Rewind button on the Recorder docker. The Current Position indicator moves to the top of the list of commands. Next apply a different fill to the text. You can use anything. My only recommendation is not to make the fill too dark. I used a weave fill from the \TILES\TEXTURE folder of the Corel CD-ROM. Click the Play button and all of the steps are applied.

What if we wanted to add some more commands to the list in the recorder? Let's do it and see how it is done.

1. Ensure the Insert New Command button at the top of the docker is enabled. Either click the Fast Forward button or double-click the last command in the list. This moves the current command marker to the last command, as shown next.

2. Click the Record button. You will notice that another SetDocumentInfo line appears. We'll remove it later. Choose Effects | Texture | Plastic. Change the settings to the following: Highlight, 60; Depth, 10; Smoothness, 90; and Light Direction, 270. Click OK and then Stop on the recorder. The result is shown next.

3. The duplicate SetDocumentInfo line doesn't cause any problems; but just for the sake of good housekeeping (not the magazine), let's remove it. Select the command by clicking it. Next, click the trash can icon at the bottom of the docker, as shown next.

18

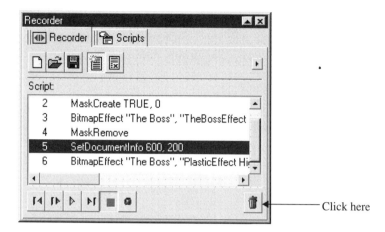

Click here

4. The script we created is shown in Figure 18-2. I have widened the docker window so that we can view all of the information that the Recorder docker has captured. Once a file works, you can save it as a script by clicking the Save Recording button at the top of the Recorder docker. I saved mine as Plastic with Edges. Default scripts are saved in either the Effects folder or the Scripts folder. They can be saved anywhere your little old heart desires, but those two folders are where the Scripts docker is expecting to find them. I saved mine in the Scripts folder, as shown next. I also included a brief description of what the script did, because it is easier later to read the description than to open the file and try to figure out just what you did. Before we conclude this chapter, let's take a brief look at the Scripts docker.

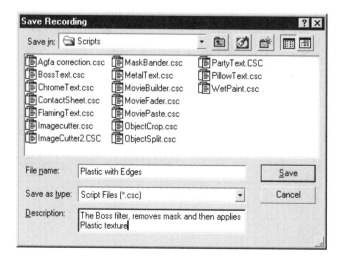

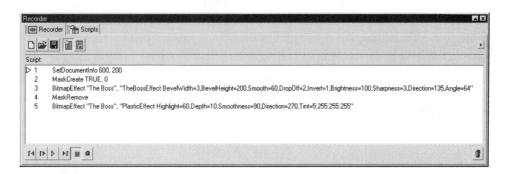

FIGURE 18-2   The script is simple, but it saves a lot of time when you're comparing effects on different fills

Scripts Docker

The Scripts docker (CTRL-F6), shown next, is where scripts are selected and launched. It is only necessary to double-click the script to launch it. The first time you open the Scripts docker, you should see two choices for folders: Scripts and Effects. The Effects folder contains scripts that are applications of the filters; the Scripts folder tends to contain more complex sequences. To launch a script, you can click the Play button shown at the bottom of the docker window, or just double-click the script in the docker.

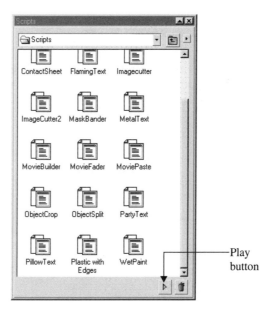

Play button

18

For a great effect, fill the text with the Texture Fill called Lava River in the Samples 6 Texture Library, and then double-click the Plastic with Edges script in the docker. You can see the result of applying the script we just created to this fill and a few others in the color insert.

In Summary

Well, now you know enough about automating PHOTO-PAINT to make some of those boring repetitive tasks less painful. In the next chapter, you'll discover how to customize PHOTO-PAINT so that it is really your own little program.

CHAPTER 19

Customizing Corel
PHOTO-PAINT 10 Preferences

My experience as a larger-than-average person taught me that one size doesn't fit all. I also know that the same is true when it comes to the default arrangement and settings of tools of any software application—this includes PHOTO-PAINT. That's why Corel allows many of the features to be moved, removed, and otherwise customized.

In this chapter, you will learn how to customize your PHOTO-PAINT workspace so that it is both comfortable and productive. Corel has put a lot of features into its product that enable you, to quote a famous fast-food chain, to "have it your way." There are literally several million combinations of tool settings possible, so we are not going to look at all of the configurable or customizable tools, just the commonly used ones.

You can configure existing toolbars, menus, and keyboard commands as well as create new ones. PHOTO-PAINT comes with 21 toolbars (plus 31 flavors of Property bars) not to mention 12, yes count them, 12 dockers. You can add, remove, and rearrange buttons on both existing and new custom toolbars. The same can be done with the commands that are available in the menu bar. Many of the default keyboard combinations can be altered, or new combinations can be made. While all three areas—toolbars, menus, and keyboard commands—offer unique benefits, one, the configurable toolbars, offers some of the greatest productivity advantages. Let's start with the toolbars.

Toolbars

Even though they look somewhat alike, don't confuse toolbars and the Property bar. Property bars are much like politicians; their content changes depending on the tool selected, whereas a toolbar, while customizable, is dedicated to a specific tool or task. Our first step when we set up PHOTO-PAINT is to get the toolbars to the right size for the display. Then we can fiddle with them.

Fitting the Toolbar to Your Monitor

Because monitors come in all sizes from 9 inches to 23 inches, Corel has made the sizes of the buttons, and therefore the sizes of the toolbars, configurable. One of the first steps in setting up PHOTO-PAINT is to find the best fit for your monitor. Every size of button except the smallest may cause a portion of the toolbar to drop off the end of a standard monitor. The rule for toolbar size is: The larger your display (physically), the larger the toolbar button settings can be—as long as the toolbar fits the screen. The quality of the icons on the buttons varies with size; I think the middle-sized buttons look the best. In Figure 19-1, I have placed the icons for all three sizes of toolbars side by side for comparison.

Changing the Toolbar Size and Shape

From the Windows menu, choose Customize. When the Options dialog box opens, select Customize, as shown next. Highlight the toolbar whose size you want to change and then from the Button dropdown list in the Size section select the desired size. Clicking the OK button in the dialog box applies the change to the toolbars. The Border setting increases or decreases the size of the border or bar that the buttons appear to sit on. Changing the Border to the maximum setting of 10 (pixels) means all button and no border; all the way to the right, and the border surrounding the buttons increases to its maximum.

FIGURE 19-1   Toolbar buttons come in three different sizes (small, medium, and large)— sorry, no extra large

19

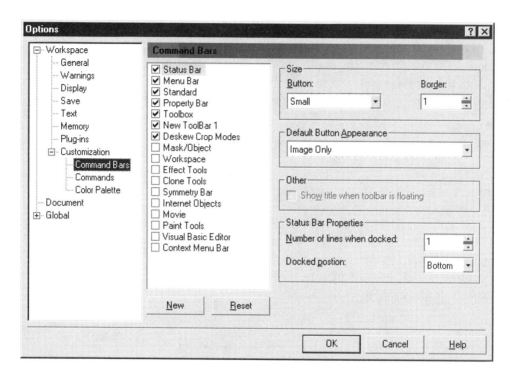

In previous releases of PHOTO-PAINT, all of the toolbar buttons would change size at the same time. In PHOTO-PAINT 10, you can make each toolbar one of the three different sizes.

Selecting Toolbars That Are Displayed

The quickest way to select which toolbars are displayed is to right-click your mouse on a toolbar (the Status bar counts), as shown in Figure 19-2.

If you choose to display all of the PHOTO-PAINT standard toolbars, you won't be able to find the image. While the image that follows may seem cluttered, even that isn't all of the toolbars. Do some of these toolbars look familiar? They should. They are the flyouts from the Toolbox.

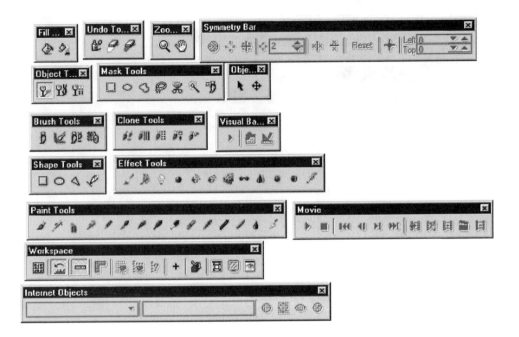

Another way to make a toolbar visible is to select Toolbars from the Window menu and place a check by the desired toolbar. The first time you launch PHOTO-PAINT, there are three toolbars checked (visible): Standard, Property Bar, and Toolbox. Because toolbars take up screen space and the Property bar provides much of the functionality of the other toolbars, I recommend that you initially keep only the default toolbars selected.

Placing and Shaping the Toolbars

You can move the toolbar anywhere on the screen. By clicking any part of the toolbar that doesn't have a button, you can drag it to any of the four sides of the window. When it gets close to a side, it will attach itself (dock) there. To make it a floating toolbar, move it away from the side.

19

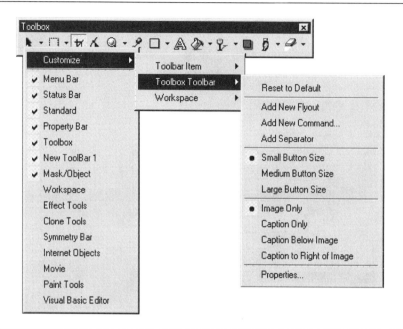

FIGURE 19-2 Right-clicking a toolbar provides a quick selection list for displaying toolbars and accessing customization controls

Be careful when docking the toolbars. PHOTO-PAINT doesn't seem to mind if the toolbar you just docked is too long and some of the buttons go beyond the edge of the monitor, making them no longer visible.

When toolbars are floating, you can change their shape to just about any shape you can imagine. In Figure 19-3, I have shown just a few of the many different possible shapes for a large multibutton toolbar such as Workspace. Changing the shape is as simple as putting the cursor on the edge of the toolbar until it turns into a two-headed arrow and then clicking and dragging the shape to the desired shape.

Customizing Toolbars

There are several ways to customize a toolbar. Here are some basic concepts about the buttons and the toolbars. Every command in PHOTO-PAINT has a button that can be placed on a toolbar. All of these buttons can be rearranged, moved to a different toolbar, or removed from a toolbar completely. To place a copy of a button, hold down the ALT key and drag the button to its new location. If you drag it off the toolbar, the button will be removed.

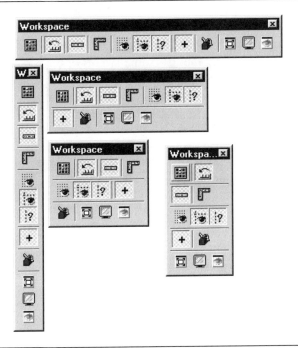

FIGURE 19-3   The toolbars can be configured to just about any shape you can imagine

I recommend that you spend some time working with PHOTO-PAINT to get a feel for what arrangement will work best for you before you begin customizing.

If you are going to be doing the projects throughout this book, here is a simple project that creates a custom toolbar to make the other projects in this book easier and get you used to creating and modifying toolbars.

Building Your Own Custom Toolbar

The following procedure creates a custom toolbar. Before any customization can be done, an image must be open. (I don't know why, but it must.) The first step is to create or load an image.

1. Open a new file (CTRL-N), click the OK button when the dialog box opens, and minimize the image by clicking the Minus button in the upper-right corner.

2. Open the Options dialog box (CTRL-J), shown next. Open Customize and select Commands. If you used PHOTO-PAINT 9 or earlier, you will find

19

this is much easier to use. Below the Command title is where you select the menu bar group where the command is currently assigned. In the example shown next, the File menu is shown and all of the commands that appear in the File menu appear on the list (some are off of the screen and you must scroll down the list to see them). The New from Clipboard command is highlighted and to the right is displayed the text that appears on the Quick Tip Help as well as a list of where else in PHOTO-PAINT this command is available.

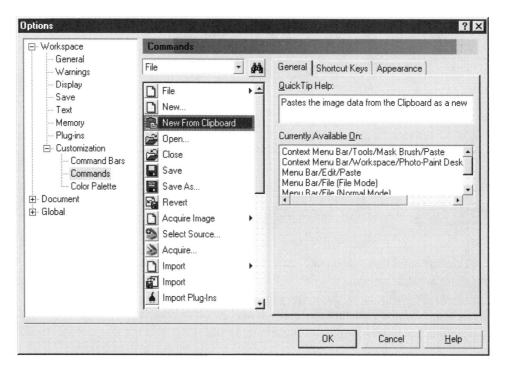

3. The Shortcut Keys tab displays the shortcut key currently assigned to the command as well as an area that allows you to assign a different one. This is discussed in greater detail in the following sections. The good news is, PHOTO-PAINT will warn you if you are about to overwrite an existing assignment. The Appearance tab shown next is a full-fledged icon bitmap editor. From here you can make your own icons. If you find this idea exciting, seek professional help.

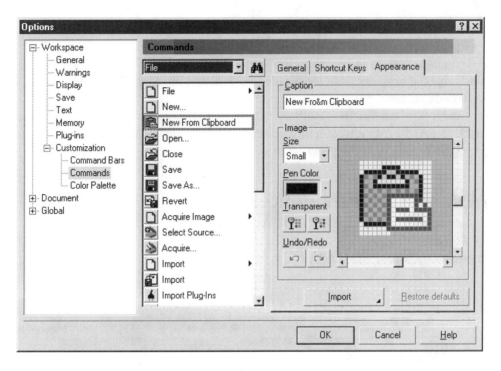

4. To drag the command to a new custom toolbar, you only need to drag the command from the dialog box into the workspace area of PHOTO-PAINT.

To remove a toolbar that you made, or if you accidentally made an extra one or two doing the preceding exercise, press CTRL-J, select Toolbars, right-click on the toolbar, and select Delete from the pop-up menu.

Menus and Keyboard Commands

The arrangement of the menus works in a similar fashion to the toolbars. An example of rearranging the menu structure would be moving a command that is nested several levels deep to the top of the menu for easy access. Another time-saver is the ability to assign a command to a keyboard shortcut. PHOTO-PAINT comes with a large set of default keyboard combinations. The operation of customizing a keyboard combination is pretty much self-explanatory. Assigning a keyboard combination to a command allows you to execute commands quickly without the

19

need to click a button or access the menu. The only disadvantage of using keyboard combinations is the need to memorize the keyboard shortcut. Also, remember that you cannot use existing reserved combinations like CTRL-S (Save). Refer to the user's manual or online help for detailed information on using either the menu or keyboard command configurations.

Each of these methods—toolbars, menus, and keyboard commands—offers the PHOTO-PAINT user a wealth of productivity enhancements that can be applied to a specific project or to the program in general.

Making Your Preferences Known

The preference settings for PHOTO-PAINT, called Options, are located in the Tools menu or by pressing CTRL-J. The user interface for this area hasn't changed considerably since PHOTO-PAINT 8, as shown in Figure 19-4. If it looks familiar,

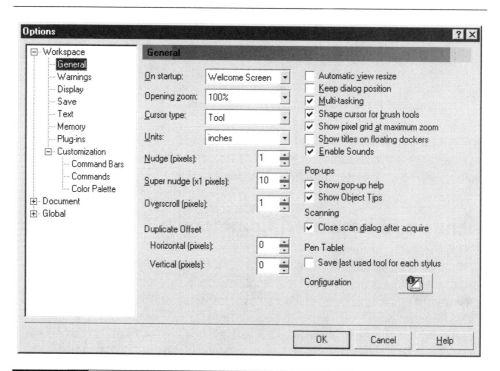

FIGURE 19-4   The Options Dialog Box

you probably have or use Netscape's Communicator for your browser. This has been designed to allow multiple configurations to be saved as individual workspaces.

The three major groups of preference settings are Workspace, Document, and Global.

The first selection in the Workspace group on the Options dialog box is called General.

The Workplace Settings

This grouping includes General, Warnings, Display, Save, Text, Memory, Plug-ins, and Customization.

The General Page

The General page, shown in Figure 19-4, contains many of the settings that determine how PHOTO-PAINT functions. The setting that determines what PHOTO-PAINT does when you launch it is found in the On Startup setting. By default, it is set to the Welcome screen.

There are a few default settings in the General page that you should consider changing. I recommend keeping the Zoom state on Open at 100 percent. If you have To Fit or some other Zoom level selected, it may increase the amount of time necessary to display an image after it is loaded on slower systems.

For Cursor Type, an important setting is the Shape Cursor for Brush Tools check box. When enabled, this changes the cursor to the size and shape of a selected Brush tool. This is important because this feature allows you to see the size of your Brush tool. The only reason I know for not selecting this feature is that the cursor shape can slow down the Brush tool action if you have a slow system.

Near the top of the page is the Automatic View Resize option. This changes the size of the image window automatically so that it always fits the current size of the image anytime you change the Zoom level. As neat as this feature is, you may want to leave it unchecked when editing an image. This option keeps the edge of the image window tight to the edge of the image, which creates a problem as the cursor approaches the edge of the image window. The program thinks you want to take action on the image window size or placement on the workspace rather than on the image, making work near the edge of the image difficult. If you will be doing the projects in this book, I recommend leaving this feature off. Having said this, I use it a lot when writing a book like this, since I do not want gray edges on my screen captures.

19

The Warnings Page

This page, new with PHOTO-PAINT 10, controls all of the little warning boxes that appear when you try to do something that PHOTO-PAINT thinks you shouldn't be doing. It used to be necessary to turn off these features from the Options page, but now, when the little warning box appears, you can check the Don't Warn Me Again box and it will change the settings in this page. For example, you will notice that in mine the Read-Only Status is unchecked. I made this change from the warning box.

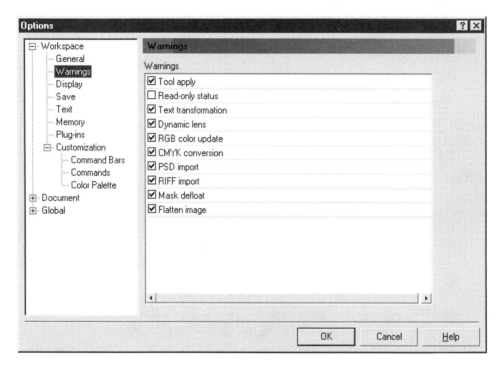

I have just a few comments about the warnings. If you work with images created with older versions of PHOTO-PAINT (but not version 5), turn off the RGB Color Update. This feature is supposed to warn you that you have loaded an image from a version of PHOTO-PAINT that used a different color space. It offers to correct the problem for you. If you select Yes, and the image was not from PHOTO-PAINT 5, the color in your image will look like someone threw it into a blender and hit the frappé button. This is because the ability of PHOTO-PAINT to distinguish images from Ventura 6 or from PHOTO-PAINT 6 is a little weak. In short, turn it off. Also, if you get a lot of your images from CD-ROMs, you will quickly tire of the very obvious warning that the CD-ROM is read-only. Your choice—it is always the first thing I turn off.

The Display Page

This page, shown next, contains the settings to change the colors, actions, and appearance of the marquees in PHOTO-PAINT. These settings are not intended to make the marquees more aesthetically appealing, but to enable adjusting their colors and shapes for the types of images you are working on. For example, the Object marquee is blue, but against a blue background you cannot see it. Generally, these settings should be left in their default state unless the color of the image makes it difficult to see the marquees.

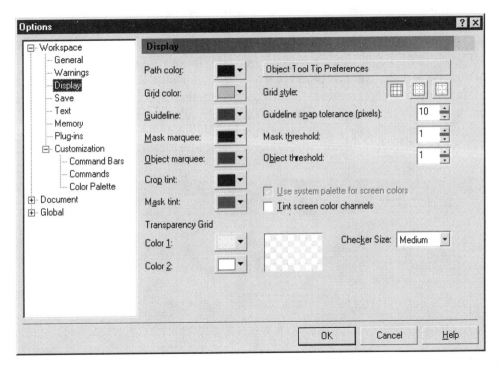

Tweaking the Marquee

Many veteran PHOTO-PAINT users are unaware that the mask marquee is customizable. You can define where on a mask boundary the marquee is displayed, and the color of its marching pixels can be changed. To change the color of the marquee, simply select a new color. A different color is often helpful in making the marquee stand out from the image. In the Threshold section, we can specify the position of the marquee for feathered masks. The range of Threshold is 1 to 255, which should be a clue. If you recall, grayscale images have a tonal range of 256

19

shades of gray. Are you getting the idea? Choosing a threshold value of 255 places the mask marquee on the most transparent (lightest) pixels in the mask's feathered boundary, which are also the innermost pixels of that edge. A value of 1, the default setting, places the mask marquee on the most opaque (darkest) pixels of the mask edge.

The Save Page

The Save page is the page where you can instruct PHOTO-PAINT to automatically back up the file you are working on at specific time intervals and enable backup copies of images to be produced when an image is saved. The automatic backup of an open image, called Auto-Save, sounds good, but keep in mind that the changes you make to the image you are working on will be saved at these intervals whether or not you actually want them to be. If you choose to enable this feature (it is off by default), I suggest setting it to Save to Checkpoint. The Checkpoint command creates a temporary copy of an image. This avoids changes being made to the original file before you are ready to save them. You should leave the other settings in their default state until you become more familiar with PHOTO-PAINT.

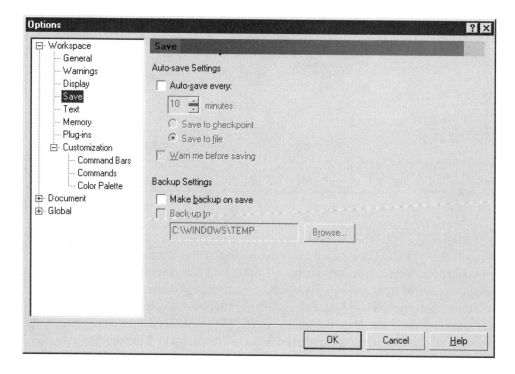

The Text Page

Another new addition to PHOTO-PAINT 10, the Text page provides several
controls for the font lists. You can select which types of fonts are displayed as well
as whether or not the font samples appear on the list (unless your system is really
strapped for resources—use it) and how many of the previously used fonts appear
at the top of the list.

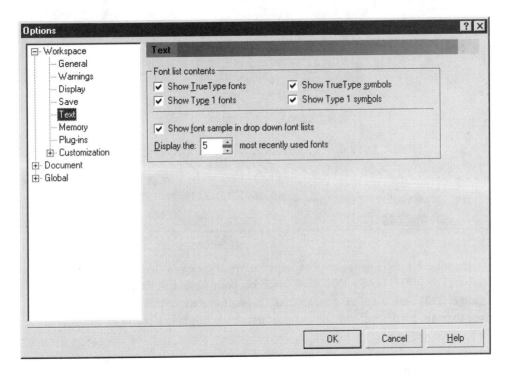

The Memory Page

The next illustration shows the Memory page, which determines how much hard
disk space on which disks is available for PHOTO-PAINT to save temporary files,
and the allocation of the system memory for image editing and Undo lists and
levels. The correct settings in this tab improve the performance of PHOTO-PAINT
by adjusting the use of system resources to the way you work.

19

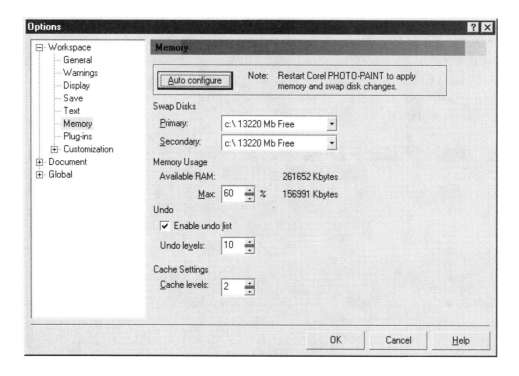

Because bitmap images require larger areas of memory than traditional Windows applications, PHOTO-PAINT uses space on your hard disk drive for temporary storage. This area is called a *swap disk*. If you have more than one hard disk drive, the program, by default, will select the first drive (alphabetically) as the primary swap disk and the second drive as the secondary swap disk regardless of the amounts of available space on the drives. Check your settings to make sure that the drive with the greatest amount of available space is set as the primary swap drive. If one of the drives is slower than the other, select the fastest drive for the primary swap drive.

The Memory page has settings to enable and disable the Undo and Undo List commands. This is an important feature. The traditional problem with a photo-editing package is the lack of multiple undo levels. With PHOTO-PAINT, you can determine how many undo levels you have. Before you decide to set the undo level to 99, be aware that each level of undo keeps a copy of the image at that level, which uses up system resources. Setting to a high level can consume a lot of swap disk space and ultimately slow down your system. I recommend keeping the undo level to less than 3. Another feature that has been improved in

PHOTO-PAINT 10 is the Undo List. Enabling this feature will allow you to undo as far back as you choose. It does this by recording each command that is applied to an image and then reapplying the commands (minus the ones you wanted to undo) in a sequential manner. While it is slower than the normal Undo, it does not consume as many system resources as undo levels.

You can also determine the amount of RAM assigned to temporarily store images when you open and edit them with the Cache Settings. Allotting too much RAM for the images can result in slower performance of other Windows applications. I recommend leaving this setting at its default state.

NOTE	*Any change you make to the settings in the Memory tab requires restarting PHOTO-PAINT for the changes to take effect.*

The Plug-in Page

For detailed information on how to use the settings in this page, see Chapter 13.

The Customization Page

This page offers selections for customization of menus, keyboard shortcuts, and toolbars discussed earlier in this chapter.

The Document Guidelines Group

This grouping contains the settings for the guidelines, grids, and rulers. The operation and configuration of rulers and guidelines is explored in Chapter 5. Settings can be accessed through this dialog box or directly through the Tools roll-up. As with many other things in Win 9x, multiple paths lead to the same destination.

The Global Bitmap Effects Group

The Global group controls bitmap effects and filters. In addition, from the top page you can set the initial preview mode of the filters.

The Bitmap Effects page

These control how the preview appears when the filter is first launched.

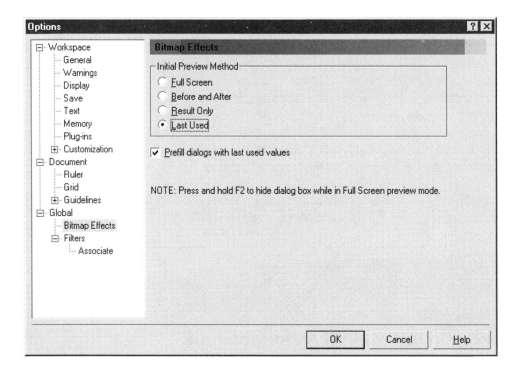

The Filters Page

This page controls two major areas of the import and export filters. First it controls what import and export filters are installed and available in PHOTO-PAINT. This feature if properly used can be a real time saver. If you are always working in a limited number of formats, you can "turn off" the filters that you are not using so that your list of choices isn't miles long. This is especially handy if the file format you use always seems to be just out of sight when you open the file dialogs.

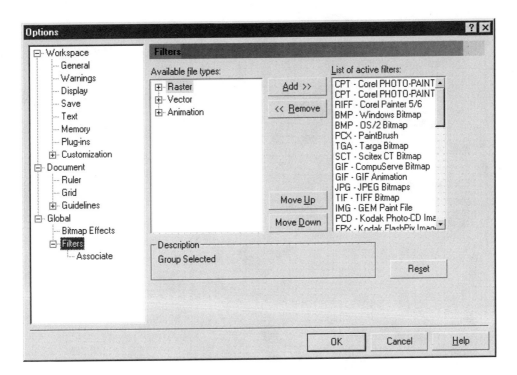

The second area controlled by this page is the file associations. How many times have you double-clicked a graphic file in My Computer or Explorer and the wrong application opened? In this page you can tell PHOTO-PAINT which file formats are associated with it by simply checking and unchecking boxes.

Onscreen Palette

Located in the Customization area are the controls for the onscreen color palette. By default, it first appears on the right side of the screen. Like the toolbars, it can be dragged and docked anywhere on the screen. You can change several of the color features by selecting Customize in the Tools menu and clicking on the Color Palette tab. From here, you can configure the color wells and control how the right button on the mouse responds when clicking one of the color wells. I recommend keeping the default setting of Set Fill Color. It offers a quick and easy way to change fill colors.

19

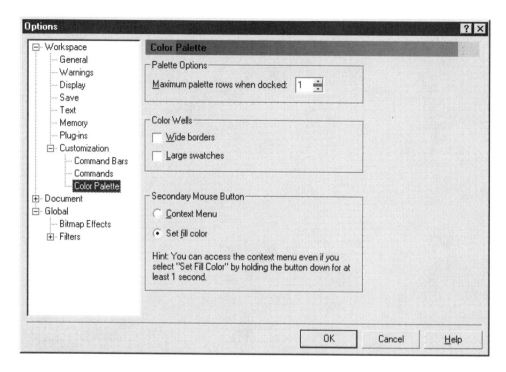

TIP

When configuring the color palette, you may want to disable the Use 3D Wells setting if you are experiencing sluggish performance from your display.

In Summary

Many Corel PHOTO-PAINT users ignore the customization features and settings discussed in this chapter and as a result waste a lot of time "fighting" PHOTO-PAINT. By that I mean that the program, by default, has certain settings that cause certain actions to occur. For example, every time you open an image on a CD-ROM, PHOTO-PAINT warns you that it is a read-only file. While it only takes a keystroke to acknowledge the message, it makes more sense in the long run to change the setting. There are so many shortcuts and custom toolbars that are possible, it makes good sense to customize PHOTO-PAINT to work for you and not against you. Of course, if you are charging your work by the hour...

CHAPTER 20

Getting the Best Printing Using PHOTO-PAINT

597

This chapter is dedicated to showing you how to make the most out of the powerful printing engine included in Corel PHOTO-PAINT 10. Many users sadly just click the print button, never realizing all of the features that Corel has spent both time and money to include. As a form of disclaimer, it should be pointed out that even though this is an official Corel book, many of the opinions expressed in this chapter are the result of talking with PHOTO-PAINT users since the days of PHOTO-PAINT 5.

When printing photographs on an ink jet printer, we are always concerned that the resulting output looks like what we see on the screen, but we also want to know how to use the features of PHOTO-PAINT to print multiple copies of photos on single sheets of (sometimes expensive) glossy photo paper. So, let's learn how this jewel works.

Color Correction vs. Ink Jet Printers

Many PHOTO-PAINT users I talk to at conferences confess that they don't get satisfactory results using Corel's color correction with their ink jet printers; others are frustrated by being unable to get color profile for their latest ink jet printer. Some of these fine folks feel guilty—a sense that they are doing something wrong, making me feel a little like I need to start taking a portable confessional with me to conferences. My answer to these users involves a secret that I will now share with you: I use the color correction that is part of my ink jet printer, and I don't use the Corel color profile. Does this make me a bad person? No. Does this mean Corel's color management isn't worth anything? Absolutely not! So, why don't I use them? Because most PHOTO-PAINT users are not preparing materials for four-color prepress, but are printing photographs on their inkjet printers. So, how do you turn off Corel's color correction? Click the Print button in the Standard toolbar and, when the dialog box opens, click the tab for the Misc page. Ensure that Apply ICC Profile is not checked, as shown next.

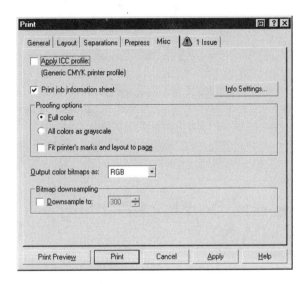

After you have turned off Corel's color management, your next step is deciding which printer color management setting achieves the best color fidelity reproduction. Here is the secret formula for determining the best setting for color settings of your printer: experiment! Feel free to share this secret with others. I use two Epson printers, which give me really nice results. I was able to come up with several excellent settings for both my Epson Stylus Color 850 (yeah, it's an older printer, but it works fine) and my Epson Stylus Photo 1200. Which leads to another question that always comes up at a conference . . . .

Color Printers vs. Color Photo Printers

Regardless of what photo-editing program you use, a major question users have is whether they need a photo printer or a regular inkjet printer. As a user who has both printers available, I can tell you the answer: little to nothing to do with the output. For example, HP currently sells a PhotoSmart™ printer, which can actually read the media of a digital camera without ever getting either the camera or the printer near a computer. The actual printing mechanism (called a print engine) of both the photo printer and the office printer is identical. Earlier ink jet printers used five to seven inks to obtain the subtle shading necessary to reproduce vivid photographic colors. Now, you can get excellent results from a printer even if it doesn't have the word photo in its name.

General Dos and Don'ts of Printing with PHOTO-PAINT

Always remember that the driving force for the features in Corel's printing engine is CorelDRAW. The reason you should remember this is that many of the neat features, when applied to a bitmap image, can produce less-than-desirable results. After printing photographs with PHOTO-PAINT for the last five years and talking with the fine Corel folk in Ottawa, I have learned a few tricks that are worth sharing.

Fit to Page: It's Not Your Friend

Located on the Layout page of the Print dialog box (shown next), Fit to Page is a great feature if you are using CorelDRAW. When selected, the print engine resizes the image so the entire image you are printing fits into the printable area of the paper. Since CorelDRAW is a vector-based program, resizing works great.

Wait! PHOTO-PAINT images are bitmaps, right? Therefore, if you use it, the PHOTO-PAINT image will be resized (not resampled) and the result will suffer various degrees of distortion, depending on just how much the image is resized and the subject matter of the photo.

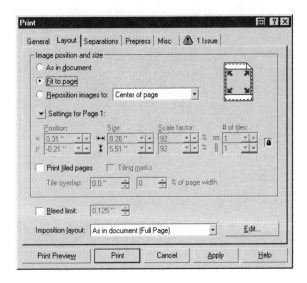

Always Check Your Printer Properties

When you are printing several images, it is always a good idea to quickly check the settings on your printer to ensure that they have not changed from the last time you used the printer. Just click Properties, as shown next, opening the properties box for the selected printer. Since the factors that determine when the printer reverts back to its default settings is dependent upon the printer used and the phases of the moon (just kidding), this little step prevents the unpleasant discovery that the printer isn't set up correctly. This is especially important when using photo glossy paper, which isn't cheap.

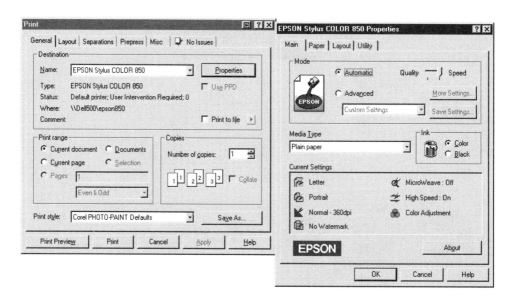

> **TIP** *A word to the wise is to make sure that the printer that appears in the Name destination box is the one you want to use to print. The most common cause for the printer to mysteriously change while you weren't looking happens when you create PDF files.*

Low Resolution May Not Be Bad

When you start to print an image from a digital camera or the picture of your brother-in-law that he downloaded to you for your birthday (oh joy), you may find that the resolution is less than 96 dots per inch (dpi)—which triggers a Preflight warning, shown next. When working with vivid colors in a photograph, don't assume that 72–96 dpi will necessarily look bad. While in most cases a low-resolution image will not look very good, my advice is not to give up when you see this warning. If your image contains mostly natural subjects—clouds, rocks, bushes, and so on—odds are that it will look OK. If it is mostly manmade stuff, then the chances are it won't look very good when you print it.

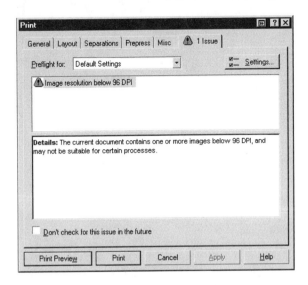

Making Your Own Wallet-Size Pictures

When you get portraits from a photo studio, they ask (read: badger) you regarding the number and size of photos that you want. Have you ever noticed that they are all multiples of standard letter-size paper (8.5 × 11 inches)? Corel PHOTO-PAINT has a built-in feature with the technically accurate but not very intuitive name Imposition Layout, which can automatically change a single photo into photo studio–style multiples. Here is how it is done.

From the Print dialog box, select the Layout tab, and at the bottom of the page is one of several ways to select the number and placement of photos on a single page. In the next illustration, the list of preset and saved imposition layouts is shown.

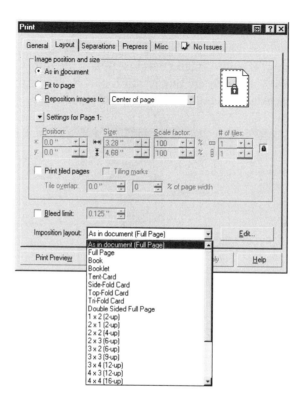

Corel provides a lot of presets: while many are for prepress, several of them serve as great starting points for creating multiple copies of photos. Changing the preset layout to 2 × 2 (4-Up) and clicking Edit opens the screen shown in Figure 20-1, which is essentially the same screen, less a few options, that opens when Print Preview is selected. In the following section, we will look at what some, not all, of these options do.

When the preview opens, you can see by the numbers in the images that we have a layout with four copies of the same image—indicated by the same number on each image. The dashed lines indicate the printable area on the printer I have selected.

TIP *If you want to actually see the image, you can click the Template | Document Preview button.*

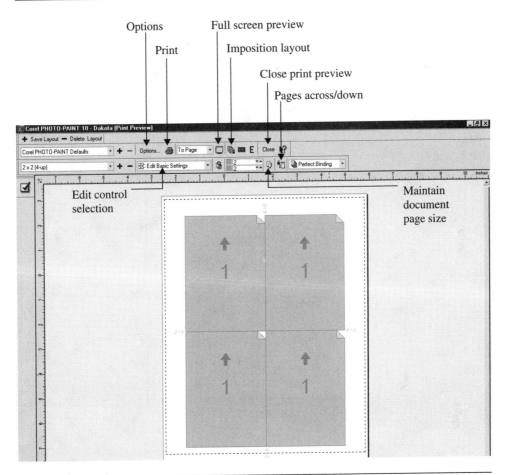

FIGURE 20-1   It is from this screen that you can make multiple copies of photos

Adding Gutters

Using the default settings of the selected imposition layout, there isn't any space (called gutters) between the four copies of the photos. If you want to add gutters so that all of the photos have a nice white border, select Edit Gutters & Finishing from the Edit Control Selection drop-down list. Click either the horizontal or the vertical space and change the width of the gutter in the Gutter Size value box. In the image shown next, both gutters have been changed to a width of 0.5 inches and the layout was saved by clicking the button with the + sign and naming it "2 × 2 (4-up) with .5 inch gutters." Any time you want to print an image using this imposition, you only have to load the custom preset.

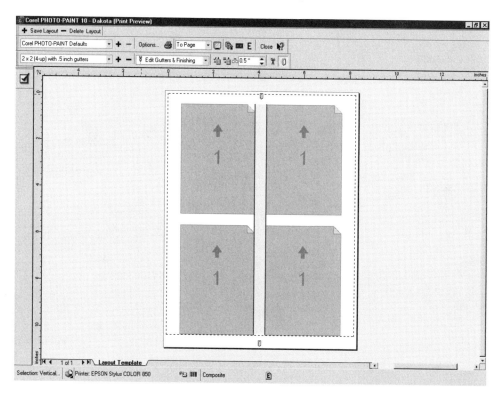

Making Photos That Fit Without Alterations

If you select an imposition that makes the photos so that they no longer fit in the printable area of the printer, PHOTO-PAINT will automatically resize (not resample) the image so that it fits. As stated earlier in this chapter, you should avoid having the print engine resize your image if possible. From this preview screen it isn't apparent that the image is being resized. To see if the image is being resized, click the Maintain Document Page Size button. This action causes the size of the preview image to be displayed in its non-resized size. In short, if you click the Maintain Document Page Size button and the preview doesn't change size, the images have not been resized.

From the Print dialog box, you will also have a warning in the Preflight page if the image size has been modified.

Fitting Several Different Photos on a Page

Another feature of Corel PHOTO-PAINT is the ability to make a contact sheet of photos that are open. To print multiple images on a single page, click the Documents button in the Print Range section of the Print dialog box, as shown next.

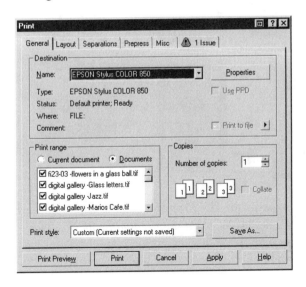

All of the open images are checked, but you can uncheck any one that you don't want printed. Next, choose an imposition that includes all, or at least most, of the images you have selected. The image shown next is an example of what the printed output looks like. Quite obviously, the images in the sheet have been resized.

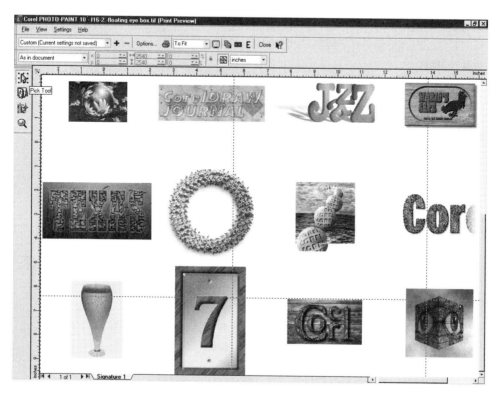

There is an option in the Prepress page of the Print dialog box that will make PHOTO-PAINT print the filename with the image. If you use this feature when multiple images are on a single page, the file information will not be under each image, but they will all be combined into a single line. In short, don't do it.

In Summary

In this chapter, I have only covered information specific to printing photographs using PHOTO-PAINT 10. Corel has provided a wealth of information about prepress printing in both the user manuals and online help. I recommend that you take advantage of these resources to make the most out of Corel's powerful printing engine.

Index

A

Adaptive Unsharp filters, 389
Add Noise filters, 404–407
  dialog box, 404–405
  noise and focus with, 407
  removing banding from radial
    fills, 406–407
  types of noise and, 406
Add to Palette button, 305–306
additive color. *See* RGB (additive color)
Additive mask mode, 146, 534
Adjust tab, Glass filter, 427–428
Adobe Photoshop
  black-and-white-images in, 30
  vs. PHOTO-PAINT, 6
Alchemy Effects filters, 457–458
aligned mode, Clone tool, 355,
  358–359

alpha channels
  managing with Channel docker,
    539, 541
  passing grayscale information
    with, 39
  saving Color masks to, 558
  saving complex masks to, 535,
    538–539
ALT key
  creating automatic brush
    strokes, 316–317
  creating straight lines, 356
Angle box, Fountain Fill options, 238
Angle controls, Glass filter, 429–430
Anti-Aliasing check box, 63
Antialiasing
  buttons, 326
  defined, 263
  shape tools, 263

Apply ICC Profile check box, 63
Art Stroke filter. *See* effect filters,
    Art Stroke
Artistic Media docker, 315–316
aspect ratio, maintaining, 96–97
Auto check box, Remove Noise
    filter, 417
Automatic View Resize Option,
    Workplace settings, 82, 587
automation tools, 563–576
        Batch Process, 564–566
        Recorder docker, creating
            scripts, 570–574
        Recorder docker, overview of,
            566–568
        Recorder docker, Scale on
            Playback, 568–570
        Recorder docker, Show
            Commands/Use Frame
            Range, 568
        Scripts docker, 575–576
Average Direction setting, 543

B

backgrounds. *See also* Corel
    TEXTURE; Paper Color setting
        Glass Block filter and, 531–532
        Motion Blur filter and, 397–398
        paint tools for, 290–291
        replacing with Color Mask,
            553–555
        restoring photographic, 200–207
BACKSPACE key, function of, 82
Band Pass Custom effect filters, 458
banding, removing

from radial fills, 406–407
    using Guassian Blur filter,
        394–395
base image, defined, 162–163
Batch Process (Playback), 564–566
beat frequency, defined, 416
Bevel Width sliders, 427
Bitmap Effects pages, 593
Bitmap Fill, 244–249
        controlling size/position of tiles,
            246–247
        function of, 231, 245–246
        loading bitmap images, 247
        working with, 248–249
Bitmap Fill dialog box, 245–247
bitmap images
        converting vector files to, 25
        creating and controlling objects
            and, 162
        display using, 22–23
        hazards of zooming, 77
        loading, 245
        opening, 61–64
        provided by Corel, 244
black-and-white images
        cropping photographs, 217–218
        keystoning photographs and,
            219–222
        overview, 30–33
        resolution settings, 47–48
        using marquee, 136
Black Matte previews, 558
Bleed attributes, 331
Blocks (Puzzle) Distort effect
    filters, 461

Blur filters, 391–403
  Directional Smooth, 400
  Gaussian Blur, depth of field using, 393–394
  Gaussian Blur, overview, 392–393
  Gaussian Blur, removal of banding using, 394–395
  Jaggy Despeckle, 398–399
  Low Pass, 403
  Motion Blur, 396–398
  overview, 391–392
  Radial Blur, 399–400
  Smart Blur, 401–402
  Smooth, 400
  Soften, 400
  Tune Blur feature, 401
  Zoom, 400
Border command, masks, 545
Boss filters
  creating 3D web page buttons, 523–528
  creating mappable objects, 528–528
  (Emboss) 3D effect filters, 438–439
  shapes of holes using Deteriorated Metal with, 549
brightness, defined, 50
Brightness sliders, 429
brush nibs. *See* nibs
Brush setting docker, 318–320
Brush Texture roll-up, 330–331
brush tools, 313–372
  Artistic Media docker and, 315–316

brush nibs, 317–318
Brush setting docker, 318–320
constraining and automating, 316–317
managing, 322
overview of, 314
selecting and configuring, 315
Stroke Style section, managing brush tools, 322
Stroke Style section, overview of, 320–321
Stroke Style section, Paint mode, 321–322
Symmetry toolbar and, 338–339
brush tools, Brush Texture roll-up, 330–331
brush tools, Clone tool (C)
  aligned/nonaligned modes, 358–359
  Clone from Fill, 361
  Clone from Saved, 360–361
  Clone mode, 359
  cloning from what to where, 355
  constraining, 356–357
  Cumulative/Merged objects operations, 362–363
  Impressionist, 359
  overview of, 353–354
  Pointillism, 359
  resetting, 355–356
  settings for, 357–358
brush tools, Dab Attributes roll-up
  Spacing setting, 328–329
  Spread setting, 329–330
brush tools, Effect tools
  Blend, 351–352

Brightness, 347
Contrast, 348
Dodge and Burn, 352–353
Hue, 348–349
Hue Replacer, 349–350
overview of, 343–345
Sharpen, 352
Smear, 345–346
Smudge, 346–347
Sponge (Saturation), 350
Tint, 350–351
Undither, 352
brush tools, Image Sprayer tool
creating image lists, 364–370
overview of, 363–364
painting with, 371–372
presets, 370
brush tools, Nib Properties roll-up,
323–326
brush tools, Orbits/Color Variation
roll-up, 331–335
Include Center button, 332
Toggle Orbits button, 332
using, 333–335
brush tools, Paint tools, 339–343
creating custom nibs, 340–343
selecting, 339
toolbar for, 340
brush tools, Pen Settings roll-up
associating paint tool to
stylus, 337
auto pen tablet configuration,
336–337
buttons, 337–338
configuring pen, 336
overview, 335–336

brush tools, Stroke Attributes roll-up
Antialiasing and Smoothing, 326
Fade Out, 327
Brush Warping screens, 466–467
Bump Map Custom effect filters,
459–460
Butt joints, 263
buttons, 3D. *See* 3D buttons

C

CAPTURE, Corel. *See* Corel CAPTURE
Capture Cursors, 513
Cardinality-Distribution, 36
CCDs (charge-coupled devices), 208
CD-ROMs
Corel Scrapbook docker
window and, 510
saving image files on, 70
Center Offset setting, 237–238
channel ops (CHOPs), 409
channels, 538–541
alpha, 538–539
Channel dockers, 539, 541
defined, 535
exploring, 539
Charcoal Art Stroke effect filters, 452
charge-coupled devices (CCDs), 208
Checkpoint commands
customizing Save page
with, 590
overview, 124
CHOPs (channel ops), 409
Circle Mask tool (J), 141
Clear button, 117
Clik drives, 507

Clip masks, 174–179
Clip to Parent icons
    blending objects with, 172
    example, 179
    overview, 171
Clipboard, Microsoft Windows, 69
Clone from Saved tools, 125–126
Clone tools (C), 353–363
    aligned/nonaligned modes,
      358–359
    Clone from Fill, 361
    Clone from Saved, 360–361
    Clone mode, 359
    constraining, 356–357
    Cumulative/Merged objects
      operations, 362–363
    Impressionist, 359
    overview of, 314, 353–354
    Pointillism, 359
    resetting, 355–356
    restoring dark photographic
      backgrounds, 201–206
    settings for, 357–358
    where to Clone, 355
CMY color models, 301
CMYK (subtractive color), 48–50
    color models for, 299–301
    color values and, 49
    converting to, 223
    overview of, 48–49
    using 32-bit color for, 39
    vs. RGB, 50
color. *See also* CMYK (subtractive
    color); RGB (additive color)
    basic theory, 47–48

black-and-white-images and,
    30–33
describing values of, 49
digital cameras and, 208–211
gamut, 51
grayscale images and, 33–36
halftone images and, 46–47
hue, saturation, and
    brightness, 50
matching, 49–50
models, 48
printers, 600
resolution settings, 47–48
Uniform Color fill mode,
    234–235
Color Blend
    Fountain Fill dialog box and,
      239–242
    mixers, 306–307, 309–310
Color controls, Glass effect filters, 429
color correction
    ink-jet printers, 598–599
    photo CDs, 59–60
    photographs, 211–217
color cubes, defined, 37
color depth
    4-bit, 27–29, 36–38
    8-bit, 27–29, 36–38, 68
    16-bit, 27–29, 38
    24-bit (True Color), 27–29,
      38, 68
    32-bit, 27–29, 39
    48-bit, 27–29, 39
    overview of, 27–29
    Palettes Mode and, 310–312

photo CDs and, 59–60
scanners and, 493
selecting, 58, 62
Color Harmonies mixer, 306–309
Color Hue, digital cameras, 210–216
Color mask, 552–561
    advantages of paths over, 559
    dialog box, 552–553
    hue tools and, 349
    overview of, 552
    replacing backgrounds with,
        553–555
    Stroke Mask/Path commands,
        559–561
    tips for using, 556–558
Color mask tools
    Lasso Mask tools (A), 149–151
    Magic Wand Mask tools (W),
        152–156
    overview, 146–148
    Scissors Mask tools (4), 151
color mode. *See* color depth
Color Mode
    Add Noise filter dialog box, 405
    New Image dialog box, 68
color models
    creating colors using, 302–303
    options for, 301–302
    selecting, 299–300
color noise, 405
color palettes
    choosing, 292–294
    Color Palette Browser, 294
    Color Swatches and, 274
    customizing, 595–596
    default RGB, 291

overview, 274
Palette Knife Art Stroke effect
    filter, 454
Palettes mode, 299–300,
    310–312
    saving colors with, 305–306
    selecting colors from, 234–235
    Web Safe technicalities, 37, 291
color paths,
    Clockwise/Counter-Clockwise, 240
Color Replacer tools (Q)
    overview, 126
    selecting paint color with,
        290–291
Color Similarity setting
    Eyedropper tool (E) and, 298
    Lasso Mask tool (A) and, 149
    Magic Wand Mask tool (W) and,
        152, 157
    overview, 148, 157
    Scissors Mask tool (4) and, 151
Color Swatches palettes, 274
Color Variation roll-up. *See*
    Orbits/Color Variation roll-up
Color Variation setting, 333
color, working with, 289–312
    changing colors, 291–292
    finding colors by name,
        294–296
    options, Color Blend, 309–310
    options, Color Harmonies,
        307–309
    options, Mixers mode, 306–307
    options, overview of, 304–305
    Paint Color dialog box, 299–300
    Palettes mode and, 310–312

picking palettes, 292–294
saving new color to palette,
    305–306
using color models options,
    301–303
using Eyedropper tool (E),
    297–299
using Paint, Paper and Fill
    colors, 290–291
Combine Objects button, 174
CompactFlash memory cards, 506
compression types, 71, 74
Conical fountain fills
    determining angle of, 238
    overview, 237
Conical setting, 261
Conté Crayon Art Stroke effect
    filters, 453
Context Help, 16
Continuous Preview options, 480–481
continuous-tone images, defined, 33
Contour filters. *See* effect filters, Contour
Contrast Enhancement, defined,
    201–204
Conversion styles, 32–36
    Cardinality-Distribution, 36
    Floyd-Steinberg, 35
    halftones, 35
    Jarvis, 34
    Ordered, 34
    Stucki, 35
Copy toolbar button, 15
copyrights, 58
Corel CAPTURE, 133–137
    creating images from Windows
        Clipboard, 69

dialog box, 511
hot keys and, 134
Image tab page and, 135
Initial Delay and Capture Cursor
    and, 135
Options page and, 136
selecting Destination and,
    135–136
Source page and, 134
Corel KNOCKOUT, 282–287
    finishing, 285–287
    overview, 282–284
    RAM requirements for, 283
    transition zone and, 284–285
Corel Scrapbook docker window, 132
Corel TEXTURE, 270–282
    Batcher and, 271
    changing texture size in,
        278–279
    color swatches and color palette
        in, 274
    form and geometry in, 274
    how to make texture in,
        274–276
    Layer-Specific Dialog box, 273
    lighting properties in, 273
    locating program for, 271
    making 3D buttons in, 279–282
    making seamless tiles in,
        276–278
    overview, 270–271
    Shader layers and, 273
    surface properties and, 273
    title bar and toolbars in, 272
    workspace and Preview area
        in, 272–273

CorelTUTOR, 16
correction tools. *See* mistakes, tools
  for correcting
corrosion effects, creating, 550
CPUs, setup, 18
Crafts Creative effect filters, 442–443
Crayon Art Stroke effect filters, 453
Create a Movie check box, 68
Create a New Image dialog box, 67–69
Create as Object from Background
  button, 174
Create Fill from Selection
  commands, 230
Create Mask from Object(s) button, 174
Create New Channel button, 539
Create Object from Mask button, 174
Creative filters. *See* effect filters,
  Creative
cropping
      opening images and, 56–57
      overview, 217–218
      tools, Crop Border Color,
        100–101
      tools, Crop to Mask, 99–100
      tools, Crop to Selection, 98
      tools, overview, 92
Crosshair cursor shape, 143
Crystallize Creative effect filters, 443
CTRL key
      constraining Clone tool, 356
      making straight lines, 316
      as Mask tool modifier key,
        139–141
      selecting mask mode, 145
CTRL-O (Open) command, 55
CTRL-Z (Undo) command, 123

Cubist Art Stroke effect filters, 453
Cumulative option, 362
Current Object with Border option, 512
Cursor Type, 587
Custom Blend setting, 240–242
Custom filters. *See* effect filters, Custom
Custom Rotate command
      Custom Rotate dialog box,
        85–86
      distortion and, 87–88
      function of, 85
      overview, 87–88
Customization page, 593
customizing, 578–595
      Bitmap Effects page and, 593
      Document Guidelines
        Group, 593
      Filters page, 594–595
      Global Bitmap Effects
        Group, 593
      menu and keyboard commands
        for, 585–586
      onscreen color palette, 595–596
      preference settings, 586–587
      toolbars, building, 583–585
      toolbars, fitting to monitor,
        578–579
      toolbars, overview, 582–583
      toolbars, placing, 581–582
      toolbars, selecting displayed,
        580–581
      toolbars, shaping and sizing,
        579–580
      Workplace settings,
        Customization page, 593

Workplace settings, Display page, 589

Workplace settings, General page, 587

Workplace settings, mask marquee, 589–590

Workplace settings, Memory page, 591–593

Workplace settings, Plug-In page, 593

Workplace settings, Save page, 590

Workplace settings, Text page, 591

Workplace settings, Warnings page, 588

Cut toolbar button, 15

Cylinder 3D effect filters, 424

D

Dab Attributes roll-up, 327–330

    setting Pointillism Clone tool, 359

    Spacing setting in, 328–329

    Spread setting in, 329–330

Dabble Art Stroke effect filters, 454

data paths, color, 39

Decrease Resolution feature, 506

Default RGB

    defined, 291

    naming colors in, 294–296

Deinterlace filters, 509

DEL key, for removing masks, 539

Delete Color option, 558

Delete (minus button), for Texture Fill, 252

Delete Object(s) button, 174

Density sliders, 404–405

depth of field, defined, 393–394

descreening filters

    removing scanning moiré patterns with, 504

    using Remove Moiré filter, 415–416

Destination page, 513

Deteriorated Metal technique

    corrosion effect, 550

    overview, 547–549

    variations, 551

diagonal lines, creating, 390

Diffuse filters, 408

Digimarc watermarks, 58

digital cameras, 506–508

    getting images from digicam to computers, 129

    Jaggy Despeckle filters and, 399

    loading images directly into PHOTO-PAINT, 130

    overview, 506

    restoring photos, changing Color Hues, 210–211

    restoring photos, color correction, 211–216

    restoring photos, color fundamentals and, 208–210

    restoring photos, overview of, 207–208

digital images, 21–51

    basic color theory for, 47–48

bitmap and vector, 22–25
black-and-white, 30–33
CMYK, compared with RGB, 50
CMYK, using, 48–49
color depth and, 27–29, 38–39
color gamut and, 51
color matching for, 49–50
color models for, 48
creating halftones for, 46–47
describing colors for, 49
gamma, 39–40
grayscale, 33–36
hue, saturation, and brightness
   for, 50
image resolution, 40–46
image resolution, defined, 41
image resolution, image size
   and, 40
image resolution, printer
   resolution and, 46
image resolution, screen
   resolution and, 41–46
overview of basic terms for, 22
pixels and, 26–27
RGB color and, 48
Direction controls, 429–430
Directional setting, 476–477
Directional Sharpen filters, 390
Directional Smooth filters, 400
Disable Fill button, 261
Displace Distort effect filters, 462–463
displacement maps, defined, 462–463
display cards
   recommended screen settings
     and, 45–46
   screen resolution and, 41–45

Display page, customizing, 589
Display Properties dialog box, 29
distortion. *See also* effect filters, Distort
   effect of Unsharp Mask
     Filters on, 389
   rotating images and, 85–86
Dithered check box, 63
dithering, defining, 33
Do Not Show Filter Dialog feature, 71
dockers, 12
Document Guidelines Group, 593
Don't Save, using, 566
downsampling, defined, 93
Drop-Off type, 428
Duplicate command, 89–90
duplication, video capture and, 509
Dust & Scratch filter, 408–409
dusting, defined, 407

E

E hot key, for Eyedropper tool,
   297–299
Edge Detect Contour effect filters, 456
Edge Level (%) sliders, 390
Edge Pads, 238
Edge Texture, 331
Edit Color option, 558
Edit Fill & Transparency (EFT)
   dialog box
     components of, 230
     fill button types and, 231
     Fountain Fill mode and,
       235–244
     selecting type of fill with,
       230–232

transparency controls and, 258–261
Uniform Color fill mode and, 234–235
Edit Gutters & Finishing option, 605–606
editing features, 6–10
overview, 6–7
virtual reality changes, 7–10
effect filters, 3D, 422–441
3D Rotate, 422–424
Boss (Emboss), 438–439
Cylinder, 424
Emboss, 424–425
Glass, 426–432
Page Curl, 433–434
Perspective, 434–435
Pinch/Punch, 435–435
Sphere, 437–438
Zig Zag, 439–442
effect filters, Art Stroke, 452–455
Charcoal, 452
Conté Crayon, 453
Crayon, 453
Cubist, 453
Dabble, 454
Impressionist, 454
Palette Knife, 454
Sketchpad, 454–455
Watercolor, 455
effect filters, Contour, 455–457
Edge Detect, 456
Find Edges, 457
Trace Contour, 457
effect filters, Creative, 442–452
Crafts, 442–443

Crystallize, 443
Fabric, 443–444
Frame, 444
Glass Block, 445–446
Mosaic, 446–448
Particles, 448
Scatter, 448
Smoked Glass, 449
Stained Glass, 449
Vignette, 449
Vortex, 449–450
Weather, 450–452
effect filters, Custom, 460–474
Alchemy, 457–458
Band Pass, 458–458
User Defined, 459
effect filters, Distort
Blocks (formerly known as Puzzle), 461
Displace, 462–463
Mesh Warp, 463–464
Offset, 467–468
Pixelate, 468–469
Ripple, 469
Shear, 469–470
SQUIZZ!, 465–467
Swirl, 470–471
Tile, 471
Wet Paint, 472
Whirlpool, 473
Wind, 473–474
effect filters, Fancy, 478–486
Julia Set Explorer 2.0, 478–479
Terazzo, Continuous Preview option, 480–481
Terazzo, Feather option, 483–484

Terazzo Filter Dialog Box, 480

Terazzo, Mode settings and
Opacity slider, 485

Terazzo, motifs, 481

Terazzo, overview of, 479

Terazzo, previewing and saving
tiles, 485–486

Terazzo, selecting symmetry,
482–483

Terazzo, tiles, motifs and
patterns, 479–480

effect filters, Render, 474–478

3D Stereo Noise, 475

Lens Flare, 475

Lighting Effects, 476–478

Effect tools, 343–353

Blend, 351–352

Brightness, 347

Contrast, 348

Dodge and Burn, 352–353

Hue, 348–349

Hue Replacer, 349–350

overview of, 314, 343–345

Sharpen, 352

Smear, 345–346

Smudge, 346–347

Sponge (Saturation), 350

Tint, 350–351

Undither, 352

Effects folder, Scripts docker, 575

EFT dialog box. *See* Edit Fill &
Transparency (EFT) dialog box

Ellipse tools, 265

Elliptical Area feature, 512

Elliptical transparency setting, 260

Emboss 3D effect filters, 424–425

Emboss Dialog box, 425

Eraser option, 360

Eraser tool (X)

Paint colors and, 290

Pen settings roll-up, 338

using, 121

Exclusive OR (XOR) mask mode, 146

Export command, 70

export filters, customizing, 594–595

Export Plug-Ins, 377

Export toolbar button, 15

Eyedropper tool (E)

best color selection using, 101

Color Replacer tool and, 126

function of, 231

getting right color with,
297–299

F

Fabric Creative effect filters, 443–444

Fade Last commands, 385

Fade Out function, brush strokes, 327

Feather masks, 542–544

Feather option, 483–484

file compression, categories of, 74

file formats, 71–73

Corel PHOTO-PAINT (CPT), 72

Graphics Interchange Format
(GIF), 72–73

overview of, 71

Photoshop (PSD), 73

PICT, 73

Tagged Image File Format
(TIFF), 73

Windows Bitmap (BMP, DIB), 72

file management, 54–66
   checking for watermarks, 58
   importing into Bitmap dialog
      boxes, 62–64
   modifying image as it opens,
      56–57
   opening 3D images, 64–66
   opening existing images, 55–57
   opening Photo CDs, 59–61
   opening vector images, 61–62
   overview of, 54
   reopening images, 58
   viewing size, format and
      notes, 58
   welcome screen for, 54–55
file structure, defined, 71
Files of Type setting
   finding files, 56
   saving files, 71
Fill color
   changing colors and, 291–292
   overview of, 290–291
   selecting right fill using, 230
Fill command, location of, 228
Fill status lines, 234
fill tools, 228–266
   button types for, 233
   property bars for, 231–232
   selecting, 230–232
   selection options, 228–230
   status bar for, 234
   types of fill, 256
fill tools, Bitmap Fill, 244–249
   applying, 248–249
   Bitmap Fill dialog box, 245–247

loading Bitmap images,
   245, 247
operating, 245–246
size and position of Bitmap tiles,
   246–247
fill tools, Fill command, 228
fill tools, Fountain Fill, 235–244
   applying, 242–244
   Center Offset setting, 237–238
   Color Blend, 239–242
   Custom Blend setting, 240–242
   Fountain Fill dialog box,
      235–236
   Options Selection, 238–239
   Presets area, 242
   Type list, 236–237
fill tools, Interactive Fill, 255–257
   overview, 230, 255–256
   Paint Mode setting, 256–257
   Style settings, 257–258
fill tools, Shape tools, 261–266
   antialiasing, 263
   Ellipse tool, 265
   joint types (Polygon tool), 263
   Line tool, 266
   overview of, 261–262
   Paint mode, 263
   Polygon tool, 265–266
   Rectangle tool, 264–265
   Roundness settings(Rectangle
      tool), 263
   Transparency setting, 262
   width, 262
fill tools, Texture Fill, 249–254
   applying, 253–255

Delete, 252
overview of, 249–250
Preview button and
    locked/unlocked
    parameters, 252
Save As, 252
Style Name and parameter
    section, 253
Texture Fill dialog box
    overview, 250–253
texture libraries, 251–252
fill tools, transparency controls
elliptical, 260
flat, 259
linear, 259
radial, 261
square, rectangle and
    conical, 261
fill tools, Uniform Color fill mode,
    234–235
Filled joints, Polygon tool, 263
fills, radial, 406–407
film scanners, 494
filters, 375–419
    dialog boxes, other effects
        available with, 384
    dialog boxes, panning and
        zooming, 381–383
    dialog boxes, preview options,
        380–381
    installation of, 376–378
    Last Effect, Repeat Effect and
        Fade Last commands,
        384–385
    managing plug-ins, 378–379
    Remove Moiré and, 415–417
    understanding plug-in, 376

filters, Blur, 392–402
    Directional Smooth filters, 400
    Gaussian Blur filters, 392–395
    Gaussian Blur filters, depth of
        field using, 393–394
    Gaussian Blur filters, removal of
        banding using, 394–395
    Jaggy Despeckle filters,
        398–399
    Low Pass filters, 403
    Motion Blur filters, 396–398
    overview, 391–392
    Radial Blur filters, 399–400
    Smart Blur filters, 401–402
    Smooth filters, 400
    Soften filters, 400
    Tune Blur feature, 401
    Zoom filters, 400
filters, Custom effect
    Bump Map filters, 459–460
    overview, 457–459
filters, Noise, 403–415
    Add Noise filters, 404–407
    Diffuse, 408
    Dust & Scratch filters, 408–409
    effects of, 406–407
    Masks, Maximum filters, 410
    Masks, Median filters, 412–415
    Masks, Minimum filters,
        411–412
    Masks, overview, 409–410
    overview, 403–404
    Remove Noise filters, 417
    removing noise with, 406–408
    Tune Noise filters, 418
Filters page, customizing, 594–595

filters, sharpening, 385–391
>Adaptive Unsharp filters, 389
>affect on noise of, 388
>Directional Sharpen filters, 390
>High Pass filters, 390–391
>overview of, 385–388
>Sharpen filters, 390
>Sharpen filters, defined, 386
>Tune Sharpen filters, 391
>Unsharp Mask filters, 389

Find Color feature, 296
Find Edges Contour effect filters, 457
Fit to Page feature, 600–601
Flashpath floppy adapters, 507
Flat drop-off, 428
flat drop shadows, defined, 180
Flat transparency setting, 259
Flatten attribute, nib shape, 324
Flip commands, 83–84
Floyd-Steinberg conversions, example of, 35
Flyout Option button, 173
fonts, customizing, 591
Fountain Fill, 235–244
>applying, 242–244
>Center Offset setting, 237–238
>Color Blend and Custom Blend settings, 239–242
>dialog box, 235–242
>Options Selection, 238–239
>overview, 231
>Presets area, 242
>Type list, 236–237
Frame Creative effect filters, 444
freehand. *See* vector images
Freehand Mask tool (K), 141–143

G

Gamma lens, 201–203
gamma setting, 39–40
Gamut alarm, 304
Gaussian Blur filters, 392–395
>changing Color Hue with, 211
>depth of field using, 393–394
>removal of banding and increase in blurring with, 406
>removal of banding using, 394–395
>restoring dark photographic backgrounds with, 201–205
Gaussian drop-off, 428
Gaussian noise, 406–407
General page, customizing, 587
geometry control layer, 274
GIF file formats. *See* Graphics Interchange Format (GIF)
Glass 3D effect filters, 426–432
Glass Block Creative effect filter
>distorting backgrounds using, 531–532
>overview, 445–446
glide reflections, defined, 480
Global Bitmap Effects Group, 593
gradient fills. *See* Fountain Fill
Graphics Interchange Format (GIF)
>file formatting and, 518–519
>overview of, 72–73
graphs
>rules about, 118–119
>using, 115–117
grayscale
>black-and-white-images and, 30–33

color model and, 302
masks using, 134–137
overview, 33–36
resolution settings for, 47–48
using Color Mask with, 558
Grid & Ruler Setup dialog box, 113
Grid Warping, 466
grids
    rules about, 118–119
    using, 115–117
Grow commands, masks, 156–157
Grow speed setting, 333
Guidelines Options dialog box,
  117–118
guns, defined, 38
gutters, defined, 603–605

H

halftones
    creating, 46–47
    example of, 35
    overview, 31
Hand tools (H), 80–81
hard disk capacity, system setup, 19
hardware, system setup and, 18
help
    locations of, 16–17
    scanners and, 493
High Pass filters, 390–391
HLS color models, 301
holes
    creating with Deteriorated
      Metal, 547–551
    removing from masks, 545
hot key, choosing, 512–513

HSB (hue, saturation and brightness)
  mode
    color masks and, 148–149, 557
    overview, 301
    Tolerance sliders and, 100–101
hue, defined, 50

I

image lists
    creating custom, 364
    creating from image with
      multiple objects, 367
    creating from image with no
      objects, 367–370
    creating from single object,
      364–366
    defined, 364
Image | Resample command
    resizing using, 93
    rulers for layout using, 112
image resolution, 40–46. *See also*
  image size
    defined, 41
    image size and, 40
    pixels and, 26
    printer resolution and, 46
    printing images with low,
      602–603
    scanners and, 492–493, 501–503
    screen resolution, 41–46
    screen resolution, color
      settings, 47
    screen resolution, recommended
      settings, 45–46
    vector images and, 63
    video capture and, 508

image size
    changing texture and, 572–573
    creating new images and, 68–69
    Custom Rotation and, 87–88
    hazards of bitmap zooming
      on, 77
    modifying objects and, 189
    opening images and, 58
    photo CDs, 59, 61
    pixels and, 26
    printing photos and, 606–608
    resolution and, 40
    vector images, 23–24, 63
    viewing and modifying, 91–92
    web graphics and, 518
Image Size value, 69
Image Sprayer tools, 363–372
    creating image lists with,
      364–370
    overview, 314, 363–364
    painting with, 371–372
    presets and, 370
image windows, 13
images, creating, 67:71
    choosing size, color and
      background, 68
    from clipboard, 69
    Create a New Image dialog
      box, 68
    options and features, 68–69
    overview, 67–69
    saving work, 69–71
images, digital. *See* digital images
images, opening, 55–67
    3D images, 64–66
    bitmap images, 61–64

    existing images, 55–57
    file opening features, checking
      watermarks, 58
    file opening features, modifying
      images while opening, 56–57
    file opening features, reopening
      images, 58
    file opening features, viewing
      file information, 58
    Import into Bitmap dialog box
      and, 62–64
    Photo CD images, 59–61
    vector images, 61–62
images, saving, 69–73
    file formats for, 72–73
    options for, 71
    Save Tile feature, 485
    vs. exporting, 69–71
images, viewing/modifying, 75–108
    color mode, converting,
      106–108
    color mode, mode command,
      105–106
    cropping, Crop Border Color,
      100–101
    cropping, Crop to Mask, 99–100
    cropping, Crop to Selection, 98
    Duplicate command, 89–90
    fitting images to your display,
      82–83
    Flip command, 83–84
    image size, 91–92
    Paper Size command,
      demonstration of, 102–104
    Paper Size command, overview
      of, 101

Paper Size command, Paper Size dialog box, 102
Resample command, overview of, 92–93
Resample command, resampling, 95–97
Resample command, resizing, 93–95
Rotate command, demonstration of, 88–89
Rotate command, distortion, 85–86
Rotate command, image size and paper color, 87–88
Rotate command, using Custom Rotate, 87
shape and placement, 83
Zoom and navigation tools for, 76–82
Import 3D Model dialog box, 64–66
import filters, customizing, 594–595
import plug-ins, 497–499
Import to Bitmap dialog box, 61–64
optimum color modes and, 62
options to consider for, 63
picking size and resolution and, 63
using transparent backgrounds and, 63–64
Import toolbar button, 15
Imposition Layout
adding gutters to, 605–606
printing multiple photos with, 603–605
Impressionist Art Stroke effect filters, 454

Include Center button, Orbits/Color Variation, 332
Initial Delay Before First Capture, 513
ink jet printers
color correction and, 598–599
vs. photo printers, 600
Input Plug-Ins, 377
Interactive Dropshadow tools (s), 180–187
managing, 185–187
overview, 180–185
rules of, 187
Interactive Fill
overview, 230, 255–256
Style settings, 257–258
interlacing, defined, 509
internal filters, 376
Internet colors, converting, 518
interpolated resolution, defined, 492
interpolation
defined, 95–96
video capture and, 509
Invert Mask command, 540, 556

J

Jaggy Despeckle filter, 398–399
Jarvis conversion, example of, 34
joint types (Polygon tool only), 263
JPEG file formats
smaller file sizes using, 518
vs. GIF, 519
Julia Set Explorer 2.0 Fancy effect filters, 478–479

K

keyboard commands, customizing, 585–586
keystoning, 219–222
KNOCKOUT, Corel. *See* Corel KNOCKOUT

L

Lab color models, 301–302
Lasso Mask tools (A), 149–151
Last Effect commands, 324–325
Layer-Specific Dialog box, 273
layers, defined, 171
layout tools
    creating guidelines, 117–119
    navigation tools and, 119–120
    overview of, 110
    Zoom tools and, 119
layout tools, correction tools
    Checkpoint command, 124
    Clone from Saved tool, 125–126
    Color Replacer tool, 126
    eraser tool, 121
    local undo tool, 121–123
    overview of, 120
    Undo/Redo docker, 124–125
layout tools, grids
    overview of, 110, 115–117
    rules for, 118–119
layout tools, rulers
    overview, 110–113
    properties of, 114–115
    rules for, 118–119

Lens Flare Render effect filters, 475
lenses, 201–203
Level sliders
    Add Noise filter dialog box and, 404
    Diffuse filters and, 408
Levels Equalization, defined, 201–204
libraries, texture, 251–252
Library List, 252
Library Name option, 252
Light Eraser option, 360
Lighting Effects Render effect filters, 476–478
lighting properties, 273
Lighting tab, Glass effect filters, 428–430
line art. *See* black-and-white images
line frequency, defined, 47
Line tools, 266
Linear fountain fills, 237–238
Linear transparency setting, 259
Load Bitmap Fill dialog box, 247
Load button, 247
Load Mask function, 536–537
Load Texture button, 331
loading, masks, 536–537
Local Undo tool, 121–123
Lock button, 252
Lock Object Transparency mode, 173
lossless compression, defined, 74
lossy compression, defined, 74
Low Pass filters, 403
luminosity. *See* brightness
LZW compression, 74

M

MacIntosh graphics
  file formatting for, 73
  gamma setting for, 40
  using 32-bit color for, 39
  Web Safe Colors palette and, 37
Magic Wand Mask tools (W)
  Color Similarity setting and, 157
  overview, 152–156
Maintain Aspect Ratio feature
  Corel CAPTURE and, 513
  using Resample command with,
    96–97
Maintain Original Image Size option
  overview, 87
  resizing using, 93
  rulers for layout using, 112
manipulation tools
  Feather masks and, 542–544
  overview, 540–541
mappable objects, creating, 528–528
marquee, mask
  comparing overlay with, 137
  customizing, 589–590
  overview, 136–137
Mask Brush tools (B), 159–160
Mask mode
  buttons, 556
  Maximum filter and, 410
  Median filter and, 412–415
  Minimum filter and, 411–412
Mask/Object toolbars
  illustration and explanation
    of, 534
  mask marquees and, 136

Mask Overlay button, 540
Mask Overlay feature, 137–138
Mask plug-Ins, 377
Mask tool modifier keys
  Freehand Mask (K) tool, 142
  Mask Transform tool (M),
    139–141
Mask Transform tools (M), 138–141,
  158–159
masks, 130–160
  black, white and gray, 134–135
  Clip, 174–179
  Color Similarity and Magic
    Wands and, 157
  converting text to, 194
  creating custom nibs from,
    340–343
  creation tools for, 138–139
  displaying, overview of, 135
  displaying, using marquee,
    136–137
  displaying, using overlay,
    137–138
  Grow and Similar commands
    and, 156–157
  icons for, 14
  Mask Brush tool (B) and,
    159–160
  Mask Transform tool (M) and,
    158–159
  modes for, 143–146
  Noise filters and, 409–410
  overview, 132–134
  properties and selection of, 158
masks, color-sensitive
  Lasso Mask tool (A), 149–151

Magic Wand Mask tool (W),
152–156
overview of, 146–148
Scissors Mask Tool (4), 151
masks, complex, 533–562
Color Mask dialog box,
552–553
Color Mask, overview, 552
Color Mask, replacing
background using, 553–555
Color Mask, Stroke Mask/Path
commands, 559–561
Color Mask, tips for using,
556–558
Color Mask, using paths, 559
Deteriorated Metal, corrosion
effect, 550
Deteriorated Metal, overview,
547–549
Deteriorated Metal, various
effects, 551
inverting, 540
manipulation tools, Feather
masks, 542–544
manipulation tools, overview,
540–541
overview, 534
removing, 539–540
Shape commands, Border, 545
Shape commands,
overview, 544
Shape commands, Remove
Holes, 545

Shape commands, Smooth,
545–546
Shape commands,
Threshold, 546
using Select All button, 540
masks, regular tools
Circle Mask (J), 141
Freehand Mask (K), 141–143
mask tool modifier keys,
139–141
Rectangle Mask (R), 139–141
masks, saving
as Alpha channel, 538
Channels docker, 539
exploring channels, 539
loading, 536–537
managing channels and,
538–539
methods of, 534–535
Maximize Work Area commands, 82
Maximum filters, 410
Median filters, 412–415
Memory Available value, 69
Memory page, customizing, 591–593
menu bars, 12, 272
menu commands, customizing,
585–586
Merge box, 174
Merge Objects with Background option
overview, 90
rulers for layout using, 111
Merge source button, 362
Mesa drop-off, 428

Mesh Warp Distort effect filters,
    463–464
Microsoft Windows
    Bitmap file formats (BMP,
        DIB), 72
    Clipboard, 69
    Metafile (WMF), 61
    Start button, 58
    Web Safe Colors palette, 37
Middle Direction setting, 543
Minimum filters, 411–412
minus button (Delete), Texture
    Fill, 252
mirror reflections, defined, 480
Mirror Symmetry mode, 338–339
mistakes, tools for correcting, 120–127
    Checkpoint command, 124
    Clone from Saved tool, 125–126
    Color Replacer tool, 126
    Eraser tool, 121
    Local Undo tool, 121–123
    overview, 120
    Undo/Redo docker, 124–125
Mixers mode, 299–306
Mode commands, 105–107
Mode drop-down lists, 485
mode icons, 14
Models mode
    naming colors, 303
    Options button, 303–305
    overview, 299–300
    saving new color to palette,
        305–306
    specifying colors with numbers
        or names, 303

moiré patterns
    overview, 415–417
    scanning printed material and
        dangers of, 503
    using descreening filter, 504
    using Remove Moiré filter,
        415–417, 504–506
monitors
    color depth and, 29
    screen resolution and, 41–45
    screen setting recommendations,
        45–46
More>> button, 556
Mosaic Creative effect filters, 446–448
motifs
    defined, 479
    Terazzo effect filters, adjusting,
        481–482
Motion Blur filters, 396–398
movies, creating, 68–69
.msk extension, 535

N

naming
    colors, 303, 306
    finding colors by, 294–296
    viewing Palette selections by,
        311–312
navigation tools
    fitting images, automatic view
        resizing, 82
    fitting images, full screen
        preview, 83

fitting images, Maximize Work
Area command, 82
Hand tool (H), 80–81, 119
Navigator Pop-Up, 81–82,
119–120
Navigator Pop-Up, 81–82, 119–120
Netscape Navigator, Web Safe Colors
palette, 37
New Lens button, 174
New Object button, 174
New toolbar button, 15
Nib Options button, 324
Nib Properties Control/Preview
section, 323–324
Nib Rotation, Toggle, 325–326
nibs, brush
defined, 317
properties and settings for,
323–324
rotating, 325–326
sizes of, 323
viewing and selecting, 318
No background check box, 68
No Symmetry mode, 338
noise
color, 405
effects of filters on, 406–407
sharpening filters and, 388
types of, 406
Noise filters
Add Noise filter dialog boxes,
404–405
Add Noise filters, 404–407
defining noise and, 393–394
Diffuse filters, 408

Dust & Scratch filter, 408–409
effects of, 406–407
masks, Maximum filter, 410
masks, Median filter, 412–415
masks, Minimum filter,
411–412
masks, overview, 409–410
removing noise and, 406–408,
417
Tune Noise and, 418
non-lossy compression, defined, 74
nonaligned Clone mode, 358–359
Normal mask mode, 144–146
Normal method, color-sensitive mask
tools, 148
Normal mode, Clone tools, 358–359
Normal Tolerance sliders, 100–101
Notify End of Capture setting, 514
numbers, color, 303
Numerical setting, Color Mask, 558

O

Object Picker tools
adjusting text using, 194
creating guidelines with, 117
grouping objects and, 189
transform modes and,
187–188, 189
Object Properties dialog box, 172
Object tools, 284
Object Transparency tools
Clip masks and, 174–179
comparing Clip masks to, 179
example of, 181
overview, 180

objects, 161–189
  additional tips for working with, 188–189
  Clip masks and, 174–179, 181
  Clip to Parent feature and, 171
  controlling size and paper color for, 88
  defined, 64, 162–164, 171
  drawbacks of bitmap programs and, 162
  grouping, 189
  Interactive Dropshadow tool, managing, 185–187
  Interactive Dropshadow tool, overview, 180–185
  Interactive Dropshadow tool, rules for, 187
  object transparency tools, 180
  overview, 162, 166–171
  transform modes and, 187–188
Objects docker, 163–179
  Clip to Parent feature, 171
  controlling blend of, 172–173
  defining objects and, 163–164
  display options of, 173
  guided tour of, 166–171
  illustration of, 166
  merge mode and opacity and, 174
  modes of, 165–166
  multifunction buttons of, 173–174
  overview, 164–165
  Thumbnail Display area of, 171–172
Offset Distort effect filters, 467–468

onscreen color palettes, 12
Opacity sliders
  Objects dockers and, 174
  overview, 428
  Terazzo effect filters, 485
Open an Image dialog box
  Crop command and, 98
  opening existing images with, 56
  reopening images with, 58
Open Palette dialog box, 294
Open toolbar button, 15
optical resolution, defined, 492–493
Options button
  Color Blend and, 309–310
  Color Harmonies mixer and, 307–309
  Mixers mode and, 306–307
  opening existing images with, 56–58
  overview, 304–305
  saving new color to palette with, 305–306
Options dialog box, customizing, 586–587
Options setting
  automatic view resize, 82
  Fountain Fill, 238–239
Orbits/Color Variation roll-up, 331–335
  Include Center button, 332
  Toggle Orbits button and, 332
  using orbits, 333–335
Orbits tab, 370
Ordered conversion, example of, 34
Origin setting, 247

Original-Result formats, 60
Outside Direction setting, 543
overlay, mask, 137–138
Overlay setting, 558

P

Packbits, 74
Page Curl 3D effect filters, 433–434
Paint color
 changing colors, 291–292
 overview of, 290–291
 Paint Color dialog box, 48,
  299–300
Paint mode
 brush tools, 321–322
 Paint Mode setting, 256–257
 shape tools, 263
Paint tools, 339–343
 creating custom nibs from
  masks, 340–343
 overview of, 314, 339–340
Palette Knife Art Stroke effect
 filters, 454
palettes. *See* color palettes
panning, 381–383
Pantone Spot color systems, 50
Paper color
 changing colors, 291–292
 selecting, 290–291
Paper Color setting
 creating background for new
  images using, 68
 creating new images
  choosing, 68

opening vector images and,
 63–64
viewing and modifying images
 and, 87–88
Paper Size command, 101–105
 example, 102–104
 overview, 92, 101
 Paper Size Dialog Box, 102
paragraph text, 190
parallel port scanners, 491
Particles Creative effect filters, 448
Paste as Object toolbar button, 15
Path tool (.), 190–194
paths
 overview, 559–561
 Path Node Edit tools and, 559
 Path tool (.), 190–194
patterns, filling. *See* fill tools
PCDs. *See* Photo CDs (PCDs)
PCs, gamma setting for, 40
Pen setting roll-up, 335–338
 associating paint tool to stylus
  and, 337
 auto pen tablet configuration
  and, 336–337
 buttons and, 337–338
 configuring pen and, 336
 overview, 335–336
Perspective 3D effect filter, 434–435
perspective drop shadows, defined, 180
Perspective mode, defined, 219–222
Photo CDs (PCDs), bitmap fills, 246
Photo CDs (PCDs), opening, 59–61
 color correction issues and, 60
 dialog box, 59–60

finding right image size
when, 61
tips and tricks for, 60
photo-editing program, 6–7
PHOTO-PAINT, history of, 4–5
PHOTO-PAINT screen elements
graphic of, 11
introduction, 11–15
menu bar, 12
onscreen color palette, 12
title bar, 12
photo printers, 600
photographs
choosing JPEGs for, 519
scanning, 417
photographs, repairing and restoring,
199–223
cropping noncolor, 217–218
dark backgrounds and, 200–207
digital cameras, changing color
hue, 210–211
digital cameras, color correction
exercise, 211–216
digital cameras, color
fundamental, 208–210
digital cameras, overview,
207–208
keystoning noncolor, 219–222
overview of noncolor, 217
summary, 223
using Contrast tool to bring out
color in, 348
using Smudge tool to remove
highlights, 347
Photoshop. *See* Adobe Photoshop
Photoshop (PSD) formats, 73

PICT formats (MacIntosh), 73
Pinch/Punch effect filters, 435–435
Pinwheel symmetry, 482
Pixelate Distort effect filters, 468–469
pixels
bitmap images and, 22–23
black-and-white-images and, 30
brightness values and, 463
overview, 26–27
resolution and printers and, 46
screen resolution and, 41–45
using, 40–41
plug-in filters. *See* filters
Plug-In page, customizing, 593
Plus button (Save As), 252
Point joints, 263
Polygon mode, 141–143
Polygon tools
closed multisided figures with,
265–266
joint types for, 263
POM mode, defined, 549
Post Script Options dialog box,
311–312
preference setting, customizing,
586–587
Preserve Colors check box, 390
Presets area, 242
Preview box, 56
Preview button, 252–253
previewing
full screen window for, 83, 273
Preview area in workspace,
272–273
scans, 496
tiles, 485

Print toolbar button, 15
printers, 597–608
    adding gutters, 605–606
    advantages of low resolution,
      602–603
    checking properties of, 601–602
    color correction with ink jet,
      598–599
    comparing color with color
      photo, 600
    Fit to Page feature, dos and
      don'ts of, 600–601
    fitting several different photos
      on page, 607–608
    making photos fit without
      alterations, 606–607
    making wallet-size pictures,
      603–604
    overview, 598
    resolution and, 46
Process button, 285
Property Bars
    customizing toolbars and, 581
    overview, 14
PSD (Photoshop) formats, 73

Q

QuickDRAW files, 3D images, 64–66

R

Radial Blur filters, 399–400
Radial fountain fills, 406–407
Radial Symmetry mode, 338–339
Radial transparency setting, 261

Radius setting, 333
RAM
    16-bit color and amount of, 37
    requirements for Corel
      KNOCKOUT, 283
    setting up your system and, 18
rasterization. *See also* bitmap images
    defined, 61
    vector images and, 25
Rate setting, 346
Recorder docker, 566–574
    creating a script and, 570–574
    overview, 566–568
    Scale on Playback, 568–570
    Show Commands/Use Frame
      Range, 568
rectangles
    Rectangle Masks (R), 139–141
    Rectangle tools, 264–265
    Rectangle transparency
      settings, 261
    Rectangular Area features, 512
    Rectangular fountain fills, 237
Redo toolbar button, 15
Refraction sliders, 427–428
Registration color models, 302
regular mask tools
    Circle Mask (J), 141
    Freehand Mask (K), 141–143
    mask tool modifier keys,
      139–141
    Rectangle Mask (R), 139–141
Remove button, 379
Remove Holes commands, 545
Remove Mask button, 539

Remove Moiré filters, 415–417,
  504–506
Remove Noise filter, 417
Render filters. *See* effect filters, Render
Render Text to Mask button, 194–195
Render to Object option, 262
reopening images, 58
Repeat Effect commands, 384–385
Resample commands, 92–97
  overview, 92–93
  resampling with, 95–97
  resizing with, 93–95
resampling
  modifying images with, 56–57
  overview, 92–93
  rulers for layout using, 112
  using Resample command,
    92–93, 95–97
Reset Colors icons, 290
resizing
  advantages of vector images for,
    23–24
  automatic view, 82
  comparing PHOTO-PAINT with
    other applications for, 91–92
  overview, 91–92
  using Resample command for,
    93–95
resolution. *See* image resolution
Restore to Checkpoint commands, 124
retouching, 82
RGB (additive color)
  color depth and, 37–39
  color models and, 299–301

color values in, 49
converting to CMYK, 223
defined, 48
overview, 48
vs. CMYK, 50
RGB (additive color) Color
  Updates, 588
Ripple Distort effect filters, 469
Rotate commands, 84–89
  controlling image size and paper
    color, 87–88
  distortion and, 85–86
  example, 88–89
  overview, 84
  using Custom Rotate, 87
rotation
  defined, 480
  Rotation attribute, nib
    shape, 324
  Rotation speed setting, Orbits
    roll-up, 333
  Toggle Nib Rotation button,
    325–326
Round joints, 263
Rounded rectangles, 264–265
Roundness setting (Rectangle
  tools), 263
Row/Column Offset setting, 247
rulers
  applying, 110–115
  overview, 12
  properties of, 114–115
  rules for, 118–119

S

Sampled Colors mode
    Color Mask preset settings
      and, 558
    default setting for Color
      masks, 558
saturation, defined, 50
Saturation tools, 350
Save an Image to Disc dialog box,
    69–71
Save As (plus button), 252
Save page, customizing, 590
Save Tile features, 485
Save toolbar button, 15
Scale Bitmap to Fit setting, 247
Scale on Playback, 568–570
scaling. *See* resizing
scanners, 490–506
    48-bit color and, 39
    avoiding moiré patterns,
      417, 503
    color depth and, 493
    descreening filters and, 399, 504
    film, 494
    overview, 490–491
    parallel ports for, 491
    previewing scanned
      material, 496
    reducing noise in images from,
      393–394
    Remove Moiré filter and,
      504–506
    resolution and, 492–493,
      501–503

    scanning lots of images, 498,
      499–500
    SCSI, 491–492
    technical support and, 493
    USB, 492
    using import plug-ins, 497–499
    using Remove Noise filter to
      improve images from,
      417–418
    using TWAIN drivers, 494–497
Scatter Creative effect filters, 448
Scissors Mask tools (4), 151
Scrambler options, 360
screen elements
    dockers, 12
    image window, 13
    mask and mode icons, 14
    property bar, 14
    rulers and guidelines, 12
    standard toolbar icons, 14–15
    status bar, 14
    toolbars, 13
    toolbox/flyouts, 13–14
screening, introduction to, 31
screens
    frequency of, 47
    full screen previews, 83
    resolution for, 41–44
    ruling of, 31
    setting recommendations for,
      45–46
Scripts docker, 575–576
Scripts folder, 575
SCSI (small computer system
    interface) scanners, 491–492

seamless tiles, 570–572
Select All commands, 540
Select button, 495–496
Select Fill dialog box
    Fountain Fill mode and,
        235–244
    overview, 230
    selecting right fill and, 231
    Uniform Color fill mode and,
        234–235
Select Source dialog box, 495–496
Selection Plug-Ins, 377
serial interface cables, 507
Set Tolerance Default values, 558
Shader layers, 273–274
shadows. *See* Interactive Dropshadow
    tools (S)
Shape commands, creating masks,
    544–546
    Border, 545
    overview, 544
    Remove Holes, 545
    Smooth, 545–546
    Threshold, 546
Shape Cursor for Brush Tools
    checkbox, 587
Shape Soft Edge, 123
Shape tools, 261–266
    antialiasing, 263
    Disable Fill button and, 261
    Ellipse tool, 265
    joint types (Polygon tool), 263
    Line tool, 266
    overview, 261–262
    Paint mode, 263
    Polygon tool, 265–266

Rectangle tool, 264–265
Roundness settings (Rectangle
    tool), 263
Transparency setting, 262
width, 262
sharpening filters, 385–391
    Adaptive Unsharp filters, 389
    affect on noise of, 388
    Directional Sharpen filters, 390
    High Pass filters, 390–391
    overview, 385–388
    Sharpen filters, 386, 390
    Tune Sharpen filters, 391
    Unsharp Mask filters, 389
    unsharp masking filters
        (USMs), 389
Sharpness sliders, 429
Shear Distort effect filters, 469–470
SHIFT key
    changing brush stroke direction
        using, 316
    changing sizes for cloning
        using, 357
    as Mask Tool Modifier Key,
        139–141
    selecting mask modes using,
        145–146
shortcut keys
    4 shortcut key, Scissors Mask
        tools, 151
    A shortcut key, Lasso Mask
        tools, 149–151
    B shortcut key, Mask Brush
        tools, 159–160
    C shortcut key, Clone tools,
        355–356

F6 keyboard shortcut, for Rectangle tool, 264

F7 keyboard shortcut, for Ellipse tool, 264–265

F9 keyboard shortcut, for full screen preview, 83

H shortcut key, Hand tools, 80–81

J shortcut key, Circle Mask tool, 141

K shortcut key, Freehand Mask tools, 141–143

M shortcut key, Mask Transform tools, 138:13, 158–159

N shortcut key, Navigator Pop-Up, 81, 120

Q shortcut key, Color Replacer tools, 126, 290–291

S shortcut key, Interactive Dropshadow tools, 180–187

Shortcut Keys tab, 584

W shortcut key, Magic Wand tools, 157, 152–156

Y keyboard shortcut, Polygon tool, 266

Show Commands, 568

Show Grid mode, 119

Show Mask Marquee button, 136

Show Ready to Capture Dialog, 514

SilverFast program, 498–499

Similar command, masks
Magic Wand Mask tool (W) and, 157
overview, 156–157

Simulate Pressure with Mouse, 338

size. *See* image size

Size setting, 246–247

Sketchpad Art Stroke effect filters, 454–455

small computer system interface (SCSI) scanners, 491–492

Smart Blur filters, 401–402

Smoked Glass Creative effect filters, 449

Smooth commands, 545–546

Smooth filters, 400

Smoothing functions, 326

Smoothness setting, 549

Smoothness sliders, 427

Snap-to-Grid mode, 115, 119

Snap to Guidelines feature, 118

Soft Edge setting, 345

Soften filters, 400

speed, showing
Jaggy Despeckle filters and, 398–399
Motion Blur filters and, 397–398

Sphere 3D effect filters, 437–438

Spike noise, 406

Spotlight setting, 476–477

Spread setting, 329–330

Square fountain fills, 13

Square transparency setting, 261

SQUIZZ! Distort effect filters
Brush Warping, 466–467
Grid Warping, 466
overview, 465–467

Stained Glass Creative effect filters, 449

standard toolbar icons, 14–15

status bars
> overview, 14
> viewing selected fill
>> color/pattern and, 234

Steps value box, 238

Stroke Attributes roll-up
> Antialiasing and Smoothing, 326
> Fade Out, 327

Stroke Mask/Path commands, 559–561

Stroke Style section
> managing brush tools, 322
> overview, 320–321
> Paint mode, 321–322

Stucki conversion example, 35

Style Name fields, 253

Styles library, 251–252

stylus, 337

Subtract Scene Balance check box, 60

subtractive color. *See* CMYK
   (subtractive color)

Subtractive mask mode, 146

Super VGA screen resolutions, 45–46

surface properties, 273

Sustain Color attributes, 331

Swap colors, 304

swap disks, defined, 592

Swap Paint/Paper colors, 290

swatch book, defined, 50

Swirl Distort effect filters, 470–471

symmetry
> creating and selection patterns
>> for, 482–483
> Feather option and, 483–484

Symmetry toolbar, 338–339

system set-up, 18–19

T

Tagged Image File Format (TIFF), 73,
   535, 538

Terazzo Fancy effect filter
> Continuous Preview option,
>> 480–481
> Feather option, 483–484
> Mode settings and Opacity
>> sliders, 485
> motifs for, 481
> overview of, 479
> previewing and saving tiles,
>> 485–486
> selecting symmetry, 482–483
> Terazzo Filter Dialog Box, 480
> tiles, motifs and patterns,
>> 479–480

text, 190–195
> adding paragraph-style, 190
> adjusting, 193–194
> choosing GIF for, 519
> overview, 190
> Path tool (.) and, 190–192, 194

Text page, customizing, 591

Text tools, 194–195

Texture Creator, 290

Texture Fill, 249–254. *See also* Corel
   TEXTURE
> calculating fill size and, 250
> Delete and, 252
> dialog box, 250–253
> editing features of, 250–251
> function of, 231
> libraries and, 251–252
> overview, 249–250

Preview button and locked/unlocked parameters and, 252
Save As and, 252
Style Name and parameter section and, 253
working with, 253–255
texture, Smudge tools, 346
3D buttons
creating gradient, 519–522
using Boss filter to create, 523–528
using Corel TEXTURE to create, 279–282
3D filters. *See* effect filters, 3D
3D images
opening images, 64–66
Rotate effect filters, 422–424
Stereo Noise Render effect filter, 475
Threshold commands, 546
Threshold sliders
Dust & Scratch filter and, 409
moving masks to black or white with, 557
Sharpen filters and, 390
Threshold values, 589
Thumbnail Display area, 171–172
thumbnail images, 418–419
TIFF (Tagged Image File Format), 73, 535, 538
tiles
seamless, 570–572
Tile Distort effect filter, 471
TILES folder, 244
Tint slider, 311

title bar
Corel TEXTURE and, 272
overview, 12
Toggle Cumulative button, 362
Toggle Nib Rotation button, 325–326
Toggle Orbits button, 332
Toggle Pen, 338
Tolerance sliders
best color selection and, 101
cropping an image with, 101
function of, 100
warnings about, 101
Tool setting roll-up, 231
toolbars
Corel TEXTURE and, 272
docking, 581–582
overview, 13
toolbars, customizing
building your own, 583–585
changing shape and size of, 579–580
fitting to your monitor, 578–579
overview of, 582–583
placing and shaping, 581–582
selecting displayed, 580–581
toolbox/flyouts, 13–14
Trace Contour effect filter, 457
transform mode, 187–188
Transform setting, 247
transition zones
defined, 284
processing completed work and, 285–287
translations, defined, 480
transparency controls, 258–261
Elliptical setting, 260

Flat setting, 259
Linear setting, 259
overview, 258
Radial setting, 261
Square, Rectangle and Conical
    settings, 261
Transparency setting
    Nib Properties roll-up and,
        323–324
    selecting right fill using, 230
    shape tools, 262
    soft edge at nib, 324
    special effects using, 123
    using Smear tool and, 345
transparency tools, object. *See* Object
    Transparency tools
Transparent Background check box,
    63–64
True Color (24-bit), 27–29, 38
Tune Blur features, 401
Tune Noise dialog box, 418–419
Tune Noise features, 418
Tune Sharpen filters, 391
TWAIN drivers
    history of, 497
    loading images into
        PHOTO-PAINT from
        digicam, 508
    overview, 494–495
    previewing scan, 496
    using select and acquire,
        495–496
Type, fill tools, 256
Type list, 236–237

U

Undo command (CTRL-Z), 123
Undo List commands, 592–593
Undo/Redo dockers, 124–125
Undo Tool flyout, 120–123
    correcting mistakes in, 121
    Eraser tool, 121
    Local Undo tool, 121–123
    overview, 120
    use of File | Revert in, 123
Undo toolbar button
    correcting mistakes and, 121
    customizing Memory page and,
        592–593
    overview, 15
Uniform Color fill mode, 231, 234–235
Uniform noise, 406
Unsharp Mask filters (USMs), 389
upsampling, defined, 93
USB
    adapters for digicams, 507
    scanners, 492
Use Frame Range commands,
    Recorder docker, 568
User Defined Custom effect filters, 459
USMs (Unsharp Mask filters), 389

V

Value 1 options button, 304
vector images
    choosing GIF for, 519
    display using, 22–25
    hazards of bitmap zooming
        with, 77

opening, choosing color mode
for, 62
opening, options for, 63
opening, photographs and, 65
opening, size and resolution
for, 63
opening, transparent
backgrounds and, 63–64
VGA screen resolution, 45–46
video capture, 130–131
Vignette Creative effect filters, 449
virtual reality changes, 7–10
Vortex Creative effect filters, 449–450

W

Warnings page, customizing, 588
Watercolor Art Stroke effect
filters, 455
watermarks, Digimarc, 58
Weather Creative effect filters,
450–452
web images, 518–532
choosing file formats for, 519
Corel CAPTURE, choosing hot
key for, 134
Corel CAPTURE, Image tab
page and, 135
Corel CAPTURE, Initial Delay
and Capture Cursor for, 135
Corel CAPTURE, Options page
for, 136
Corel CAPTURE, selecting
Destination for, 135–136
Corel CAPTURE, Source page
for, 134

Corel Scrapbook docker
window, 132
creating 3D buttons using Boss
filter, 523–528
creating 3D gradient buttons,
519–522
creating mappable objects using
Boss filter, 528–528
distorting backgrounds with
Glass Block filter, 531–532
gamma settings for, 40
Internet colors for, 518
smaller image sizes and, 518
Web Safe Color palettes, 37
Wet Paint Distort effect filters, 472
What's This; message, 16–17
Whirlpool Distort effect filters, 473
White Matte preview, Color Mask, 558
Width setting
Feather Mask command
using, 543
shape tools using, 262
Wind Distort effect filters, 473–474
Window |Tile command, modifying
images, 89
Windows. *See* Microsoft Windows
Workplace setting, customizing,
587–593
Customization page, 593
Display page, 589
General page, 587
mask marquee, 589–590
Memory page, 591–593
Plug-In page, 593
Save page, 590
Text page, 591
Warnings page, 588

X

XOR (Exclusive OR) mask mode, 146

Y

YIQ color models, 302

Z

Zig Zag 3D effect filters, 439–442
Zoom filters, blurring, 400
Zoom levels
    customizing Workplace settings
      and, 587
    features of grids and, 117
    rulers for layout using, 113, 115
    screen resolution and, 41
    tools for working with, 77–79

Zoom tools, 76–81
    To Active/To Selected/To All
      setting, 80
    hazards of bitmap zooming
      with, 77
    layout and, 119
    overview of, 76–77
    previewing filter options,
      381–383
    To Width/To Height setting, 79
    working with Zoom levels,
      77–79
    Zoom 100 percent vs. Zoom 1 to
      1, 79
    Zoom property bar, 79
    Zoom to Fit setting, 79
Zoom tool (Z), 80

INTERNATIONAL CONTACT INFORMATION

AUSTRALIA
McGraw-Hill Book Company Australia Pty. Ltd.
TEL +61-2-9417-9899
FAX +61-2-9417-5687
http://www.mcgraw-hill.com.au
books-it_sydney@mcgraw-hill.com

CANADA
McGraw-Hill Ryerson Ltd.
TEL +905-430-5000
FAX +905-430-5020
http://www.mcgrawhill.ca

GREECE, MIDDLE EAST,
NORTHERN AFRICA
McGraw-Hill Hellas
TEL +30-1-656-0990-3-4
FAX +30-1-654-5525

MEXICO (Also serving Latin America)
McGraw-Hill Interamericana Editores S.A. de C.V.
TEL +525-117-1583
FAX +525-117-1589
http://www.mcgraw-hill.com.mx
fernando_castellanos@mcgraw-hill.com

SINGAPORE (Serving Asia)
McGraw-Hill Book Company
TEL +65-863-1580
FAX +65-862-3354
http://www.mcgraw-hill.com.sg
mghasia@mcgraw-hill.com

SOUTH AFRICA
McGraw-Hill South Africa
TEL +27-11-622-7512
FAX +27-11-622-9045
robyn_swanepoel@mcgraw-hill.com

UNITED KINGDOM & EUROPE
(Excluding Southern Europe)
McGraw-Hill Education Europe
TEL +44-1-628-502500
FAX +44-1-628-770224
http://www.mcgraw-hill.co.uk
computing_neurope@mcgraw-hill.com

ALL OTHER INQUIRIES Contact:
Osborne/McGraw-Hill
TEL +1-510-549-6600
FAX +1-510-883-7600
http://www.osborne.com
omg_international@mcgraw-hill.com

THE MOUSE IS DEAD.
LONG LIVE THE GRAPHIRE.

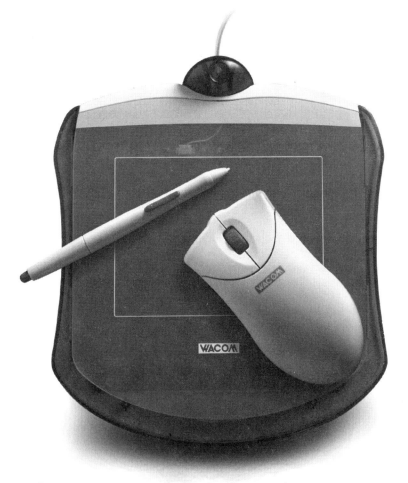

Graphire's pressure-sensitive pen and cordless mouse combine to give you more control, accuracy and flexibility than you thought possible. Comes with Corel's powerful Painter Classic to give you the Painter/Photo-Paint one-two punch. Available in many colors and, best of all, it all comes at a revolutionary price of just **$99**^{95}. Visit our website at www.wacom.com/photopaint to find out how the Graphire changes everything.

graphire BY **WACOM**